THE DEAD SEA SCROLLS AND THE NEW TESTAMENT

George J. Brooke is Rylands Professor of Biblical Criticism and Exegesis in the University of Manchester where he has taught Biblical Studies and Early Judaism since 1984, specializing in the Dead Sea Scrolls. He is co-director of the Manchester-Sheffield Centre for Dead Sea Scrolls Research and since 1992 has been a member of the Israel Antiquities Authority's international team of editors of the scrolls. In 1999 he was the President of the British Association for Jewish Studies. He was a founding editor of the journal *Dead Sea Discoveries* (Leiden: Brill, 1994–) and is an editor of the University of Manchester's *Journal of Semitic Studies* (Oxford: Oxford University Press). Among his many publications are *Exegesis at Qumran* (1985), *The Allegro Qumran Collection* (1996), *The Complete World of the Dead Sea Scrolls* (co-author; 2002). Since 2001 Brooke has edited the Society for Old Testament Study *Book List*.

For Jane

The Dead Sea Scrolls *and the* New Testament

George J. Brooke

Fortress Press
Minneapolis

Fortress Press edition 2005

Cover images:
    A few lines (in Hebrew square writing) from one of the two scrolls of Isaiah found in the cave of the scrolls of Qumran, northwest of the Dead Sea. Herodian period. Israel Museum (IDAM), Jerusalem, Israel. Photo © Erich Lessing/Art Resource, NY.
    The purple Codex Rossanensis, a sixth-century manuscript on purple parchment, contains the gospel of Matthew and almost the entire gospel of Mark. Biblioteca Arcivescoveile, Rossano, Italy. Photo © Erich Lessing/Art Resource, NY.

Cover design: James Korsmo

ISBN 0-8006-3723-2 (hc)
ISBN 0-8006-3724-0 (pb)

Typeset by Kenneth Burnley, Wirral, Cheshire
Printed in Great Britain

10 09 08 07 06 05   1 2 3 4 5 6 7 8 9 10

Contents

Preface

I am pleased to acknowledge the prompting of both Ruth McCurry, commissioning editor of SPCK, and K. C. Hanson, editor at Fortress Press, in encouraging me to put together this collection of essays on the broad theme of the Dead Sea Scrolls and the New Testament. Some colleagues have remarked over the years that they have had difficulty in locating some of my work and I hope that the availability of this collection will alleviate that problem as well as making some of my work accessible to a wider readership. It will also permit the reader to see more clearly the character of one of the directions which my research on the Dead Sea Scrolls has taken since I first became involved with them as a student, to begin with at the feet of Geza Vermes in Oxford in the academic year 1971–2 and then under the supervision of William H. Brownlee in Claremont between 1974 and 1977. In ways too numerous to list here, I am also indebted to many other friends, colleagues and scholars who have shared their enthusiasm with me for the Dead Sea Scrolls and related matters.

Throughout this collection the essays have been brought into a consistent style based upon the *SBL Handbook of Style for Ancient Near Eastern, Biblical, and Early Christian Studies* (ed. P. H. Alexander, J. F. Kutsko, J. D. Ernest, S. A. Decker-Lucke and for the Society of Biblical Literature D. L. Petersen; Peabody: Hendrickson Publishers, 1999). Abbreviations follow those cited in the *SBL Handbook*. All Akkadian, Aramaic, Greek and Hebrew has been transliterated according to the systems of the *SBL Handbook*, Chapter 5, so that even some of the more technical studies in this collection can be widely accessible.

Most of the essays have been revised and updated in minor ways; for some the revision has been more extensive. I have largely kept the same paragraphs as in the originals and also the same footnote numbers so that users should be able to locate the corresponding sections of earlier forms of these essays with ease. All the designations of particular compositions and the references to the manuscript fragments from the Qumran caves and elsewhere have been altered to correspond accurately with the principal editions of the manuscripts in the Discoveries in the Judaean Desert series (referred to in detail or as DJD with volume number, and page number).

The system for referring to the scrolls has been adopted from the *SBL Handbook* (p. 76).

> When a manuscript is referred to by column and line number, roman numerals are used for the column number, followed by a space, with the line number set as arabic numerals (e.g., 1QS III, 12; 1QpHab I, 2). Manuscripts of biblical texts can include the biblical citation of chapter and verse in parentheses: 4QpaleoExod^m V, 4 (9:7).
>
> When there are several fragments and they are numbered separately within a work, the fragments should be in arabic numerals. Thus 1Q27 1 II, 25 means text 27 from Qumran Cave 1, fragment 1, column II, line 25; 4QpIsa^c 4–7 II, 2–4 means the third copy (copy *c*) of a pesher on Isaiah from Qumran Cave 4, joined fragments 4 to 7, column II, lines 2 to 4. Fragments are also identified by uppercase letters (e.g., 11Q1 A [Lev. 4:24–6]).

Those working with some translations of the scrolls will need to operate with two or more numbering systems, but the SBL system is increasingly widely used and is generally applied also in the principal editions of these fragmentary manuscripts.

Biblical quotations are either my own translations or are cited from the *New Revised Standard Version*, copyrighted, 1989 by the Division of Christian Education of the National Council of the Churches of Christ in the United States of America, and are used by permission (all rights reserved).

I am grateful to all those who originally commissioned these essays for conferences or publication projects of various kinds over the last 15 years or more. I am also grateful to all the original publishers who have given permission for the essays to be reproduced here; a separate list of the original places of publication can be found in the list of Acknowledgements. The dedication of this collection to my wife, Jane, is the least she merits for giving me many years of loving supportive encouragement.

George J. Brooke
Manchester

Acknowledgements

I am grateful to the various publishers who have willingly given permission for me to reproduce material which I have contributed to their publications.

Chapter 1 first appeared as 'The Scrolls and the Study of the New Testament', in *The Dead Sea Scrolls at Fifty* (ed. R. A. Kugler and E. M. Schuller; SBLEJL 15; Atlanta: Scholars Press, 1999), 61–76.

Chapter 2 first appeared in a slightly shorter form as 'Dead Sea Scrolls', in *Jesus in History, Culture and Thought: An Encyclopedia* (ed. J. L. Houlden; Santa Barbara/Oxford: ABC–Clio, 2003), 201–6.

Chapter 3 first appeared as '"The Canon within the Canon" at Qumran and in the New Testament', in *The Scrolls and the Scriptures: Qumran Fifty Years After* (ed. S. E. Porter and C. A. Evans; JSPSup 26; Roehampton Institute London Papers 3; Sheffield: Sheffield Academic Press, 1997), 242–66.

Chapter 4 first appeared as 'Biblical Interpretation in the Qumran Scrolls and the New Testament', in *The Dead Sea Scrolls Fifty Years after their Discovery: Proceedings of the Jerusalem Congress, July 20–25, 1997* (ed. L. H. Schiffman, E. Tov and J. C. VanderKam; Jerusalem: Israel Exploration Society and the Shrine of the Book, Israel Museum, 2000), 60–73.

Chapter 5 first appeared as 'Shared Intertextual Interpretations in the Dead Sea Scrolls and the New Testament', in *Biblical Perspectives: Early Use and Interpretation of the Bible in Light of the Dead Sea Scrolls: Proceedings of the First International Symposium of the Orion Center for the Study of the Dead Sea Scrolls and Associated Literature, 12–14 May, 1996* (ed. M. E. Stone and E. G. Chazon; STDJ 28; Leiden: Brill, 1998), 35–57; it was subsequently published in French as 'Interprétations intertextuelles communes dans les manuscrits de la Mer Morte et le Nouveau Testament', in *Intertexualités: La Bible en échos* (ed. A. H. W. Curtis and D. Marguerat; Le Monde de la Bible 40; Geneva: Labor et Fides, 2000), 97–120.

Chapter 6 first appeared as 'The Temple Scroll and the New Testament', in *Temple Scroll Studies: Papers Presented at the International Symposium on the Temple Scroll (Manchester, December 1987)* (ed. G. J. Brooke; JSPSup 7; Sheffield: JSOT Press, 1989), 181–99.

Chapter 7 first appeared as 'Levi and the Levites in the Dead Sea Scrolls and the New Testament', in *Mogilany 1989. Papers on the Dead Sea Scrolls offered in memory of Jean Carmignac: Part I, General Research on the Dead Sea Scrolls; Qumran and the New Testament; the Present State of Qumranology* (ed. Z. J. Kapera; Qumranica Mogilanensia 2; Kraków: Enigma Press, 1993), 105–29.

Chapter 8 first appeared as '4QTestament of Levi^d(?) and the Messianic Servant High Priest', in *From Jesus to John: Essays on Jesus and New Testament Christology in Honour of Marinus de Jonge* (ed. M.C. de Boer; JSNTSup 84; Sheffield: Sheffield Academic Press, 1993), 83–100.

Chapter 9 first appeared as 'Luke–Acts and the Qumran Scrolls: the Case of MMT', in *Luke's Literary Achievement: Collected Essays* (ed. C. M. Tuckett; JSNTSup 116; Sheffield: Sheffield Academic Press, 1995), 72–90.

Chapter 10 first appeared in French as '4Q252 et le Nouveau Testament', in *Le déchirement: Juifs et chrétiens au premier siècle* (ed. D. Marguerat; Le Monde de la Bible 32; Geneva: Labor et Fides, 1996), 221–42.

Chapter 11 first appeared as 'Between Qumran and Corinth: Embroidered Allusions to Women's Authority', in *The Dead Sea Scrolls as Background to Postbiblical Judaism and Early Christianity: Papers from an International Conference at St Andrews in 2001* (ed. J. Davila; STDJ 46; Leiden: Brill, 2003), 157–76.

Chapter 12 first appeared as 'The Wisdom of Matthew's Beatitudes (4QBeat and Mt. 5.3–12)', in *Scripture Bulletin* 19 (1989): 35–41.

Chapter 13 first appeared as '4Q500 1 and the Use of Scripture in the Parable of the Vineyard', *Dead Sea Discoveries* 2 (1995): 268–94.

Chapter 14 first appeared as 'Qumran: The Cradle of the Christ?', in *The Birth of Jesus: Biblical and Theological Reflections* (ed. G. J. Brooke; Edinburgh: T & T Clark, 2000), 23–34.

Chapter 15 first appeared in a shorter form as 'Power to the Powerless: A Long-Lost Song of Miriam', *Biblical Archaeology Review* 20/3 (May/June 1994): 62–5.

Chapter 16 first appeared as '4Q252 and the 153 Fish of John 21.11', in *Antikes Judentum und Frühes Christentum: Festschrift für Hartmut Stegemann zum 65. Geburtstag* (ed. B. Kollmann, W. Reinbold, A. Steudel; BZNW 97; Berlin: de Gruyter, 1999), 253–65.

Abbreviations

AASOR	Annual of the American Schools of Oriental Research
AB	Anchor Bible
AGJU	Arbeiten zur Geschichte des antiken Judentums und des Urchristentums
AnBib	Analecta biblica
AOAT	Alter orient und Altes Testament
APOT	*The Apocrypha and Pseudepigrapha of the Old Testament*, ed. R. H. Charles. 2 vols. Oxford, 1913
ar	Aramaic
BARev	*Biblical Archaeology Review*
B.C.E.	Before the Common/Christian Era
BDAG	Bauer, W., F. W. Danker, W. F. Arndt and F. W. Gingrich, *Greek–English Lexicon of the New Testament and Other Early Christian Literature*. 3rd edn, Chicago, 1999
BDB	Brown, F., S. R. Driver and C. A. Briggs, *A Hebrew and English Lexicon of the Old Testament*. Oxford, 1907
BETL	Bibliotheca ephemeridum theologicarum lovaniensium
Bib	*Biblica*
BJRL	*Bulletin of the John Rylands (University) Library*
BJS	Brown Judaic Studies
BNTC	Black's New Testament Commentaries
BRev	*Bible Review*
BZ	*Biblische Zeitschrift*
BZAW	Beihefte zur Zeitschrift für die alttestamentliche Wissenschaft
CahRB	Cahiers de la Revue Biblique
CBQ	*Catholic Biblical Quarterly*
CBQMS	Catholic Biblical Quarterly Monograph Series
C.E.	Common/Christian Era
CGTC	Cambridge Greek Testament Commentary
CRAI	Comptes rendus de l'Académie des inscriptions et belles-lettres
CRINT	Compendia rerum iudaicarum ad Novum Testamentum

DJD	Discoveries in the Judaean Desert
DSD	*Dead Sea Discoveries*
EB	Etudes bibliques
EKK	Evangelisch-katholischer Kommentar
ErIsr	*Eretz-Israel*
EstEcl	*Estudios eclesiásticos*
ET	English Translation
EV	English Version
ExpTim	*Expository Times*
Gk	Greek
HNT	Handbuch zum Neuen Testament
HSM	Harvard Semitic Monographs
HSS	Harvard Semitic Studies
HTR	*Harvard Theological Review*
HUCA	*Hebrew Union College Annual*
ICC	International Critical Commentary
IDBSup	*Interpreter's Dictionary of the Bible: Supplementary Volume*, ed. K. Crim. Nashville, 1976
IEJ	*Israel Exploration Journal*
IOS	*Israel Oriental Studies*
JANESCU	*Journal of the Ancient Near Eastern Society of Columbia University*
JBL	*Journal of Biblical Literature*
JJS	*Journal of Jewish Studies*
JQR	*Jewish Quarterly Review*
JSJ	*Journal for the Study of Judaism in the Persian, Hellenistic, and Roman Periods*
JSNT	*Journal for the Study of the New Testament*
JSNTSup	Journal for the Study of the New Testament: Supplement Series
JSOT	*Journal for the Study of the Old Testament*
JSOTSup	Journal for the Study of the Old Testament: Supplement Series
JSP	*Journal for the Study of the Pseudepigrapha*
JSPSup	Journal for the Study of the Pseudepigrapha: Supplement Series
JSS	*Journal of Semitic Studies*
JTS	*Journal of Theological Studies*
KBL	Koehler, L. and W. Baumgartner, *Lexicon in Veteris Testamentii libros*. 2nd edn, Leiden, 1958.
LCL	Loeb Classical Library
LSJ	Liddell, H. G., R. Scott, H. S. Jones, *A Greek–English Lexicon*, 9th edn with revised supplement. Oxford, 1996
LXX	The Septuagint

MHUC   Monographs of the Hebrew Union College
MT   Masoretic Text
NCB   New Century Bible
NICNT   New International Commentary on the New Testament
NJBC   *The New Jerome Biblical Commentary*, ed. R. E. Brown
            et al. Englewood Cliffs, 1990
NKZ   *Neue kirkliche Zeitschrift*
NovT   *Novum Testamentum*
NTS   *New Testament Studies*
OTP   *Old Testament Pseudepigrapha*, ed. J. H. Charlesworth.
            2 vols. New York, 1983
PTMS   Pittsburgh Theological Monograph Series
RB   *Revue biblique*
RevQ   *Revue de Qumrân*
RHPR   *Revue d'histoire et de philosophie religieuses*
SBFLA   *Studii biblici Franciscani liber annus*
SBL   Society of Biblical Literature
SBLDS   SBL Dissertation Series
SBLEJL   SBL Early Judaism and Its Literature
SBLMS   SBL Monograph Series
SBLRBS   SBL Resources for Biblical Study
SBLSCS   SBL Septuagint and Cognate Studies
ScrB   *Scripture Bulletin*
SJLA   Studies in Judaism in Late Antiquity
SNTSMS   Society for New Testament Studies Monograph Series
ST   *Studia theologica*
STDJ   Studies on the Texts of the Desert of Judah
StPB   Studia post-biblica
SUNT   Studien zur Umwelt des Neuen Testaments
SVTP   Studia in Veteris Testamenti pseudepigrapha
TD   *Theology Digest*
TDNT   *Theological Dictionary of the New Testament*, ed. G. Kittel and
            G. Friedrich; trans. G. W. Bromiley. 10 vols. Grand Rapids,
            1964–76
TJ   *Trinity Journal*
TLZ   *Theologische Literaturzeitung*
TPI   Trinity Press International
TS   *Theological Studies*
TZ   *Theologische Zeitschrift*
UTB   Uni-Taschenbücher
VD   *Verbum domini*
VT   *Vetus Testamentum*
VTSup   Vetus Testamentum Supplements
WUNT   Wissenschaftliche Untersuchungen zum Neuen Testament

| ZNW | *Zeitschrift für die neutestamentliche Wissenschaft und die Kunde der älteren Kirche* |
| ZST | *Zeitschrift für systematische Theologie* |

Abbreviations of Dead Sea Scrolls most widely referred to in this book

CD	*Cairo Damascus Document*
1QapGen	*Genesis Apocryphon*
1QH	*Hodayot* or *Thanksgiving Hymns*
1QM	*Milḥamah* or *War Scroll*
1QpHab	*Pesher Habakkuk*
1QS	*Rule of the Community* (from Cave 1)
1QSa (1Q28a)	*Rule of the Congregation*
4QpIsa	*Pesher Isaiah*
4Q174	*Florilegium* or *Eschatological Midrash*
4Q175	*Testimonia*
4Q246	*Daniel Apocryphon*
4Q252	*Commentary on Genesis A*
4Q285	*Sefer ha-Milḥamah*
4Q365	*Reworked Pentateuch*
4Q385	*Pseudo-Ezekiel*
4Q394–98	*Miqsat Maʿaśê ha-Torah* (MMT)
4Q521	*Messianic Apocalypse*
4Q525	*Beatitudes*
4Q541	*Apocryphon of Levi*
11QApPsᵃ	*Apocryphal Psalms*
11QT	*Temple Scroll*

Abbreviations of some other ancient texts

Ant.	*Antiquities* (Josephus)
Apoc. Abr.	*Apocalypse of Abraham*
Apos. Con.	*Apostolic Constitutions and Canons*
Jos. Asen.	*Joseph and Aseneth*
Jub.	*Jubilees*
L.A.B.	*Liber antiquitatum biblicarum*
L.A.E.	*Life of Adam and Eve*
Pr. Jos.	*Prayer of Joseph*
Ps. Sol.	*Psalms of Solomon*
Rab.	*Rabbah*
Targ.	*Targum*
T. Ab.	*Testament of Abraham*
T. Levi	*Testament of Levi*
War	*Jewish War* (Josephus)

Introduction

My doctoral work was a detailed study of 4Q174, a thematic eschatological commentary on various scriptural passages which are cited explicitly. I was much exercised over the character of early Jewish scriptural interpretation in that fragmentary manuscript. Ever since, my research has been concerned in one way or another with the texts, transmission and interpretation of Scripture in the Dead Sea Scrolls and other Jewish literature contemporary in particular with the scrolls that have come from the Qumran caves on the north-west shore of the Dead Sea. The essays collected here are mostly concerned with how scriptural interpretation, commentary or exegesis as found in the Dead Sea Scrolls might illuminate similar matters of interpretation in the writings of the New Testament and vice versa.

The Dead Sea Scrolls from the Qumran caves, probably in their entirety, pre-date the writings of the New Testament. The 11 caves at and near Qumran have produced the remains of between 850 and 900 manuscripts. These manuscripts have been dated through a range of techniques to a period from the late third century B.C.E. to the middle of the first century C.E.; the majority of them come from the first century B.C.E., give or take a generation. The site at Qumran was occupied by a sectarian group, almost certainly to be associated with the Essenes in some form, between the first quarter of the first century B.C.E. (100–75 B.C.E.) and the destruction of the site by the Romans in 68 C.E. It is thus clear that the manuscripts that are earlier than the occupation of the site must have been penned elsewhere. It is also likely that many of those dated as contemporaneous with the occupation of the site were brought there from outside, since the manuscripts attest to more than one set of scribal practices. Intriguingly, those compositions which are clearly sectarian, describing the beliefs and practices of the group which lived at Qumran and the wider movement of which it was a part, are mostly written using distinctive scribal conventions. This suggests that those manuscripts reflecting other scribal practices were brought to Qumran from elsewhere.

Although there are some compositions in the 11 Qumran caves which do not entirely fit with the ethos of the community who lived there, the vast majority of compositions found in the caves reflect a coherent ideology. As a result, it is not inappropriate to call this collection of manuscripts from the 11 caves a library. However, it should also be kept in mind that not all the caves were filled with manuscripts at the same time, as is commonly supposed, but that the caves seem to have had varying functions, some (such as Cave 1) serving as burial places (*genizot*) for worn-out or damaged manuscripts, others (such as Cave 4) serving as working depositories, others (such as Cave 7) apparently housing special collections, and yet others (such as Cave 8) possibly serving as workshops of some kind.

The library collection as a whole contains compositions which are usually grouped under three headings. First, about a quarter of the manuscripts are copies of the Jewish Scriptures in some form; there are several copies of some scriptural books which subsequently became almost universally authoritative, none of others, and there are several copies of certain compositions, such as the *Book of Jubilees*, which seem to have had scriptural authority for the Qumran community and its wider movement, but which had limited circulation after the destruction of the temple. Second, about a quarter of the manuscripts are copies of sectarian compositions, such as the *Damascus Document* or the *Rule of the Community*; these disclose the particular religious concerns of the group that lived at Qumran and the wider movement from which it originated and of which it was a part. The third group of compositions reflects general Jewish literature of the late second temple period; a few items were known before the discoveries in 1947 and thereafter, but most of this literature is new to the modern world. There are some noticeable absences from the library: the Books of Maccabees do not feature, nor is there any sign of any non-Jewish Greek or Roman literature, even though some of the collection is in Greek. Furthermore, there are very few business items, such as legal transactions, minutes of meetings, letters, inventory lists, or business dockets. The scrolls from the 11 Qumran caves are a Jewish religious library with particular religious concerns and ideological tendencies.

A few features of the Qumran library are worth noting in relation to the general themes of this collection of essays. Three points of particular significance for the better appreciation of the New Testament need to be stated. The first is a very general point. Until the discoveries of the Dead Sea Scrolls the only writing from Hasmonean and Roman Palestine was to be found on coin inscriptions and ossuaries. The scrolls from Qumran have provided about 900 manuscripts in Aramaic, Hebrew and Greek from the place and time when Jesus and his followers lived. This alone means that the Judaism of the period, the Judaism of which Jesus was a part, has had to be reconsidered. Although many of the essays in this volume argue that the scrolls shed considerable light on individual words and phrases in the New Testament, the general picture should not be forgotten. It can be no coincidence, for example, that the last 25 years have seen an increasing concern among New Testament scholars with the Jewish Law in the late second temple period as it might illuminate Jesus' halakhic practice or Paul's understanding of Torah; to my mind this has been directly and indirectly stimulated by the large number of legal compositions which have come to light among the scrolls, not least since the publication of the *Temple Scroll* in 1977. Because of the scrolls found at Qumran much more is known about how the interpretation of the Law was a focus of the daily concerns of at least one group of Jews in the three centuries before the fall of the temple in 70 C.E.

The second point concerns the details to be found in many of the scrolls, not just the sectarian ones. The fascination with the Dead Sea Scrolls among scholars of the New Testament arose not least because of the messianic and eschatological views to be found in some Qumran sectarian compositions together with there being some apparent similarities in community organization and practice which could explain various matters in the early Christian communities. However, what has emerged with the complete publication of what has survived in the Qumran caves is that the overriding character of the religious self-expression of those who lived at Qumran and of the Judaism of which they were a part was their concern with tradition. Attitudes to the Law were certainly a part of that concern, but it was much broader than the Law alone. The majority of compositions from the Qumran caves are concerned one way or another with the transmission of scriptural traditions. The dominant issue is the transmission and interpretation of authoritative Scriptures. The Dead Sea Scrolls show that this was a far more complicated matter in second temple Judaism than could have been imagined. The complexity rests not only in the variety of the forms of scriptural texts, but also in the richness of their interpretative transmission in rewritten parabiblical compositions of all kinds, as well as in commentaries which relate to their sources explicitly. It is the wealth of this exegetical activity which should now inform the reading of traditions in a collection of Jewish or Jewish Christian texts such as the New Testament.

Lastly, though some few manuscripts in Caves 4 and 7 are in Greek (in Cave 7 exclusively so), almost certainly no copies of any of the writings of the New Testament have come from any of the caves. Those few scholars who persist in the view that a direct link can be made between Qumran and the New Testament are probably constructing an approach to the evidence which cannot be sustained. The links between the Dead Sea Scrolls and the New Testament are more likely to be indirect. Although it is indeed possible that a few second- and third-generation Christians had at some time had Essene or even Qumran affiliation, they have left only slender traces of their former lives in the New Testament; they have had their outlooks oriented towards what their Christian companions had seen of the activity of God in the life, death and resurrection of Jesus, a reorientation which was a major shift away from their concerns as those might be reconstructed from the fragmentary remains found in the Qumran caves. The overall implication of this observation is that those using the scrolls to illuminate the writings of the New Testament should be as much concerned with the differences as with the similarities.

Concern with differences as well as similarities makes comparison both more complicated as well as in the end more fruitful. It could be that the complexity of the data now available from the Qumran caves has inhibited New Testament scholars from venturing down the road towards the Dead Sea. In the first chapter in this collection I outline some of the principal features of the history of the study of the New Testament in the light of the Dead Sea Scrolls. Although all would acknowledge the need to take account of the Jewish origins of much of Christianity, few nowadays engage with the most authentic sources for reconstructing those very origins. My hope is that the publication of a set of essays like this might contribute to a fresh engagement with the scrolls not only for the fascination which they have in themselves, but also for what they can contribute to the better understanding of the writings of the New Testament and the multifarious sources they reflect.

Undoubtedly, much in the New Testament is appropriately set in the complex world of the eastern Mediterranean in late antiquity. Although widely acknowledged it needs to be reaffirmed that late second temple period Judaism can no longer be neatly distinguished from the Graeco-Roman culture of which it was a part. Even at Qumran the influence of the wider culture is visible in many aspects of life: from the existence of manuscripts in Greek to the concerns with the latest knowledge about the sun, the moon and the stars; from the likely support for crucifixion as a form of punishment to knowledge of Roman military tactics; from the structures of community organization to the necessity to formulate a view about the Gentile, whether as the agent of God or as the object of divine annihilation. Nevertheless, the Qumran library has an undeniable and distinctive Jewishness about it, which can be located in place and time. As a result it is not surprising that it is John the Baptist and Jesus, Jews of Roman Palestine, on whom the scrolls might be thought to shed most light. How that might be done, especially in the case of Jesus, is the subject of the second short chapter. Jesus was not an Essene, but neither can it be denied that some aspects of his life and teaching can be informed by what we know from the Qumran caves.

From what has been preserved of the teaching of Jesus it is likely that he based his message of both the immanence and the imminence of the kingship of God on some Jewish Scriptures more than others. The New Testament as a whole seems to have a similar set of preferences to those found in the Qumran library collection. Chapter 3 is an attempt to underline the character of the similarities and differences in the selection of some Scriptures over against others. The similar place given to some traditions from Genesis, Deuteronomy, Isaiah, the Twelve and the Psalms in both collections is remarkable. For the members of the Qumran community those traditions reflect an understanding of God's ways with humanity which puts a distinctive onus on the true Israel in its very particularity, a responsibility which is known to be celebrated in heaven but is recognized as only to be fully lived out in the eschatological age which seems to be already dawning. For the early Christian writers working with similar scriptural preferences the not dissimilar onus of responsibility of the Christian communities is constantly directed towards Jesus as the hermeneutical key whose life and message are seen as both an unattainable ideal, but also as the means to realizing the sovereignty of God on earth through the life of discipleship.

Although there are similar scriptural starting points, there are also some distinct emphases. For example, the use of Isaiah in the scrolls is far more comprehensive than the seemingly more selective use of Isaianic proof-texts by the writers of the New Testament. The appeal to Deuteronomy both in legal traditions and in poetry and prayer is more energetically serious in the Qumran community and the wider movement of which it was a part than the Deuteronomic cherry-picking observable in New Testament authors who are still feeling their way in relation to the place of the Law in their new forms of Judaism. The same goes for the methods through which the Scriptures are handled; there are several similarities in both literary corpora, but the fourth chapter on biblical interpretation in the Qumran scrolls and the New Testament, as well as pointing out some of the similarities, also argues that there are certain fundamental differences which need to be accounted for.

Differences also underpin the contribution of Chapter 5 on shared intertextual interpretations in the Dead Sea Scrolls and the New Testament. There are several instances in the scrolls and in the New Testament in which the same two or more scriptural texts are combined together for some reason. The thesis of the chapter is that seldom, if ever, is this the result of either direct or indirect literary dependence of one author upon another, in this case of the New Testament author upon the interpretative traditions found in the scrolls. Rather, when the scriptural combinations are looked at closely, the exegetical differences in detail are usually more significant than any apparent similarities. The solution to this conundrum may rest in the way in which the same combinations of authoritative texts suggest themselves independently to a range of authors. Those who know their Scriptures well and who are trained in similar exegetical techniques will often seemingly spontaneously put items together. All texts have intertexts; it is not surprising that different authors with similar starting points end up elaborating their insights by using the same secondary supporting texts.

If differences between the Dead Sea Scrolls and the New Testament characterize several of the five essays in the first section of this book, in the second section of this collection there is greater emphasis on the similarities. The six studies assembled in Part Two juxtapose particular compositions from the Qumran caves with their New Testament counterparts. The overall aim is not to argue for any kind of literary dependence but to disclose something of the rich exegetical tapestry present in late second temple Jewish circles in Palestine and to show that the New Testament authors were aware of some of the threads which made up the warp and woof. The juxtaposition of the *Temple Scroll* (11Q19) with the Gospel of John in particular shows that a few traditions connected with Jacob lie on the surface of both compositions, but that many more may lie in a seam which has yet to be mined just beneath the surface. Some of those Jacob traditions are probably evident elsewhere in the New Testament when all the references to Levi and the Levites in both sets of texts are put alongside each other; in this case such traditions may also disclose the identity of a few people who made the transition from Essenism to Christianity.

It cannot be denied that some subtlety has to be used in the analysis of individual Dead Sea Scrolls and particular sections of the New Testament texts. It is not always straightforward to see how texts might illuminate one another. In Chapter 8 I suggest that the collection of references to Isaiah in the *Apocryphon of Levi* (4Q541) indicates that its compiler was aware of traditions about an eschatological high priest who could have the language of the Suffering Servant applied to him. Such a combination of descriptors provides an argument that scholars should revisit the issue of the place of the Suffering Servant as a description of Jesus in the New Testament; perhaps its limited use can be explained by its strong associations with cultic motifs in contemporary Jewish interpretation. Given that many details in Luke–Acts were illuminated by the first generation of Qumran scholars, in Chapter 9 attention to the ideological assumptions of *Miqsat Ma'aśê ha-Torah* (4Q394–398) is used to illuminate some of the cultic concerns of the author of Luke–Acts, from the place of Jerusalem to the interest in who should be included in temple worship; from some similar premises, the two compositions reach radically different answers. Chapter 10 highlights the exegetical interests which exercised the compiler of the *Commentary on Genesis* (4Q252) and asks whether any of the same interests or the ways in which they are expressed are discernible in the New Testament. Some are, some are not; those that are can now be set within a broader exegetical framework. The juxtaposition of two words in specific contexts in Chapter 11, *rwqmh* in the *Damascus Document* (4Q270 7 I, 14) and *exousia* in 1 Corinthians 11.10, demonstrates how in some cases interpretative difficulties can receive mutual illumination, even if they cannot necessarily be decisively solved.

The third section of this book contains five essays which are focused on the mutual illumination of the Scrolls and the Gospels. In Chapter 12 I argue that in the light of *Beatitudes* (4Q525) the beatitudes in Matthew's Gospel in particular should be seen as the development of a traditional pattern of Wisdom instruction in contemporary Judaism and, vice versa, in light of Matthew's use of the beatitudes at the opening of the Sermon on the Mount, their use in 4Q525 might be understood in terms of religious initiation. In Chapter 13 the detailed analysis of the parable of the vineyard (Mk 12.1–12 //) in light of 4Q500 puts the parable realistically into a tradition of Jewish exegesis with which even Jesus himself could have been familiar; the parable in turn supports the discernment of various features of the vineyard in 4Q500, Fragment 1, a piece which otherwise might have easily been ignored by New Testament scholars.

The closing three chapters contain some attractive exegetical surprises. In Chapter 14, among other matters, there is discussion of the begetting of the Messiah by God. The *Rule of the Congregation* (1QSa (1Q28a) II, 11–12) shows that the divine engendering of the Messiah was conceptually possible though not in a literal sense, while the birth narratives in the Gospels give permission for this particular reading of a very difficult Qumran text. Chapter 15 highlights the possible significance of a few very partial lines in the *Reworked Pentateuch* (4Q365 6a II, 1–7) for the better appreciation of revolutionary songs of reversal associated with women such as Miriam, Judith and Mary; the Magnificat in turn helps explain some of the terse phraseology of the Song of Miriam. In Chapter 16 one item of the calendrical data in the *Commentary on Genesis* (4Q252) is used to help further support a particular understanding of the enigmatic 153 fish in John 21.11; in turn, the Pythagorean calculations behind some of the Johannine mathematics can be added to the appreciation of the apt association of the Essenes with the Pythagoreans by Josephus.

As pointed out at the opening of this Introduction the concern of these essays with the ways in which scriptural traditions are transmitted and interpreted in the Dead Sea Scrolls and the New Testament is true to my own longstanding research interests in early Jewish exegesis. However, these essays should also be taken as indicating two new directions for scholars to take. Those concerned to appreciate some of the exegetical details preserved in the Dead Sea Scrolls would do well not to omit the evidence of the New Testament in their search of contemporary Jewish literature which might help in the explanation of challenging fragmentary passages. New Testament scholars in turn should recognize that the value of the Dead Sea Scrolls for the better appreciation of the Jewish background of much in the New Testament does not lie exclusively in particular matters of organization or messianic belief, but much more broadly in the ways in which Jews contemporary with Jesus and Paul constructed their own self-understandings and identities through highly intricate and sophisticated interpretations of inherited traditions, interpretations which gave life to texts written in earlier generations. With attention to such matters it can readily be seen that the Dead Sea Scrolls and the New Testament are entering a new era of mutual illumination.

PART ONE

GENERALLY
ILLUMINATING

1

The Qumran Scrolls and the Study of the New Testament

How can one summarize briefly 50 years or more of scholarship on the Qumran scrolls and the study of the New Testament?[1] I propose to use the periodization of the Qumran site which has been offered to us by Père Roland de Vaux and with which most biblical scholars and others might have some familiarity.[2] Like most matters to do with the Qumran scrolls this historical schematization is itself currently under review and so, no doubt, some aspects of the use of it in this summary will also be subject to revision by others.

PRE-QUMRAN

To begin with there is the pre-Qumran Israelite period. For the discussion of the scrolls and the New Testament two features of the pre-1947, pre-Qumran period are worth highlighting. First, the classical sources on

---

1 The bibliography is vast. Some few items will be referred to during the course of this brief survey. More complete details can be found in the standard bibliographies: W. S. LaSor, *Bibliography of the Dead Sea Scrolls 1948–1957* (Fuller Theological Seminary Bibliographical Series 2; Pasadena: Fuller Theological Seminary, 1958), esp. 82–9; C. Burchard, *Bibliographie zu den Handschriften vom Toten Meer* (BZAW 76; Berlin: A. Töpelmann, 1959); C. Burchard, *Bibliographie zu den Handschriften vom Toten Meer II* (BZAW 89; Berlin: A. Töpelmann, 1965); B. Jongeling, *A Classified Bibliography of the Finds in the Desert of Judah 1958–1969* (STDJ 7; Leiden: Brill, 1971), esp. 111–29; F. García Martínez and D. W. Parry, *A Bibliography of the Finds in the Desert of Judah 1970–95* (STDJ 19; Leiden: Brill, 1996), see the indexes; A. Pinnick, *The Orion Center Bibliography of the Dead Sea Scrolls (1995–2000)* (STDJ 41; Leiden: Brill, 2001), see the indexes. Also useful is J. A. Fitzmyer, *The Dead Sea Scrolls: Major Publications and Tools for Study* (SBLRBS 20; Atlanta: Scholars Press, 1990), 168–79.
2 First published in book form in R. de Vaux, *L'archéologie et les manuscrits de la Mer Morte* (Schweich Lectures; London: Oxford University Press for the British Academy, 1961), 1–39.

the Essenes were sometimes discussed in relation to Jesus and the early church communities. The most well-known conclusion in this regard has been E. Renan's dictum that Christianity was an Essenism which had largely succeeded;[3] few would agree with this nowadays. Of the three obvious possibilities, that the Essenes and the New Testament have nothing to do with each other, that the New Testament shows that the early Christians were Essenes in some form, and that while distinct it is nevertheless possible that some Essenes became members of some early Christian communities, it is the last which is most commonly recognized as closest to the truth in light of the scrolls.[4]

Second, there was the publication of the *Cairo Damascus Document* or Zadokite Work.[5] In addition to a general comment on the relationship between the Pseudepigrapha whose ideology seemed to lie behind the *Damascus Document* and the sectarian character of early Christianity,[6] S. Schechter made ten specific references to the New Testament, among which are a reference to Matthew with regard to what Schechter understood as the ruling against polygamy in CD IV, 21,[7] references to 1 Corinthians 11.25 and Hebrews 8.8 with regard to the new covenant in CD VI, 19, references to John 13.34, 15.12 and Romans 12.10 with regard to the use of Leviticus 19.18 in CD VI, 21, and the mention of Abraham as friend of God in CD III, 3 and James 2.23.[8] R. H. Charles, in his version of the same text,[9] offered an overall opinion of what happened to the Sons of Zadok:

---

3 E. Renan, *Histoire du people d'Israël* (Paris: Calman, 1891), 5.70. Among others, this view was endorsed by A. Dupont-Sommer, *The Essene Writings from Qumran* (Oxford: Blackwell, 1961), 13, 368–78.

4 Note the representative comment of J. H. Charlesworth, 'The Dead Sea Scrolls and the Gospel according to John', in *Exploring the Gospel of John: In Honor of D. Moody Smith* (ed. R. A. Culpepper and C. C. Black; Louisville: Westminster John Knox Press, 1996), 89: 'It seems widely, and wisely, acknowledged that some Essenes became Christians.'

5 First published in 1910 and reissued as S. Schechter, *Documents of Jewish Sectaries: Volume I: Fragments of a Zadokite Work* (with a prolegomenon by J. A. Fitzmyer; New York: Ktav, 1970).

6 *Documents of Jewish Sectaries*, 61 (= xxix).

7 Schechter referred to Matt. 21.3, but this is an error for Matt. 19.3–9, especially 19.4 where Gen. 1.27 is used as in CD IV, 21. The parallel in Mk 10.1–12 should also be considered.

8 On Abraham as friend of God, see also 4Q252 II, 8. Schechter's other comparisons with the New Testament were CD VII, 3 (Rom. 12.19); CD V, 19 (2 Tim. 3.8); CD II, 16 (2 Pet. 2.14).

9 R. H. Charles, 'The Fragments of a Zadokite Work', *APOT* 2.785–834.

The later history of the Sons of Zadok is buried in all but impenetrable gloom. It is, however, not at all improbable that many of their members joined the Christian Church. For their appreciation of the Prophets – unparalleled in legalistic Judaism; their insistent preaching on the need of repentance; their constant proclamation of God's readiness to forgive the repentant; their expectation of a Messiah (and just at his period) and of a future life – all these beliefs and hopes prepared them to accept Christianity, and accordingly it is not unreasonable to conclude that they formed part of the 'great company of the *priests* that became obedient to the faith' (Acts vi. 7).[10]

Charles extended Schechter's list of suggestive parallels somewhat. Intriguingly, however, despite Schechter's hints, he did not mention any New Testament parallel for the new covenant of CD VI, 19, though he did suggest that the *mebaqqer* was the same kind of official as the *episkopos* of the early churches.[11] Other scholars also wrote on the *Damascus Document* and early Christianity in the pre-Qumran period.[12]

PERIOD IA

Period Ia at Qumran is that of small beginnings. For the purposes of this study these small beginnings in juxtaposing the scrolls emerging from the Qumran caves with the New Testament run from the earliest publications in 1948 up to about 1952 or a little beyond. The majority of the early articles on the scrolls and the New Testament or Christian origins were written in French or German. Although one should beware of national stereotypes in scholarship, we may suspect that those in French resulted chiefly from the proximity of French scholars to unfolding events in the Qumran region and that those in German reflect an interest of some German New Testament scholarship in a somewhat positivist view of the historical circumstances of first-century Palestine. This concern is still apparent in Germany with regard to the

---

10 *APOT* 2.786.
11 *APOT* 2.824.
12 See the bibliography by J. A. Fitzmyer in S. Schechter, *Documents of Jewish Sectaries*, 25–34.

scrolls, though not really as part of mainstream German New Testament scholarship.[13]

This period's articles were the product of the excitement of the increasingly justified realization that the scrolls were genuinely 2,000 years old or more and of noticing that in places there were some significant parallels with the New Testament writings. K. G. Kuhn's short article 'Zur Bedeutung der neuen palästinischen Handschriftenfunde für die neutestamentliche Wissenschaft', published in early 1950, is a good example of the genre.[14] He discussed briefly at the outset the likely date of the manuscripts from Cave 1: he sides with those who have identified the scrolls with the *Damascus Document* and related Pseudepigrapha. Then he offered a detailed analysis of 1QS I, 11–13 in a pointed form.[15] In his comments on the text he drew attention to some verbal parallels in the New Testament and comments more generally on what 1QS seems to be saying about the organization of the Church according to Acts and the kind of offering which Ananias and Sapphira should have made. There was no attempt to argue that members of the community reflected in 1QS had joined the early Christian Church, though the possibility was admitted; rather 1QS I, 11–13 was used solely to illuminate the meaning of a few details in the New Testament narrative.

---

13 See, e.g., R. Riesner, 'Essener und Urkirche in Jerusalem', in *Christen und Christliches in Qumran?* (ed. B. Mayer; Regensburg: Pustet, 1992), 139–55; C. P. Thiede, *The Earliest Gospel Manuscript? The Qumran Fragment 7Q5 and Its Significance for New Testament Studies* (Carlisle: Paternoster Press, 1992); C. P. Thiede, *Rekindling the Word: In Search of Gospel Truth* (Valley Forge: Trinity Press International, 1995), 158–204. This attitude is reflected in the way in which M. Baigent and R. Leigh, *The Dead Sea Scroll Deception* (London: Jonathan Cape, 1991), was entitled in its German edition *Verschlußsache Jesus: Die Qumranrollen und die Wahrheit über das frühe Christentum* (Munich: Drömer Knaur, 1991); and the same happened with R. H. Eisenman and M. Wise, *The Dead Sea Scrolls Uncovered* (Rockport: Element Books, 1992), which in German became *Jesus und die Urchristen: Die Qumran-Rollen entschlüsselt* (Munich: Bretelsmann, 1993).

14 K. G. Kuhn, 'Der gegenwärtige Stand der Erforschung der in Palästina neu gefundenen hebräischen Handschriften: 9. Zur Bedeutung der neuen palästinischen Handschriftenfunde für die neutestamentliche Wissenschaft', *TLZ* 75 (1950) cols 81–6.

15 The concern to encourage New Testament scholars to engage with the scrolls in Hebrew by presenting them in a pointed form is praiseworthy. The same can be noted of the German parallel edition of scrolls by the New Testament scholar E. Lohse, *Die Texte aus Qumran: Hebräisch und Deutsch* (Munich: Kösel Verlag, 1964, 2nd edn 1971).

PERIOD IB

Period Ib saw the rapid expansion of activity. With regard to the study of the scrolls and the New Testament it seems to me that this period lasted for about 25 years, from the early 1950s until the publication in 1976 of G. Vermes' essay 'The Impact of the Dead Sea Scrolls on the Study of the New Testament',[16] and in 1977 of E. P. Sanders' *Paul and Palestinian Judaism*.[17] As with the pre-Qumran view on the relationship between the Essenes and the early Christians, so this period of scholarly endeavour has three options in it with regard to the scrolls from Qumran and the New Testament writings, each of which is an attempt to deal with the problem which S. Sandmel so eloquently labelled 'parallelomania'.[18] The first option was to say that the scrolls are the background to the life and thought of the early churches, or even more strongly, to say that John the Baptist[19] and Jesus both had Essene connections.[20] For some scholars and others this option was played as if the scrolls prefigured nearly all the key

---

16 G. Vermes, 'The Impact of the Dead Sea Scrolls on the Study of the New Testament', *JJS* 27 (1976): 107–16; reprinted in G. Vermes, *Jesus and the World of Judaism* (London: SCM Press, 1983), 115–25, 182. The summary review by J. A. Fitzmyer can also be cited as indicating the end of this period of research, since, apart from Fitzmyer's own writings, it refers to nothing published after 1976: J. A. Fitzmyer, 'The Dead Sea Scrolls and the New Testament after Thirty Years', *TD* 29 (1981): 351–67.

17 E. P. Sanders, *Paul and Palestinian Judaism* (London: SCM Press, 1977).

18 S. Sandmel, 'Parallelomania', *JBL* 81 (1962): 1–13; see also S. Sandmel, 'Palestinian and Hellenistic Judaism and Christianity: the Question of a Comfortable Theory', *HUCA* 50 (1979): 137–48.

19 The literature on John the Baptist and Qumran is extensive; see the items mentioned by L. F. Badia, *The Qumran Baptism and John the Baptist's Baptism* (Lanham: University Press of America, 1980), 78–87, and R. L. Webb, *John the Baptizer and Prophet: A Socio-Historical Study* (Sheffield: Sheffield Academic Press, 1991), 213, n. 137; for a balanced survey see J. E. Taylor, *The Immerser: John the Baptist within Second Temple Judaism* (Grand Rapids: Eerdmans, 1997), 15–48.

20 Linking Jesus directly with the Essenes or the Qumran community is much more problematic. See the balanced summary assessments of H. Stegemann, *Die Essener, Qumran, Johannes der Täufer und Jesus: Ein Sachbuch* (Spektrum 4249; Freiburg: Herder, 1993), 314–52; J. A. Fitzmyer, 'The Dead Sea Scrolls and Early Christianity', *TD* 42 (1995): 305–7. Both Stegemann and Fitzmyer write against some of the more bizarre theories of recent years such as those put forward by B. Thiering, *Jesus and the Riddle of the Scrolls: Unlocking the Secrets of his Life Story* (San Francisco: HarperSanFrancisco, 1992).

items in the New Testament, from John's priestly relations to Jesus' crucifixion. The second option, sometimes a doctrinal over-reaction to the
first by those concerned to preserve the uniqueness of the New Testament
message[21] and especially of Jesus and the divine revelation located in him,
was to suggest that there was really very little relationship between the
scrolls and what was now visible in the New Testament.[22]

The third option was an emerging consensus view that there was some
kind of relationship between the sectarian scrolls and the early Christian
writings, but that this did not involve the simple equation of the two.[23]
This is worth describing further because it is in the process of being
revived. There are four major elements to it.[24] The first is that, with the
possible exception of John the Baptist, the principal time where the scrolls
assist in understanding the New Testament is in the post-70 C.E. period.
The second is that it is predominantly in matters of community organization (e.g., a group of 12;[25] *mebaqqer* = *episkopos*) and practice (e.g.,
community of goods) that suitable parallels can be found. The third is that
there is some shared worldview between the scrolls and the New Testament, especially in relation to the temple,[26] some aspects of eschatology

---

21 E.g., in general H. H. Rowley concluded that 'to suppose that the Scrolls can give
us any evidence of the nature of early Christianity is fantastic': *The Dead Sea Scrolls
and the New Testament* (London: SPCK, 1957), 30. And with regard to John the
Baptist, Rowley concluded that 'in all that is most characteristic of John's baptism
complete independence of both proselyte baptism and Essene baptism is to be recognized': 'The Baptism of John and the Qumran Sect', in *New Testament Essays* (ed. A. J.
B. Higgins; Manchester: Manchester University Press, 1959), 228.

22 See, e.g., G. Graystone, *The Dead Sea Scrolls and the Originality of Christ*
(London: Sheed & Ward, 1956).

23 This option is exemplified in the writings of F. F. Bruce, as in his study 'Qumran
and the New Testament', *Faith and Thought* 90 (1958): 92–102.

24 These are described by Vermes, 'The Impact of the Dead Sea Scrolls on the Study
of the New Testament'.

25 1QS VIII, 1. There are several noteworthy variations on the number 12, notably
in 11QT[a] LVII, 11–13 and 4QpIsa[d]. On the latter see among others D. Flusser,
'Qumran und die Zwölf', in *Initiation* (ed. C. J. Bleeker; Studies in the History of
Religions 10; Leiden: Brill, 1965), 134–46; reprinted in *Judaism and the Origins of
Christianity* (Jerusalem: Magnes Press, 1988), 173–85; J. M. Baumgarten, 'The
Duodecimal Courts of Qumran, Revelation, and the Sanhedrin', *JBL* 95 (1976):
59–78; reprinted in J. M. Baumgarten, *Studies in Qumran Law* (SJLA 24; Leiden:
Brill, 1977), 145–71.

26 See the oft-cited study of B. Gärtner, *The Temple and the Community in Qumran and
the New Testament: A Comparative Study in the Temple Symbolism of the Qumran Texts
and the New Testament* (SNTSMS 1; Cambridge: Cambridge University Press, 1965).

(notably messianism), and various other concepts.[27] The fourth is that the scrolls triggered a widespread appreciation for the varieties of early Church communities, just as they widened the parameters of the description of the Judaism which was developing contemporaneously.

The hallmark of this period of study is the surprising absence of books that represent the consensus view. No overall synthesis on the scrolls and the New Testament was written, nor has yet been written, but several key studies took centre stage. Among these one can be invidious and single out a few that remain significant and are sometimes cited: D. Flusser's manifold suggestive notes from 1953 onwards,[28] cautious studies by F. F. Bruce from 1956,[29] R. E. Brown's study on Qumran and the Fourth Gospel and Johannine Epistles,[30] J. Daniélou's small book on early Christianity,[31] M. Black's study of the scrolls, the classical sources, and Christian origins,[32] J. A. Fitzmyer's work on the quotation formulae in the scrolls and the New Testament,[33] H. Braun's compendium of parallels,[34] the monographs of the Heidelberg School in the series Studien zur Umwelt des Neuen Testaments, each written with a view to providing information for the Jewish setting of the New

---

27 See, e.g., F. C. Fensham, '"Camp" in the New Testament and Milḥamah', RevQ 4 (1963–4): 557–62.

28 See now, D. Flusser, Judaism and the Origins of Christianity (Jerusalem: Magnes Press, 1988) where many of the most significant studies are brought together and reprinted.

29 F. F. Bruce, 'Qumrân and Early Christianity', NTS 2 (1955–6): 176–90.

30 R. E. Brown, 'The Qumran Scrolls and the Johannine Gospel and Epistles', CBQ 17 (1955): 403–19, 559–74; reprinted in K. Stendahl, ed., The Scrolls and the New Testament (New York: Harper, 1957), 183–207, and in R. E. Brown, New Testament Essays (London: Geoffrey Chapman, 1967), 102–31.

31 J. Daniélou, Les manuscrits de la Mer Morte et les origines du Christianisme (Paris: Editions de l'Orange, 1957); ET The Dead Sea Scrolls and Primitive Christianity (New York: New American Library, 1958).

32 M. Black, The Scrolls and Christian Origins: Studies in the Jewish Background of the New Testament (London: T. Nelson & Sons, 1961).

33 J. A. Fitzmyer, 'The Use of Explicit Old Testament Quotations in Qumran Literature and in the New Testament', NTS 7 (1960–1): 297–333; reprinted in J. A. Fitzmyer, Essays on the Semitic Background of the New Testament (London: Geoffrey Chapman, 1971), 3–58, and most recently in J. A. Fitzmyer, The Semitic Background of the New Testament (Grand Rapids: Eerdmans; Livonia: Dove, 1997), 3–58.

34 H. Braun, Qumran und das Neue Testament I–II (Tübingen: J. C. B. Mohr, 1966).

Testament,[35] all coming to a fruitful climax in E. P. Sanders' insightful appreciation of the role of genre in describing the Qumran sectarian worldview such that salvation by grace and by rigorous obedience could be seen as two sides of the same coin.[36]

ABANDONMENT

Then the site was abandoned. We may debate for the 1980s about the precise duration of the period of abandonment or even whether there really was complete abandonment, but New Testament studies and research on the Qumran scrolls seem to have gone their separate ways. For New Testament studies the 1980s see a shift away from purely historical readings of the early Church documents towards the use of all manner of other techniques and critical approaches. One wonders whether part of the lack of interest in the scrolls was engendered by the way in which the continuing failure to publish the manuscripts was considered an inhibiting factor: why should scholars risk their reputations on specifying some kind of relationship between the scrolls and the New Testament if they might be refuted by new material which a handful of scholars already knew about? More significantly, it is possible to construe the relative silence among New Testament scholars concerning the scrolls as the result in part of the publication of the *Temple Scroll* in 1977.[37] Its first publication in Modern Hebrew may have added to New Testament scholarly inhibitions. Certainly the publication of the *Temple Scroll* led to many scrolls scholars reorienting themselves away from questions narrowly defined in terms of historical or ideological trajectories towards a complete reconsideration of the transmission and application of the Law in the second temple period. The consensus, and in relation to the New Testament, largely Christian reading of the scrolls no longer seemed

---

35 H.-W. Kuhn, *Enderwartung und gegenwärtiges Heil* (SUNT 4; Göttingen: Vandenhoeck & Ruprecht, 1966); P. von der Osten-Sacken, *Gott und Belial* (SUNT 6; Göttingen: Vandenhoeck & Ruprecht, 1969); G. Klinzing, *Die Umdeutung des Kultus in der Qumrangemeinde und im Neuen Testament* (SUNT 7; Göttingen: Vandenhoeck & Ruprecht, 1971); and latterly H. Lichtenberger, *Studien zum Menschenbild in Texten der Qumrangemeinde* (SUNT 15; Göttingen: Vandenhoeck & Ruprecht, 1980).

36 E. P. Sanders, *Paul and Palestinian Judaism* (London: SCM Press, 1977), 233–328.

37 Y. Yadin, *The Temple Scroll (Hebrew Edition)* (Jerusalem: Israel Exploration Society, Institute of Archaeology of the Hebrew University, Shrine of the Book, 1977); the English version did not become available until 1983.

so self-evident. The *Temple Scroll* has shown clearly that the disputes which were at the heart of what distinguished one group from another in the 200 years before the destruction of the temple in 70 C.E. were halakhic in kind rather than doctrinal. The subsequent publication of other legal texts found at Qumran, especially the six copies of *Miqṣat Ma'aśê ha-Torah*,[38] has further increased the gap between many New Testament scholars and the scrolls from Qumran. More and more it is becoming apparent that to appreciate the scrolls properly scholars must have some secure knowledge of Jewish legal traditions in the late second temple period. Few New Testament scholars are trained in these matters nowadays, and so it could be that some scholars will remain permanently shy of coming to terms with the significance of the complete corpus of Qumran scrolls for the better understanding of the New Testament.

PERIOD II

Period II saw the reoccupation of the site. For scholarship on the significance of the scrolls for the study of the New Testament this began shortly before the general release of all the unpublished scrolls in 1991 with the publication of a few small fragments, notably a part of 4Q525, the Wisdom text with beatitudes.[39] However, since the open access policy of the Israeli authorities in 1991, and especially since the availability of the microfiche edition of all the photographs of the Dead Sea Scrolls,[40] there has been a new spate of activity in their research at least part of which has involved reconsideration of the relationship between the scrolls and the New Testament writings.

Several intriguing developments have taken place. First, it has become obvious that the consensus view of Period Ib was largely on the right

---

38 E. Qimron and J. Strugnell, *Qumran Cave 4.V: Miqṣat Ma'aśe Ha-Torah* (DJD 10; Oxford: Clarendon Press, 1994).

39 E. Puech, 'Un Hymne essénien en partie retrouvé et les Béatitudes: 1QH V 12–VI 18 (= col. XIII–XIV 7) et 4QBéat', *RevQ* 13 (1988): 59–88; cf. G. J. Brooke, 'The Wisdom of Matthew's Beatitudes (4QBéat and Mt. 5.3–12)', *ScrB* 19 (1988–9): 35–41 (slightly revised as Chapter 12 in this volume); J. A. Fitzmyer, 'A Palestinian Collection of Beatitudes', in *The Four Gospels 1992: Festschrift Frans Neirynck* (ed. F. Van Segbroeck, C. M. Tuckett, G. Van Belle, J. Verheyden; BETL 100; Leuven: Leuven University Press & Peeters, 1992), 509–15.

40 E. Tov with the collaboration of S. J. Pfann, *The Dead Sea Scrolls on Microfiche: A Comprehensive Facsimile Edition of the Texts from the Judean Desert* (Leiden: Brill/IDC, 1993).

track,[41] though its views are now in need of adjustment, especially with regard to legal traditions. Some scholars have been well intentioned in reviving the study of the scrolls and the New Testament along lines not that dissimilar from the mainstream approaches of Periods Ia and Ib. For example, J. H. Charlesworth has seen to the republication of three significant volumes of essays from Period Ib, *The Scrolls and the New Testament*,[42] *Paul and Qumran*,[43] and *John and Qumran*.[44] H.-W. Kuhn's Munich project continues to work on Pauline parallels.[45] These acts have stressed the continuity of scholarly opinion between Period Ib and Period II, but there is some considerable evidence that this is not an adequate approach in itself.

So two other matters have emerged alongside this restatement of continuity. First, one feature of the consensus view of Period Ib was that the scrolls were chiefly helpful in providing an anterior or contemporary Jewish framework for the organization and beliefs of the second or especially the third generation of early Church members. It was largely in the period after 70 C.E. that the influence of the scrolls on various early Church writings could be seen: not in Mark, but perhaps in Matthew with its use of fulfilment quotations or the Fourth Gospel with its dualism; not in Paul, but perhaps in Ephesians with its mysteries or in

---

41 As is helpfully summarized by J. C. VanderKam, *The Dead Sea Scrolls Today* (Grand Rapids: Eerdmans, 1994), 159–85.

42 K. Stendahl, *The Scrolls and the New Testament* (New York: Harper, 1957; London: SCM Press, 1958); republished New York: Crossroad, 1992.

43 J. Murphy-O'Connor, ed., *Paul and Qumran* (London: Geoffrey Chapman, 1968); republished as J. Murphy-O'Connor and J. H. Charlesworth, eds, *Paul and the Dead Sea Scrolls* (New York: Crossroad, 1990).

44 J. H. Charlesworth, ed., *John and Qumran* (London: Geoffrey Chapman, 1972); republished as J. H. Charlesworth, ed., *John and the Dead Sea Scrolls* (New York: Crossroad, 1990).

45 See H.-W. Kuhn, 'Die Bedeutung der Qumrantexte für das Verständnis des Ersten Thessalonicherbriefes: Vorstellung des Münchener Projekts Qumran und das Neue Testament', in *The Madrid Qumran Congress: Proceedings of the International Congress on the Dead Sea Scrolls, Madrid, 18–21 March 1991* (ed. J. Trebolle Barrera and L. Vegas Montaner; STDJ 11; Leiden: Brill, 1992) 339–53; 'The Impact of the Qumran Scrolls on the Understanding of Paul', in *The Dead Sea Scrolls: Forty Years of Research* (ed. D. Dimant and U. Rappaport; STDJ 10; Leiden: Brill, 1992), 327–39; 'Die Bedeutung der Qumrantexte für das Verständnis des Galaterbriefes aus dem Münchener Projekt: Qumran und das Neue Testament', in *New Qumran Texts and Studies: Proceedings of the First Meeting of the International Organization for Qumran Studies, Paris 1992* (ed. G. J. Brooke with F. García Martínez; STDJ 15; Leiden: Brill, 1994), 169–221.

Hebrews with Melchizedek.[46] But the influence, both direct and indirect of the compositions found in the scrolls and these later New Testament writings is being reconsidered. Despite some protestations, preliminary results indicate that the influence is far less dominant than might have been supposed. For the Fourth Gospel, for example, there is little in its concern with light and darkness that cannot be derived from Scripture itself or from standard contemporary Jewish meditations on the Scriptures;[47] even the phrase 'sons of light' is no more characteristic of the Gospel and its community than it is for Paul (or even Luke).[48] Or again, as Franco Manzi has recently shown,[49] the portrayal of Melchizedek in Hebrews may have been influenced by currents in Jewish angelology which are also visible in the scrolls, but overall the differences in the form and function of the two portrayals of the same figure are far greater than the similarities. It has even been suggested that the closer a New Testament passage and a Qumran scroll seem to be, the more likely is it that both merely share a feature of Palestinian Judaism common at the time.[50] The scrolls have helped us to see the Jewishness of much of the New Testament at all levels, but they have not provided the source material scholars so often seek.[51]

---

46 See J. H. Charlesworth, 'The Dead Sea Scrolls and the Gospel according to John', in *Exploring the Gospel of John: In Honor of D. Moody Smith* (ed. R. A. Culpepper and C. C. Black; Louisville: Westminster John Knox Press, 1996), 89, where he considers the most obvious parallels between the Dead Sea Scrolls and the New Testament to lie in the Pauline school, the Matthean school and the Johannine school.

47 See, e.g., R. Bauckham, 'Qumran and the Fourth Gospel: Is There a Connection?', in *The Scrolls and the Scriptures: Qumran Fifty Years After* (ed. S. E. Porter and C. A. Evans; JSPSup 26; Roehampton Institute London Papers 3; Sheffield: Sheffield Academic Press, 1997), 267–79.

48 'Sons of light' or 'children of light' occurs only four times in the New Testament: Luke 16.8; John 12.36; Eph. 5.8; 1 Thess. 5.5.

49 F. Manzi, *Melchisedek e l'angelologia nell'Epistola agli Ebrei e a Qumran* (AnBib 136; Rome: Pontifical Biblical Institute, 1997).

50 G. J. Brooke, 'Shared Intertextual Interpretations in the Dead Sea Scrolls and the New Testament', in *Biblical Perspectives: Early Use and Interpretation of the Bible in Light of the Dead Sea Scrolls: Proceedings of the First International Symposium of the Orion Center for the Study of the Dead Sea Scrolls and Associated Literature, 12–14 May, 1996* (ed. M. E. Stone and E. G. Chazon; STDJ 28; Leiden: Brill, 1998), 35–57 (Chapter 5 in this book).

51 See the helpful summary statement by H. Lichtenberger, 'Qumran', *TRE* 28 (1997), 75: 'Lebensordnungen des frühen Christentums wie Gütergemeinschaft, Gemeinschaftsmahl, Gemeindeordnung und -zucht weisen zwar Parallelen auf, sind jedoch unterschiedlich begründet.'

Second, with the possible exception of the phrase *m'śy htwrh* in 4QMMT,[52] it is striking that many of the so-called parallels with the New Testament which have become available since 1991 have involved the Jesus tradition. All these so-called parallels with the Jesus tradition come predominantly from non-sectarian texts and so say little or nothing about Jesus' relationship with Qumranians or Essenes.[53] Rather they show us something of the broader religious and cultural context of Judaism in Palestine in the late second temple period. The recently available scrolls have offered a set of beatitudes (4Q525) whose form and content, and possibly even purpose, looks somewhat like those particularly of Matthew, especially in what they share in concluding with an extensive blessing concerning persecution.[54] 4Q521, the so-called messianic apocalypse, describes either God or his eschatological agent as the one who 'will heal the wounded, will make the dead live, will proclaim good news to the meek' for which the parallels in Luke/Q 7.22 are so striking that J. J. Collins has concluded that 'it is quite possible that the author of the Sayings source knew 4Q521; at least he drew on a common tradition'.[55] Jesus cries formally

52 On the significance of this phrase for the study of the New Testament see J. D. G. Dunn, '4QMMT and Galatians', *NTS* 43 (1997): 147–53, and the literature cited there.
53 The discerning of the relationship between Jesus and the Essenes is still the driving force behind worthwhile works such as *Jesus and the Dead Sea Scrolls* (ed. J. H. Charlesworth; New York: Doubleday, 1992). For example, in his own contribution to the book Charlesworth concludes: 'I am convinced that Jesus was closer to the non-Qumran Essenes than to the strict and withdrawn Essenes living in the desert of Judea' (p. 40).
54 In addition to the studies in n. 39 see also E. Puech, '4Q525 et les péricopes des Béatitudes in Ben Sira et Matthieu', *RB* 98 (1991): 80–106; H.-J. Fabry, 'Der makarismus: Mehr als nur eine Weisheitliche Lehrform: Gedanken zu den neuedierten Text 4Q525', in *Alttestamentliche Glaube und Biblische Theologie: Festschrift für Horst Dietrich Preuß zum 65. Geburtstag* (ed. J. Hausmann and H.-J. Zobel; Stuttgart: Kohlhammer, 1992); E. Puech, 'The Collection of Beatitudes in Hebrew and in Greek (4Q525 1–4 and Mt 5, 3–12)', in *Early Christianity in Context: Monuments and Documents* (ed. F. Manns and E. Alliata; Jerusalem: Franciscan Printing Press, 1993), 353–68.
55 J. J. Collins, 'The Works of the Messiah', *DSD* 1 (1994): 107; see also the discussions of this parallel by J. D. Tabor and M. O. Wise, '4Q521 "On Resurrection" and the Synoptic Gospel Tradition: A Preliminary Study', *JSP* 10 (1994): 149–62; C. M. Tuckett, 'Scripture and Q', in *The Scriptures in the Gospels* (ed. C. M. Tuckett; BETL 131; Leuven: University Press and Peeters, 1997), 3–26; F. Nierynck, 'Q 6,20b-21 and Isaiah 61', in *The Scriptures in the Gospels* (ed. C. M. Tuckett; BETL 131; Leuven: University Press and Peeters, 1997), 27–64.

to Abba in prayer; 4Q372 has Joseph address God, 'my father and my God'.[56] The small principal fragment of 4Q500 has recently been reconsidered to suggest that the parable of the vineyard is based on a Palestinian combination of scriptural passages concerning who may be heirs to the temple and its environs.[57] All these examples are from non-sectarian compositions; we can conclude this brief list by referring to a sectarian example. The concluding exhortation of the *Damascus Document* (4QD[e] 7 I, 13–14) mentions fathers and mothers as having particular official status in the movement; the multiple attestation of the Synoptics is that Jesus reworked these traditional family labels too (Mk 3.31–5; Matt. 12.46–50; Lk. 8.19–21). Further examples from both non-sectarian and sectarian compositions could also be cited.

On other matters the jury is still out. It has not yet been determined whether 4Q246's 'Son of God' and 'Son of the Most High' should be read as referring to a positive human figure or as somebody else. It is also difficult to assess what role, if any, Luke 1.32–5 should play in the debate.[58] It has not yet been decided precisely where Jesus stood politically and whether his few violent sayings align him with the kind of Messiah to be found in 4Q285 Fragment 5 who will kill his enemy.[59] It may never be settled whether the so-called Prayer of Nabonidus is restored correctly when it reflects divine rather than human agency in the healing of the king which is linked with the remission of sin; and it is difficult to decide how the New Testament evidence concerning how Jesus' practice was understood should be included in determining the most suitable reading.[60]

Overall the Jewishness of Jesus is now always accepted as the starting point for understanding him, and the discoveries of the Qumran scrolls can take responsibility for that in some measure. Qumran was neither his

---

56 E. M. Schuller, 'A Preliminary Study of 4Q372 1', *RevQ* 14 (1989–90): 349–76.

57 G. J. Brooke, '4Q500 1 and the Use of Scripture in the Parable of the Vineyard', *DSD* 2 (1995): 268–94 (Chapter 15 in this book); C. A. Evans, 'Jesus and the Dead Sea Scrolls from Qumran Cave 4', in *Eschatology, Messianism, and the Dead Sea Scrolls* (ed. C. A. Evans and P. W. Flint; Studies in the Dead Sea Scrolls and Related Literature 1; Grand Rapids: Eerdmans, 1997), 91–100.

58 On 4Q246 see especially J. J. Collins, *The Scepter and the Star: the Messiahs of the Dead Sea Scrolls and Other Ancient Literature* (New York: Doubleday, 1995), 154–72.

59 See J. J. Collins, *The Scepter and the Star*, 58–60.

60 See J. J. Collins, '242. 4QPrayer of Nabonidus ar', in *Qumran Cave 4.XVII: Parabiblical Texts, Part 3* (ed. J. C. VanderKam; DJD 22; Oxford: Clarendon Press, 1996), 83–93.

cradle nor his apparent grave,[61] but as much as later rabbinic texts, the non-sectarian scrolls illuminate the kinds of Judaism he was part of and distinctively renewed.[62]

PERIOD III

Period III at Qumran was of intermittent times of occupation. The future may well contain only the sporadic interaction of New Testament scholars with the Qumran scrolls. After all, when will the Jesus Seminar or the Society of Biblical Literature's Q section make it a requirement that members must have advanced postdoctoral qualifications in Qumran Aramaic before they are allowed to vote on the meaning or authenticity of a logion?[63] Or when will there ever be more than a few New Testament scholars who feel comfortable both in a class reading unpointed Hebrew fragments and in a group working on Greek or Latin sources? Despite these likely problems, it can be hoped that three matters will feature in this sporadic future interaction between New Testament scholars and the scrolls.

First, scrolls scholars are just beginning to appreciate the full range of exegetical traditions which are preserved in all manner of scrolls, within biblical manuscripts, within the pseudo-biblical and parabiblical materials, the rewritten Bible materials, and in all manner of other free-standing compositions, Wisdom texts, testaments, narratives, apocalypses, exhortations, hymns and prayers. There will soon be a place for a considered study of the many exegetical traditions which are shared between the scrolls' authors and traditors and the New Testament writers. Here we shall not look for literary dependence, but for intertextual sensitivity as the better understanding of one text illuminates another.[64]

---

61 Despite the ongoing but partially arbitrary arguments of B. Thiering, 'Jesus and the Dead Sea Scrolls: The Question of Method', *The Journal of Higher Criticism* 3 (1996): 215–36.

62 It is surprising how little reference there is to the scrolls in G. Vermes, *The Religion of Jesus the Jew* (London: SCM Press, 1993).

63 And not just Qumran Aramaic, since the corpus is relatively small: see G. Vermes, 'Jewish Literature and New Testament Exegesis: Reflections on Methodology', *JJS* 33 (1982): 361–76; reprinted in G. Vermes, *Jesus and the World of Judaism* (London: SCM Press, 1983), 74–88.

64 Indications of a way forward in this respect can be seen in some of my own studies: 'The Temple Scroll and the New Testament', in *Temple Scroll Studies: Papers Presented at the International Symposium on the Temple Scroll (Manchester, December*

Second, several biblical scholars have variously applied the social sciences to books of the Hebrew Bible/Old Testament and the New Testament. Those who have worked with the New Testament from such perspectives seem to have produced more of specific value and insight than their Old Testament counterparts, perhaps because the New Testament literature can generally be more closely dated and provided with a suitable social and historical setting more readily than can the parts of the Hebrew Bible. But the 850 or more manuscripts from the 11 caves at Qumran, almost certainly to be taken together with the site itself, provide an unbelievable opportunity for the good social scientist or social historian.[65] Here are the deposits of a single community in its various forms, remains of which are expressed in their own terms. Unless the last members to leave the community took with them all the copies of Esther, and 1 and 2 Maccabees,[66] distorting the picture for all time, then there is much room for the New Testament social scientists to assist Qumranologists in the reading of the fragments from a jargon-free social scientific point of view. Such might be very illuminating in both directions: how should the material on fathers and mothers in the *Damascus Document* be understood with regard to the social history of the groups it purports to reflect, and how might such material improve our understanding of the saying in the Synoptics concerning who is a mother or brother?

Third, the breadth of material in the scrolls concerning the Law and its right practice in the communities of those compositions will force a reassessment of the place of the Law in the concerns of the New

---

1987) (ed. G. J. Brooke; JSPSup 7; Sheffield: Sheffield Academic Press, 1989), 181–99 (Chapter 6 in this book); 'Ezekiel in Some Qumran and New Testament Texts', in *The Madrid Qumran Congress: Proceedings of the International Congress on the Dead Sea Scrolls, Madrid 18–21 March 1991* (ed. J. Trebolle Barrera and L. Vegas Montaner; STDJ 11; Leiden: Brill, 1992), 317–37; 'Luke–Acts and the Qumran Scrolls: the Case of MMT', in *Luke's Literary Achievement: Collected Essays* (ed. C. M. Tuckett; JSNTSup 116; Sheffield: Sheffield Academic Press, 1995), 72–90 (Chapter 9 in this book); '4Q252 et le Nouveau Testament', in *Le déchirement: Juifs et chrétiens au premier siècle* (ed. D. Marguerat; Geneva: Labor et Fides, 1996), 221–42 (in English as Chapter 10 in this book).

65 This approach has long been advocated by S. Talmon; see the Preface to his collected essays *The World of Qumran from Within* (Jerusalem: Magnes Press, 1989), 7–9. Other examples are beginning to appear, e.g., G. Stanton, 'Matthew's Gospel and the Damascus Document in Sociological Perspective', in *A Gospel for a New People: Studies in Matthew* (Edinburgh: T & T Clark, 1992), 85–107.

66 And even nearly all the New Testament books from Cave 7!

Testament authors.[67] Indeed, despite several shelves of recent studies on Paul and the Law, the debate is really only just beginning. What is generally becoming apparent is that both the several forms of Qumran Judaism and the various forms of community belief and practice in the early churches are both exemplars of religious movements concerned with grace and law. By studying how the Law was handled and interpreted in the scrolls from Qumran one can begin to appreciate how it was viewed as a gracious gift from God and by considering the *Hodayot* one can sense that it was clearly recognized that a relationship with God was not possible without an adequate covenantal framework.

PERIOD IV?

And is there a Period IV? Apart from the occasional shepherd or traveller, the site was left alone until the archaeologists occupied the site just over 1,800 years later. Maybe in the distant future scholarly observers will look back and ask why it was that in the second half of the twentieth century so many New Testament members of the Society of Biblical Literature either had suffered from that strange compulsion to take a course on the Qumran scrolls as part of their graduate requirements or had contracted an even weirder malady, 'chapter two-itis'; that is, after a standard introductory chapter, they had succumbed to the writing of a compulsory Chapter 2 in their dissertations on the background to their particular topic in Qumran and its scrolls. Those who look back from our future may also note that nearly every New Testament scholar seemed to recover from both maladies and left the scrolls behind as child's play; a few of us, however, have remained permanently afflicted, doggedly determined to show that the scrolls are of major significance for the better understanding of the New Testament and that sometimes the New Testament may help in the better understanding of some aspects of the scrolls.

---

67 Something of the dynamic of the place of the Torah is already clearly articulated by H. Stegemann, 'Some Aspects of Eschatology in Texts from the Qumran Community and in the Teachings of Jesus', in *Biblical Archaeology Today: Proceedings of the International Congress on Biblical Archaeology, Jerusalem, April 1984* (Jerusalem: Israel Exploration Society, Israel Academy of Sciences and Humanities, American Schools of Oriental Research, 1985), 408–26.

2

Jesus, the Dead Sea Scrolls and Scrolls Scholarship

INTRODUCTION

The term Dead Sea Scrolls refers to manuscripts discovered in several places since 1947 in the region of the Dead Sea, from Wadi ed-Daliyeh about 14 kilometres north of Jericho to Masada near the south-west shore of the Dead Sea. These manuscripts date from between the fourth century B.C.E. and the seventh century C.E. Most commonly, however, the term Dead Sea Scrolls is used to refer to the collection of about 850 manuscripts found between 1947 and 1956 in 11 caves at or near Qumran on the north-west shore of the Dead Sea. The Qumran scrolls seem to be the remains of a library that consisted of authoritative texts (many of which would later be included in the Hebrew Bible), sectarian compositions and general Jewish literature. The owners of this library are most often and most suitably identified with some part of the Essenes. Some Essenes lived at Qumran between about 100 B.C.E. and 68 C.E.; others lived throughout Judaea in small conventicles.

Nowhere in any of the scrolls is Jesus mentioned, nor are there any references to any early Christians. Furthermore, it is highly unlikely that any of the Greek fragments found in Qumran Cave 7 are copies of any of the books of the New Testament.[1] Likewise, nowhere in the New Testament

---

1 First proposed by J. O'Callaghan, 'Papiros neotestamentarios en la cueva 7 de Qumran?', *Bib* 53 (1972): 91–100; and extensively in numerous articles and his monograph *Los papiros griegos de la cueva 7 de Qumran* (Madrid: Editorial Católica, 1974). O'Callaghan's proposals have been most enthusiastically supported by C. P. Thiede, *The Earliest Gospel Manuscript? The Qumran Fragment 7Q5 and Its Significance for New Testament Studies* (Carlisle: Paternoster Press, 1992); C. P. Thiede, *Rekindling the Word: In Search of Gospel Truth* (Valley Forge: Trinity Press International, 1995), 158–204. Several scholars have challenged the identifications and offered preferable ones; see especially, E. Puech, 'Notes sur les fragments grecs du manuscrit 7Q4 1 Hénoch 103 et 105', *RB* 103 (1996): 592–600.

are there any unambiguous references to the Essenes. Nevertheless, there are several striking parallels between the Gospel portrayals of what Jesus said and did and the Dead Sea Scrolls. These parallels have enjoyed much prominence, especially among those who have been interested in reconstructing the Jewish world in which Jesus lived, a feature of Jesus research that was prompted in part by wanting to assert the Jewishness of Jesus in face of the Holocaust. The interest has also been exploited by scholars, motivated more by faith than reason, who have had narrow historicist concerns linked with the desire to demonstrate the veracity of divine revelation as that is supposed to reside in the writings of the New Testament.

At each stage in the scholarly discussion of the significance of the Dead Sea Scrolls for understanding Jesus there have been three approaches. Most of this short study will consider the dominant view that there is some significant relationship, even if only because the Dead Sea Scrolls are the largest body of Jewish textual evidence from Palestine that is contemporary with Jesus.[2] They thus speak eloquently of much of the character of Palestinian Judaism at the time of Jesus. The other two less widespread views are that Jesus and the Dead Sea Scrolls have no relationship at all, and that such a lack should be noted forcefully, or that the relationship is so close that Jesus can be viewed as akin to an Essene.

THREE VIEWS

A relationship between Jesus and the Dead Sea Scrolls[3]

There have been at least four principal ways of construing that there is some kind of relationship between Jesus and the Dead Sea Scrolls, and that the Dead Sea Scrolls enhance how Jesus' Jewishness is best understood.[4]

---

2 Similarities and differences are laid out thematically by H.-W. Kuhn, 'Jesus', in *Encyclopedia of the Dead Sea Scrolls* (ed. L. H. Schiffman and J. C. VanderKam; New York: Oxford University Press, 2000), 404–8.

3 The discerning of the relationship between Jesus and the Essenes is still the driving force behind worthwhile works such as *Jesus and the Dead Sea Scrolls* (ed. J. H. Charlesworth; New York: Doubleday, 1992). For example, in his own contribution to the book Charlesworth concludes: 'I am convinced that Jesus was closer to the non-Qumran Essenes than to the strict and withdrawn Essenes living in the desert of Judea' (p. 40).

4 Further bibliography can be found in C. A. Evans, 'The Recently Published Dead Sea Scrolls and the Historical Jesus', in *Studying the Historical Jesus: Evaluations of the State of Current Research* (ed. B. Chilton and C. A. Evans; Leiden: Brill, 1994), 547–65.

1. Most often, in some of his deeds and words, Jesus is thought merely to be echoing contemporary Jewish teachings and practices, which are also coincidentally found in the scrolls. For example, Jesus' emphasis on the reign ('kingdom') of God echoes in some ways the declaration of the sovereignty of God found in the Qumran *Songs of the Sabbath Sacrifice*; the debates about his messianic self-understanding can be informed by the kinds of messianic hopes present in several of the sectarian scrolls;[5] the organization of his close followers as a group of 12 echoes the way the Qumran community also tried to be heirs of the tribes of Israel;[6] and his celibacy seems to have its nearest counterpart in the asceticism of some Essenes.[7]

Or, more precisely, 4Q525 2–3 II, 1–6 contains a set of beatitudes, one of which mentions the 'pure in heart' and the last of which is a meditation on persecution.[8] In Matthew 5.8 Jesus' sixth beatitude concerns the 'pure in heart', and the eighth and ninth concern persecution. Here seems to be a common Jewish form of Wisdom instruction with no necessary dependence of one text upon the other. Or again, both the authors of the Dead Sea Scrolls and Jesus seem to be the heirs of a common

---

5 See J. J. Collins, *The Scepter and the Star: The Messiahs of the Dead Sea Scrolls and Other Ancient Literature* (Anchor Bible Reference Library; New York: Doubleday, 1995); G. G. Xeravits, *King, Priest, Prophet: Positive Eschatological Protagonists of the Qumran Library* (STDJ 47; Leiden: Brill, 2002).

6 See, e.g., D. Flusser, 'Qumran und die Zwölf', in *Initiation* (ed. C. J. Bleeker; Studies in the History of Religions 10; Leiden: Brill, 1965), 134–46; reprinted in *Judaism and the Origins of Christianity* (Jerusalem: Magnes Press, 1988), 173–85; J. M. Baumgarten, 'The Duodecimal Courts of Qumran, Revelation, and the Sanhedrin', *JBL* 95 (1976): 59–78; reprinted in J. M. Baumgarten, *Studies in Qumran Law* (SJLA 24; Leiden: Brill, 1977), 145–71.

7 See J. M. Baumgarten, 'Celibacy', in *Encyclopedia of the Dead Sea Scrolls* (ed. L. H. Schiffman and J. C. VanderKam; New York: Oxford University Press, 2000), 122–5; P. W. van der Horst, 'Der Zölibat im Frühjudentum', in *Frühjudentum und Neues Testament im Horizont Biblischer Theologie* (ed. W. Kraus and K.-W. Niebuhr; WUNT 162; Tübingen: Mohr Siebeck, 2003), 3–14.

8 See, e.g., E. Puech, 'Un Hymne essénien en partie retrouvé et les Béatitudes: 1QH V 12–VI 18 (= col. XIII–XIV 7) et 4QBéat', *RevQ* 13 (1988): 59–88; cf. G. J. Brooke, 'The Wisdom of Matthew's Beatitudes (4QBéat and Mt. 5.3–12)', *ScrB* 19 (1988–1989): 35–41 (slightly revised as Chapter 12 in this volume); J. A. Fitzmyer, 'A Palestinian Collection of Beatitudes', in *The Four Gospels 1992: Festschrift Frans Neirynck* (ed. F. Van Segbroeck, C. M. Tuckett, G. Van Belle, J. Verheyden; BETL 100; Leuven: Leuven University Press and Peeters, 1992), 509–15. See also the further studies in Chapter 1, n. 54.

exegetical tradition concerning the vineyard in Isaiah 5 (the motif is developed in similar ways in 4Q500 1 and Lk. 20.9–19)[9] and concerning the anointed proclaimer of good news of Isaiah 52 and 61 (the author of 11QMelchizedek and Jesus in Luke 4.18–19 both understand the figure eschatologically). In terms of religious pratices, Jesus' exorcisms reflect common views of the link between sickness and demons, a view also known at Qumran (e.g., 4Q242),[10] as was the therapeutic technique of laying on of hands (1QapGen XX, 29). This overall approach is often neglected by those who research the life and teachings of Jesus because of the common abuse of the criterion of dissimilarity; however, it should not be thought that the authentic Jesus can only be found in items for which there is no parallel elsewhere, otherwise Jesus would never have been understood by his Jewish contemporaries.

2. Some scholars have argued that Jesus adopted certain insights from the compositions that the Essenes preserved or even composed. This approach to Jesus commonly stresses the eclectic character of his teaching, proposing that it is his combination of ideas (especially those of the Pharisees and Essenes) that is distinctive, rather than any particular element. Four examples indicate the range of Jesus' possible dependence on Essene ideas. In Luke ('Q') 7.22 Jesus answers the disciples of John the Baptist about his identity by quoting Isaiah 61 in an adapted form; the same adaptation can only be found elsewhere in 4Q521 2 II + 4, 2: 'the dead are raised, the poor have good news brought to them'.[11] In Mark 10.2–9 Jesus justifies his strict interpretation of divorce law by appealing to Genesis 1.27 and 2.24; in the sectarian *Damascus Document* (CD IV, 20–V, 1) a similar justification is given for monogamy and

9 G. J. Brooke, '4Q500 1 and the Use of Scripture in the Parable of the Vineyard', *DSD* 2 (1995): 268–94 (Chapter 13 in this book).
10 See J. J. Collins, '242. 4QPrayer of Nabonidus ar', in *Qumran Cave 4.XVII: Parabiblical Texts, Part 3* (ed. J. C. VanderKam; DJD 22; Oxford: Clarendon Press, 1996), 83–93.
11 See especially J. J. Collins, 'The Works of the Messiah', *DSD* 1 (1994): 107; see also the discussions of this parallel by J. D. Tabor and M. O. Wise, '4Q521 "On Resurrection" and the Synoptic Gospel Tradition: A Preliminary Study', *JSP* 10 (1994): 149–62; C. M. Tuckett, 'Scripture and Q', in *The Scriptures in the Gospels* (ed. C. M. Tuckett; BETL 131; Leuven: University Press and Peeters, 1997), 3–26; F. Nierynck, 'Q 6,20b-21 and Isaiah 61', in *The Scriptures in the Gospels* (ed. C. M. Tuckett; BETL 131; Leuven: University Press and Peeters, 1997), 27–64.

against divorce.[12] In Matthew 5.33 Jesus advises against endorsing oaths by appealing to the deity, a practice also attacked in CD XV, 1–2. Jesus' use of 'Abba', 'Father', as an address to God is matched most closely in contemporary Palestinian Jewish prayer in 4Q372 1, 16 ('my Father and my God') and 4Q460 9 I, 6 ('my Father and my Lord').[13]

3. Some scholars have stressed the view that rather than being directly dependent upon Essene teaching Jesus may have known it and reacted against it. In Matthew 5.43 Jesus reproaches those who love their neighbours and hate their enemies, as seems to be the case in some sectarian compositions (e.g., 1QS I, 10). In Luke 16.8 Jesus appears to be telling the parable of the dishonest manager to discourage imitation of the 'sons of light', a term used as a self-designation of the community of the Dead Sea Scrolls. The quasi-sectarian 4QInstruction (4Q416 2 III, 3–5) teaches that it is better not to touch money entrusted to one than to risk losing it; Jesus seems to teach just the opposite (Matt. 25.14–30; Lk. 19.11–27). Whereas MMT (4Q394 8 III–IV 4), the *War Scroll* (1QM VII, 4–5) and the *Rule of the Congregation* (1QSa (1Q28a) II, 5–8) all variously speak against the blind, deaf and lame, Jesus seems to go out of his way to demonstrate that just such people should be restored to the worshipping community.

Some scholars have combined both the second and third approaches outlined above to show that Jesus was part of first-century Jewish debates, knowingly agreeing and disagreeing with Essene views as suited his own principles; this approach has been taken not least by several prominent Jewish scholars.

4. Some scholars have suggested that Jesus capitalized on the model of leadership provided by the Teacher of Righteousness of the sectarian Dead Sea Scrolls (especially as described in the *Damascus Document* and the *pesharim* (biblical commentaries)). In its most controversial and least substantiated form this view proposes that Jesus was recognized as the

---

12 See also 11QT[a] LVII, 15–19. P. R. Davies, *Behind the Essenes: History and Ideology in the Dead Sea Scrolls* (BJS 94; Atlanta: Scholars Press, 1987), 73–85; J. A. Fitzmyer, 'The Matthean Divorce Texts and Some New Palestinian Evidence', *TS* 37 (1976): 197–226; J. A. Fitzmyer, 'Divorce among First-Century Palestinian Jews', *ErIsr* 14 (1978): 103–10; J. R. Mueller, 'The Temple Scroll and the Gospel Divorce Texts', *RevQ* 10 (1979–81): 247–75. For the broader picture and recent bibliography see also D. Instone-Brewer, *Divorce and Remarriage in the Bible: The Social and Literary Context* (Grand Rapids: Eerdmans, 2002).
13 See E. M. Schuller, 'The Psalm of 4Q372 1 within the Context of Second Temple Prayer', *CBQ* 54 (1992): 67–79.

Teacher returned from the dead; though few, if any, would hold to this nowadays, its possibility shows how some of the parallels between the Dead Sea Scrolls and Jesus can be construed. More generally, the Teacher can be viewed as an embodiment of the eschatological prophet and/or priest expected by some Jews; Jesus likewise may have embodied some aspects of such a role for himself (Mk 6.4; Jn 6.14).

Explanations for these parallels between the Dead Sea Scrolls and Jesus have taken various routes. Most often it is proposed that it was Jesus' encounter with John the Baptist that provided his link to Essene teaching and practice. Although John was probably not an Essene,[14] the geographical proximity of his ministry to Qumran and his attention to divine judgement, repentance and ritual washing show that John is likely to have known about Essene teaching and rituals, and possibly even adapted them for his own purposes.

While not denying that Essene views could have been mediated through John the Baptist, other scholars suggest that Jesus encountered Essenes during his ministry and that he particularly approved of some of their ethical views, such as those on divorce and poverty. In light of this, it is supposed by some that Jesus used buildings close to the Essene quarter when he stayed in Jerusalem and that the house used for the Last Supper was possibly owned by an Essene.[15]

Rather than speaking of 'Jesus and the Dead Sea Scrolls', other scholars have preferred to analyse the many parallels between the Dead Sea Scrolls and the writings of the New Testament. Since none of the written works of the New Testament is earlier than the 50s C.E., the main point of contact between the Essenes and early Christianity can be portrayed as taking place in the second half of the first century C.E. Any supposed Essene influence in the teaching of Jesus can then be explained as the later influence of Essenes on the second generation of Christians who were attempting to record Jesus' deeds and sayings; Essene influence on the New Testament authors was read back into earlier layers of the tradition. On the one hand, this view makes some satisfactory sense of the

---

14 The literature on John the Baptist and Qumran is extensive; see the items mentioned by L. F. Badia, *The Qumran Baptism and John the Baptist's Baptism* (Lanham: University Press of America, 1980), 78–87, and R. L. Webb, *John the Baptizer and Prophet: A Socio-Historical Study* (Sheffield: Sheffield Academic Press, 1991), 213 n. 137; for a balanced survey see J. E. Taylor, *The Immerser: John the Baptist within Second Temple Judaism* (Grand Rapids: Eerdmans, 1997), 15–48.

15 See, e.g., R. Riesner, 'Essener und Urkirche in Jerusalem', in *Christen und Christliches in Qumran?* (ed. B. Mayer; Regensburg: Pustet, 1992), 139–55.

dominant historical reconstructions, which locate Jesus chiefly in Galilee and stress his message of the inclusiveness and immediacy of the kingdom of God; the influence of the ideas in the Dead Sea Scrolls is seen as minimal. On the other hand, this approach conveniently preserves much of the distinctiveness of Jesus' message and his likely self-understanding. Some Christian scholars have been happy to adopt this approach as an implicit way of protecting Jesus' uniqueness.[16]

No relationship between Jesus and the Dead Sea Scrolls

The second overall approach to assessing the significance of the Dead Sea Scrolls for understanding Jesus has been to deny any connection between the two.[17] Several factors support the view. Most obviously, nowhere in the Dead Sea Scrolls is there mention of Jesus or any of his disciples; conversely, nowhere in the New Testament is there any clear reference to the Essenes or their texts. Furthermore, Jesus was from Galilee and apparently of lower artisan status; the scrolls from Qumran belonged to an educated and predominantly priestly elite whose main focus was Jerusalem. Jesus preached a message of inclusivity and probably regularly ate with many Jews whom others marginalized; the Qumran Essenes were among those most ready to maintain purity through rigid rules of exclusion. Thus for geographical, sociological and theological reasons Jesus can be distanced from the collectors and authors of the Dead Sea Scrolls. This lack of clear evidence has resulted in some overly sceptical conclusions that reflect an unrealistic construction of first-century Judaism as if its distinctive groupings seldom interacted.

Jesus the Essene

The third approach, the opposite of the second, has asserted that in some way Jesus and his followers should be identified with those who collected the scrolls. The lack of explicit evidence permits those who take this approach to present elaborate and largely unverifiable (and therefore also irrefutable) reconstructions of Palestinian Judaism and Jesus' place in it.

---

16 E.g., G. Graystone, *The Dead Sea Scrolls and the Originality of Christ* (London: Sheed & Ward, 1956).

17 H. H. Rowley concluded that 'to suppose that the Scrolls can give us any evidence of the nature of early Christianity is fantastic': *The Dead Sea Scrolls and the New Testament* (London: SPCK, 1957), 30.

The general public's yearning for historical certainties, however unlikely, and its fascination with conspiracy theories have often given pride of place to approaches such as those of B. Thiering (for whom Jesus is a disgraced member of the Qumran community).[18] More plausible, but suffering from vast over-simplification, is the approach of R. Eisenman; he sweepingly classifies all first-century Judaism as either nationalist (like the Zealots) or assimilationist (like Paul).[19] For Eisenman there are hints in the Gospels and Acts that Jesus and his first followers were nationalist xenophobic Jews like the Essenes; only after Paul's victory in early Christianity were the sources adapted to minimize these features and stress that Jesus was outward-looking and inclusive in his preaching and practice.

18 B. Thiering, *Jesus and the Riddle of the Scrolls: Unlocking the Secrets of his Life Story* (San Francisco: HarperSanFrancisco, 1992); also published as *Jesus the Man: A New Interpretation from the Dead Sea Scrolls*. Thiering is criticized suitably by O. Betz and R. Riesner, *Jesus, Qumran and the Vatican* (London: SCM Press, 1994), 99–113; H. Stegemann, *The Library of Qumran: On the Essenes, Qumran, John the Baptist, and Jesus* (Leiden: Brill/Grand Rapids: Eerdmans, 1998), 28–30.

19 Eisenman popularized his views in R. H. Eisenman and M. Wise, *The Dead Sea Scrolls Uncovered* (Rockport: Element Books, 1992); *Jesus und die Urchristen: Die Qumran-Rollen entschlüsselt* (Munich: Bretelsmann, 1993). Eisenman's views were further spread in association with conspiracy theories by M. Baigent and R. Leigh, *The Dead Sea Scroll Deception* (London: Jonathan Cape, 1991); *Verschlußsache Jesus: Die Qumranrollen und die Wahrheit über das frühe Christentum* (Munich: Drömer Knaur, 1991). Eisenman has restated his views in *The Dead Sea Scrolls and the First Christians: Essays and Translations* (Shaftesbury: Element Books, 1996). Eisenman has been criticized suitably by O. Betz and R. Riesner, *Jesus, Qumran and the Vatican* (London: SCM Press, 1994), 69–81.

3

The 'Canon within the Canon' at Qumran and in the New Testament

INTRODUCTION

It is necessary to begin by clarifying what this chapter is about. It is not concerned directly with the extent and contents of the canon of the Hebrew Bible as that may be evident in the Dead Sea Scrolls and the New Testament. Nor is it concerned directly with the processes by which one book rather than another becomes authoritative and normative, nor with how groups of books also come to take priority over others. To this extent no apologies need be offered for using the word 'canon', even in inverted commas, since it is clearly both anachronistic and out of place.[1] Furthermore, to focus on how canons of writings emerge is naturally to describe negative matters, since canons are usually formed in a reactionary way, against other people's preferences. It is no accident that the firmest delimitations of the canon in Christian circles, even the earliest uses of the word in a technical sense, come at the same time as the creeds are emerging: authoritative texts are produced to protect and project orthodoxy against what are perceived as the wild assertions of heresy.

The subject matter of this chapter is altogether more positive, however, for to speak of a 'canon within the canon' is to focus on those writings or books, or parts of them, which a community considered especially important for one reason or another. The term 'canon within the canon' is used loosely to assert that within the range of books which were emerging as authoritative in a general way, for some groups a few works

---

1 For a useful summary treatment of technical terminology in relation to the canon of the Old Testament and for views on the place of the Old Testament in the early churches see E. E. Ellis, 'The Old Testament Canon in the Early Church', in *Mikra: Text, Translation, Reading and Interpretation of the Hebrew Bible in Ancient Judaism and Early Christianity* (ed. M. J. Mulder; CRINT 2/1; Assen: van Gorcum; Philadelphia: Fortress Press, 1988), 653–90.

were especially significant, and not just whole books, but parts of them. Against a backdrop of the canonical process proper,[2] the purpose of this study is to ask why certain books were being cherished and used at the centre of the life of various communities, not to worry about whether a particular document was deemed to be part of a canon, thought to be divinely inspired, or considered to control one's lifestyle.

With regard to the Dead Sea Scrolls found in the 11 Qumran caves two other preliminary matters need to be made clear immediately. First, it will be assumed in this study that the 900 or so manuscripts found between 1947 and 1956 in the 11 caves near to the Qumran settlement and in the adjoining foothills form some kind of collection. It may certainly be true that some caves had distinctive purposes: the manuscripts in Cave 1 were neatly wrapped in linen and placed in jars almost like a genizah or time capsule, those in Cave 7 were all in Greek, not all those in Cave 4 could have been in the dozen or so jars of which fragments were found, and so on. Nevertheless, there is a coherence in the collection from three aspects.

1   There are no copies of clearly non-Jewish literature, such as any of the Greek classics, nor are there any copies of particular Jewish texts which we have good reason to think were in circulation in Palestine in the first century B.C.E., such as 1 and 2 Maccabees or Judith.

2   In the three caves which have produced most manuscripts, 1, 4 and 11, there is an evenness of distribution, both in proportion – about 30 per cent biblical, 30 per cent sectarian and 40 per cent other

---

2 This canonical process has been delineated suitably by E. Ulrich, 'The Canonical Process, Textual Criticism, and Latter Stages in the Composition of the Bible', in '*Sha'arei Talmon': Studies in the Bible, Qumran, and the Ancient Near East Presented to Shemaryahu Talmon* (ed. M. Fishbane and E. Tov; Winona Lake: Eisenbrauns, 1992), 267–91, see esp. p. 274: 'Prior to the end of the first century, we do not have a canon in either Judaism or Christianity. We have a canon-in-the-making, but we do not have a canon. We have, well documented by practice, the concept of authoritative sacred books which are to be preserved very faithfully. And we have a "canonical process", that is, the activity by which books later to become accepted as the canon were produced and treated as sacred and authoritative. But we do not have a canon or a canonical text before the end of the first century.'

3 This has been pointed out most clearly by D. Dimant, 'The Qumran Manuscripts: Contents and Significance', in *Time to Prepare the Way in the Wilderness: Papers on the Qumran Scrolls by Fellows of the Institute for Advanced Studies of the Hebrew University, Jerusalem, 1989–1990* (ed. D. Dimant and L. H. Schiffman; STDJ 16; Leiden: Brill, 1995), 23–58, esp. p. 58.

materials[3] – and also in the way in which the same composition recurs in the various caves, such as the *Serek ha-Yaḥad* (*Rule of the Community*), the *War Scroll* and the *Hodayot* being found in Caves 1 and 4, the *Temple Scroll* in Caves 4 and 11, and *Jubilees* and the *New Jerusalem* text in Caves 1, 4 and 11; some of these compositions are found in other caves as well.

3   There is a consistency among the compositions concerning the calendar; not that only one calendar is known, but it seems as if only one calendar was normative.

The second assumption concerning the Qumran collection concerns its relationship to the Qumran settlement. It is most plausible to suggest that the caves and their scrolls are to be associated with the site, so that in discussing the Dead Sea Scrolls from the 11 caves, it is reasonable to talk about the community and the wider movement of which it was probably a part. If the recently discovered ostracon is being correctly read,[4] then there is some evidence from very near the site itself that the *yaḥad* lived there, but even if not, it must be recalled that the only way to some of the caves was through or past the site itself.

THE 'CANON WITHIN THE CANON' AT QUMRAN

Establishing the 'canon within the canon' at Qumran

Given the assumptions just outlined and in the hope that the evidence from the Qumran caves to be described is not distorted unduly by the accidents of preservation and survival, it is possible to move directly to describe the 'canon within the canon' at Qumran. There are four ways to establish such a 'canon within the canon'; these four ways must be taken together.

1. Notwithstanding the ravages of insects and earthquakes, it is possible to count up the number of extant copies of particular compositions to see what kind of popularity they might have had among the group which preserved them. There is naturally some uncertainty about whether a particular fragment has been correctly

---

4 See F. M. Cross and E. Eshel, 'Ostraca from Khirbet Qumran', *IEJ* 47 (1997): 17–28; and the alternative readings proposed by A. Yardeni, 'A Draft of a Deed on an Ostracon from Khirbet Qumrân', *IEJ* 47 (1997): 233–7.

identified[5] and so statistics, as always, are susceptible to economical truth, but a rough guideline can be presented as follows. When the various compositions from the Qumran caves are counted up, there are more than 20 copies of Genesis, Deuteronomy, Isaiah and the Psalms. There are approximately 17 copies of Exodus and at least 15 of the *Book of Jubilees*, so these come a close second. Then still in double figures we have Leviticus, the *Hodayot* and the *Rule of the Community*.[6]

2. The second way to discern the popularity of any work is to see how many times it is referred to in other compositions. Here we are faced with a problem, because certain genres lend themselves to being quoted explicitly, and certain types of writing may be more inclined to quote explicitly than implicitly. Thus a legal text may more readily quote another authority explicitly, whereas a hymnic composition is likely only to allude implicitly to a poetic source. No detailed comprehensive analysis of the use of Scripture in the compositions found at Qumran has yet been completed.[7] For explicit quotations a basic starting point can be found in J. A. Fitzmyer's classic study of the 43 quotations in the *Rule of*

---

5 A small fragment containing what looks like a biblical text could belong to a composition which is explicitly citing Scripture. Even some manuscripts, such as 4QDeut[n], which contain nothing but biblical material can be better understood as excerpted texts: see the large number of such manuscripts listed and described by E. Tov, 'Excerpted and Abbreviated Biblical Texts from Qumran', *RevQ* 16 (1993–5): 581–600.

6 With some minor adjustments in light of the most recent volumes in the Discoveries in the Judaean Desert series, these figures are worked out on the basis of the manuscripts as listed by F. García Martínez, *The Dead Sea Scrolls Translated: The Qumran Texts in English* (Leiden: Brill; Grand Rapids: 2nd edn Eerdmans, 1994), 467–519. Helpful lists of the biblical manuscripts and their contents can be found in U. Glessmer, 'Liste der biblischen Texte aus Qumran', *RevQ* 16 (1993–5): 153–92; E. Ulrich, 'An Index of the Passages in the Biblical Manuscripts from the Judean Desert (Genesis–Kings)', *DSD* 1 (1994): 113–29; E. Ulrich, 'An Index of the Passages in the Biblical Manuscripts from the Judean Desert (Part 2: Isaiah–Chronicles)', *DSD* 2 (1995): 86–107; D. L. Washburn, *A Catalog of Biblical Passages in the Dead Sea Scrolls* (SBL Text-Critical Studies 2; Atlanta: SBL, 2002).

7 The most helpful recent index of scriptural passages in the Dead Sea Scrolls is that produced by J. Maier, *Die Qumran-Essener: Die Texte vom Toten Meer* Band III (UTB 1916; München: Ernst Reinhardt Verlag, 1996), 161–82. However, it is difficult to know how to use the information in Maier's index without attempting to classify it somehow; explicit quotations are listed alongside rewritten texts and implicit allusions without any differentiation.

the Community, the *War Scroll*, the *Damascus Document* and 4Q174.[8] These texts contain a variety of genres and the quotations are used for a variety of purposes; indeed Fitzmyer offers a preliminary classification of uses ('literal', 'modernized', 'accommodated', 'eschatological'). These four compositions may all be identified closely with the Qumran community and its wider movement. Of the 43 citations 11 are from the Twelve Minor Prophets, nine from Deuteronomy, seven from Isaiah, five from Numbers. Only one comes from Genesis, none from the Psalms.

Alongside these explicit allusions, one should put a work which because of its genre is using Scripture in a more intricate implicit fashion. For want of a more accessible way into this, we may take the index of scriptural allusions in S. Holm-Nielsen's analysis of the Cave 1 version of the *Hodayot* (1QH[a]).[9] He counts 48 passages from the Psalms to which there are clear allusions in 1QH[a],[10] some of them more than once, and 97 passages from the Psalms which may be alluded to but about which there cannot be any certainty.[11] For Isaiah, there are 68 clear allusions and 53 uncertain ones.[12] There are also 31 passages from the Twelve Minor Prophets (together with 18 uncertain ones),[13] 18 passages from Jeremiah (together with 13 uncertain ones),[14] and ten from Job (together with 21 uncertain ones).[15] For the Pentateuch, Holm-Nielsen notes seven passages from Genesis (together with eight uncertain allusions), six from Exodus (together with seven uncertain allusions), none from Numbers

---

8 J. A. Fitzmyer, 'The Use of Explicit Old Testament Quotations in Qumran Literature and in the New Testament', *NTS* 7 (1960–1): 297–333; reprinted in J. A. Fitzmyer, *Essays on the Semitic Background of the New Testament* (London: Chapman, 1971), 3–58 (republished in *The Semitic Background of the New Testament* [Grand Rapids: Eerdmans, 1997]).

9 S. Holm-Nielsen, *Hodayot: Psalms from Qumran* (Acta Theologica Danica 2; Aarhus: Universitetsforlaget, 1960). Holm-Nielsen's chapter on 'The Use of the Old Testament in the Hodayot' (pp. 301–15) is especially important, since he justifiably concludes that the use of Scripture in the *Hodayot* does not depend on previously existing collections of extracts.

10 Maier lists 26 allusions to the Psalms in 1QH[a], not all of which correspond with Holm-Nielsen's identifications.

11 He also notes ten passages where phrasing from a biblical Psalm could be used suitably to make a restoration in the scroll.

12 Maier lists 31 passages of Isaiah to which there are clear allusions in 1QH[a].

13 Maier lists eight passages in the Twelve Minor Prophets to which allusion is made in 1QH[a].

14 Maier lists 13 passages from Jeremiah to which there is allusion in 1QH[a].

15 For 1QH[a] Maier lists three passages from Job.

(but five uncertain allusions), seven from Deuteronomy (together with four uncertain allusions); the poets who composed the *Hodayot* do not seem keen to cite Leviticus![16] Other scriptural books are also alluded to but only a very few times. Thus among one collection of the community's poetry the Psalms, Isaiah and the Twelve seem to be particularly influential.

3. The next way to appreciate which compositions are significant for the Qumran community and its wider movement is to take any one composition and assess its dependence on other texts in detail. Let us briefly take the *Damascus Document* as an example. If one looks at the explicit quotations of Scripture in the *Damascus Document*, at least 40 citations can be isolated: two from Genesis, four from Leviticus, four from Numbers, nine from Deuteronomy, one from 1 Samuel, six from Isaiah, three from Ezekiel, 12 from the Twelve Minor Prophets and one from Proverbs.[17] Deuteronomy, Isaiah and the Twelve are clearly significant, but so too are Leviticus, Numbers and Ezekiel. However, when one turns to consider the dominant implicit allusions, even in the section of the Admonition alone, then the picture changes somewhat. In his detailed study J. G. Campbell has been able to point out the principal uses of Scripture in CD I–VIII and XIX–XX.[18] Deuteronomy is evidently the most important of the books of the Torah, especially sections of Deuteronomy 27—32, and Leviticus, especially Chapter 26, is also prominent. The number of allusions to Isaiah is almost equalled by the number to Ezekiel. Citations of or allusions to Hosea and Micah also feature prominently in almost all the sections of the Admonition. Most significantly, however, the Psalms are also important, especially Psalms 37, 78 and 106, a fact that one cannot recognize from concentrating on explicit quotations alone.[19]

Thus in any particular work various scriptural passages may play a part; some of these may be used explicitly, some implicitly. An overall study of the use of the biblical books in all the Dead Sea Scrolls has yet to be undertaken, but each composition from the Qumran caves, whether

16 Maier's index of citations lists two for Genesis, three for Exodus and four for Deuteronomy.

17 See G. Vermes, 'Biblical Proof-Texts in Qumran Literature', *JSS* 34 (1989): 493–508.

18 J. G. Campbell, *The Use of Scripture in the Damascus Document 1–8, 19–20* (BZAW 228; Berlin: W. de Gruyter, 1995).

19 See especially the chart in Campbell's book, *The Use of Scripture in the Damascus Document 1–8, 19–20*, 179–82.

sectarian or not, even though part of the overall Qumran collection, may have patterns of scriptural exegesis which are distinctive. So, for the *Damascus Document*, Genesis plays only a small role, while parts of Leviticus, Deuteronomy, Isaiah, Ezekiel, the Twelve and a few select Psalms are all significant. By taking note of one composition in this way, even though only briefly, the limitations of generalizations become all too apparent.

4. The final way to appreciate which compositions are significant for the Qumran community and its wider movement is to consider briefly the number of compositions which seem to be dependent in some way upon earlier models. The process of evaluation here is much more subjective, but among the matters to be considered are the following. Only since all the Dead Sea Scrolls have become generally available has it become apparent just how significant the traditions contained in Genesis and the first part of Exodus were for the community. There are many texts which retell, rework, rewrite and comment upon Genesis in particular. Foremost among these is the *Book of Jubilees*, a second-century B.C.E. composition which is dependent upon Genesis and Exodus for the most part but which contains other traditions as well; there are apparently at least 15 copies of this work in the Qumran caves.[20] Furthermore, there are compositions very like it, known as *Pseudo-Jubilees*, and importantly for our purposes *Jubilees* seems to be cited as some kind of authority, both in the well-known section of the *Damascus Document* ('And the explication of their times, when Israel was blind to all these; behold, it is specified in the Book of the Divisions of the Times in their Jubilees and in their Weeks' CD XVI, 2–4) and also in 4Q228 which has even come to be known as the *Text with a Citation of Jubilees* ('for thus it is written in the Divisions' 4Q228 1 I, 9).[21] In addition to these *Jubilees*

---

20 For the copies from Caves 1, 2, 3 and 11 see J. C. VanderKam, *Textual and Historical Studies in the Book of Jubilees* (HSM 14; Missoula: Scholars Press, 1977); for the Cave 4 manuscripts see J. C. VanderKam and J. T. Milik, 'Jubilees', in *Qumran Cave 4.VIII: Parabiblical Texts, Part 1* (ed. H. Attridge et al.; DJD 13; Oxford: Clarendon Press, 1994), 1–140. VanderKam and Milik do not include the three fragments of 4Q176 identified as from the *Book of Jubilees* by M. Kister, 'Newly-identified Fragments of the Book of Jubilees: Jub. 23, 21–23, 30–31', *RevQ* 12 (1985–7): 529–36; these fragments were probably written by the same scribe who copied 4QJub^f. In addition 4Q482 and 4Q483 may be copies of the *Book of Jubilees*: see M. Baillet, *Qumran Cave 4.III* (DJD 7; Oxford: Clarendon Press, 1982), 1–2.

21 J. C. VanderKam and J. T. Milik, '4QText with a Citation of Jubilees', in *Qumran Cave 4.VIII: Parabiblical Texts, Part 1* (DJD 13), 177–85.

manuscripts, one should associate with Genesis in some way the *Enoch* manuscripts (4Q201–12; also 4Q247), the *Book of Giants* (1Q23; 1Q24; 2Q26; 4Q530–33; 6Q8), those which concern Noah (1Q19; 1Q19bis; 4Q534–36), the *Admonition based on the Flood* (4Q370), the Aramaic retelling of Genesis in the *Genesis Apocryphon* (1QapGen ar), the Genesis–Exodus paraphrase (4Q422), the *Reworked Pentateuch* manuscripts (4Q158; 4Q364–67) which also form some kind of biblical paraphrase, the compositions associated with various patriarchal figures (1Q21; 3Q7; 4Q213–15; 4Q369; 4Q371–73; 4Q464; 4Q537; 4Q538–41), the *Ages of Creation* (4Q180–81), and last but not least, the *Genesis Commentaries* (4Q252; 4Q253; 4Q254; 4Q254a). In addition, several of the Wisdom and poetic texts allude to various materials in Genesis.

For Deuteronomy, a similar list of secondary uses of the work can be summoned up. There are rewritings such as in the *Reworked Pentateuch* manuscripts already mentioned, and parts of the *Temple Scroll* (4Q524; 11Q19; 11Q20). There are at least two manuscripts which have adapted sections of Deuteronomy probably for liturgical purposes (4QDeut[n,q]). Furthermore, there are a significant number of phylacteries that have survived from the caves; these generally contain Deuteronomy 5. There are several apocryphal texts which can be associated with Moses (1Q22; 1Q29; 2Q21; 4Q374–77; 4Q385a; 4Q387a; 4Q388a; 4Q389–90). More obliquely, Deuteronomy may be envisaged as providing the framework for key community texts like MMT (4Q394–99) and the *Rule of the Community*. It is also certainly the case that the paraphrases of Joshua (4Q378–79) and various admonition texts weave into their presentations the ideology and the phraseology of Deuteronomy.

For the Psalms, the same is the case. The Dead Sea Scrolls are replete with hymnic compositions (e.g., 4Q380–81, as well as all the copies of the *Hodayot*, 1QH[a]; 1Q35–39; 4Q427–33), some of which copy out large chunks of what we would identify as biblical psalms or which use hymnic compositions which appear elsewhere in the Scriptures. The *Commentaries on the Psalms* (4Q171; 4Q173) are also evidence of the importance in which these texts were held. The Psalms probably also played a key role in the structure of exegetical texts like 4Q174 and 177, as well as 11QMelchizedek. In addition, there are many liturgical compositions which echo the Psalms, sometimes quite explicitly (e.g., 11QApPs[a]).

The story with the Prophets is rather different. We have noticed in the previous two points that both Isaiah and the Twelve have featured significantly, both with respect to the number of manuscripts and in the number of times in which in particular community texts they are quoted. However, for neither Isaiah nor the Twelve is it clear that there are any rewritten forms as there are for the Pentateuch, the Psalms and for both Jeremiah and Ezekiel. It is even likely that some manuscripts are best understood as reworked forms of the lives of other prophets, especially Elijah and Elisha. But Isaiah and the Twelve seem to have escaped such treatment. Conversely, it is remarkable that to date nothing resembling the formal *pesher* kind of commentary has been found in which Jeremiah and Ezekiel are exegeted in a consistent running fashion. Yet such commentaries are found on both Isaiah and on half of the books of the Twelve (Hosea, Micah, Nahum, Habakkuk, Zephaniah, Malachi).

Taking the four criteria together it seems evident that 'the canon within the canon' at Qumran is formed from the biblical books of Genesis, Deuteronomy, Isaiah and the Psalms, although in certain compositions other scriptural texts also play a role.[22] Together with Genesis one should include all the various forms of its traditions and also the pre-Sinaitic parts of Exodus. Together with Deuteronomy one should include the various rewritten forms of the text and those compositions which are controlled by its structure and ideology. Together with the Psalms proper, one should leave open the question of whether there was more than one Psalter at Qumran, but one should also include a wide range of poetic compositions which depend on the Psalms for their inspiration. Together with Isaiah one should associate the Twelve Minor Prophets. The two collections seem to be treated in a similar way by the Qumran community and may have had similar functions.

The significance of Qumran's 'canon within the canon'

What does this fourfold 'canon within the canon' signify for the better understanding of the developing community which copied and preserved these texts?

---

22 This means that the standard view that it is Deuteronomy, Isaiah and the Psalms which are the most favoured biblical books at Qumran needs adjustment. In the first edition of his popular introduction J. G. Campbell wrote 'Deuteronomy, Isaiah and the Psalms stand out from the list as of prime significance' (*Deciphering the Dead Sea Scrolls* [London: Fontana, 1996], 41,), but in the second edition this was very suitably altered to 'Genesis, Deuteronomy, Isaiah and the Psalms stand out from the list as of prime significance' (*Deciphering the Dead Sea Scrolls* [Oxford: Blackwell, 2nd edn, 2002], 34.

1. For Genesis and pre-Sinaitic Exodus several issues seem to be at stake. First, as with many contemporary groups in the Hellenistic world, there is a concern with antiquity. An appeal to the covenant at Sinai was clearly considered important, but it was felt necessary by some to look before Sinai to explain the movement's unique place in the divine scheme of things. From a certain perspective the community and its wider movement viewed itself as established by God to be for him what he had originally intended for humanity as a whole. Those who hold fast to the sure house which God has established in Israel 'are destined to live for ever and all the glory of Adam shall be theirs' (CD III, 20). Or, put another way, God has commanded 'that a sanctuary of Adam be built for himself, that there they may send up, like the smoke of incense, the works of thanksgiving' (4Q174 III, 6–7).[23] The community's *Endzeit* experience is to be an *Urzeit* realization.

But the appeal to Genesis does more than this. It raises acutely the problem of the inadequacy of the preaching and practice of the priestly tradition which finalized its form and passed it on. To read the creation accounts solely as presented in the Pentateuch is to be forced to admit human inadequacy. Humanity's only desert is to be expelled from the garden; there is no escaping human responsibility for the state of things. However, here is a movement that wants to say that it qualifies for a place in the garden once again; it even thinks of itself as the garden replanted.[24] While the individual may confess his own wrongdoings, responsibility for the overall sorry state of things is thought to lie elsewhere. Hence much of the interest in the traditions in Genesis is with those parallel attempts to handle the problem of evil (Gen. 6.1–4), which reduce the role of human inadequacy and present a myth of angelic responsibility for the chaos around. Here the Watchers play a significant role as the first to go astray and lead others with them (CD II, 17–19). Those who continue to sin have fallen prey to the snares of Belial. Thus in several texts found at Qumran there is a concern to remythologize or represent the old myths which allow for the possibility that humanity, that is the community, may once again have a place in the garden, become truly *homo horticultor*.

As a corollary to this remythologization of the Genesis narratives, the whole book comes to be recognized as a text not of history per se so much

---

23 Using the column and line numbering of the edition of 4Q174 by A. Steudel, *Der Midrasch zur Eschatologie aus der Qumrangemeinde (4QMidrEschat*[a.b]*)* (STDJ 13; Leiden: Brill, 1994), 23–9.
24 Cf. 1QH[a] XIV, 16–17; XVI, 20–22.

as of the actualization of divine blessing and curse in history. The interest in the Qumran collection in the narratives of Genesis and in the fortunes and fates of various patriarchs exemplifies this. Notably there is an interest in Noah, Abraham, Jacob and Levi, all those to whom particular promises were made or divine blessings given. It is salutary to recall D. Clines' recognition of this in the Pentateuch as a whole:

> The theme of the Pentateuch is the partial fulfilment – which implies also the partial non-fulfilment – of the promise to or blessing of the patriarchs. The promise or blessing is both the divine initiative in a world where human initiatives always lead to disaster, and a re-affirmation of the primal divine intentions for man.[25]

For the Qumranites, this was how and why Genesis and Deuteronomy were to be read: as partially fulfilled blessings and, of course, curses. What remained to be fulfilled was being completed in the life and times of the community itself and its immediate future.

Part of the blessings of Genesis involve the replacement of those things which have distorted the order of the cosmos as God intended it and a reaffirmation of the harmony of creation in its sabbatarian balance. With regard to Genesis, especially the first creation account, mention should also be made of the community's concern for the right calendar and its strict Sabbath-keeping which is a reflection of its concern to imitate the intended created order.[26]

2. With Deuteronomy the appeal rests in several matters. First, if Genesis provides the ideology of Paradise regained, then Deuteronomy provides the ideology of place for the localization of the garden. The several descriptions of the atonement of the land in the community texts

---

25 D. J. A. Clines, *The Theme of the Pentateuch* (JSOTSup 10; Sheffield: JSOT Press, 1978), 29.

26 Many texts could be cited under these headings. On keeping the right calendar note especially 1QS X, 1–8 and the calendrical sections of the *Temple Scroll* and 4QMMT[a] (4Q394); note too, among many calendrical compositions, *Astronomical Enoch* (4Q208–211); *Genesis Commentary A* on dating the events of the flood (4Q252 I, 4–II, 4); *Phases of the Moon* (4Q317); the *Otot Text* (4Q319); Calendrical Documents (4Q320–30); Astronomical fragments (4Q335–37). On the Sabbath, see especially CD X, 14–XI, 18; concern with the right observance of the Sabbath is also a dominant feature of the *Book of Jubilees* which is represented in the Qumran collection in at least 15 copies.

disclose how important the suitable occupation of the land is for the community.[27] The gift of the land to Abram is a promise that has been actualized and so the land is a reality to be protected and restored. Whether or not the *Temple Scroll* is a community composition, its preservation in the caves, probably both Caves 4 and 11, shows that it was studied there with some attention. The use of Deuteronomy 12—22 in Columns LI–LXVI is based on the understanding that these chapters define the law that should be applied in the land.[28] The correct practice of the king is paramount.

Indeed many scholars have noted how the so-called Law of the King in the *Temple Scroll* (11QT[a] LVI, 12–LIX, 21) serves a useful purpose in helping to date the period of the text's compilation, but it is worth juxtaposing this law with a section of MMT which also discusses kingship. There two things are said about the place of the addressee (a ruler?). On the one hand, he is to take to heart the way '[the blessings have (already) befallen in . . .] in the days of Solomon the son of David. And the curses [that] have (already) befallen from the days of Jeroboam the son of Nebat and up to when Jerusalem and Zedekiah King of Judah went into captivity'; thus all leaders are to 'think of the kings of Israel and contemplate their deeds: whoever among them feared [the To]rah was delivered from troubles'.[29] On the other, he is to 'think of David who was a man of righteous deeds and who was (therefore) delivered from many troubles and was forgiven'.[30] With the exception of David and one or two others, the Deuteronomistic view of Israel's history is to be taken seriously. Indeed, that the period from Solomon to the exile is so bad may account for why the Books of Kings and Chronicles are largely absent from the Qumran library; little or none of the history of that period could be construed as normative in any way for those who were the members of the renewed covenant.

In addition to Deuteronomy providing the law for the land, it also

---

27 Note especially 1QS VIII, 6: 'They shall be witnesses to the truth at the Judgment, and shall be the elect of Goodwill who shall atone for the Land, and pay to the wicked their reward' (trans. G. Vermes, *The Dead Sea Scrolls in English* [London: Penguin Books, 1998], 109); cf. 1QS VIII, 10; 4Q265 7 II, 9.

28 On the *Temple Scroll* and the land see M. O. Wise, *A Critical Study of the Temple Scroll from Qumran Cave 11* (Studies in Ancient Oriental Civilization 49; Chicago: Oriental Institute of the University of Chicago, 1990), esp. pp. 200–1.

29 4Q398 11–13, 6–7; trans. E. Qimron and J. Strugnell, *Qumran Cave 4.V: Miqṣat Ma'aśe Ha-Torah* (DJD 10; Oxford: Clarendon Press, 1994), 61.

30 Qimron and Strugnell (trans.), *Qumran Cave 4.V*, 63.

reveals two tendencies which were avidly taken up in the community's writings. The first is that it offers permission for the rewriting of normative texts, and perhaps in some cases the model for how such rewriting should be done. The order of the books in the Pentateuch as we now know it was also known at least in the third century B.C.E.[31] The narrative of Deuteronomy itself places it after that of Exodus in any case. Thus it was recognized that Deuteronomy was a re-presentation of much of the material in the earlier books of the Pentateuch. This permission to rewrite was exploited to the full. It was not an innovation among the Qumranites. The author of the *Book of Jubilees* took the same opportunity and others may have done as well, depending upon how the relationship of texts is viewed.[32] The *Temple Scroll*, in its overall representation of material from Exodus 34 to Deuteronomy 22, has been labelled a sixth book of the Torah;[33] whatever it is generically, it contains rewritten biblical material. J. Strugnell, in his revised pronouncements on MMT,[34] has drawn attention to the Deuteronomic structure of the non-calendrical parts of the work, opening with phrasing that resembles Deuteronomy 1.1 and closing with recollections of blessings and curses. Even the *Rule of the Community* in its 1QS form, in part another collection of laws, begins with an appeal based on the Shema: 'The Master shall teach the saints to live according to the Book of the Community Rule, that they may seek God with a whole heart and soul.'

The second tendency which Deuteronomy encourages is that of the toughening of laws. For example, while the Law at Sinai according to Exodus clearly prohibits idolatry, Deuteronomy goes into more detail and extends the severity of the Law; in Deuteronomy 13.7–12 (EVV 13.6–11) whoever even attempts to entice another into idolatry, even if it is a close relative, shall surely be put to death. So it is that in many of the

---

31 And is reflected in some of the Qumran biblical manuscripts (4QGen–Exod[a]; 4QpaleoGen–Exod[l]; 4QExod–Lev[f]; 4QLev–Num[a]) as well as the Reworked Pentateuch (4Q158; 4Q364–67).

32 For example, it has yet to be finally determined how the relationship between Genesis and the *Books of Enoch* is to be best understood; for what they have in common, both may contain reworked traditions from earlier sources.

33 H. Stegemann, 'Is the Temple Scroll a Sixth Book of the Torah – Lost for 2,500 Years?', *BARev* 13 (1987): 28–35.

34 J. Strugnell, 'MMT: Second Thoughts on a Forthcoming Edition', in *The Community of the Renewed Covenant: The Notre Dame Symposium on the Dead Sea Scrolls* (ed. E. Ulrich and J. VanderKam; Christianity and Judaism in Antiquity Series 10; Notre Dame: University of Notre Dame Press, 1994), 62–70.

texts found at Qumran the legislation of some parts of the Pentateuch is extended or made more severe. For example, the Sabbath laws in CD X, 14–XI, 18 are both a clarification and an extension of scriptural Law: work must cease well before sunset on the sixth day (CD X, 14–16) so as to avoid any risk of working on the Sabbath; or again, the ban on handling any kind of tool on the Sabbath was strictly promulgated so that even if a person should be in danger of death, no implement should be used to save them (CD XI, 16–17). Of the laws of purification in the *Temple Scroll*, Y. Yadin writes, 'The laws of the scroll are very harsh here, in diametrical opposition to the definitive rabbinic laws on the matter.'[35] Many more cases of such stringency could be cited.

A last issue arises especially in Deuteronomy and is of interest in relation to how the community and its wider movement determined the correct interpretation, application and extension of the Law. It is Deuteronomy which deals most explicitly with the status of Moses. He is obviously recognized as the mediator of the Law, not as priest or lay leader, but as prophet. Thus Deuteronomy becomes a key indicator for how the hidden law should be revealed in the community. Such revelation is a matter of prophetic activity: 'This is the interpretation of the Law which God commanded through Moses to observe, according to everything that is revealed from time to time, and as the prophets have revealed by his holy spirit' (1QS VIII, 15–16). Moses is a type of the prophet to come, as Deuteronomy 18.15–18 itself claims.[36] The corollary to this is that there are texts which clearly define the nature of false prophecy (4Q375), and even provide us with a list of the worst false prophets in Israel's history (4Q339). The relationship between the lawgiver and the prophet is an intimate one: through both God makes known his will and his mysterious purposes. With strictness, through God's prophets, humanity is called to obey; Deuteronomy helps make humanity *homo oboediens*.

3. The motif of prophecy links Deuteronomy both with the Psalms and with Isaiah and the Twelve. The Psalms are considered prophecy: the account of David's compositions in 11QPs³ XXVII, 2–11 concludes that David composed 4,050 psalms and songs and 'uttered all these through prophecy which was given him from before the Most High'. As prophetic texts they can be exegeted through the form of commentary peculiar to

---

35 Y. Yadin, *The Temple Scroll*, Vol. I (Jerusalem: Israel Exploration Society, Institute of Archaeology of the Hebrew University, Shrine of the Book, 1983), 333.
36 Deut. 18.15–18 is important in 4Q175 5–8.

the Qumran community, that which describes the interpretation proper as *pesher*. *Pesher* is reserved for the interpretation of unfulfilled blessings, curses, visions and auditions. The Psalms belong in the category of texts which inform the community of the meaning of its own history and its imminent completion.

The prophetic activity of David is a particular concern of the 11QPs[a] scroll, but this is just one facet of the significance of David for the community. He is the prophetic poet par excellence, but he is also the one figure whose behaviour needs to be squared with the Law: with regard to polygamy 'David had not read the sealed book of the Law which was in the ark, for it was not opened in Israel from the death of Eleazar and Joshua, and the elders who worshipped Ashtoreth' (CD V, 1–5). He also plays a key role, perhaps in later compositions only,[37] as the progenitor of the Messiah, who is occasionally described as the shoot of David. The unique role of David in these three respects is highlighted when one considers the almost total absence of any influence of Solomon in the Dead Sea Scrolls: not only are his Proverbs extant in only two very fragmentary manuscripts, but there is only one explicit reference to the book in the entire corpus (Prov. 15.8 in CD XI, 21). Furthermore, there is some ambiguity in the passages which actually use his name.[38]

But the Psalms and their numerous related poetic and liturgical texts are important not just for their association with David, but for another reason too. In light of the use of Deuteronomy in the Dead Sea Scrolls and its strict interpretation, the modern commentator might be tempted to conclude that the covenanters were a bunch of hard-liners. One should reserve judgement on such matters until one has read all the poetic texts which seek to encourage and inspire readers to place themselves before God with confidence; though confession is common, as in the biblical Psalms, the salvific power of God is recognized again and again. This is an oft-repeated motif in the *Hodayot*.

Through the Sabbath songs arranged in a group of 13 and the list of

---

37 As is the thesis of K. Pomykala, *The Davidic Tradition in Early Judaism: Its History and Significance for Messianism* (SBLEJL 7; Atlanta: Scholars Press, 1995).

38 Solomon features in 4Q398 (MMT) 11–13, 1 ('in the days of Solomon the son of David'); also in 11QApPs[a] the opening of column 1 is unclear: '. . .] of Solomon, and he will invoke [. . .'; it is quite likely that this collection of Psalms was considered Davidic, like 11QPs[a] and others, and so the mention of Solomon is incidental. He appears lastly in a fragment of 4Q385 which seems to describe the end of David's reign and that Solomon was his successor, though perhaps something is taken from his hand (13, 4).

David's compositions stating clearly that he composed 364 songs for the daily offering throughout the year,[39] the worship of the community reflects a deep concern with the way things are, with the reality of the presence of God and his angels to which the only adequate response is praise and adoration. Thus all the poetry of the Psalms serves to realize what is contained in the blessings of Genesis and Deuteronomy, that the worshipping community is the location of God's mercy, and praise is the activity of the moment which combines heaven and earth. Humanity adjusted aright is also *homo laudans*.

4. And what of the prophets, especially Isaiah and the Twelve? More of these texts was of concern to the community than might be thought at first. The *pesharim* allow us to see that for the most part, like the Psalms or some of them at least, Isaiah and the Twelve were taken seriously in their entirety. Perhaps the preservation of the whole of a copy of the Book of Isaiah (1QIsa[a]) and a partial copy of a second (1QIsa[b]) in Cave 1, in which the scrolls seem to have been placed with particular care, signals a reverence for the whole text. However, a minority of the *pesharim* also shows us that the commentator could at times work through selected portions of the text (4QpIsa[b]). Another surprising feature of the handling of Isaiah and the Twelve in the *pesharim* is that the two are somewhat interdependent. In 4QpIsa[c] we have the rare phenomenon of the secondary quotation of Zechariah 11.11 (21, 7–8) and Hosea 6.9 (23 II, 14); conversely in 1QpHab VI, 11–12 there is a virtual quotation of Isaiah 13.18. The implication of this is that both Isaiah and the Twelve seem to have been considered as mutually informative of the covenanters' experiences. Knowledge and use of the majority of the pericopae in Isaiah and the Twelve show that the covenanters were able to handle both judgement and consolation, the former for those outside the community, the latter for those inside.

As mentioned, it is not the past history of Israel with which the covenanters identified. The history of which they considered themselves a part, that they thought God was making actual in their own time and in their very experiences, was that foretold in the prophets. This needed to be exposed by gifted and learned interpreters, such as the Teacher of

---

39 On the Qumran Psalter (11QPs[a]) as in some way reflecting a solar calendar, see M. Chyutin, 'The Redaction of the Qumranic and the Traditional Book of Psalms as a Calendar', *RevQ* 16 (1993–5): 367–95. For another view see R. T. Beckwith, *Calendar and Chronology, Jewish and Christian: Biblical, Intertestamental and Patristic Studies* (AGJU 33; Leiden: Brill, 1996), Chapter 6.

Righteousness 'through whom God made known all the secrets of his servants the prophets' (1QpHab VII, 4–5). Such comforting exegesis could make sense of abuse and persecution and could counter the dissonance resulting from a sense of being in the right but not in power. Thus despite circumstances, Isaiah and the Twelve allowed the community to think of itself as consisting of *homo electus*.

THE 'CANON WITHIN THE CANON' IN THE NEW TESTAMENT

Establishing the 'canon within the canon' in the New Testament

Material on the use of the Old Testament in the New is voluminous.[40] There is neither space nor reason to rehearse it all again here, not even in as much detail as for the Qumran Dead Sea Scrolls. However, three matters can be described in outline: the range of texts to which reference is made, the manner of such use, and the likely date when such usage might have begun.

1. The overall array of texts that are cited with some authority by the authors of the various books of the New Testament is not that dissimilar from that found in the compositions discovered at Qumran. No selection of biblical manuscripts as kept by some early Christian community has yet been unearthed, nor for the first century C.E. is there any vast selection of pseudo-biblical Christian materials, so the primary resource for discovering the early Christian 'canon within the canon' is the New Testament itself, both its explicit quotations of and its implicit allusions to other works.

The explicit quotations can be listed readily. As in the Dead Sea Scrolls, citations from texts deemed to carry some weight are often introduced by some kind of technical formula. The fourth edition of the United Bible Societies Text of the Greek New Testament (*UBSGNT*[4])[41] has two indices concerning the use of the Old Testament in the New

---

40 Among many other items reference might be made to D. A. Carson and H. G. M. Williamson (eds.), *It is Written: Scripture Citing Scripture* (Cambridge: Cambridge University Press, 1988), Chs 11–19; E. E. Ellis, 'Biblical Interpretation in the New Testament Church', in *Mikra: Text, Translation, Reading and Interpretation of the Hebrew Bible in Ancient Judaism and Early Christianity* (ed. M. J. Mulder; CRINT 2/1; Assen: van Gorcum; Philadelphia: Fortress Press, 1988), 691–725.

41 B. Aland, K. Aland, J. Karavidopoulos, C. M. Martini, B. M. Metzger, *The Greek New Testament* (Stuttgart: United Bible Societies, 4th edn, 1993).

Testament as its editors have understood it. One index lists supposed explicit quotations. Two viewpoints need to be set side by side, a straightforward enumeration of the quotations and a preliminary appreciation of their selectivity. For the Pentateuch, 26 texts of Genesis are quoted, 30 from Exodus, eight from Leviticus, three from Numbers and 36 from Deuteronomy. The explicit references to the history books are almost non-existent either as Joshua—Kings or as Chronicles and Ezra—Nehemiah, apart from 2 Samuel 7 and 1 Kings 19 (Rom. 11.3–4), both prophetic items. For the prophets proper including Daniel, there are 54 texts from Isaiah, four from Jeremiah, two from Ezekiel, 24 from the Twelve Minor Prophets, and one from Daniel. Fifty-eight texts from the Psalms are quoted, some several times; for the rest of the Writings there are only five references from Proverbs and two from Job. On this basis Isaiah and the Psalms are the runaway favourites with Genesis, Exodus and Deuteronomy featuring respectably, together with the Twelve Minor Prophets.

In addition to simply counting the number of explicit quotations it is important to note something of where the quotations are taken. It is noticeable, for example, that in terms of the explicit citation of Genesis there is nothing from the Noah cycle, almost nothing from the Jacob traditions, and nothing from the Joseph cycle. As for Deuteronomy, most of the passages cited are from the Decalogue and the Shema, from Deuteronomy 18 on the prophet who is to come, and from the Song of Moses. Quotations from the Psalms are spread throughout all five books, but chief among those which are quoted more than once are Psalms 2, 16, 69, 110 and 118, the relevant sections of each of which can be understood as referring to an individual, anointed or otherwise. For Isaiah, the Twelve and Daniel, as with the Psalms, the majority of passages cited can be taken as having to do with an individual figure, whether Emmanuel (Isaiah 7), the Servant (Isaiah 40; 42; 49; 52—3), the son of man (Daniel 7), Son (Hosea 11), David (Amos 9) or the king (Zechariah 9).

As for allusions and other verbal parallels, the index in the *UBSGNT*[4] is very extensive. The proportions for various books of the Old Testament are similar to the proportions already enumerated for the explicit quotations. It is necessary, however, to be aware that the profile of passages to which allusion is made is somewhat different than with the explicit quotations, at least for certain books of the New Testament. This makes it necessary to nuance how various traditions may have been of influence, at least for some authors and audiences, if not more generally throughout all the churches. So, for example, whereas in the whole New

Testament there are no explicit quotations from Leviticus concerning sacrifice, there are several allusions to such passages, not only in the Letter to the Hebrews in which Leviticus 16 plays a major role, but also in the letters of Paul and Luke–Acts.[42] Or again, though there are no explicit quotations from the Former Prophets in the Gospels and Acts, there are many important allusions to them in a range of different genres, in the genealogies, in the poetry of Luke's infancy narrative, in the miracle stories and in the speeches of Peter and Paul in Acts. For another example, the very restricted explicit use of Jeremiah and Ezekiel in the New Testament, almost limited for the former to the new covenant passage and for the latter to Ezekiel 20.34, 41 and 37.27 in 2 Corinthians 6.16–17, is replaced by a wealth of allusions to both prophetic books, most notably in Revelation.[43] A range of other works also features, almost exclusively from the Apocrypha and *1 Enoch*, but with no hint of *Jubilees*.

2. Bearing in mind the ideological points which the particular use of certain books of Scripture in the Dead Sea Scrolls found at Qumran suggests, what can be said about the manner in which the books of the New Testament use their selected Old Testament passages? Some aspects of the use of Scripture in the New Testament are similar to that found in the Dead Sea Scrolls. For example, though the subject matter is Jesus, as Son or as the Word, there is some attempt in the appeal to the Scriptures in some sense to argue for the antiquity of what the Christ event might mean (for example, Heb. 1.1–4; Jn 1.1–14). The appeal to earliest times, to creation itself, does three things: it suggests that what God had originally intended is somehow comprehensible for the reader, that what God had intended all along was only partially known to intervening generations, and that therefore what is now to be understood is superior to that which was recognized by previous generations. All these matters can be seen in the Dead Sea Scrolls' handling of the scriptural traditions about the earliest times.

In another matter, to do with the use of Genesis in particular, there is a similarity between the Dead Sea Scrolls and the New Testament. In the Dead Sea Scrolls, appeal to the patriarchs is a matter both of providing pre-Mosaic examples for particular matters of obedience, and also of providing typological models for expressing contemporary

---

42 See esp. Lev. 3.17 in Acts 15.20, 29; Lev. 6.16, 26 in 1 Cor. 9.13; Lev. 7.6, 15 in 1 Cor. 10.18.

43 Among many others, see especially M. D. Goulder, 'The Apocalypse as an Annual Cycle of Prophecies', *NTS* 27 (1981): 342–67.

understandings and aspirations.[44] In the New Testament, too, there is both exemplary usage of patriarchal figures and others,[45] and there is also a wide-ranging typological use of figures such as Adam and Noah, Abraham and Sarah, Hagar and Jacob. In both the Dead Sea Scrolls and the New Testament these types are used to present a similar *Urzeit und Endzeit* fulfilment, and to argue that the Mosaic covenant is in constant need of interpretation. However, as soon as one passes from method to content, then differences between the two corpora emerge, as the scriptural types in the New Testament are almost exclusively related to Jesus Christ and the new era he is thought to have inaugurated.[46] Furthermore, in relation to promise and fulfilment, the New Testament authors focus on universalist aspects of unfulfilled blessings given to the patriarchs and thereby creatively redirect the particularism of the Mosaic covenant: both the blessings and curses are read as referring to all people. The physical shift away from Palestine to the dispersion and into the Gentile world also means that this universalism is not generally expressed in the particular alternative mythologies available within Palestinian Jewish tradition, but, for example, through appeal to conscience and aspects of natural law. Thus allusions to Enoch are largely restricted to texts which belong to or reflect Palestinian Jewish Christian communities, notably Jude 14.

The universalist reading of Genesis also controls the reading of Deuteronomy. Here the differences between the Dead Sea Scrolls and the New Testament become all the more apparent. The use of Deuteronomy in the New Testament is in no way tied to the gift of the land which needs to be lived out appropriately, nor is it read as guiding strict obedience. There is much appeal to the Decalogue of Deuteronomy 5 and a few other pertinent laws[47] as a way of providing an effective summary of the Law for Christians. Deuteronomy 18.15–18 on the status of Moses as a prophet recurs in several places, and as such is a key concept in

---

44 For example, in some texts the community describes itself as 'the House of Judah' (1QpHab VIII, 1; 4QpPs[a] 1–10 II, 14); in others the movement aspires to 'all the glory of Adam' (1QS IV, 23; CD III, 20).

45 See especially the appeal to the exemplary faith of Abel, Enoch, Noah, Abraham and others in Heb. 11.4–40.

46 Similarity between the Dead Sea Scrolls and the New Testament is most obvious in how both communities variously claim to be the true Israel.

47 Notably the rule against bribery in Deut. 10.17 based on the impartiality of God himself which is alluded to in several New Testament passages: Acts 10.34; Rom. 2.11; Gal. 2.6; Eph. 6.9; Col. 3.25; 1 Tim. 6.15; Rev. 17.14; 19.16.

understanding the various portrayals of the figure of Jesus. The blessings of the Song of Moses are also set in contexts of universal fulfilment.

The christological use of parts of Deuteronomy is reflected in the way in which the text of Isaiah is handled in the New Testament. Whereas in the Dead Sea Scrolls it is difficult to specify which sections of the book were of key importance to the community and its wider movement, in the New Testament Isaiah is explicitly used overwhelmingly because of the messianic readings in Isaiah 7, 9 and 11 and the individualistic significance of the Servant Songs. Judgement is retained through the use of Isaiah 6.9–10 in several places and one or two other passages. Rather than providing a sense of election for the community, the Book of Isaiah is searched for texts that relate to one specific elect individual.

As for the Psalms, their use is primarily in line with the view of them in the Dead Sea Scrolls as prophetic texts in need of fulfilment. Especially is this the case in the passion narratives, but also the overall structure of the argument of Hebrews has been seen to be based on Psalms 95, 110 and 40. However, Psalms 2, 110, 118 and others are cited and alluded to often, confirming the particularist interest of the New Testament authors in searching the Scriptures for texts that could be used christologically of Jesus. Furthermore, it is noticeable that those Psalms in the New Testament which are almost certainly Jewish compositions slightly adapted, such as the canticles in Luke's infancy narrative, are indeed replete with implicit allusions to the Psalms, but only very occasionally are hints of the Psalms to be found in the newly composed hymns such as are found in Philippians 2, Colossians 1 or scattered through the Book of Revelation. Again, the christocentricity of early Christian worship has provoked a break with longstanding traditions of how God is suitably worshipped.

3. The third matter to focus on in the prevalence of this quartet of scriptural books in the New Testament concerns the likely date of and reason for their predominance. Three examples follow in the next section of this chapter. They are all taken from the earliest layers of the New Testament, from the source common to Matthew and Luke, from Mark, and from a pre-Pauline hymn which Paul probably adapted. These examples show that the four leading scriptural books – Genesis, Deuteronomy, Isaiah and the Psalms – were prominent in the earliest layers of the tradition and are not the result of generations of reflection. The question to ask, then, is whether the similar pattern of the canon within the canon in the New Testament as in the Dead Sea Scrolls results from the dependence of one upon the other, or whether it is merely the

case that eschatologically oriented, perhaps somewhat marginalized, forms of Judaism tended to look to the same Scriptures for their self-understanding. Though from the time of John the Baptist onwards some of those responsible for the copying and preservation of the Dead Sea Scrolls may indeed have joined the Jesus movement or the early Christian communities in Palestine and elsewhere, the subtle differences – in which parts of the favourite scriptural books were chosen and in the ways in which much of the handling of the texts occurred – suggest that the differences in content should be noted as much as the similarities in method.

The working and significance of the 'canon within the canon' in the New Testament

In this short section, three examples of the early Christian use of Old Testament texts will be given. Though selected to illustrate the prominence of Genesis, Deuteronomy, Isaiah and the Psalms, the texts discussed could be substituted with many others.

Luke 7.22–3 (Matt. 11.4–6)

The disciples of John the Baptist have come to Jesus to inquire about whether Jesus was the expected one. Jesus' answer to them is a combination of scriptural allusions. The precise phraseology of 'the blind see' combines the language of Isaiah 35.5 with Isaiah 61.1; 'the lame walk' is partly Isaiah 35.6; 'lepers are cleansed' may allude to Leviticus 14.2–3 or 4 Kings 5.3; 'the deaf hear' is Isaiah 35.5 again; 'the dead are raised' may allude to Deuteronomy 32.39[48] or Isaiah 26.19;[49] 'the poor have good news preached to them' is a form of Isaiah 61.1. Here is a combination of Isaianic passages with some hints of motifs to be found in the Law. The passages are associated with the anointed prophet of the last days and so in their New Testament context exemplify how scriptural promises are fulfilled through Jesus. Some of these ideas are also portrayed in 4Q521 in relation to divine activity in the time of his anointed one, but there

---

48 As pointed out for the parallel in 4Q521 by E. Puech, 'Une apocalypse messianique (4Q521)', *RevQ* 15 (1990–2): 493.
49 As claimed, for example, by J. A. Fitzmyer, *The Gospel according to Luke I–XI* (AB 28; Garden City: Doubleday, 2nd edn, 1983), 668.

Isaiah 61.1 is expanded through reference to Psalms 107.9 and 146.7.[50] Since this saying is shared between Luke and Matthew it may well come from a common source and possibly even stem in some form from Jesus himself.

Mark 12.1–12 (Matt. 21.33–6; Lk. 20.9–19)

Elsewhere it has been argued that the combination of the parabolic use of the vineyard material from Isaiah 5.1–7 and the proof-text concerning the cornerstone from Psalm 118.22–3 was a natural juxtaposition of texts, and in something like the form of the tradition as presented in Mark 12 and parallels may have originated with Jesus himself.[51] The details of that argument need not be rehearsed here. It is only important to notice that two other scriptural matters are commonly discussed in relation to the parable. First, two items of Genesis need to be noted. The term 'beloved' (Mk 12.6; Lk. 20.13) is to be understood against a background of scriptural passages, foremost among which is Genesis 22.2.[52] The words of the tenants, 'Come, let us kill him', are also the words of Joseph's brothers in Genesis 37.20. Second, if the parable should be interpreted with respect to the laws and practices concerning inheritance, then clearly with regard to what the vineyard symbolizes the many references to the land as Israel's inheritance in Deuteronomy come readily to mind. Thus, in this pericope there is a subtle combination of themes from Genesis, Deuteronomy, Isaiah and the Psalms; furthermore, the particular usage of the material from Genesis and Psalm 118 is focused on Jesus. The selection of scriptural passages according to their christological potential is evident. Nevertheless all four books of the 'canon within the canon' are represented. A general allusion to the Twelve may also be present in the sending of the servants, one after the other, just as the prophets had also been sent, some of whom are explicitly called 'servant' (Amos 3.7; Zech. 1.6).

---

50 For comments on the relationship between 4Q521 and Lk. 7.22–3, see G. J. Brooke, 'Shared Intertextual Interpretations in the Dead Sea Scrolls and the New Testament', in *Biblical Perspectives: Early Use and Interpretation of the Bible in Light of the Dead Sea Scrolls: Proceedings of the First International Symposium of the Orion Center for the Study of the Dead Sea Scrolls and Associated Literature, 12–14 May, 1996* (ed. M. E. Stone and E. G. Chazon; STDJ 28; Leiden: Brill, 1998), 35–57 (Chapter 5 in this book).

51 G. J. Brooke, '4Q500 1 and the Use of Scripture in the Parable of the Vineyard', *DSD* 2 (1995): 268–94.

52 The epithet also occurs in Mk 1.11 and parallels; it may also reflect the description of Israel in Isa. 44.2.

Philippians 2.6–11

This early Christian hymn, either composed or more probably adapted by Paul, is replete with scriptural allusions. Often pointed out are the references to Genesis 1—3: in the contrast between the form of God and the form of a slave, in the temptation to be like God, implicitly in the contrast between Christ's obedience and Adam's disobedience, and in Christ's acceptance of Adam's lot, mortality, for himself, so that through his exaltation, glory could once again become visible.[53] Alongside the Genesis allusions are also some motifs from Isaiah: the precise word for 'servant' is used of Israel in Isaiah 49.3 and 5; the motif of kenosis in Philippians 2.7 may be a suitable rendering of Isaiah 53.12, 'he emptied out his life to death'; most obviously Isaiah 45.23 is poetically adapted in Philippians 2.10–11. Allusions to Deuteronomy can also be recognized in the passage: the Decalogue (Deut. 5.6–21) and the Shema (Deut. 6.4–5) both insist on the singularity of God and that nothing should be made in his likeness, and the name of God is not to be taken in vain (Deut. 5.11). The Shema also insists on the importance of obedience, and the glory of God is revealed as the Decalogue is given (Deut. 5.24). Furthermore, Paul seems aware of these Deuteronomic allusions as he sets the hymn within the context of an exhortation to obedience (Phil. 2.12) with fear and trembling (cf. Exod. 15.15–16) endorsed by his own self-sacrifice (Phil. 2.17). As mentioned earlier, there are few allusions, if any, to the Psalms in these new early Christian hymns.[54] Nevertheless, here once again are Genesis, Deuteronomy and Isaiah combined through an obvious christological purpose with universalist implications.

CONCLUSION

Four scriptural books and their extras were particularly popular among those connected with the Dead Sea Scrolls and the various New Testament authors: Genesis, Deuteronomy, Isaiah and the Psalms. To both groups these books in various ways guaranteed the antiquity of their claims, allowed them to justify their positions as the true representatives

---

53 See, for example, J. D. G. Dunn, *Christology in the Making: A New Testament Inquiry into the Origins of the Doctrine of the Incarnation* (London: SCM Press, 1980), 114–21.

54 There is a possibility that Phil. 2.10 contains an allusion to Ps. 67.15 LXX in which Shaddai is rendered by the very distinctive 'heavenly one'. The context in the Psalm describes God as at Sinai.

of Israel, strongly suggested they were living at the time of the fulfilment of God's promises, that his blessings were theirs despite persecutions and misunderstandings.

The covenanters of the Dead Sea Scrolls thought of how in them humanity was restored, that through God's mercy correct obedience was possible, and that in purity they could join the worship of the angels; God was about to complete his consolation of them. For many of the early Christians too, humanity seemed restored, God's mercy enabled correct response and thanksgiving became a community characteristic. For the covenanters the interpretative myths associated with these four authoritative books were shattered when the land was irretrievably occupied and the locus of worship destroyed; for the Christians the interpretative myth, somewhat similarly based, came to reflect a continuing reality because it was made of universal significance through the recollection of the death of one man.

4

Biblical Interpretation in the
Qumran Scrolls and the New Testament

In this chapter the aim is to juxtapose various issues in the way in which authoritative scriptural texts are handled in both the Qumran corpus and the New Testament in order to suggest more clearly where the similarities and differences between the two bodies of literature may lie. Biblical interpretation in both sets of texts appears in many guises and under many forms. Sometimes it has seemed to those who have studied the subject that the two share much in common, not only in a common background and method, but even in detail and content.[1]

THE ATTITUDE TO THE CANON

This is not the place to address the issue of what constituted the authoritative collection of texts either for the Qumran community and the movement of which it was a part or for the authors of the New

---

1 There is a vast literature on biblical interpretation in the Dead Sea Scrolls: items published since 1970 are listed in F. García Martínez and D. W. Parry, *A Bibliography of the Finds in the Desert of Judah 1970–1995* (STDJ 19; Leiden: Brill, 1996); A. Pinnick, *The Orion Center Bibliography of the Dead Sea Scrolls (1995–2000)* (STDJ 41; Leiden: Brill, 2001); and regularly in *RevQ*. For a good survey and summary bibliography, see J. Maier, 'Early Jewish Biblical Interpretation in the Qumran Literature', in *Hebrew Bible/Old Testament: The History of Its Interpretation*, Vol. I/1 *Antiquity* (ed. M. Sæbø; Göttingen: Vandenhoeck & Ruprecht, 1996), 108–29. For biblical interpretation in the New Testament see the contribution by H. Hübner, 'New Testament Interpretation of the Old Testament', in the same volume (pp. 332–72), to whose Select Bibliography should be added the impressive collection of essays in D. A. Carson and H. G. M. Williamson (ed.), *It is Written: Scripture Citing Scripture. Essays in Honour of Barnabas Lindars* (Cambridge: University Press, 1988).

Testament.[2] It is clear that both sets of literature recognized the authority of the five books of the Law of Moses, held the prophetic literature in high regard, could quote from the Psalms and most other works among the Writings assuming audience approval, and that each movement had considerable respect for other compositions such as at Qumran the *Book of Jubilees* or the *Hodayot*,[3] in Paul some of the Greek philosophers, or in both the traditions variously associated with Enoch.[4]

Against this general agreement as to what constituted an authoritative collection of books which could be quoted both to fellow members of the two movements and to those outside, there are nevertheless two important differences to note.

The first derives from what may be considered almost accidental evidence. Reflecting the general agreement as to the extent of the collection of authoritative works, there is a remarkable correspondence between the two most explicit so-called canon notices in both corpora. For the Qumran materials this comes in 4QMMT.[5] The text of 4Q397 14–21, 10–11 is very broken but two, three or four collections of works could be referred to: the Book of Moses, the Books of the Prophets, David, and the writings about the deeds of succeeding generations

---

2 For more on this matter see G. J. Brooke, '"The Canon within the Canon" at Qumran and in the New Testament', *The Scrolls and the Scriptures: Qumran Fifty Years After* (ed. S. E. Porter and C. A. Evans; JSPSup 26; Roehampton Institute London Papers 3; Sheffield: Sheffield Academic Press, 1997), 242–66 (Chapter 3 in this book).

3 Preserved in the Qumran caves are more than 20 copies of Genesis, Deuteronomy, Isaiah and the Psalms, approximately 17 copies of Exodus and at least 15 of the *Book of Jubilees*. Then still in double figures are manuscript copies of Leviticus, the *Hodayot* and the *Rule of the Community*. Whether the *Hodayot* and the *Rule of the Community* are referred to in other texts as authoritative sources has yet to be definitively determined, but for the probable use of the *Hodayot*, see the stimulating study by P. R. Davies, 'History and Hagiography: The Life of the "Teacher" in Hymn and *Pesher*', in *Behind the Essenes: The History and Ideology in the Dead Sea Scrolls* (BJS 94; Atlanta: Scholars Press, 1987), 87–105. For the possible use of the *Rule of the Community* in another composition, see 4Q265 (*Miscellaneous Rules*).

4 At Qumran not only evident in all the *Enoch* manuscripts (esp. 4Q201–12) but in compositions such as CD and the *Book of Jubilees*; in the New Testament the writings associated with Enoch are most explicit in Jude 14–15.

5 Even if MMT predates the occupation of the Qumran site, it nevertheless has enough in common with other sectarian compositions, especially CD and the *Temple Scroll*, to permit us to take it as representative of the Qumran corpus.

(perhaps some of the history books).[6] There need be no problem in understanding the Book of Moses to be a reference to the five books of the Law. There is a range of ways in which the Law is designated: sometimes simply as the Law,[7] sometimes as the Books of the Law,[8] or the Law of Moses,[9] or the Book of Moses.[10] To understand the label 'Prophets' in 4QMMT correctly it is most appropriate to consider the use of the term in the plural in other compositions. There are several references to the Prophets, nearly all of which can be understood to refer to written traditions, such as 1QS I, 3 ('by means of the hand of Moses and his servants the Prophets'); that the label refers to books is explicit in CD VII, 17 (4Q266 3 III, 18), 'the books of the Prophets', and is clearly implied in a reference such as 1QpHab VII, 5 in which the Teacher's God-given knowledge of 'all the mysteries of the words of his servants the Prophets' is described. Given this stress on the words of the prophets as servants, it seems quite likely that the so-called canon notice in 4QMMT should be understood as using the term Prophets to refer principally to the writings of the Prophets themselves, that is the Latter Prophets, rather than also to the Former Prophets. The prophetic collection of texts might, however, be considered as a somewhat open-ended, but overarching category, and so could include by extension the remaining one or two groups of writings. By David, 4QMMT refers presumably to a Psalter of some kind, though possibly to a developing collection of books of which the Psalter was considered the first. As for what can be salvaged of the rest of the very fragmentary context at the end of the line and start of the next (4Q397 14–21, 10–11), there may be a reference to a collection of historical writings under a title including the phrase *dwr wdwr*.

---

6 See the principal edition of these fragments in E. Qimron and J. Strugnell, *Qumran Cave 4.V: Miqṣat Ma'aśe Ha-Torah* (DJD 10; Oxford: Clarendon Press, 1994), 27 and Plate VI. Qimron and Strugnell consider that the relevant line 'is a significant piece of evidence for the history of the tripartite division of the Canon' (p. 59), but the suggestion adopted tentatively here is that of G. Brin in his review of DJD 10 in *JSS* 40 (1995): 341–2, namely that there may be reference to four sets of written materials. Others prefer to see a reference to just two sets of authoritative Scriptures, with the second set being further defined and extended; see, e.g., E. Ulrich, 'The Non-attestation of a Tripartite Canon in 4QMMT', *CBQ* 65 (2003): 202–14.
7 Sometimes also the 'Law of God' as at 1QpHab I, 11.
8 CD VII, 15; 4Q273 2, 2.
9 Esp. in CD XV, 2, 9, 12 (4Q266 8 I, 3); XVI, 2 (4Q271 4 II, 4), 5 (4Q270 6 II, 18; 4Q271 4 II, 6); 4Q266 11, 6.
10 4Q397 14–21, 15; 4Q398 14–17 I, 2.

Apart from appreciating what may be referred to as authoritative in 4QMMT, notice should be taken of the context in which the reference is made. The appeal to the addressee to study and understand these writings is part of an exhortation which emphasizes the correctness of the daily life of the community. To avoid abomination it is separated from the majority of the people and from its own perspective no treachery or deceit or evil is to be found in its midst. Here appeal is made to shared authoritative texts *as a whole* to argue the point that the community of the author is keeping to the written traditions sufficiently faithfully to believe that it would be the heir of the blessings promised in those self-same traditions. In this way it can be clearly understood that the community stands under the authority of the whole tradition.

The most striking parallel to the canon notice of 4QMMT is to be found in Luke 24.44–47:

> Then he said to them, 'These are my words that I spoke to you while I was still with you – that everything written about me in the law of Moses, the prophets, and the psalms must be fulfilled.' Then he opened their minds to understand the scriptures, and he said to them, 'Thus it is written, that the Messiah is to suffer and to rise from the dead on the third day, and that repentance and forgiveness of sins is to be proclaimed in his name to all nations.'

The appeal is very similar to that made in 4QMMT. There is an earnest desire for understanding of the Scriptures, the Law, the Prophets,[11] and the Psalms. But the literary context of the appeal to Scripture is strikingly different. First, it is surely not accidental that this exposition of Scripture by Jesus takes place according to the Lukan narrative in the context of a resurrection appearance.[12] Whatever modern theologians may make of the resurrection of Jesus, this narrative implies that it is the basis of the

11 The pair, 'the Law and the Prophets', occurs in several places in the Gospels and Acts (Matt. 5.17; 7.12; 11.13; 22.40; Lk. 16.16, 29, 31; 24.44; Jn 1.45; Acts 13.15; 24.4), providing further evidence that even in the Qumran texts the label 'Prophets' in the plural probably refers to the books of the so-called literary prophets.
12 In organizing his study of the use of Scripture in the New Testament, B. Lindars made the striking and suitable decision to treat 'The Resurrection' as the principal starting point for understanding the early Christian construction of arguments from Scripture for the messiahship of Jesus: *New Testament Apologetic: The Doctrinal Significance of the Old Testament Quotations* (London: SCM Press, 1961), 32–74.

disciples' experience and provides the correct backdrop to the interpretation and understanding of the Scriptures. Second, Jesus' words as represented by Luke show that the adequate reading of Scripture is selective. It is what is written in the Scriptures 'about me' that matters, 'that the Messiah is to suffer and to rise from the dead on the third day'. Paul writes something similar in addressing the Corinthians: 'Christ died for our sins in accordance with the scriptures . . . he was raised on the third day in accordance with the scriptures' (1 Cor. 15.3–4).[13]

The second matter can be expressed somewhat crudely in terms of the comparison of Qumran exegesis with Christian eisegesis. The basic attitude to the authoritative texts in the Qumran community and its wider movement concerned the suitable handling of the tradition which itself set the agenda for daily living. The Law needed to be applied to daily life in the land and in particular to the temple as properly constructed and ordered. For all that the agreed core of Scripture remained the same so that dialogue could be maintained with those outside, the Qumranic exegetical approach led to the extension of the tradition, not its reduction. This is attested, for example, by the very existence of the so-called *Temple Scroll*. This is a text which purports largely to be a direct address of God to Moses about the temple and about how life in the land should be lived. Because these matters were not adequately covered in the Law, the scroll is compiled so as to present itself as having an authority equal to or greater than that of the Law itself.[14] The agenda is set by scriptural texts and new compositions derived by thoroughgoing exegesis. Thus the Law is extended and completed, not replaced. Later Jewish codifications of opinions on various aspects of the Law were compiled with a similar purpose.

In the New Testament, however, the experiential and christological starting point led to a searching in the Scriptures for passages which were consistent with that view that God had been and continued to be active in Jesus with universal effect. Thus while the whole of an emerging canon remained significant for Christianity in its continuing dialogue with

---

13 There is extensive debate about which Scriptures Paul is referring to. Perhaps it is best to think of the plural as referring to the Scriptures as a whole, within which there are proof-texts for the death and resurrection of Jesus, such as Isa. 53 and Hos. 6.2: see, e.g., H. Conzelmann, *1 Corinthians: A Commentary on the First Epistle to the Corinthians* (Hermeneia; Philadelphia: Fortress Press, 1975), 255–6.

14 B. Z. Wacholder has insisted on calling the composition 11QTorah to indicate this: *The Dawn of Qumran: The Sectarian Torah and the Teacher of Righteousness* (MHUC 8; Cincinnati: Hebrew Union College Press, 1983), esp. 17–21.

Judaism and its continuing need to understand its own roots, certain passages which could be understood as fulfilled in the life, death and resurrection of Jesus were focused on to the exclusion of much else. Part of the excluding process rested in that much of the New Testament was finally written up after the fall of the temple and the occupation of the land by the Romans and others. Once identified on the basis of the content of the early kerygma, scriptural passages could be interpreted in manners similar to the handling of texts in Judaism more broadly, but the agenda was set not primarily by Scripture itself, but by the early Christian experience kerygmatically formulated.

Thus the Qumranic evidence suggests an attitude to Scripture which leads to its extension; the New Testament suggests an attitude which leads to a minimalist approach. Naturally, the actual circumstances lying behind any particular composition could be different from this overall picture. At Qumran, experiences and eschatological views could affect the reading of texts eisegetically. Among the early Christian authors,[15] some aspects of what was written up no doubt depended upon the exegesis of various scriptural passages which might be derived from the teaching of Jesus himself.

CATEGORIES OF INTERPRETATION

The Law

Whereas about 50 years ago the immediate availability of non-biblical sectarian rules in 1QS and the prophetic interpretation in 1QpHab suggested that the dominant means of handling Scripture in the movement responsible for these texts was to do with the realization of prophecy, the availability of the complete corpus has allowed scholars to see that the dominant element in its attention to Scripture was indeed the right interpretation of the Law. In fact, this was obvious from the outset, once it became clear that the *Cairo Damascus Document* was in some way related to the other community texts, though until recently the majority of studies of the *Damascus Document* has concentrated on the so-called Admonition (CD I–VIII; XIX–XX) rather than the Laws. But the *Damascus Document* makes one thing plain: it is not for the wrong view

---

15 One thinks especially of Jesus as portrayed in Matt. 5.17: the Law and the Prophets are not 'abolished' but 'fulfilled'.

of prophecy that the community member can be expelled, but for not following the right interpretation of the Law.[16]

Furthermore, according to texts like 1QS VI, 6–7, it was incumbent upon members of the community to engage in the study of the Law. Nowhere is it explicit that membership entailed the study of the Prophets with a similar vigour though, as has already been pointed out, the leadership of the community encouraged understanding of the whole breadth of the written tradition. The community and its wider movement, like Israel of old, was covenantal, obtained its identity through the Law enshrined ritually. As S. Talmon has very suitably noted with regard to the occurrence of the phrase in CD, it was the community of the 'renewed covenant'.[17]

What emerges from the study of the Law at Qumran is a consistent *Tendenz*. In almost every area, legal prescriptions are interpreted in a rigorous and hard-line manner, such that in some regards the Law is extended to every aspect of life, whether it be sexual relations or the keeping of the Sabbath, meal practice or business dealings. Here one can sense a basic premise behind the interpretation of scriptural rulings, namely, that the Law is all-pervasive, it affects every area of life and can be extended so to do.

In the New Testament some particular matters in the Law are indeed debated, especially in the Jesus traditions, and it is important to observe that a method similar to that visible in many of the scrolls can be seen. In both sets of literature legal texts are expounded through their juxtaposition with others. However, the majority perspective on the Law in the New Testament is that it is a problem in itself. The opening of the churches to Gentiles in the second generation meant that apart from some items which might be of ongoing significance for some in debates with fellow Jews, only those commandments of obvious universal significance are projected afresh.

Compared with the sense of the all-pervasive character of the Law which can be found in the Qumran scrolls at every stage of its development, the focus in the New Testament on the few laws of universal significance, such as can be found in the Decalogue or one reading of

16 See, e.g., CD VI, 18; XX, 32–33; cf. 4Q266 11, 20–21 = 4Q270 7 II, 15.

17 S. Talmon, 'The Community of the Renewed Covenant: Between Judaism and Christianity', in *The Community of the Renewed Covenant: The Notre Dame Symposium on the Dead Sea Scrolls* (ed. E. Ulrich and J. VanderKam; Christianity and Judaism in Antiquity Series 10; Notre Dame: University of Notre Dame Press, 1994), 3–24.

Leviticus 19.18 (read in a certain way) results in those New Testament authors who attempt ethical instruction either making an appeal to conscience as an arbiter in determining suitable behaviour, or making use of the more widely accessible Wisdom traditions of the Writings, such as with the patience of Job (Jas 5.11), the need to tell the truth, the need for love (1 Pet. 4.8 on Prov. 10.12), or making use of Graeco-Roman traditions, as in the household codes.

Whereas with respect to the Law and its own self-understanding the Qumran community and its wider movement was the community of the renewed covenant, the early Christian declaration of the universal significance of the death of Jesus meant that the interpretation of the Law in the New Testament depended upon a (new) covenant.[18] Put another way, in the life of the Qumran community and its wider movement there was no covenantal anamnesis other than that described in Scripture itself, so the community stood under the authority of the whole Law. In the early Christian communities focus was variously on 'the death of the Lord until he comes' (1 Cor. 11.26) and that anticipated hope governed how the Law should be universalized.

Prophecy

This concern with the Law in the Qumran scrolls is matched with a concern to understand the prophets aright too. The character of the canon described above is its concentration on the Law and the Prophets. Indeed the two categories are mentioned together in a number of places (e.g., 1QS VIII, 15–16). There is little interest in the Qumran community or its wider movement in repeating and interpreting Israel's history writing, nor is there much concern with Wisdom materials, except in as much as the traditions can be particularized for the community.[19]

Prophetic interpretation, especially in the form of the *pesharim*, has often been considered to have been the most characteristic of the uses of Scripture in the Qumran scrolls. Partly this view has arisen because one of the first manuscripts to come to light and also one of the best preserved was the *Habakkuk Commentary* (1QpHab). Partly this is the result of a scholarly abuse of the material as the atomistic but cryptic interpretations in the commentaries have been plundered in order supposedly to provide the history of the community.

---

18 'New' in 1 Cor. 11.25; Lk. 22.20.
19 Hence the dominant motif of 'the secrets/mysteries of existence' in the sapiential texts found at Qumran, secrets presumably to which only the community had access.

There are many variations on the forms of prophetic interpretation in the Qumran scrolls, ranging from the thoroughgoing continuous commentary as in 1QpHab to commentaries that are either selective in the sections of the Prophets upon which they comment or which juxtapose texts thematically. Some prophetic texts are used as proof-texts; some are used only in poetic allusions.[20] Nevertheless in explicit Qumran prophetic interpretation the aspect of most of these compositions which is commonly overlooked is the way in which the text of Scripture acts as a control on the content of the commentary. It is not just that in the *Habakkuk Commentary* (1QpHab) the whole text has to receive *pesher* sequentially; rather, the commentator is neatly aware of the structure and purpose of the first two chapters of Habakkuk in themselves and readily allows such awareness to influence his composition.[21] Or again, in the more thematic compositions, texts are not woven arbitrarily together, but are commonly to be found presented in such a way that the same scriptural verses recur in several places (cf. 11QMelch) or extensive, more or less complete pericopae are commented upon (cf. 4Q174).

There is nothing quite like this to be found in the New Testament where explicit use of prophecy is largely a matter of the application of proof-texts to matters which are based on some other grounds. The use of some Psalms in a thematic way in the Letter to the Hebrews may be something of an exception. Furthermore, this controlling influence of Scripture in the *pesharim* needs to be stressed, not least because many New Testament commentators have been tempted to describe the interpretative activity of many of the New Testament authors as *pesher*-like. It can be put quite simply: in the *pesher* the primary or base scriptural text always precedes the interpretation; in the New Testament, such as in Matthew's infancy narrative or in the use of the Psalms in the passion narratives, the scriptural text, in the way the narrative is presented, follows after the event.

All this is to suggest that the fulfilment interpretation which is found in the Qumran commentaries is somewhat different from that to be found in the use of proof-texts in certain sections of the New Testament. That said, the chief characteristic of prophetic interpretation in both bodies of literature is the atomistic identification of one or more items in the scriptural text with something else: 'This is That'.

---

20 As in the use of much of Isaiah in the *Hodayot*.
21 See, e.g., W. H. Brownlee, 'The Composition of Habakkuk', in *Hommages à André Dupont-Sommer* (ed. A. Caquot and M. Philonenko; Paris: Librairie d'Amérique et d'Orient Adrien-Maisonneuve, 1971), 255–75.

Narrative

Narrative interpretation is evident in several compositions found at Qumran. Its chief characteristic is to explain incidents in the base narrative so as to make them more easily understood by or acceptable to a particular audience. Often such explanation is done through careful exegesis of which the narrative only presents the end result. Commonly there is a polemical edge to the retelling, such as with the treatment of Genesis and Exodus in the *Book of Jubilees*.

Narrative interpretation in the scrolls often appears to be most concerned with explanatory clarification of the plain meaning of the text. This seems to be the case whether the issue is what might explain Noah's preeminence, or Abraham's activity in Egypt (1QapGen), or the chronology of the flood (4Q252), or the date of the entry into the land (*Jubilees*). The interest is in re-presenting the story correctly according to a particular viewpoint.

In the New Testament the majority of uses of scriptural narrative is either typological (as in the use by Jesus and others of the Sodom and Gomorrah story as a warning) or symbolic (as in the allusion to the Jacob cycle in the Fourth Gospel) or allegorical (as in Paul's use of Sarah and Hagar for freedom and slavery (Gal. 4.21–31)). The only extensive interpretation of scriptural narrative in the New Testament occurs in Stephen's speech in Acts 7. There the narrative is retold in a much reduced form with attention to its plain meaning in order to make a negative point about the temple.

Poetic and liturgical scriptural interpretation

Poetic scriptural interpretation is apparent in many compositions found at Qumran. Above all, there are collections of apocryphal psalms, various liturgical texts and the *Hodayot*. To some extent, whether lesser or greater, all these poetic texts are rooted in the imitation of biblical genres of poetry, especially as found in the Book of Psalms, but also elsewhere. Thus, for example, 4Q365 seems to contain a victory song which has affinities with the Song of the Sea but also with the Song of Judith.[22] This rebirth of images in imitative allusion is both paying respect to tradition

---

22 See G. J. Brooke, 'Power to the Powerless: A Long-Lost Song of Miriam', *BARev* 20/3 (May/June 1994): 62–5; a longer form of this paper is included as Chapter 15 in the book.

and permitting the contemporary application of an image to the present spiritual needs of the community. Thus on the one hand there are plenty of phrases which are used with sensitivity to their original contexts, while on the other, dominant concerns – such as the need to pray within the covenant[23] aright – are suitably interwoven.

There are poetic passages in the New Testament too and several points can be made about the handling of scriptural traditions in them. Some of the New Testament poems are almost certainly taken over from contemporary Judaism and adjusted very slightly to fit their new christologically oriented context. Among such poems should be included those in the Lukan infancy narrative known as the Magnificat and the Benedictus. These poems are replete with scriptural allusions in a manner almost indistinguishable from some of the poems found at Qumran. The Magnificat, in any case, is closely modelled on the Song of Hannah. But there is another group of poems in the New Testament which have little to do with scriptural precedents. Such, for example, is the hymn in Colossians 1.15–20, which may be vaguely inspired by the role of Wisdom in Proverbs 8.22–31, but which is generally interpreted in detail by commentators with little reference to scriptural antecedents. Or again, the short narrative poem in 1 Timothy 3.16 which is usually expounded with reference to other New Testament and early Christian formulations of the kerygma.[24]

Thus with regard to poetic interpretation, while it is hard to find any extensive passage in the Qumran corpus which does not depend on Scripture in some way or other, in the limited poetic corpus of the New Testament there are already some non-scriptural poems which are the result of reflection on the life, death and resurrection of Jesus rather than meditations on Scripture.

Homiletic interpretation

Homiletic interpretation consists in the advocacy of a particular point through the supportive use of Scripture. This use of Scripture is common both in the compositions found at Qumran and in the New Testament.

---

23 Note, e.g., that the term 'covenant' occurs over 25 times in 1QH[a], but less than 20 times in the whole Psalter and only a dozen times in Isaiah, the two scriptural books upon which 1QH[a] most depends.

24 See, e.g., the classic work of M. Dibelius and H. Conzelmann, *The Pastoral Epistles* (Hermeneia; Philadelphia: Fortress Press, 1972), 61–3.

Authors of the sectarian compositions and of the early Christian letters and Gospels seem to have commonly derived their written forms from instructions or debates which had taken place in a didactic setting. Sometimes the point at issue was derived from Scripture and as such the particular scriptural passage acted as the control of the discourse. At other times scriptural items were introduced to support an argument which had begun on other grounds.

The character and purpose of this homiletical use of Scripture is rhetorical recollection. The audience is invited to recall various events and figures from the past in order to identify with them or repudiate them. Such is the use of the flood narrative in the Admonition of 4Q370: there is recollection of the creative and destructive activity of God in order to encourage the correct response, the determination to live aright and so come under God's blessing, avoiding the curses which have befallen others in the past. A similar exhortation is clear in the third address at the opening of the *Cairo Damascus Document* (CD II, 14—III, 12): there is recollection of the misdeeds of the watchers, the sons of Noah, the sons of Jacob, the sons of those who entered the land and so on, and there are the exceptional and positive examples of Abraham, Isaac and Jacob, and those who have remained steadfast in God's precepts. It is clear which example the audience is being encouraged to follow. In all this the references to Scripture demand that the audience know something of the original context of the circumstances which are being held up as exemplary.

It is this kind of scriptural interpretation which is consistently most like that of a similar type in the New Testament, such as the appeal in Hebrews 11 to the great examples of the faithful of ages past. The similarity rests in part on the fact that homiletic interpretation is generally selective. The events and figures recalled from the tradition are selected to make the point suitably. Since selectivity is one of the hallmarks of the scriptural interpretation of the New Testament in other forms of interpretation as well, it is not surprising that when selectivity is called for by the genre of interpretation, then Qumran interpretations resemble scripturally based exhortations found elsewhere.

METHODS OF INTERPRETATION

Having considered all too briefly some of the similarities and dissimilarities between the Qumran corpus and the New Testament in terms of the varieties of scriptural interpretation, this next section will consider equally briefly some items to do with exegetical methodology.

With regard to the interpretation of Scripture, once allowance has been made for some of the differences in premises outlined above, then it is necessary to stress that in many respects the Qumran corpus and the New Testament writings share much in terms of exegetical methodology, though some differences appear here too.

On the larger scale, one of the most obvious methods of interpretation in the Qumran corpus involves the presentation of new material in a form which looks in most respects like that which is being interpreted. New laws, which in themselves are matters of legal interpretation, are presented in the form of Torah. New forms of narrative are presented in manner like the narratives upon which they are a commentary. New poems wear similar structural garments to those from which they take their phrasing. So effective is this methodology on the grand scale that nowadays some may even dispute, for example, whether the so-called *Reworked Pentateuch* texts are interpretation or more simply versions of the Torah itself.[25] A similar argument has taken place with respect to the *Temple Scroll*: should it not rather be called 11QTorah? Some of the narrative compositions found in the Qumran caves also take the form of narrative rather than of explicit commentary, so that the story is rehearsed with suitable rephrasing and interpolation. In the Bible the rewritings of Exodus in Deuteronomy and of Samuel—Kings in Chronicles provide the classic prototypes for this activity. In the Greek Bible this is clearly evident also in the additions to Esther. Many of the scripturally based Psalms and interpretative poetic compositions present themselves as new Psalms, even with appropriate superscriptions.[26]

---

25 See, e.g., M. Segal, '4QReworked Pentateuch or 4QPentateuch?', in *The Dead Sea Scrolls Fifty Years after their Discovery: Proceedings of the Jerusalem Congress, July 20–25, 1997* (ed. L. H. Schiffman, E. Tov and J. C. VanderKam; Jerusalem: Israel Exploration Society and the Shrine of the Book, Israel Museum, 2000), 391–9.

26 The standard commentaries on Deuteronomy and Chronicles address these issues; for the Additions to Esther see C. A. Moore, *Daniel, Esther and Jeremiah: The Additions* (AB 44; Garden City: Doubleday, 1977), 153–252; for Psalms, see Ps. 105.1–15, 96.1–13 and 106.1, 47–8 in 1 Chr. 16.8–36, and also, e.g., the re-use of Ps. 18 in 4Q381 24, 7–11 (DJD 11, 111–12).

Whereas some of the compositions found at Qumran are clearly imitative of scriptural genres, the same cannot be said of much of the New Testament. That may be because the New Testament is constituted primarily of some kind of biography, collections of letters and an apocalypse (or collection of visions and auditions with an overall epistolary preface), none of which genres is widely present in the Hebrew Bible. However, in the light of the number of compositions which seem to be best defined through their association with one particular biblical figure – whether Noah, Abraham, Moses, David, Elijah, Jeremiah or Ezekiel – it is a genuine possibility that the kind of combination of words and deeds which make up both the Gospels and Acts should be reviewed anew against the backdrop of such Jewish texts. And the scrolls provide justification for a fresh consideration of whether Matthew's Gospel is a deliberate attempt to imitate a Pentateuch,[27] or whether Luke structures his Gospel on the narrative framework of Deuteronomy.[28]

In matters of detailed exegetical methodology, there is much that the Qumran scrolls share with the New Testament. However, because there is so much overlap in exegetical techniques but not so much in actual content, it is most likely that both bodies of literature share much of a common Jewish heritage, rather than that the New Testament authors were dependent in some direct way upon the exegetical examples found in the scrolls.

The shared exegetical methodology is evident in the handling of the scriptural text which on occasion is altered so as to fit the interpretation more neatly. In the Qumran material the most obvious possible example of this is to be seen in the change of 'enemies of' (*yby*) to 'friends of' (*'whby*) in the citation of Psalm 37.20b in 4Q171 3–4 III, 5a. In the New Testament this minor adjustment of Scripture so as to fit better the context is most evident in Paul.[29] There is also evidence that the exegete

---

27 The emerging pentateuchs of Enochic material and the Books of Psalms, together with the widely acknowledged rewritten forms of the Law of Moses make this a real possibility as a contemporary Jewish literary activity.

28 For the latter see J. Drury, *Tradition and Design in Luke's Gospel: A Study in Early Christian Historiography* (London: Darton, Longman & Todd, 1976), esp. Chapter 4.

29 See the list of examples compiled by C. D. Stanley, *Paul and the Language of Scripture: Citation Technique in the Pauline Epistles and Contemporary Literature* (SNTSMS 74; Cambridge: University Press, 1992), Part II.

could make use of known variant readings, as in the case of the author of the Habakkuk Commentary in relation to Habakkuk 2.16.[30]

The interpretation of the legal sections of the Torah is most obviously carried out through the juxtaposition of two or more texts. On that basis the exegete can take his student from the general to the particular and vice versa; the breadth and particularity of any ruling can be made apparent. But the juxtaposition of texts is not done arbitrarily; it depends often upon the various texts sharing a common theme or being linked to one another through catchword association. This is the case also in the New Testament.

Exegesis through catchword is common too in other genres of scriptural interpretation. The links between the various scriptural citations in the principal fragment of 4Q174 have been pointed out several times, but the same is evident in many other texts too. In the New Testament two fine examples of the catchword association of texts can be seen in the catenae in Romans 3.10–18 where Paul defines a sinful person through various physical features in a catalogue of Psalm verses which are linked to one another, though not always by a word which is explicit in the citation. The author of the Letter to the Hebrews does something similar in listing those texts which help him distinguish Jesus from the angels (Heb. 1.5–14).

It becomes apparent from the use of catchword techniques that the interpreter was commonly aware of the context from which any particular citation was taken and usually that context was treated with respect. Combinations of texts in both the scrolls and the New Testament are thus particularly rich fields for those interested in early Jewish exegetical methodology. A fine example in the scrolls from Qumran is to be found in 4QD^a (4Q266) 11, 3–5. After a section dealing with how an individual is to be disciplined, the author continues with reference to Israel in a series of three quotations, each formally introduced by 'it is written' (*ktwb*):

> And concerning Israel it is written, I will get me to the ends of heaven and will not smell the savour of your sweet odours. And elsewhere it is written, To return to God with weeping

---

30 MT Hab 2.16 reads *h'rl*, but 1QpHab reads (with the LXX) *hr'l*. Yet the commentary that follows the verse offers an interpretation which includes the consonants *'wrlt*; see W. H. Brownlee, *The Midrash Pesher of Habakkuk* (SBLMS 24; Missoula: Scholars Press, 1979), 190–2.

and fasting. And in <another> place it is written, Rend your hearts, not your garments.[31]

The first quotation is a combination of the hope of Deuteronomy 30.4 ('Even if you are expelled to the ends of heavens, from there the Lord your God will gather you') and the threat of Leviticus 26.31 ('If you disobey me . . . I will lay waste your cities, will make your sanctuaries desolate, and I will not smell the savour of your sweet odours'). The second and third are citations of parts of Joel 2.12 and 13. Although a catchword link between the two principal quotations is not clear, the combination of the two texts may depend upon the notion of what God does for those who return to him, a feature of the wider contexts of the passages cited (Deut. 30.2 and Joel 2.13). In the New Testament the effect of finding so many exegetical combinations in the scrolls is to see that not only early Christian authors might do this, but also Jesus himself could have created or used already existent combinations with effect.[32]

The exegetical combination of scriptural texts is not always explicit. Both the scrolls and the New Testament are replete with much implicit combination of texts. Thus, for example, the kinds of harmonization present in the Samaritan Pentateuch are attested widely, both in biblical and in parabiblical manuscripts. Or again, the combination of Ezekiel 1 and 10 with parts of Isaiah 6 is evident in both 4Q385 and Revelation 4.[33]

There are several examples where the same scriptural passage is cited in both a Qumran composition and in a New Testament passage but, despite some similarities in eschatological outlook, the different assumptions behind the uses of such passages in the two literary corpora force us to conclude that it is not so much with regard to such examples that scriptural interpretation in both bodies of literature might be mutually illuminating. Rather, the exegetical methodologies used in both sets of texts show how much was common in early Judaism's handling of

---

31 Tr. J. M. Baumgarten, *Qumran Cave 4.XIII: The Damascus Document (4Q266–273)* (DJD 18; Oxford: Clarendon Press, 1996), 76–7.

32 See, e.g., G. J. Brooke, '4Q500 1 and the Use of Scripture in the Parable of the Vineyard', *DSD* 2 (1995): 268–94; Chapter 13 in this book.

33 See G. J. Brooke, 'Ezekiel in Some Qumran and New Testament Texts', in *The Madrid Qumran Congress: Proceedings of the International Congress on the Dead Sea Scrolls, Madrid 18–21 March 1991* (ed. J. Trebolle Barrera and L. Vegas Montaner; STDJ 11; Leiden: Brill/ Madrid: Universidad Complutense, 1993), 333–6.

Scripture. Primarily on that basis, taking account of both the scrolls and the New Testament, scholars will be able to draw a better understanding of the transmission and interpretation of Scripture in the late second temple period and beyond.

CONCLUSIONS

First among our conclusions must be an acknowledgement of the breadth and diversity of biblical interpretation in both the scrolls and the New Testament. Too often biblical interpretation in the scrolls is reduced to study of the *pesharim*, as if that was somehow definitive of the movement's handling of the traditions; likewise in the New Testament, most attention is paid to particular kinds of proof-texting. The publication of the whole range of compositions found at Qumran with their overwhelming dependence on textual precursors should encourage New Testament scholars to consider afresh the kinds of treatment of the Scriptures of which the authors of the New Testament could be capable.

Second, it can be noted that there is indeed some similarity between the two literary corpora in what is perceived as the core of works on to which new ideas and experiences can be attached. Genesis, Deuteronomy, Isaiah and the Psalms are the focus of attention. But it should also be noted that despite this seeming similarity in the contents of the so-called 'canon within the canon', in fact the two corpora for the most part focus on rather different sections of these various biblical books.

Third, the different assumptions which lie behind the approaches of the scrolls' authors and those of the New Testament need to be carefully noted. The methods in the handling of Scripture may be very similar in both sets of texts, but the purpose and resultant character of the scriptural interpretation in both bodies of literature means that in the end with regard to content the differences are more obvious than the similarities.

Fourth, against these conclusions a difficult problem arises. The scrolls from Qumran present an immense range of compositions which use biblical traditions in an extremely rich and variegated way. These new compositions, for all that some of them may be exclusively sectarian in authorship and orientation, provide a new context for the assessment of the use of biblical traditions in the New Testament. While some few scholars still look to Alexandria or Athens to explain the context of the form and content of much of the New Testament, for more than a generation, indeed partly spurred on by the Qumran finds, most New

Testament scholars have earnestly desired to set much in an appropriate Judaean and Galilean context. A tension emerges not only for scholars concerned with the history and religion of early Judaism but for those dealing with the New Testament also. Where should the continuities and discontinuities be located? The problematic of appropriate contextualization covers every single item, down to the very terminology that modern exegetes may suitably use of the interpretative processes they observe: for example, is 'midrash' a suitable term for use by either Qumranologists or Neutestamentlers?

Fifth, despite the attention that needs to be paid to differences, it remains the case that with regard to biblical interpretation the scrolls and the New Testament need each other. The scrolls are not merely a quarry of instruction for the better appreciation of the use of the Bible in the New Testament; the New Testament, as a repository of much early Jewish exegesis, may sometimes provide the key for the better understanding of the scrolls.

5

Shared Intertextual Interpretations in the Dead Sea Scrolls and the New Testament

INTRODUCTION

The primary purpose of this chapter is to begin to describe the literary character of similar combinations of scriptural passages which appear in some Qumran and some New Testament texts. There have been many studies on individual scriptural passages which are found in a text from Qumran and in the New Testament,[1] sometimes with strikingly similar intentions, and there are also extensive studies on some texts like 4Q175 (4QTestimonia) which use scriptural texts in a combination, the parts of which are then variously used in diverse places in the New Testament.[2] However, there has been little attempt so far to isolate those passages in both Qumran texts and in the New Testament where a common *combination* of scriptural passages seems to be used. Various reasons might be given to explain the lack of study of this phenomenon: maybe this is because there are relatively few cases of such shared combinations, or maybe it is because the recent generation of New Testament scholars has tended to focus on explicit quotations alone, thereby reducing the possibility of perceiving combinations of the use of scriptural passages, one of which may be explicit while others are somewhat concealed in allusion.

There is indeed a certain danger inherent in this task. It is often difficult to be certain that particular scriptural passages lie behind certain Qumran or New Testament phrases. And yet the need for undertaking a

---

1 The most significant starting point is the essay by J. A. Fitzmyer, 'The Use of Explicit Old Testament Quotations in Qumran Literature and in the New Testament', *NTS* 7 (1960–1): 297–333; reprinted in *Essays on the Semitic Background of the New Testament* (London: Chapman, 1971), 3–58. Further bibliography can be found in J. A. Fitzmyer, *The Dead Sea Scrolls: Major Publications and Tools for Study* (SBLRBS 20; Atlanta: Scholars Press, 1990), 173–9.

2 See, e.g., J. A. Fitzmyer, '4QTestimonia and the New Testament', *TS* 18 (1957): 513–37; reprinted in *Essays on the Semitic Background of the New Testament*, 59–89.

study such as this arises in order to underline the complexity of the evidence when faced with claims that the movement reflected in the sectarian texts left its mark in very concrete ways on the early churches and even on Jesus himself. The starting point in an investigation of this sort must be the literary character of the presentation of combined scriptural passages, not the simple question of whether New Testament authors have simply copied the combination of scriptural passages they variously use from a text now found at Qumran. This starting point requires a literary sensitivity which is not immediately drawn towards making assertions about the possibility of the dependence of one author upon another, about the possible historical connections between texts, about cause and effect. Thus, because a literary approach like this makes more of each author's own integrity, undoubtedly the tendency in this investigation is to discern more of the differences between the early Christian writers and the authors of the compositions which have been found at Qumran.

The very paucity of texts in both the Qumran corpus and the New Testament where a solid case can be made that the latter is quoting from the former (or something very like it) goes some way towards demonstrating the point. So, for example, it is intriguing that in CD IV, 19–V, 2 four scriptural passages (Mic. 2.6; Gen. 1.27; 7.9; Deut. 17.17) are used in close proximity in an argument against divorce or polygamy or both; the similar use of Genesis 1.27 both there and in Mark 10.6 has often been highlighted to underline the proximity of Jesus' reasoning to that of the Damascus covenanters, even to the point that the Genesis verse is introduced in a similar fashion in both texts.[3] Even though the subsequent use of Genesis 2.24 in Mark 10.7–8 seems somewhat redundant to the argument that Mark represents Jesus as making and so implies that the New Testament passage is quoting from a source,[4] since Genesis 2.24 does not feature in the argument of CD IV, 19–V, 2, we must conclude that the CD passage cannot be that source. The similar introductory phraseology in both passages (CD IV, 21: *yswd hbry'h*; Mk 10.6: *apo de archēs ktiseōs*) may also suggest some commonality between them. However, it is also notable that it is only the one scriptural passage that both texts actually share.

---

3 The statement of J. A. Fitzmyer can be considered typical: 'One of the most striking cases of accommodation which occurs in the Qumran literature is found in the following passage [CD IV, 19–V, 2], in which four Old Testament passages are used. It also has a striking parallel in the New Testament' (*Essays on the Semitic Background of the New Testament*, 36).

4 This possibility was drawn to my attention by D. R. Schwartz.

Another important introductory point also needs to be made. The recent tendency among New Testament scholars in particular to focus on explicit quotations[5] has often resulted in studies that do little more than discuss the textual affinity of the quotation in its New Testament setting.[6] Furthermore such an approach tends to lead to discussion of the use of such scriptural quotations as if they were generally taken directly from a scriptural text. There is little concern to show how scriptural passages may be meaningful, not just in themselves in isolation but because of the interpretative traditions associated with them over generations. A search for common exegetical combinations is thus an attempt to say that it is likely that most Scripture is used by individuals and their communities as mediated to them by their contemporaries and immediate forebears.

The study of so-called comparative midrash, which may include New Testament examples, has been around for a long time but, again, this has generally been carried out in relation to single scriptural phrases, verses or pericope.[7] It is the arrival of intertextuality[8] on the scholarly scene which enables the kind of study proposed here to be undertaken with some awareness of methodological insights gained from a variety of literary-critical approaches.[9] In light of this it is only right to define what

---

5 As, e.g., C. D. Stanley, *Paul and the Language of Scripture: Citation Technique in the Pauline Epistles and Contemporary Literature* (SNTSMS 74; Cambridge: University Press, 1992).

6 This was the intended hallmark of the study by J. de Waard, *A Comparative Study of the Old Testament Text in the Dead Sea Scrolls and in the New Testament* (STDJ 4; Leiden: Brill, 1965), but many studies proceed little further.

7 See the landmark studies by G. Vermes as collected in his *Scripture and Tradition in Judaism: Haggadic Studies* (StPB 4; Leiden: Brill, 2nd edn, 1983).

8 The term was adopted and adapted for literary theory by J. Kristeva in her essay 'Word, Dialogue and Novel', first published in French in *Séméiotiké: recherches pour une sémanalyse* (Paris: Seuil, 1969) and available in English in *The Kristeva Reader* (ed. T. Moi; Oxford: Blackwell, 1986), 35–61; see also J. Kristeva, *La Révolution du langue poétique* (Paris: Seuil, 1974), 59–60.

9 The literature on intertextuality is very extensive: a useful guide is M. Worton and J. Still, eds, *Intertextuality: Theories and Practices* (Manchester: University Press, 1990); there are also some very instructive comments in S. Stewart, *Nonsense: Aspects of Intertextuality in Folklore and Literature* (Baltimore: Johns Hopkins University Press, 1978). Particularly influential on some aspects of the current study have been R. B. Hays, *Echoes of Scripture in the Letters of Paul* (New Haven: Yale University Press, 1989) with respect to the New Testament, and D. Boyarin, *Intertextuality and the Reading of Midrash* (Indiana Studies in Biblical Literature; Bloomington: Indiana University Press, 1990) with respect to Jewish exegetical traditions; also noteworthy is *Intertextuality in Biblical Writings: Essays in Honour of Bas van Iersel* (ed. S. Draisma; Kampen: Kok, 1989).

is intended here by the term intertextuality. What I mean is that all texts present their own meanings only in as much as they are in dialogue, primarily with other texts. Diachronically this dialogue is nearly exclusively with other texts, though this should not be understood as a matter of any author simply having sources; rather there is 'transposition' of earlier material into something new.[10] This means that intertextuality is not primarily about identifying what has influenced any writer, but about observing the transformation of influences. The tendency, therefore, is to notice the distinctiveness of the new text while acknowledging that no text is a closed system. Synchronically the dialogue can be with social reality apprehended in a variety of verbal forms. The dialogue may sometimes be on a one-to-one basis, though those concerned with intertextuality would suggest this was seldom the case. More commonly a text reflects the outcome of a dialogue with several partners who in turn are the products of their own dialogues; moreover as the texts from Qumran show only too well, the continuous dialogue produces multiple redactions and recensions.

The explicit citation of other texts is the most obvious way in which the dialogue between texts is visible to the reader. But generally a whole range of other allusions informs a text's representation of ideas. This can be seen most readily in poetry, so that it is not surprising that critics concerned with intertextuality often begin with poetry, but it is no less the case with nearly all non-poetic genres. So the purpose of this study is not to investigate any text's single dialogue partner, but to expose how similar intertextual clusters may recur in more than one place. This analysis may say little or nothing about the dialogue partner's original intention, but in juxtaposing texts from Qumran and the New Testament will show, on the one hand, something of where the common exegetical traditions may most pertinently lie and, on the other (by default), where the differences are between these two groups of roughly contemporaneous literature.

---

10 'The term *intertextuality* denotes this transposition of one (or several) sign-system(s) into another; but since this term has often been understood in the banal sense of 'study of sources,' we prefer the term *transposition* because it specifies that the passage from one signifying system to another demands a new articulation of the thetic – of enunciative and denotative positionality'; J. Kristeva, 'Revolution in Poetic Language', in *The Kristeva Reader*, 111.

SHARED INTERTEXTUAL INTERPRETATIONS

The examples of shared intertextual interpretations listed and described briefly here are presented in the canonical order of the principal base text which is quoted first. Since there are common features in many of the examples, there is no attempt at this stage to present the material in some kind of taxonomy.

2 Samuel 7 and Psalm 2 in 4Q174 and Hebrews 1[11]

The principal fragment of 4Q174 contains two sections of explicit scriptural interpretation.[12] The first seems to be the end of an eschatological exegesis of the oracle of Nathan in 2 Samuel 7.5–16. The precise extent and structure of the exegesis is difficult to discern. The extant lines 4Q174 III, 1–2 contain a citation of 2 Samuel 7.10–11a$^\alpha$ which is then interpreted through the subsidiary quotation of phrases from Exodus 15.17 and Deuteronomy 23.3–4. Then in the middle of line 7 without a break, 2 Samuel 7.11a$^\beta$ is quoted after the introductory formula *w'šr 'mr*; in turn this is interpreted, the interpretation being introduced solely by *'šr*. Line 9 ends approximately 18 letter-spaces short of the average left-hand margin. Lines 10–11 then present an abbreviated quotation of 2 Samuel 7.11b–14a, the interpretation of which is introduced by a pronoun and which contains a secondary quotation of Amos 9.11. It is worth noting both that the term *pšr* is nowhere used in this section of interpretation and also that although the oracle of Nathan appears to provide the running text for the thematic exegesis, it is not cited in its entirety, nor are all parts of this base text presented in the same way.

A new section of interpretation then begins at the right-hand margin in line 14 of this principal fragment of 4Q174. This section opens with the striking formula *mdrš mn* which introduces a quotation of Psalm

---

11 See G. J. Brooke, *Exegesis at Qumran: 4QFlorilegium in its Jewish Context* (JSOTS 29; Sheffield: JSOT Press, 1985), 209–10.

12 For the text of 4Q174 see now E. Puech, *La Croyance des Esséniens en la vie future: immortalité, résurrection, vie éternelle? Histoire d'une croyance dans le Judaïsme ancien* (EB 22; Paris: J. Gabalda, 1993), 572–87; A. Steudel, *Der Midrasch zur Eschatologie aus der Qumrangemeinde (4QMidrEchat$^{a.b}$): Materielle Rekonstruktion, Textbestand, Gattung und traditionsgeschichtliche Einordnung des durch 4Q174 ('Florilegium') und 4Q177 ('Catena A') repräsentierten Werkes aus den Qumranfunden* (STDJ 13; Leiden: Brill, 1994), 5–53. For Steudel the principal fragment of 4Q174 forms what can be labelled as Columns III and IV of a reconstructed manuscript.

1.1a which is followed by an interpretation introduced by a formula containing the technical term *pšr*. This interpretation contains explicit subsidiary quotations of parts of Isaiah 8.11 and Ezekiel 37.23. The interpretation ends a few letter-spaces before the average left-hand margin in line 17. Line 18 seems to begin a new section by citing Psalm 2.1–2; the first words are missing from both lines 18 and 19, but it is widely agreed that Psalm 2.1 was not introduced formulaically and that the whole of Psalm 2.2 including the last word *mšyḥw* was cited. As with Psalm 1.1 the interpretation is introduced with a formula including the word *pšr*. Although there is little or nothing individualistic about the interpretation which survives at the top of 4Q174 IV, it seems likely not only that *mšyḥw* is understood to refer to an individual, but also that it is a major part of the link between the midrash on Psalms 1 and 2 and the exegesis of Nathan's oracle in 2 Samuel 7.

This detailed description is necessary to establish the connection between the two sections of exegesis in this principal fragment of 4Q174, since elsewhere in each separate section it is more or less clear how the various subsidiary quotations can be associated with the principal text which they are being used to interpret. Sometimes this is done through catchword association, sometimes through other means.[13] But the two sections of exegesis, that on 2 Samuel 7 and that on Psalms 1 and 2, display distinctive characteristics and so may not automatically and deliberately follow on one from the other. This is most obvious in that none of the interpretations in the first section is introduced with technical formulae using the word *pšr*, whereas it is consistently used in the interpretations of the Psalms. Might it be the case that the two sections of interpretation are no more closely related than that one represents exegesis of the prophetic section of an emerging collection of Scriptures, the other the Writings, as E. Puech has suggested?[14]

That there is some closer link between the two sections of exegesis on this principal fragment of 4Q174 seems to emerge from consideration of the content of the interpretations themselves. It is clear that in both the phrase *'ḥryt hymym* features prominently, so much so indeed that A. Steudel's analysis of the text has used the phrase, as have others before her, to determine the character of the whole manuscript and how it may be related to other manuscripts.[15] Given this minimal thematic

---

13 See G. J. Brooke, *Exegesis at Qumran*, 166–9.

14 E. Puech, *La Croyance des Esséniens*, 573, n. 20.

15 A. Steudel, *Der Midrasch zur Eschatologie aus der Qumrangemeinde*, 161–3.

relationship, it is then possible to argue that in fact the citations of the opening verses of Psalms 1 and 2 function merely as incipit phrases, phrases which imply the rest of the Psalm. The intertextual relationship of the two exegetical sections becomes a little clearer as a result. It is noticeable that in the final section of the citation and interpretation of 2 Samuel 7, which comes to consider the son of David talked of in 2 Samuel 7.14 as referring to the Shoot of David, the kingly Messiah, all those phrases which might imply that the text of Samuel was only referring to the actual physical son of David, namely Solomon, are omitted.[16] The subsequent implied citation of the whole of Psalm 2 makes the interpretative purpose clear, since from Psalm 2.2 it is obvious that the son of Psalm 2.7 also refers to the Messiah, the kingly one, as Psalm 2.6 makes clear.

Thus 4Q174 seems to offer citations and interpretations of 2 Samuel 7 and Psalm 2 which show that the two scriptural passages are mutually interdependent, are held together through mutual intertextuality.[17] That 2 Samuel 7 and Psalm 2 were thought of in this way as mutually illuminating is confirmed by the New Testament counterpart to the primary citations in 4Q174. In the Letter to the Hebrews the opening argument concerns the place of the son in the hierarchy of things. The author sets out immediately to argue that the son is superior to the angels through presenting a catena of proofs from the Psalms and other texts. The catena begins with the citation of Psalm 2.7, which is followed immediately by 2 Samuel 7.14. Perhaps Psalm 2 was used because of the mention of the inheritor, the heir (cf. Ps. 2.8), in Hebrews 1.2; or maybe Psalm 2 was used because its usage elsewhere in early Christian circles (cf. Mk 1.11; Acts 13.33) was well known to the author of Hebrews. Whatever prompted its usage, the author reinforced the purpose of citing it by referring immediately to 2 Samuel 7.14.

It must be noted that the evidence of Hebrews 1 does not imply any form of literary dependence of the author of Hebrews on some Qumranic forebear, even though there may be plenty of scrolls' influence detectable in the work as a whole.[18] The point in drawing attention to the

16 See G. J. Brooke, *Exegesis at Qumran*, 111–13.

17 As described by J. J. Collins, *The Scepter and the Star: The Messiahs of the Dead Sea Scrolls and Other Ancient Literature* (Anchor Bible Reference Library; New York: Doubleday, 1995), 61, cf. 23.

18 Influence initially outlined most extensively by Y. Yadin, 'The Dead Sea Scrolls and the Epistle to the Hebrews', in *Aspects of the Dead Sea Scrolls* (ed. C. Rabin and Y. Yadin; Scripta Hierosolymitana 4; Jerusalem: Magnes Press, 2nd edn, 1965), 36–55; and continued subsequently in the extensive debate over whether the figure

parallel is to show that both authors were acquainted with a tradition whereby 2 Samuel 7 and Psalm 2 belong together. The two texts are mutually suggestive of one another and need not be considered to have come from a written source. Thus we are dealing here with intertextual exegetical tradition rather than literary dependence.[19] This seems to be confirmed in as much as 4Q174 begins with 2 Samuel 7, whereas in Hebrews Psalm 2 comes first. Also, as argued above, the author of 4Q174 is presenting material which he took to refer to the kingly Messiah. The author of Hebrews knows this to be the case too since, although the term Christ is not used until Hebrews 3.6, as soon as the term is used it is explicated in terms of sonship: 'Christ, however, was faithful over God's house as a son.'

On first impression the similar conjunction of 2 Samuel 7 and Psalm 2 in passages discussing the role and status of the Messiah seems striking. On closer analysis the similarities are not so great. Most notably the texts are cited in a different order, and for Psalm 2 each text explicitly cites a different element, even though those elements both describe something of the one who is taken to be the Messiah. There is no need to suppose any literary dependence of Hebrews upon Qumran messianism; rather, in contexts of messianic discussion, two texts have independently used a combination of scriptural passages which are in themselves mutually illuminating. Their intertextuality is self-suggested. Nevertheless, it is quite reasonable to suppose that the general setting of messianic debate within turn-of-the-era Palestinian Judaism contributed to the parameters of what might have been found to be useful in both secondary exegetical contexts.

---

of Melchizedek in 11Q13 (11QMelchizedek) lies behind the same name in Hebrews 5—7, on which see P. J. Kobelski, *Melchizedek and Melchireša'* (CBQMS 10; Washington: Catholic Biblical Association of America, 1981), 115–29.

19 Nor need we suppose a middle way, as for example does H. W. Attridge, *The Epistle to the Hebrews: A Commentary on the Epistle to the Hebrews* (Hermeneia; Philadelphia: Fortress Press, 1989), 50: 'The form of this material resembles the catenae or florilegia found at Qumran, which share some of the texts found here. Such collections of messianic proof texts probably circulated in early Christian circles and it is likely that the author used such a traditional collection at this point.' Attridge also notes the widespread criticism of such a view.

Isaiah 5 in 4Q500 and with Psalm 118 in Mark 12[20]

This example of shared intertextual interpretation is of a rather different kind. 4Q500 fragment 1 contains the remnants of just a few lines which J. M. Baumgarten has discussed most fully.[21] He has proposed convincingly that the text is part of a blessing addressed to God, based principally on the metaphor of the vineyard in Isaiah 5. It is interesting to note that clearly other scriptural passages have also influenced the reworking of Isaiah 5 as it is represented in the new way now visible in the fragment. Several features of the fragmentary lines echo Isaiah 5: the winepress (*yqb*, line 3; Isa. 5.2), the planting (*mṭ'*, line 5; *nṭ'*, Isa. 5.7), the delights (*š'šw'ym*, line 6; Isa. 5.7) and even the vineyard itself (*[k]rmkh*, line 7; *krm*, Isa. 5.1). As a liturgical text, it is poetic and lacks any obvious explicit citation of Scripture, but in association with allusions to Isaiah 5 there are several other phrases which in particular recall certain Psalms.[22] Overall the principal fragment of 4Q500 belongs in the tradition of those texts which link the vineyard with Jerusalem and the various features of the vineyard with parts of the temple mount and the sanctuary.[23] 4Q500 uses the Isaiah 5 vineyard material in intertextual interpretative association with other scriptural phrases which then allow for the whole text to be 'a description of the temple, either heavenly, or, more probably, earthly, which is the suitable place for the people (Isaiah's own interpretation) to bless God (possibly the genre of 4Q500)'.[24]

Notable in this line of interpretation is the language of building. In Isaiah 5.2 the beloved builds a watch tower; in *Tg. Ps.-Jon.* Isaiah 5.2 this is referred to the building of the sanctuary with its altar.[25] It seems natural that the particular understanding of the vineyard as Jerusalem, or the temple mount or part of it, should require an emphasis on the buildings in it. Part of this emphasis may arise out of the need of those who use this image from Isaiah 5 to interact with Isaiah 5.7 in a particular way; there

---

20 See my detailed study: G. J. Brooke, '4Q500 1 and the Use of Scripture in the Parable of the Vineyard', *DSD* 2 (1995): 268–94 (Chapter 13 in this book).

21 J. M. Baumgarten, '4Q500 and the Ancient Conception of the Lord's Vineyard', *JJS* 40 (1989): 1–6.

22 Baumgarten points to Ps. 84.7 (*bk'*; cf. 4Q500 1, 2); Ps. 65.10 (*plg 'lhym*; cf. *plgy kbwdkh*, 4Q500 1, 5); Ps. 46.5 (*nhr plgyw yśmḥw 'yr 'lhym*).

23 Cf. Isa. 32.2; Ezek. 47.1–12; *Tg. Ps.-Jon.* Isa. 5.2 (*wbnyt mqdšy bynyhwn w'p mdbḥy yhbyt lkpr' 'l ḥṭ'yhwn*); *t. Suk.* 3.15 (*wybn mgdl btwky zh hykl yqb ḥsb bh zh mzbḥ wgm yqb ḥsb bw zh hšt*); *1 Enoch* 89.50.

24 G. J. Brooke, '4Q500 1 and the Use of Scripture in the Parable of the Vineyard', 272.

25 See notes 22 and 23 above.

Isaiah's own interpretation of the vineyard is that the vineyard is the house of Israel, 'the people of Judah are his pleasant planting'. The stress on building facilitates the interpretative transition to refer the vineyard to Jerusalem and the temple. This same exegetical development can be seen in the New Testament in Mark 12.1–12 (// Matt. 21.33–45; Lk. 20.9–19) where the vineyard of Isaiah 5.1–7 is used in a parable and is interpreted as referring to Jerusalem and/or the temple from which the beloved son is cast out (Mk 12.6–8 //). The building motif is to be found in the parable in the secondary use of Psalm 118.22–3 which is linked to Isaiah 5.2 through the catchword of building (*oikodomeō*): 'the stone which the builders rejected has become the head of the corner'.

As with the previous example there is no need to suggest the literary dependence of the New Testament exegetical tradition upon its Qumran parallel. Both reflect the understanding of Isaiah 5 as referring to Jerusalem and the temple, and both seem to clarify those references by drawing on the motif of building in various ways. The interpretative approach in each seems to be based on similar intertextual resonances. In the parable of the vineyard in the New Testament these resonances become explicit, and christologically so, through the use of Psalm 118 which features elsewhere in early Christian thought (Acts 4.11; 1 Pet. 2.7). The modern interpreter's task is to perceive the suggestive elements in the source text and to hear their echoes in other texts. When this is done with sensitivity, then the intertextual associations discerned in one text assist in the better understanding of others.

Isaiah 35 and 61 and Psalm 146 in 4Q521 and Luke 7

Since its preliminary edition by E. Puech in 1992,[26] 4Q521 has attracted very wide attention.[27] Such interest has been focused around the identity of the Messiah and whether it is he or God himself who 'makes the dead

---

26 E. Puech, 'Une apocalypse messianique (*4Q521*)', *RevQ* 15 (1990–2): 475–519; reprinted in an adjusted form in E. Puech, *La Croyance des Esséniens en la vie future*, 627–92.

27 See especially M. Wise and J. Tabor, 'The Messiah at Qumran', *BARev* 18/6 (1992): 60–5; J. D. Tabor and M. O. Wise, '4Q251 "On Resurrection" and the Synoptic Gospel Tradition: A Preliminary Study', *JSP* 10 (1992): 149–62; J. J. Collins, 'The Works of the Messiah', *DSD* 1 (1994): 98–112; J. J. Collins, *The Scepter and the Star*, 117–22; G. J. Brooke, 'Luke–Acts and the Qumran Scrolls: the Case of MMT', in *Luke's Literary Achievement: Collected Essays* (ed. C. M. Tuckett; JSNTSup 116; Sheffield: Sheffield Academic Press, 1995), 75–6.

live' (*wmtym yḥyh*, 4Q521 2 II + 4, 12). In fact, apart from all the parallels listed at the outset by Puech, little detailed work has yet been done on the scriptural phrases alluded to in 4Q521 Fragments 2 II and 4. For the sake of this study the parallels in Luke 7.18–23 and Matt. 11.2–6 will be allowed to control which lines of these two fragments of 4Q521 are investigated here. The picture is very complicated and it is surely far from certain that because both 4Q521 and the Jesus saying both contain reference to 'giving life to/raising the dead' and 'preaching good news to the poor', in that order, we must conclude, as J. J. Collins has done, that 'it is quite possible that the author of the Sayings source knew 4Q521'.[28]

If Luke 7 is taken as the starting point for comparison, then there are six elements in what Jesus is supposed to have said to John the Baptist's disciples concerning how they and their master should be able to recognize the significance of who he is:

1   'the blind see (*tuphloi anablepousin*)';[29]
2   'the lame walk';[30]
3   'lepers are cleansed';
4   'the deaf hear';[31]
5   'the dead are raised';
6   'the poor have good news preached to them'.[32]

This list is commonly supposed to be based on a combination of LXX Isaiah 35.5, which mentions 'the blind', 'the deaf hearing' and 'the lame', together with LXX Isaiah 61.1, which mentions the poor having good news preached to them and the blind seeing.[33] There seems to be no

28 J. J. Collins, 'The Works of the Messiah', 107; *The Scepter and the Star*, 122.

29 This is not a direct quotation of Isa. 35.5, since the verbal phrase there is *anoichthēsontai ophthalmoi tuphlōn*; *anablepō* occurs in Isa. 61.1.

30 Only the noun is the same in both Lk. 7.22 // and Isa. 35.5.

31 Both verb and noun are the same as in Isa. 35.5.

32 This is clearly an allusion to Isa. 61.1, but the structure of the Gospel saying means that in each phrase the noun precedes the verb, whereas in Isa. 61.1 the verb precedes the noun. The grammatical forms are not quite the same in any case. The influence of Isa. 61.1 in other parts of the Gospel tradition (e.g., Matt. 5.3 // Lk. 6.20) and the possible influence of those passages on Lk. 7.22 // should also be borne in mind, but cannot be dealt with in detail here.

33 There is no overall counterpart to the LXX's *tuphlois anablepsin* in the MT or Qumran MSS of Isaiah; perhaps this is an example of intertextual influence of some kind within the transmission of Isaiah, not necessarily at the stage of translation. Though it seems as if *pqḥ* is taken to refer to the opening of the eyes as in Isa. 35.5, the

parallel in the LXX for the lepers being cleansed nor for the dead being raised. The former does recur in Matthew 10.8, an independent version of the saying which makes the picture more complex still as it lists healing the sick, raising the dead, cleansing lepers and casting out demons. The latter, giving life to the dead, is common to Luke 7.22 (// Matt. 11.5) and 4Q521.

There are two lists in 4Q521 2 II and 4 in close proximity to one another which are relevant to this discussion. In the first, in line 8, there is mention of the release of captives, giving sight to the blind, and raising up the bowed down (*mtyr 'swrym pwqḥ 'wrym zwqp kp[wpym]*). This list is an almost verbatim representation of Psalm 146.7–8 (*yhwh mtyr 'swrym yhwh pqḥ 'wrym yhwh zqp kpwpym*),[34] though giving sight to the blind is also in Isaiah 35.5 and 61.1 (LXX). The second list in 4Q521 is in lines 12–13:

1   'heal the wounded (*yrph ḥllym*)' (cf. Matt. 10.8, 'heal the sick');
2   'give life to the dead (*mtym yḥyh*)' (cf. Lk. 7.22 // Matt. 11.5; Matt. 10.8);
3   'preach good news to the poor (*'nwym ybśr*)' (cf. Isa. 61.1; Lk. 7.22 // Matt. 11.5);
4   'satisfy the weak ([*dly*]*m yśb*[*y*])';
5   'lead the outcast (*ntwśym ynhl*)';
6   'enrich the hungry (*r'bym y'śr*)' (cf. Ps. 146.7).

The opening item in this second list is intriguing, since it is echoed in the list in the independent saying in Matthew 10.8, but more significantly seems itself to echo Isaiah 61.1, but not in the form found in the MT or the Qumran manuscripts, but in the *Vorlage* of Isaiah 61.1 LXX, the second element of which is 'to heal (*iasasthai*) the broken-hearted', an element which strangely is not in any witness for the programmatic quotation of Isaiah 61.1 in Luke 4.18 or the lists in Luke 7.22 // Matthew 11.5. Furthermore, as Puech has noted,[35] the combination of 'healing' and 'giving life' is to be found in Deuteronomy 32.39.

Greek of Isa. 61.1 does not use a form of *anoigō*. Other secondary Isaianic influences should also be considered (Isa. 26.19; 29.18–19; 42.7, 18) as well as possible allusions to the Elijah and Elisha stories for items 3 and 5 (1 Kgs 17.17–24; 2 Kgs 4.18–37; 5.1–24).
34 The influence of Psalm 146 is visible elsewhere in the fragment too: e.g., with lines 1–2 compare Psalm 146.6.
35 'Une apocalypse messianique', 493.

Only two elements are common to the second list in 4Q521 and Luke 7.22 // Matthew 11.5, 'giving life/raising the dead', and 'preaching good news to the poor'. The first of these elements is unique to these two lists, and the order of the two elements is the same in both. Beyond that the parallels end. Luke 7.22 // Matthew 11.5 is a complex combination of parts of Isaiah 35.5 and 61.1. Apart from 'preaching good news to the poor', 4Q521 is a combination of different elements of Isaiah 61.1 with motifs from other passages, possibly Isaiah 49.9, Psalm 107.9, and Psalm 146.7, the last of which, if correctly restored, neatly ties the second list in 4Q521 back to the first which is exclusively from that Psalm.[36]

What can be made of all of this? When it is remembered that in the one striking parallel pair, 'giving life to/raising the dead' and 'preaching good news to the poor', the first element is represented in the two traditions partially in synonymous translation, then the similarity of the pair is slightly weakened. Overall strings of scriptural passages mostly from Isaiah and the Psalms lie behind the two developments in 4Q521 and Luke 7.22 // Matthew 11.5. In one pair of elements there seems to be a striking similarity which needs to be qualified slightly; in the rest the scriptural passages are re-presented in a rich variety of ways, suggesting anything but literary dependence. Here is a collection of scriptural passages to be associated with the activity of God (and his anointed agent) in the last days. The scriptural texts suggest each other, and this suggestive intertextuality is inherited and expressed variously in these later traditions.[37]

Isaiah 61 and Leviticus 25 in 11Q13 and Luke 4[38]

In this instance the juxtaposition of two scriptural texts is quite explicit in the text from Cave 11, but less clear in the New Testament counter-

---

36 The three elements in the list from line 13 are somewhat uncertain. Tabor and Wise read only *qd]wšym ynhl yr'h [b]m y'šh*, 'he will lead the [Ho]ly Ones, he will shepherd [th]em. He will do' ('4Q521 "On Resurrection"', 150–1).

37 It would be unwarranted indeed to suggest in light of 4Q521 and the possible links of John the Baptist with the movement part of which is reflected in the Qumran texts that the reply Jesus gives to John's disciples in the Gospel tradition was deliberately meant to fit John's expectations with a precise literary allusion to a text found at Qumran.

38 See M. de Jonge and A. S. van der Woude, '11Q Melchizedek and the New Testament', *NTS* 12 (1965–6): 301–26; J. A. Fitzmyer, 'Further Light on Melchizedek from Qumran Cave 11', *JBL* 86 (1967): 25–41 (reprinted in *Essays on the Semitic*

part. In 11Q13, 11QMelchizedek, there are remnants of three columns of writing, but it is Column II that is most substantial.[39] The use of Scripture in this column has often been studied,[40] but its intertextual significance in comparison with Luke 4 bears some further comment.

Although the precise placing of a few fragments remains debatable, it is clear enough that in 11Q13 II the exegesis is dependent upon Leviticus 25.9–13 as its base text. At the top of Column II Leviticus 25.13 is supplemented with explicit reference to Deuteronomy 15.2 in which the sabbatical year is described as a time for the remission of debts, in a way similar to that which should take place in the jubilee year according to Leviticus 25.[41] The use of the idiom *qr' drwr* in Leviticus 25.10, 'you shall proclaim liberty throughout the land to all its inhabitants', is echoed, possibly deliberately on the part of the composer of the oracle, in Isaiah 61.1. The author of 11Q13 knew this and throughout the rest of the column there are allusions to Isaiah 61.1–3 as description of the ultimate jubilee which is linked to the end of the tenth jubilee period and initiated on the Day of Atonement.

According to the story in Luke 4 at the very outset of his public ministry Jesus is in the synagogue at Nazareth and is handed the scroll of the prophet Isaiah from which he seems to read Isaiah 61.1–2, but in fact reads a conflation of Isaiah 61.1a, b, d; 58.6d; 61.2a. The presence of this conflated text is one of the keys to appreciating how Luke may have intended an allusion to the jubilee material of Leviticus 25, even includ-

---

Background of the New Testament, 245–67); J. Carmignac, 'Le document de Qumrân sur Melkisédeq,' *RevQ* 7 (1969–71): 343–78; J. T. Milik, 'Milkî-ṣedeq et Melkî-reša' dans les anciens écrits juifs et chrétiens', *JJS* 23 (1972): 95–144; G. J. Brooke, *Exegesis at Qumran*, 319–23; T. H. Lim, '11QMelch, Luke 4 and the Dying Messiah', *JJS* 43 (1992): 90–2.

39 For the text of 11Q13 see E. Puech, 'Notes sur le manuscrit 11QMelkîsédeq', *RevQ* 12 (1985–7): 483–513; *La Croyance des Esséniens en la vie future*, 516–26; DJD 23, 221–42.

40 In addition to the studies listed in note 31 see, e.g., M. P. Miller, 'The Function of Isa. 61.1–2 in 11Q Melchizedek', *JBL* 88 (1969): 467–9; D. F. Miner, 'A Suggested Reading for 11Q Melchizedek 17', *JSJ* 2 (1971): 144–8; J. A. Sanders, 'The Old Testament in 11Q Melchizedek,' *JANESCU* 5 (1973): 373–82; J. A. Sanders, 'From Isaiah 61 to Luke 4', in *Christianity, Judaism and Other Greco-Roman Cults: Studies for Morton Smith at Sixty* (ed. J. Neusner; SJLA 12; Leiden: Brill, 1975) 1.75–106.

41 The LXX makes the connection too, using *aphesis* to render both *ywbl* of Lev. 25.13 and *šmṭh* of Deut. 15.2; also 1Q22 III may be best restored with reference to both Leviticus 25 and Deuteronomy 15. See J. A. Fitzmyer, *Essays on the Semitic Background of the New Testament*, 256.

ing its association with Deuteronomy 15.2. The key word which links
the phrase from Isaiah 58.6 to Isaiah 61.1 is *aphesis*, the word used in
Leviticus 25 for both *drwr* and *ywbl*. The same Greek term is used in
Deuteronomy 15.2 to render *šmṭh*. Through the stress on this word Luke
seems to make a connection with the jubilee legislation of Leviticus 25
which Isaiah 61.1–2 may itself do. In the same way that the author of
11Q13 makes the connection between Isaiah 61 and Leviticus 25
explicit, so the conflated quotation in Luke 4.18–19 implies something
similar.[42]

In addition to this intertextual allusion which is virtually suggested by
the text of Scripture itself, either in Hebrew or in Greek, various arguments have been adduced concerning the possible connection of this
prophetic reading with the Day of Atonement; apart from hints in
1Q22, they are all problematic, given that little or nothing is known
about what might have formed part of a lectionary cycle in the first
century C.E.[43] But two other matters should be noticed. First, if Isaiah
61.1–2 is designed to be programmatic for Jesus' ministry as depicted in
Luke, then one can justifiably ask at what point Jesus may be considered
to release prisoners. In light of 11Q13 J. A. Fitzmyer wonders whether
this phrase does not rather refer to imprisoned debtors.[44] A concern with
debt is visible at several places in the traditions associated with Jesus,
notably in the Lord's Prayer (Lk. 11.4 // Matt. 6.12), but it does not seem
to be a special feature of Luke's writings as the programmatic use of Isaiah
61.1–2 in Luke 4 might have implied. Although a link with the jubilee
may be possible, it may be preferable to see the reference to the release of
prisoners as programmatic for the activities of the apostles in Acts.

---

42 This is well brought out in relation to the whole text of Luke–Acts by A. Finkel,
'Jesus' Preaching in the Synagogue on the Sabbath (Lk. 4.16–28)', in *The Gospels and
the Scriptures of Israel* (ed. C. A. Evans and W. R. Stegner; JSNTSup 104; Sheffield:
Sheffield Academic Press, 1994), 325–41.

43 See especially C. Perrot, 'Luc 4,16–30 et la lecture biblique de l'ancienne Synagogue', in *Exégèse biblique et Judaisme* (ed. J.-E. Ménard; Strasbourg: Palais
Universitaire, 1973), 170–86; and more generally his essay 'The Reading of the Bible
in the Ancient Synagogue', in *Mikra: Text, Translation, Reading and Interpretation of
the Hebrew Bible in Ancient Judaism and Early Christianity* (ed. M. J. Mulder; CRINT
2/1; Assen: van Gorcum; Philadelphia: Fortress Press, 1988), 137–59.

44 J. A. Fitzmyer, *The Gospel According to Luke I—IX: a New Translation with Introduction and Commentary* (AB 28; Garden City: Doubleday, 2nd edn, 1983), 532.

A second matter is also intriguing. In Luke Jesus' ministry begins in the synagogue at Nazareth rather than with the call of the disciples as in the other Synoptic Gospels. There is a deliberate reordering of tradition at this point. Reordering has also taken place in an earlier section of material so that, directly before the temptation account which Luke adjusts for his own purposes and places immediately before the public ministry of Jesus, Luke has placed the genealogy of Jesus. The genealogy of Jesus is immediately relevant to the debate which follows the reading and interpretation of Isaiah 61.1 at Nazareth: in Luke 4.22 all speak well of Jesus, but inquire (rhetorically?[45]) 'Is not this Joseph's son?' The content of the genealogy also gives some grounds for reading the adjusted quotation of Isaiah 61.1–2 in Luke 4.18–19 as to be understood in terms of the jubilee.

Luke's genealogy consists of 77 generations from Adam to Jesus. R. J. Bauckham has pointed out that the key to understanding the Lukan schematization does not depend upon seeing Jesus as inaugurating a twelfth set of seven generations, but in noticing that something Enochic lies behind the composition.[46] The seventh and seventy-seventh places are significant (cf. Gen. 4.24; Matt. 18.22), the one occupied by Enoch, the other by Jesus; 'furthermore, we should remember that for a mind concerned with the symbolic significance of sevens special significance also attaches to *seven times seven* – the jubilee figure of 49. It cannot be accidental that in the Lukan genealogy the name Jesus occurs not only in seventy-seventh place, but also in forty-ninth place – where the only namesake of Jesus among his ancestors appears (Luke 3.29).'[47] In *1 Enoch* 10.12 Michael is instructed to bind the Watchers for 70 generations until the great day of their judgement, the day of judgement at the end of world history. Thus as in Luke's genealogy so in *1 Enoch* world history is schematized into 77 generations. Much detailed analysis is required to discover how Luke's genealogy is constructed, especially the view that the Messiah is descended from David through his son Nathan, but the schematic parallel with 11Q13 is what is significant for the purposes of the best understanding of the use of Isaiah 61.1–2 in Luke 4. In 11Q13

---

45 Fitzmyer says of the question in Lk. 4.22: 'The query could in itself be one of cynical indignation or one of pleasant surprise or admiration; in my opinion, it records the latter' (*The Gospel According to Luke I–IX*, 535). Fitzmyer also refers back to Lk. 3.23 for appreciating the significance of the question.
46 R. J. Bauckham, *Jude and the Relatives of Jesus in the Early Church* (Edinburgh: T & T Clark, 1990), 315–73.
47 *Jude and the Relatives of Jesus*, 319.

the great Day of Atonement occurs at the end of the tenth jubilee period, just as the judgement of the Watchers in *1 Enoch* 10 occurs at the end of ten periods of seven generations each. The periodization of history in all three texts (*1 Enoch*, 11Q13, Luke) is similar and for understanding the genealogy of Luke these Jewish parallels disclose that Luke's Jesus can be understood to belong at the end of the tenth jubilee period from Enoch.

What is the significance of this similar usage of the combination of Levitcus 25 and Isaiah 61 in both 11Q13 and Luke 4? The texts are mutually illuminating in several respects, with regard to the eschatological fulfilment of the jubilee chronology in the activity of an anointed one. But the similarities are not so great when the two texts are looked at closely. In 11Q13 Leviticus 25 is the base text with which other secondary texts from the Law, Prophets and the Psalms are associated through a variety of means, mostly in terms of explicit citation, often with introductory formulae. There are no significant variants from the MT in the forms of text which are cited. In Luke 4, on the other hand, it is Isaiah 61 which controls the narrative and secondary allusions (Isa. 58; Lev. 25; Deut. 15) are contained not within the narrative as explicit scriptural quotations but within the form in which Isaiah 61.1–2 is itself cited. The intertextual combination of scriptural passages is somewhat similar in both passages as is the exegetical outlook, but the detailed means of quoting the texts differs and the application of the passages in relation to different figures (Melchizedek and Jesus) is obvious.

Ezekiel 1 and 10 in 4Q385 and Revelation 4[48]

4Q385, known as Pseudo-Ezekiel[a], has six fragments assigned to it.[49] Fragment 6 contains a rewritten version of the throne chariot vision of Ezekiel 1. As the text of Ezekiel 1 is re-presented there appear to be

---

48 See especially G. J. Brooke, 'Ezekiel in Some Qumran and New Testament Texts', in *The Madrid Qumran Congress: Proceedings of the International Congress on the Dead Sea Scrolls, Madrid 18–21 March 1991* (ed. J. Trebolle Barrera and L. Vegas Montaner; STDJ 11; Leiden: Brill; Madrid: Universidad Complutense, 1993), 332–6.

49 See D. Dimant, *Qumran Cave 4.XXI: Parabiblical Texts, Part 4: Pseudo-Prophetic Texts* (DJD 30; Oxford: Clarendon Press, 2001), 17–51. Earlier versions of the information provided in the principal edition were provided in J. Strugnell and D. Dimant, '4Q *Second Ezekiel* (4Q385)', *RevQ* 13 (1988): 45–58; D. Dimant and J. Strugnell, 'The Merkabah Vision in *Second Ezekiel* (4Q385 4)', *RevQ* 14 (1989–90): 331–48.

identifiable elements of the parallel visionary passage in Ezekiel 10. By tabulating the parallels between the scriptural texts of Ezekiel 1 and 10 and the rewritten form in Pseudo-Ezekiel, the editors of the text have been able to show that it is precisely at the point where there is the most obvious overlap between the phraseology of Ezekiel 10 and Pseudo-Ezekiel that the order of Ezekiel 1 seems to be disregarded. This happens in lines 9–12 of Fragment 6.[50] With regard to this process they comment: 'Another interesting addition refers to what is seen on both sides of the wheels. This is one of the few details which seems to betray the influence of the parallel Merkabah vision in Ezekiel 10, especially 10, 2, 6–7, where the place of the coals of fire amidst the Cherubim is repeatedly referred to.'[51] A similar clarificatory intertextual interweaving can be seen in 4Q405, 20–22.[52]

The same kind of interweaving of elements from Ezekiel 1 and 10 can be found in Revelation 4. Elsewhere I have set out the details in a tabulated form.[53] At the end of 4Q385, 6 there is allusion to Ezekiel 1.25; Revelation 4.2 has Ezekiel 1.26–8 controlling the vision from 4.2 onwards, with a secondary allusion to Ezekiel 10.1. Revelation 4.5 alludes to the lightning of Ezekiel 1.13, a verse used in the summary of 4Q385 6, 12. Revelation 4.6 refers to the sea of glass, like crystal, with a possible allusion to Ezekiel 1.22, a verse in fact associated with Ezekiel 1.13 in 4Q385 as well. Then Revelation 4.6b introduces the four living creatures (Ezek. 1.8) who have eyes in front and behind like the wheels of Ezekiel 1.18; this same juxtaposition of creatures and wheels can be seen in 4Q385 6, 12. Although referring to the creatures in series, the four faces of Revelation 4.7 correspond with those mentioned in Ezekiel 1.10 and 4Q385 6, 8–9. The six wings of Revelation 4.8 are almost certainly derived from Isaiah 6.[54] It is noticeable that when Pseudo-Ezekiel and Revelation 4 are laid side by side, the only significant differences concern the use of Ezekiel 1.8 and 16 in 4Q385 6, 9–11. Thus these two verses alone are out of order in 4Q385 and of the verses of Ezekiel 1 represented in 4Q385 they are the only ones not represented in Revelation 4.

---

50 D. Dimant and J. Strugnell, 'The Merkabah Vision in *Second Ezekiel*', 344–5 (there the fragment is labelled number 4); DJD 30, 49–51.

51 'The Merkabah Vision in *Second Ezekiel*', 345; DJD 30, 50.

52 See C. Newsom, *Songs of the Sabbath Sacrifice: A Critical Edition* (HSS 27; Atlanta: Scholars Press, 1985), 307–21, esp. 315 on lines 9–10.

53 G. J. Brooke, 'Ezekiel in Some Qumran and New Testament Texts', 333–4.

54 Enoch's vision in *1 Enoch* 14 is a similar combination of elements from Isaiah 6 and Ezekiel 1 and 10, together with other scriptural passages.

One feature of the close analysis of this kind of shared intertextuality is its possible use in the correct reading of some of the fragmentary exegetical material from Qumran. In other words, where the juxtaposition of texts seems clear in the New Testament passage, it might be possible to use such juxtaposition to provide suitable readings and restorations in a fragmentary Qumran passage. A case in point concerns the problematic line 7 in 4Q385 6. According to D. Dimant this reads *'ḥwr 'l štym tlk hḥyh h'ḥt wšty rgl[yh*. She understands that the phrase refers to legs: 'backwards; upon two (legs) each living creature was walking, and [its] two legs [.'[55] Since Ezekiel does not refer to the number of legs each creature had, Dimant has drawn attention to the possible similarity between the description in this line concerning legs and the description of the Seraphim's six wings in Isaiah 6.2, where the function of each pair is described.[56] In light of the clear use of Isaiah 6.2–3 in Revelation 4.8 where each of the four living creatures is described as having six wings, it seems appropriate to view 4Q385 6, 7 in this way.[57] However, the reading of *rgl* at the end of the extant line is far from certain. None of its letters are obvious on PAM 43.503, and it may be preferable to restore the last word of the line with some form of *hknpym*.[58] This means that the whole line could refer not to the legs or feet of the living creatures but to their wings. Ezekiel 1 and 10 seem to agree that the creatures each had four of these, two for movement, touching the wings of their neighbour, and two to cover their bodies (Ezek. 1.11; 10.21). Revelation might then be the earliest text to introduce the idea of each creature having six wings.

As a result of paying attention to these details, the similarity to one another of 4Q385 6 and Revelation 4 can be assessed cautiously. Both texts show evidence of weaving Ezekiel 1 and 10 together. 4Q385 includes some allusions to Ezekiel 1 out of order and, intriguingly, Revelation 4 makes no reference to those same Ezekiel passages. In Revelation 4 there is clear reference to Isaiah 6.2–3. That same passage is hinted at in

---

55 DJD 30, 44; cf. D. Dimant and J. Strugnell, 'The Merkabah Vision in *Second Ezekiel*', 335.

56 DJD 30, 46; cf. D. Dimant and J. Strugnell, 'The Merkabah Vision in *Second Ezekiel*', 338.

57 C. Newsom (*Songs of the Sabbath Sacrifice*, 316) also finds traces of Isa. 6.3 in 4Q400 20–23, 10. 4Q385 6, 3 seems to combine part of Ezekiel (Ezek. 16.47) with part of Isaiah (Isa. 26.20).

58 B. Z. Wacholder and M. Abegg (*A Preliminary Edition of the Unpublished Dead Sea Scrolls*, 230) have proposed *wšty hk[npym*. The *Preliminary Concordance* makes no suggestion, though the traces of letters are registered.

4Q405 and may possibly lie behind a phrase in 4Q385 6. Furthermore, it should be noted that the order of the four living creatures is different in all the sources – Ezekiel, 4Q385 and Revelation 4. There is no literary dependence here, but a complex variable exegetical representation of a spiritual experience which can only be adequately expressed by reference to more than one scriptural text.

Ezekiel 37 and Leviticus 26 in 4Q119, 11Q19 and 2 Corinthians 6

Some scriptural phrases become almost proverbial as they are used and reused, so that it is not always clear which passage may be the source of the allusion and which the passage which is making the allusion. Something of this kind of intertextuality can be seen in the way in which the text of Leviticus 26.9 in 4Q119 (4QLXXLev[a]) seems to reflect something of Ezekiel. 37.26.[59] 4Q119 reads *kai estai mou ē diathēkē en humin* whereas the LXX reads *kai stēsō tēn diathēkēn mou meth' humōn.* The relevant phrase of Ezekiel 37.26 is *bryt 'wlm yhyh 'wtm* (*diathēkē aiōnia estai met'autōn*).

Something similar can be seen in 11Q19 (11QT[a]) XXIX, 7–8: *hyw ly l'm w'nwky 'hyh lhm l'wlm.* As Y. Yadin observed the closest parallel to this is Ezekiel 37.23: *hyw ly l'm w'ny 'hyh lhm l'lhym.*[60] Leviticus 26.12 may also be in mind (*whyyty lkm l'lhym w'tm thyw ly l'm*) as also Jeremiah 31.33 (*whyyty lhm l'lhym whmh yhyw ly l'm*). The justification of making a reference to Leviticus at this point may come from noticing that it is the covenantal language of the closely proximate passage, Leviticus 26.42, which can best explain some elements in 11Q19 XXIX, 10. In other words, this redactional passage of the *Temple Scroll* seems to give us a good example of the intertextual relationship between Leviticus 26 and Ezekiel 37.

---

59 See E. C. Ulrich, 'The Septuagint Manuscripts from Qumran: A Reappraisal of Their Value', in *Septuagint, Scrolls and Cognate Writings: Papers Presented to the International Symposium on the Septuagint and Its Relations to the Dead Sea Scrolls and Other Writings (Manchester, 1990)* (ed. G. J. Brooke and B. Lindars; SBLSCS 33; Atlanta: Scholars Press, 1992), 58–9. In the principal edition of 4Q119 nothing is made of the possible influence of Ezekiel on this manuscript of Leviticus at this point: P. W. Skehan, E. Ulrich, J. E. Sanderson, *Qumran Cave 4.IV: Palaeo-Hebrew and Greek Biblical Manuscripts* (DJD 9; Oxford: Clarendon Press, 1992), 161–5.
60 Y. Yadin, *The Temple Scroll* (Jerusalem: Israel Exploration Society, Hebrew University, Shrine of the Book, 1983), 128.

This same relationship features in 2 Corinthians 6.14—7.1,[61] a passage which has commonly been discussed in relation to the Dead Sea Scrolls, especially 4Q174.[62] The text contains a string of scriptural quotations, beginning with Leviticus 26.12 and Ezekiel 37.27, followed by Isaiah 52.11 and 2 Samuel 7.14.[63] It seems as if there is a common set of passages which are mutually suggestive and represent the ideology of a particular tradition. But again, attention to detail hints at a more complex picture. Uniquely of the witnesses to Leviticus 26.12 4Q119 reads *ethn*[*os*] instead of *laos*; as Ulrich comments, 'it is very difficult to imagine *ethnos* being substituted – intentionally or in error – for an original *laos* . . . Thus it would appear that *ethnos* was the OG translation here at 26.12, with *laos* as the routine revisional substitution.'[64] In other words, the very manuscript of Scripture at Qumran in which there seems to be something of the intertextual cross-fertilization of Leviticus and Ezekiel represents a unique form of text. Once again, it is not possible to compare like with like in the scrolls and the New Testament but to see as with the relationship between Leviticus 25 and Isaiah 61 that a shared intertextual interpretation is rooted in the text of Scripture itself and that is variously used in later and almost contemporary exegetical passages.

Psalm 82 in 11Q13 and John 10

As part of the subsidiary argument in Column II of the principal fragments of 11Q13 Psalm 82.1–2 is cited, though the two verses of the

61 There is an extensive literature on this pericope: J. A. Fitzmyer, 'Qumran and the Interpolated Paragraph in 2 Cor. 6.14—7.1', *CBQ* 23 (1961): 271–80; reprinted in *Essays on the Semitic Background of the New Testament*, 205–17; B. Gärtner, *The Temple and the Community in Qumran and the New Testament* (SNTSMS 1; Cambridge: Cambridge University Press, 1965), 49–56; J. Gnilka, '2 Cor, 6.14—7.1 in Light of the Qumran Texts and the Testaments of the Twelve Patriarchs', in *Paul and Qumran* (ed. J. Murphy-O'Connor; Chicago: Priory Press, 1968), 48–68; reprinted in *Paul and the Dead Sea Scrolls* (ed. J. Murphy-O'Connor and J. H. Charlesworth; New York: Crossroad, 1990), 48–68; G. Klinzing, *Das Umdeutung des Kultus in der Qumrangemeinde und im Neuen Testament* (SUNT 7; Göttingen: Vandenhoeck & Ruprecht, 1971), 175–82; H. D. Betz, '2 Cor. 6.14—7.1. An Anti-Pauline Fragment?', *JBL* 92 (1973): 88–108; M. E. Thrall, 'The Problem of II Cor. vi.14—vii.1 in Some Recent Discussion', *NTS* 24 (1977–8): 132–48; G. J. Brooke, 'Ezekiel in Some Qumran and New Testament Texts', 331–2.

62 See, e.g., G. J. Brooke, *Exegesis at Qumran*, 211–17.

63 Cf. the proximity of Ezek. 37.27 and 2 Sam. 7.14 in Rev. 21.3 and 7 respectively.

64 E. Ulrich, 'The Septuagint Manuscripts from Qumran', 61.

Psalm are split by some secondary argument that refers to Psalm 7.7–8. Psalm 82 is also quoted in John 10.34. In 11Q13 the purpose of the reference is to highlight who are the suitable angelic judges. The use of Psalm 7.7–8 makes this clear.[65] It is not Belial (and those of his lot) but Melchizedek who is the heavenly judge, acting as God's agent.

In its address Psalm 82.6 repeats the initial suggestion of verse 1, that the angels are 'gods'. Too often the use of Psalm 82.6 in John 10.34 has been read in ontological terms concerning the nature of Jesus' relationship to God. The passage is read as being a debate about Jesus' status in an argument from the lesser to the greater, namely, that since in the lesser case the angels are called gods, so therefore in the greater case must the one whom the Father has sanctified and sent into the world, and who himself does the works of the Father, be considered as in a more intimate relationship to God than the angels, a more proximate expression of the nature of God himself, even though he is a man (Jn 10.33). But it is also noticeable that according to John 10.34, in citing Psalm 82.6, Jesus refers to the text as written in the Law. Some have taken the term Law here as implying simply a shorthand for the Scriptures as a whole,[66] but others have sought a passage in the Law which suggests something similar to the content of Psalm 82.6, such as Deuteronomy 32.43 as in 4QDeut^q: 'Worship him, all you gods.'[67]

For the better understanding of how John 10.32–9 reflects an interest in judges and right judgement R. E. Brown shows how, when taken in context, Psalm 82.6 is part of the castigation of unjust judges.[68] Since one of the Fourth Gospel's themes is that Jesus is the judge par excellence, passages in the Hebrew Bible describing how judgement belongs to God (e.g., Deut. 1.17) or which speak of Israel coming before their human judges as appearing before God himself (e.g., Deut. 19.17; Exod. 21.6; 22.9) can be assumed as part of the setting for how Jesus' audience should perceive that through Jesus divine judgement has come upon them. Although the same verse is not cited in both 11Q13 and John 10.34, the overall subject matter which lies behind the use of the Psalm in both contexts is probably to be understood as very similar.[69]

---

65 As highlighted by P. J. Kobelski, *Melchizedek and Melkireša'*, 62–3.

66 As, e.g., R. E. Brown, *The Gospel According to John I–XII* (AB; Garden City: Doubleday, 1966), 403.

67 Cf. LXX *proskunēsatōsan autō pantes huioi theou*.

68 *The Gospel According to John I–XII*, 409–11.

69 This is brought out best in studies by J. A. Emerton, 'Some New Testament Notes', *JTS* 11 (1960): 329–32; 'Melchizedek and the Gods: Fresh Evidence for the Jewish Background of John x.34–36', *JTS* 17 (1966): 399–401.

As with the previous examples here are two exegetical uses of the same Psalm, and the theme of the intepretations is very similar in the two contexts where the Psalm is cited. In 11Q13 another Psalm is interwoven to draw out the meaning of the reference to Psalm 82; in John 10 the broader context of Jesus as judge assumes allusions to other scriptural passages as is implied in the use of the term 'your Law'. There is much that is shared, but much is common simply because of the way Psalm 82 is understood as part of the argument in both passages.

CONCLUSIONS

Seven passages in the New Testament have been considered in this study. They have been set alongside a slightly larger number of passages from the scrolls found at Qumran. In both contexts the scrolls and the New Testament seem to share combined references or allusions to Scripture. It is not a matter of a single quotation alone, but of shared intertextual interpretations. What can be said by way of conclusion in drawing out the significance of this investigation?

First, it needs to be stated clearly that no New Testament work explicitly cites any literary work found in the Qumran caves. Some scriptural passages, such as the famous Isaiah 40.3, are indeed found quoted explicitly in both corpora, but the literary contexts of each usage are distinct. Perhaps the closest a New Testament work comes to citing a Qumran text is Mark 10.6 (// Matt. 19.4) on divorce, where not only is Genesis 1.27 cited explicitly as in CD IV, 21, but also the preliminary phraseology, 'from the beginning of creation' is indeed not unlike what is found in CD's *yswd hbry'h*. But we have noticed that these similarities need to be handled carefully.

Second, some Qumran and New Testament quotations of scriptural passages clearly represent the same text form, even though the former is in Hebrew and the latter in Greek. So, for example, Amos 9.11 in 4Q174, CD VII, 16 and Acts 15.16.[70] However, this similarity in text form does not mean that the New Testament author is quoting from a Qumran version of the text and translating appropriately as he goes. It is much more likely that we are now just beginning to realize what every New Testament scholar should have known all along, that in the first century C.E., while there is a move towards some kind of standardization

---

70 See the discussion in J. de Waard, *A Comparative Study of the Old Testament Text in the Dead Sea Scrolls and in the New Testament*, 24–6.

of the Hebrew text form, there remains plenty of evidence for a plurality of text types extant in Palestine during the first centuries B.C.E. and C.E. This omnipresent diversity means that the coincidence of variant readings in more than one source is not all that remarkable.

Third, perhaps the most intriguing and significant conclusion of this investigation can be expressed as follows. In several examples there is considerable overlap in shared intertextual exegetical combinations in the text found at Qumran and the New Testament, but it is also obvious that there are many differences which should not be forgotten. Having more than one exegetical matter in common with a contemporary text does not necessarily imply that there is any direct literary relationship between those two texts. This unexpected conclusion needs some elaboration. The increasingly sophisticated methodological awareness of those interested in intertextuality, that all texts reflect a dialogue with other texts, written and unwritten, has enabled students of texts to perceive that texts which assume some kind of authority often produce or are the products of echoes of other texts. As is well known, the Hebrew Bible is its own witness to developing literary traditions and the scrolls found at Qumran attest how scribes in copying its books often behaved intertextually themselves, introducing phraseology that was reminiscent of other passages of Scripture. This may happen both deliberately as two scriptural texts with related subject matter are associated with one another; or it may happen unconsciously as the idiomatic phraseology of one passage comes to influence the scribe as he works on another. This attests to the phenomenon that some scriptural texts (and no doubt others too) readily suggest their own intertextual spheres. Those that reappear most intricately in subsequent traditions are primarily attesting the suggestiveness of the exegetical base text, rather than defining a particular social group or groups who read the text in an exclusive way through the generations. Thus the more shared intertextual combinations there are between groups of various persuasions, the greater is the suggestiveness of the base text and the less the likelihood of direct literary dependence of one group upon another – unless, of course, quotation of a literary source can be unequivocally demonstrated.

There are many similar concerns in the scrolls, both the so-called sectarian ones and the non-scriptural non-sectarian ones, and in the New Testament writings. These are most obvious in the common features of their community organization and the common elements of their eschatologies, especially when messianic hopes and claims are the issue. However, these seem to be the common inheritance of the

Judaisms that live primarily under eschatological motivation, rather than the products of the self-reflection of limited numbers of people, isolated in well-defined groups, familiar with one another's ideas. In those very passages in both the Dead Sea Scrolls and the New Testament where there are similar intertextual echoes, this study has observed that the interpretative differences are as numerous as the similarities. Attention to intertextuality shows the distinctiveness of each set of writings but also that much in the New Testament is the common stock of eschatologically oriented first-century Palestinian Judaism; the scriptural exegesis in the extant texts of the first two generations of Christians does not show that Christianity is an Essenism that has largely succeeded.[71]

---

71 To paraphrase Renan. I am grateful to A. Lerner for discovering the precise reference in Renan's writings: *Histoire du peuple d'Isräl* (Paris: Calman Lévy, 1891), 5.70.

PART TWO

PARTICULAR SCROLLS ILLUMINATE THEIR NEW TESTAMENT COUNTERPARTS

6

The *Temple Scroll* and the New Testament

INTRODUCTION

This chapter is not an attempt to provide a comprehensive guide to the parallels between the *Temple Scroll* and the New Testament. For the most part discussion of their similarities has focused on the topics of crucifixion and Jesus' teaching on divorce. There are, however, some intriguing similarities in exegetical traditions, similarities sufficiently close to warrant the speculation that some parts of the New Testament documents, at least at some stage in their history, were written with the group of people in mind who may have been responsible for the 'republication' of the *Temple Scroll* at the turn of the era.

CRUCIFIXION AND DIVORCE

Crucifixion

Before the principal edition of the *Temple Scroll* was ever published Yigael Yadin had already let it be known that in his opinion the reference to Deuteronomy 21.22 in 11QT^a LXIV, 6–9 meant that the author of the scroll and the group to which he belonged approved of hanging on the tree, almost certainly crucifixion, as the most dishonourable punishment reserved for political traitors.[1] Since Yadin associated the Scroll with mainline Qumran opinion, he suggested that the lacunae in 4QpNahum should be adjusted to allow for its author to be expressing approval for Alexander Jannaeus' mass crucifixion of Pharisees.[2]

---

1 'Pesher Nahum (4QpNahum) Reconsidered', *IEJ* 21 (1971): 1–12.
2 M. Hengel for one (*Crucifixion in the Ancient World and the Folly of the Message of the Cross* [London: SCM Press, 1977], 84–5) approves of Yadin's understanding and supposes that the tradition of the hanging of the sorceresses in Ashkelon, preserved in

Several studies have been written on what the approval of death by hanging on a tree might imply for our understanding of the scriptural interpretations applied to the death of Jesus.[3] There is no need to rehearse all the scholarly insight that has resulted from the publication of 11QT[a], but two comments deserve underlining here. First, the dating of the manuscript of 11QT[a] to Herodian times means that, unless it was copied for purely antiquarian interest,[4] there were some Jews at a time close to that of Jesus' death who could have approved of crucifixion; undoubtedly it was because of Roman practice that the crucifixion actually took place, but perhaps the reading of Deuteronomy 21.22 in the tradition of the *Temple Scroll* meant that those concerned to rid themselves of Jesus may have realized that it should be on a political charge that a death sentence of the sort that the Romans would carry out would be particularly appropriate.

---

m. Sanh. 6.5, is so unusual that it may well reflect an actual event, perhaps the Pharisees getting their own back when they came into favour once again under Alexandra Salome.

3   J. M. Baumgarten, 'Does *TLH* in the Temple Scroll Refer to Crucifixion?', *JBL* 91 (1972): 472–81; reprinted in *Studies in Qumran Law* (SJLA 24; Leiden: Brill, 1977), 172–82; J. M. Baumgarten, 'Hanging and Treason in Qumran and Roman Law', *ErIsr* 16 (1982): 7–16; A. Dupont-Sommer, 'Observations nouvelles sur l'expression "suspendu vivant sur le bois" dans le Commentaire de Nahum (4QpNah II 8) à la lumière du Rouleau du Temple (11Q Temple Scroll LXIV 6–13)', *CRAIBL* (1972): 709–20; J. A. Fitzmyer, 'Crucifixion in Ancient Palestine, Qumran Literature, and the New Testament', *CBQ* 40 (1978): 493–513; J. M. Ford, '"Crucify him, crucify him" and the Temple Scroll', *ExpTim* 87 (1975–6): 275–8; D. J. Halperin, 'Crucifixion, the Nahum Pesher and the Rabbinic Penalty of Strangulation', *JJS* 32 (1981): 32–46; M. Hengel, *Crucifixion*, 84–5; L. Merino Díez, 'La crucifixíon en la antigua literatura judía (Período Intertestamental)', *EstEcl* 51 (1976): 5–27; L. Merino Díez, 'El suplicion de la cruz en la litertura judía intertestamental', *SBFLA* 26 (1976): 31–120; L. Rosso, 'Deuteronomio 21, 22: contributo del rotolo del tempio all valutazione di una variante medievale dei settanta', *RevQ* 9 (1977–8): 231–6; R. Vincent Saera, 'La halaká de Dt. 21, 22–23 y su interpretación en Qumrán y en Jn 19, 31–42', in *Salvación en la palabra: targum–derash–berith: homenaje al prof. A. Díez Macho* (ed. D. Munoz Léon; Madrid: Ediciones Cristianidad, 1986), 699–709; M. Wilcox, '"Upon the Tree" – Deut. 21.22–23 in the New Testament', *JBL* 96 (1977): 85–99.

4   As suggested by H. Stegemann, 'The Literary Composition of the Temple Scroll and its Status at Qumran', in *Temple Scroll Studies: Papers Presented to the International Symposium on the Temple Scroll, Manchester, December 1987* (ed. G. J. Brooke; JSPSup 7; Sheffield: JSOT Press, 1989), 123–48.

Second, as M. Wilcox and J. A. Fitzmyer have argued,[5] it is clear that our understanding of the allusions to Deuteronomy 21.22 in early Christian apologetic should acknowledge the possibility that such apologetic was based on a similar text of Deuteronomy. In Acts 5.30 Peter declares, 'The God of our fathers raised Jesus whom you killed by hanging on a tree'; this is echoed in another speech of Peter's (Acts 10.39): 'And we are witnesses to all that he did both in the country of the Jews and in Jerusalem. They put him to death by hanging him on a tree.' In Galatians 3.13 the text is actually cited in the argument that asserts that because Jesus has taken upon himself the curse of the Law, so the blessing of Abraham is to be available to all who believe in him. There is nothing in any of these texts that supposes that Deuteronomy 21.22 could not apply to Jesus because he was not killed before he was hung on the tree. The reading of a text-type like that of the *Temple Scroll* is probable, indeed likely, given that none of these texts is exactly a representation of the LXX,[6] which for the order of the verbs agrees with the MT. The overall point is that here we are on the very borderline between what represents different text-types and what represents different interpretations of texts considered more rather than less fixed. In so many places the *Temple Scroll*

---

5 J. A. Fitzmyer, 'Crucifixion in Ancient Palestine', 509–10; M. Wilcox, '"Upon the Tree" – Deut. 21.22–23 in the New Testament', 90–1, 99.

6 E. Haenchen (*The Acts of the Apostles: A Commentary* [ed. R. McL. Wilson; Oxford: Blackwell; Philadelphia: Westminster Press, 1971) says Acts 5.30 alludes to Deut. 21.22–3 in the LXX (p. 251) and that the same text in Acts 10.39 belongs to early Christian scriptural proof (p. 353); H. Conzelmann (*Die Apostelgeschichte* [HNT 7; 2nd edn, Tübingen: J. C. B. Mohr, 1972]; ET *Acts of the Apostles* [Hermeneia; Philadelphia: Fortress Press, 1987], p. 42) does not mention the LXX and more aptly asks whether Deut. 21.22–3 in Acts 5.30; 10.39; and Gal. 3.13 belongs to a traditional Christian apologetic tradition. More recently, R. Pesch (*Die Apostelgeschichte* [EKK 5/1; Neukirchen-Vluyn: Neukirchener Verlag, 1986], 217 n. 31) refers not to the LXX but to the interpretation of Deut. 21.22–3 in 11QT[a] for understanding the text of Acts. Yadin himself drew attention to the significance of 11QT[a] for the better understanding of Gal. 3.13 (*The Temple Scroll*, I, 379 [Heb. I, 290]). H. D. Betz (*Galatians* [Hermeneia; Philadelphia: Fortress, 1979], 151–2, n. 133) allows that Paul's use of Deut. 21.22–3 may have been based on a *Vorlage* like that of 11QT[a]. The version of Deut. 21.22–3 in the *Temple Scroll* eases the difficulties in all these New Testament passages. Of the four Passion Narratives it is those of Mark and John that came closest to representing something of Deut. 21.22–3 in their description, Mark in the stress on the need to take Jesus from the cross because evening had come (Mk 15.42–4), John by having the soldiers break the legs of those not dead so that the Law might be kept (Jn 19.31–3).

forces us to reconsider not just the interpretation of Law in the late second temple period, but also the polemic of textual recensions.

Divorce

The other matter in the New Testament which the *Temple Scroll* has illuminated and concerning which several scholars have expressed opinions is Jesus' teaching on divorce.[7] 11QT[a] LVII, 17–18 prohibits polygamy and by saying that the queen shall be with the king all the days of her life implies that divorce is not allowed, at least for the king; a second wife may be taken, only if the first dies. In CD V, 2 this law for the king, after Deuteronomy 17.17, is democratized and an excuse is offered for David's polygamous behaviour, namely his ignorance of the law-book that some have supposed to be the *Temple Scroll* itself. Yadin has commented that the *Temple Scroll* and CD together provide pre-Christian evidence that some Jews would support the view of Jesus on divorce as expressed in Mark's version of his teaching (10.1–12), whereas Matthew's version with the exception clause (19.1–12) is closer to the Shammaite ruling.[8]

---

7 A. Ammassari, 'Lo statuto matrimoniale del re di Israele (Deut. 17,17) secondo l'esegesi del "Rotolo del Tempio" (57, 15–19) e le risonanze neotestamentarie (Ef. 5, 23–33; Apoc. 21, 9–10)', *Euntes Docete* 34 (1981): 123–7; P. R. Davies, *Behind the Essenes: History and Ideology in the Dead Sea Scrolls* (BJS 94; Atlanta: Scholars Press, 1987), 73–85; J. A. Fitzmyer, 'The Matthean Divorce Texts and Some New Palestinian Evidence', *TS* 37 (1976): 197–226; J. A. Fitzmyer, 'Divorce among First-Century Palestinian Jews', *ErIsr* 14 (1978): 103–10; J. R. Mueller, 'The Temple Scroll and the Gospel Divorce Texts', *RevQ* 10 (1979–81): 247–56; J. Murphy-O'Connor, 'Remarques sur l'exposé du Professeur Y. Yadin', *RB* 79 (1972): 99–100; C. Schedl, 'Zur Ehebruchklausel der Bergpredigt im Lichte der neugefundenen Tempelrolle', *Theologisch-praktische Quartalschrift* 130 (1982): 362–5; G. Vermes, 'Sectarian Matrimonial Halakhah in the Damascus Rule', *JJS* 25 (1974): 197–202; reprinted in *Post-Biblical Jewish Studies* (SJLA 8; Leiden: Brill, 1975), 50–6; Y. Yadin, 'L'attitude essénienne envers la polygamie et le divorce', *RB* 79 (1972): 98–100. See also the article on divorce by H. A. Mink in *Tekster og tolkninger – ti studieri Det gamle Testamente* (ed. K. Jeppesen and F. H. Cryer; Aarhus: Anis, 1986). See also D. Instone-Brewer, *Divorce and Remarriage in the Bible: The Social and Literary Context* (Grand Rapids: Eerdmans, 2002), especially Chapter 4 on the Intertestamental Period, and the Bibliography.

8 Y. Yadin, *The Temple Scroll: The Hidden Law of the Dead Sea Sect* (London: Weidenfeld & Nicolson, 1985), 201–2; cf. *The Temple Scroll*, I, 357 (Heb. I, 272–3). Although when he discusses divorce, E. P. Sanders (*Jesus and Judaism* [London: SCM, 1985], 256–60) makes no mention of 11QT[a], he does refer in detail to CD IV–V and his conclusions are significant: he shows that Jesus in his teaching on divorce neither contradicts the Law nor is entirely satisfied with it – this is exactly the position of 11QT[a] in relation to the Pentateuch on many matters.

What needs to be underlined here is that it is the Marcan tradition that is closer to what 11QT^a proposes; furthermore, in the juxtaposition of CD and 11QT^a, the law for the king, at least with respect to polygamy with excuses made for David, is applied to everybody.

THE *TEMPLE SCROLL* AND THE GOSPEL OF MARK

The preeminence of the Marcan tradition and the reference to the figure of David in discussing the application of the Law are both significant factors in a set of motifs that have yet to be thoroughly examined. Yadin has subscribed to the view that the Herodians in the New Testament (Matt. 22.16; Mk 3.6; 8.15) are to be identified with the Essenes.[9] Yadin's argument rests on reading the seven baskets of bread of Mark 8.8 and 20 in the light of 11QT^a XV, 3–5, a text requiring much restoration but which seems to imply that at the feast of consecration or ordination there were to be seven baskets of bread, one for each daily offering of a ram. Yadin's identification also assumes that the Essenes were responsible in some way for the *Temple Scroll*; even if we might be tempted to be sympathetic to Yadin's use of 11QT^a for supporting the identification of the Herodians, they would only be those responsible for the scroll, not necessarily Essenes proper. In relation to the actual text of Mark the logic of Yadin's argument for identifying the Herodians requires that an identification be made in a similar way for the five loaves and 12 baskets of crumbs mentioned in Mark 8.19. If the identification of the Herodians by the seven loaves and seven baskets of crumbs is correct, then, because of Jesus' warning in Mark 8.15 ('Beware of the leaven of the Pharisees and the leaven of Herod'),[10] we should expect the combination of five and 12 to be the hallmark of the Pharisees. Now this combination of five and 12 may be found by implication in one other place in the Gospel, in Mark 2.25–6, in the context of a debate with the Pharisees. Whether addressed by Jesus in his lifetime to Pharisees or by someone in the Marcan tradition to Pharisees or Pharisaic Jewish Christians, it is assumed that the Pharisees or Mark's readership at least will grant the line of argument involving the story of David and the shewbread. According to 1 Samuel 21.3 (MT) David asks for five loaves from Ahimelech and is given the shewbread (12 loaves).

---

9 *The Temple Scroll*, I, 138–9 (Heb. I, 111–12); *The Temple Scroll: The Hidden Law*, 80–3. Yadin also mentions how Jn 6.4 explictly speaks of the feeding of the 5,000 happening as Passover drew near; this corresponds with the timing of the 11QT^a Feast of Ordination.

10 Instead of *Herodou*, P^{45}, W, Θ and others read *Hērōdianōn*.

A closer look at Mark 2.23–8 suggests some other parallels with the traditions represented in the *Temple Scroll*. Four preliminary points might be noteworthy. First, this is a Sabbath controversy; there need be nothing unusual about that except that observance of the Sabbath is stressed quite explicitly in the *Book of Jubilees*, especially Chapter 50, and in the *Damascus Document* (XII, 4–6). Those responsible for those two works had much in common at some stage with those responsible for the *Temple Scroll*.[11] Their attitude to the Law was stricter than many of their contemporaries, just as Mark's version of Jesus' saying on divorce is stricter than Matthew's version. Second, Mark 2.26 mentions that a certain Abiathar was high priest when David entered the house of God and ate the bread of the presence. Matthew and Luke omit this identification, presumably thinking it was an embarrassing error. According to the Samuel narrative Abiathar, son of Ahimelech,[12] was joint high priest with Zadok during David's reign until he backed the wrong horse in the race for the succession; but in the tradition in 1 Chronicles (18.16; 24.6), Ahimelech is son of Abiathar. Furthermore, with Zadok (in 1 Chr. 15.11), Abiathar and some Levites are addressed by David as 'The heads of the father's houses of the Levites'; the connection with Levitical interests and the allegiance to the tradition of Chronicles are both features of 11QTᵃ and it looks certain here that the Marcan tradition is working with information from the Chronicler and not directly with 1 Samuel as

---

11 In commenting on Mk 2.23–8, J. D. G. Dunn ('Mark 2.1—3.6: Between Jesus and Paul', *NTS* 30 [1984]: 402) draws attention to *Jub.* 2.29–30; 50.6–13 to illuminate the position concerning the Sabbath in contemporary Judaism, but he does not draw out the significance of his remarks. For more on *Jubilees*, CD and 11QTᵃ see J. C. VanderKam, 'The Temple Scroll and the Book of Jubilees', in *Temple Scroll Studies* (ed. G. J. Brooke; JSPSup 7; Sheffield: JSOT Press, 1989), 211–36 and P. R. Davies, 'The Temple Scroll and the Damascus Document', in *Temple Scroll Studies*, 201–10; see also P. R. Davies, *Behind the Essenes*, 107–34.

12 D, W, it, syˢ and others omit the phrase referring to Abiathar, as do Matthew and Luke, sensing its difficulty. Several scholars reflect the statement of V. Taylor (*The Gospel according to St. Mark* [London: Macmillan, 2nd edn, 1966], 217): 'The statement about Abiathar is either a primitive error or a copyist's gloss occasioned by the fact that, in association with David, Abiathar was better known than his father.' C. E. B. Cranfield (*The Gospel according to St. Mark* [CGTC; Cambridge: Cambridge University Press, 1959], 116) helps Jesus out of the difficulty by suggesting that the phrase could mean 'in the days of Abiathar the High Priest' and so need not refer to his actual high priesthood; more helpfully he says: 'It may be that there is some confusion between Ahimelech and Abiathar in the O.T. itself – cf. I Sam. xxii. 20 with II Sam. viii. 17, I Chr. xviii. 16, xxiv. 6.'

represented by either the MT or the LXX.[13] Third, Matthew inserts a tradition about those priests in the temple who profane the Sabbath and, citing Hosea 6.6, underlines that God desires mercy, not sacrifice, an attitude which is echoed in 1QS IX, 3–6. In this way Matthew makes the tradition reflect a more straightforward Qumran Essene attitude than does the Marcan pericope. Fourth, and of least significance, I have argued elsewhere that the preceding pericope (Mk 2.18–22) may reflect knowledge of the feast of new wine (11QT^a XIX, 11–XXI, 10); while John's disciples and the Pharisees fast, Jesus suggests a feast: 'And no one puts new wine into old wineskins' (Mk 2.22).[14]

These little points may not add up to very much, but for our purposes there is a more important aspect to the argument that Jesus uses in Mark 2.23–6. This is the very use of David's actions for interpreting the Law. Yadin has rightly observed that David features in the *Temple Scroll*, implicitly of course, as an authoritative interpreter of Law; not only could 1 Chronicles 28.11–19 be construed as evidence that there was a plan for the building of the temple such as the *Temple Scroll* might be, a plan which supplements and completes the Law and is entrusted to David,[15] but also in particular matters of legal interpretation what David does is taken as normative in some way. So, for example, the law concerning spoils of battle in 11QT^a XLIII, 11–15 (interpreting Num. 31.27–30) uses 1 Samuel 30.24–5 to produce an interpretation which takes account of how David made provision for exactly equal shares for warriors and those who stay at home by securing the levy for the priests and Levites *before* the division takes place, not after, as Numbers suggests; yet priests and Levites get exactly the same amount whichever way the sums are done –

---

13 In *Ant.* 6.243–4 Josephus fails to mention the giving of the shewbread to David; perhaps this illustrates that there was some debate about the suitability and significance of the action. J. D. G. Dunn ('Mark 2.1—3.6: Between Jesus and Paul') argues persuasively that the whole section in Mark reflects debates within Judaism and Jewish Christianity before the time of Paul. The Samuel passage concerned is not preserved among the Qumran fragments of Samuel: E. C. Ulrich, *The Qumran Text of Samuel and Josephus* (HSM 19; Missoula: Scholars Press, 1978), 273.

14 'The Feast of New Wine and the Question of Fasting', *ExpTim* 95 (1983–4): 175–6.

15 On the supplementary nature of the *Temple Scroll* see H. Stegemann, 'The Literary Composition of the Temple Scroll and its Status at Qumran', in *Temple Scroll Studies*, 123–48; on the importance of 1 Chr. 28.11–19 for understanding the function of 11QT^a see Y. Yadin, *The Temple Scroll*, I, 81–2, 182, 403 (Heb. I, 70, 141, 308); *The Temple Scroll: The Hidden Law*, 115–17.

'Ingenious indeed', comments Yadin.[16] Other examples could be cited, though it is important also to add that David is not used in any way in the formulation of the law concerning the number of wives the king might have: one only, says the scroll firmly! Thus David is not the sole authority in legal interpretation, but to some extent his actions are taken as normative.[17]

The significance of this for Mark 2.25–6 is that it is important for scholars to note that in some measure Torah and haggadah can be interwoven in the very formulation of Law or precedent. For example, D. Cohn-Sherbok has argued that Jesus' argument in Mark 2 cannot be valid from a rabbinic point of view, first because David's action did not take place on the Sabbath, so the analogy was not apt, and second because haggadah cannot be used to formulate precept, only to illustrate it.[18] That may be correct from a rabbinic point of view, but the use of Davidic haggadah in the formulation of the rules in the *Temple Scroll* suggests that the argument in this Gospel tradition may be valid from a different perspective. I would suggest that taken with all the minor signals mentioned above this Gospel pericope may contain an argument that would not have been out of line with those whose sympathies might lie somewhere on the Levitical edges of Essenism and Pharisaism, close to those responsible for the republication of the *Temple Scroll*. Furthermore, all these connections with the traditions of the *Temple Scroll* lead me to suspect that Yadin's use of the ordination material in 11QT^a to support the identification of the Herodians is not altogether inappropriate.

THE *TEMPLE SCROLL* AND THE GOSPEL OF JOHN

Together with these several similarities in Mark to exegetical traditions in the *Temple Scroll*, traditions that belong to the main literary components in the text of 11QT^a,[19] there are also some similarities between 11QT^a

---

16 *The Temple Scroll: The Hidden Law*, 78; for the details see *The Temple Scroll*, I, 76, 360–1 (Heb. I, 57, 276).

17 In a similar way, according to 11QPs^a XXVII, 2–11, David's psalmodic compositions are a demonstration of the correct calendric attitude; see W. H. Brownlee, 'The Significance of David's Compositions', *RevQ* 5 (1964–6): 569–74.

18 D. Cohn-Sherbok, 'An Analysis of Jesus' Arguments Concerning the Plucking of Grain on the Sabbath', *JSNT* 2 (1979): 31–41, esp. 36.

19 See the definition of the main sources and redactional sections of 11QT^a identified by A. M. Wilson and L. Wills, 'Literary Sources of the *Temple Scroll*', *HTR* 75 (1982): 275–88. On 11QT^a XXIX, 7–10 in particular see Yadin, *The Temple Scroll*, I, 182–6 (Heb. I, 140–4); P. Callaway, 'Exegetische Erwägungen zur Tempelrolle XXIX, 7–10', *RevQ* 12 (1985–7): 95–104.

and the Fourth Gospel. These similarities belong to the more self-evidently redactional parts of the scroll, 11QT^a I–III; XXIX, 8–10. When taken together these redactional parts of the *Temple Scroll* can be seen deliberately to juxtapose exegetical traditions based on Exodus 34 with exegetical materials based on the Jacob cycle. Unfortunately at least the first column of the scroll is missing, but the part of the introduction which survives uses the language of Exodus 34 and Deuteronomy 7 (the parallel passage) as its base. The whole of the scroll is thus to be viewed as the contents of a speech to Moses, as divine revelation, as the supplementary Law actually received but described neither fully nor accurately in the proto-Masoretic Pentateuch. In Column XXIX on the other hand it is the covenant with Jacob at Bethel that is mentioned, not that with Moses at Sinai. What might be the relationship of these two covenants?

The Fourth Gospel has two introductions. There are allusions to various scriptural passages in each. In the Prologue proper, John 1.1–18, Exodus 34.6 (in a version other than the LXX) lies behind the 'grace and truth' of 1.14 and 17.[20] Furthermore the emphasis in the Greek version of Exodus 33 and 34 on the 'glory' that is to be revealed to Moses may have influenced the Prologue's author's stress that 'grace and truth' define the type of glory to be seen in the word made flesh. Other prominent scriptural passages in John 1.1–18 are the allusions to Genesis 1 and the figure of Wisdom in Proverbs 8.27–30 in John 1.1–5; both these texts and the pillar of cloud in Exodus 33.9–10 are also taken up in the hymn of Sirach 24. Part of that hymn may well be echoed in John 1.14; Sirach 24.8 reads: 'Then the creator of all things gave me a commandment, and the one who created me assigned a place for my tent. And he said, "Make your dwelling in Jacob, and in Israel receive your inheritance".' It is possible to construe Sirach 24 so that Wisdom's song in praise of herself ends at verse 22 to be followed immediately by the comment: 'All this is the book of the covenant of the Most High God, the law which Moses commanded us as an inheritance for the congregations of Jacob.'[21]

---

20 Many scholars accept this identification: e.g., C. K. Barrett, *The Gospel According to St. John* (London: SPCK, 2nd edn, 1978), 167, 169; R. E. Brown, *The Gospel According to John I–XII* (AB 29; Garden City: Doubleday, 1966), 14; R. Schnackenburg, *The Gospel according to St John* (New York: Herder & Herder; London: Burns & Oates, 1968), IV, 272.

21 To find Genesis 1 linked with Exodus 34 and the temple is to see another example in support of the view that the temple is to be understood as a microcosm; see, e.g., M. Weinfeld, 'Sabbath, Temple, and the Enthronement of the Lord – The Problems of the Sitz im Leben of Genesis 1.1—2.3', in *Mélanges bibliques et orientaux en*

The allusions to these creation and Wisdom texts in association with Exodus 33—4 are not just coincidental. To begin with it must be noted that *Jubilees* opens with a restatement of Exodus 34 linked with Genesis 1. The association of Exodus 34 with the presentation of a supplemented or rewritten Law in both *Jubilees* and the *Temple Scroll* suggests that allusion to Exodus 34 may serve a similar function in the Johannine Prologue. When the references to the Wisdom texts are also taken into account, then the association of the figure of Wisdom with the Law in some form[22] confirms the suspicion that the Prologue is out to suggest that the incarnate Logos is the very content of the Law as it was revealed to Moses the second time he went up Mount Sinai. In this light John 1.18 reapplies the experience of Moses to what is now available for anyone through Jesus: 'No one has ever seen God' – not even Moses – as is made quite clear in Exodus 33.20; perhaps only Jacob at Peniel (Gen. 32.30): 'the only God who is in the bosom of the Father, he has made him known' (Jn 1.18). For the author of the Fourth Gospel Jesus Christ is the means of making explicit the character of God which was the content of the Law revealed to Moses. Here again is support for those who would see nothing antithetical in John 1.17: what was given to Moses has come through Jesus Christ. Earlier Paul may also have used Exodus 34 to identify what Moses saw with Christ himself.[23]

For the Prologue Sirach 24 is a key text. Following the premise that allusions should more often than not be understood in their original contexts, it is worth recalling that twice in Sirach 24 there are explicit references to Jacob, once as the place of Wisdom's dwelling (Sir. 24.8), and once Jacob's congregations are the inheritors of the book of the covenant, the Law which Moses commanded (Sir. 24.23). In 11QT[a] the covenant with Jacob is mentioned after the detailed listing of the festivals and their offerings; chapters 5—10 in the Fourth Gospel are also about the right ordering of the cult through the healing on the Sabbath and the interpretations of the Feasts of Passover, Tabernacles and Dedication.

But this parallel is enhanced when the use of the Jacob traditions are

---

l'honneur de M. Henri Cazelles (ed. A. Caquot and M. Delcor; AOAT 212; Neukirchen-Vluyn: Neukirchener Verlag, 1981), 501–12.

22 As proposed, for example, by B. Lindars, *Behind the Fourth Gospel* (Studies in Creative Criticism 3; London: SPCK, 1971), 48; R. E. Brown, *John I–XII*, cxxii–cxxv.

23 See the detailed analyses of 2 Cor. 3.1–8 by A. T. Hanson, *Jesus Christ in the Old Testament* (London: SPCK, 1965), 25–35; 'The Midrash in II Corinthians 3: A Reconsideration', *JSNT* 9 (1980): 2–28. Cf. Rom. 11.7, 25.

compared. In 11QT^a XXIX God recalls the covenant he made with Jacob at Bethel (Gen. 28.13–15). That covenant reads as a renewal of the covenant made with Abraham (Gen. 12.2–3, 7); in the second account of God's appearance to Jacob (Gen. 35.10–12) this Abrahamic covenant is combined with language from the priestly blessing of Genesis 1.22.[24] In this way Genesis 1 and Jacob at Bethel can be associated indirectly. Furthermore, as mentioned already, in John 1.18 there is the insistence that no one has ever seen God; yet Jacob does claim to have seen God face to face. For the Johannine Prologue as a whole we have Genesis 1, traditions identifying Wisdom with the Law entrusted to Jacob, Exodus 34, and a veiled allusion to or play upon Jacob's vision; these texts also lie behind the redaction of the *Temple Scroll*.

The Gospel's second introduction strengthens the function of these combined scriptural allusions. As the Gospel stands at the moment John 1.19–51, the second introduction, together with the sign at the marriage at Cana may form a week that matches that of Genesis 1.[25] The point to notice is not only the possible allusion to Genesis 1, but the way in which the Cana sign is preceded by material with allusions to the Jacob cycle, an effect reproduced for the second Cana sign at the end of John 4.

In the first case (John 1.19–51) the author of the Gospel has the priests and Levites[26] sent from Jerusalem to find out who John the Baptist is by way of a prelude to introducing Jesus. The climax of this introduction in John 1.51 is Jesus as the Son of Man with the promised vision of the angels of God ascending and descending on him. For all that 1.51 may be an independent saying (cf. Matt. 26.64; 16.27–8), since the time of Augustine commentators have seen in this verse an allusion to Genesis 28.12, Jacob's dream: 'And he dreamed that there was a ladder set up on the earth, and the top of it reached to heaven; and behold, the angels of God were ascending and descending on it.'

---

24 Similarly, in 4Q158 1, Gen. 32.29–30 includes phraseology of Isaac's blessing of Jacob in Gen. 28.3.

25 R. E. Brown, *John I–XII*, 105–6, cautiously agrees with other scholars who have proposed this.

26 Few commentators attempt any explanation of why Levites are mentioned in John 1.19; e.g., E. Haenchen (*John* 1 [Hermeneia; Philadelphia: Fortress Press, 1984], 143) argues that they are present neither as temple police nor as the party interested in purity, but simply to stress the religious significance of the scene. The Levitical bias of 11QT^a suggests that they may have been mentioned in John 1.19 because they formed part of the author's readership; the bias towards the Levites in 11QT^a was first summed up by J. Milgrom, 'Studies in the Temple Scroll', *JBL* 97 (1978): 501–6.

There is some very considerable confusion among scholars as to how to interpret this allusion to Jacob's dream.[27] First, some commentators have argued on the basis of *Genesis Rabbah* 69.3 (on Gen. 28.13) that the angels were descending on Jacob, reading 'on him' for 'on it'; applied to the Fourth Gospel this makes Jesus as Son of Man the replacement of Israel. Second, there are those who have relied on *Genesis Rabbah* 68.12 (on Gen. 28.12) in which Jacob appears in heaven while his body is on earth to make John 1.51 mean that Jesus as Son of Man is really with the Father, yet he is on earth at the same time. Third, there are some scholars who have been influenced by the targumic reading in which God's shekinah appears on the ladder; applied to the Fourth Gospel this tradition shows that Jesus is the localization of the shekinah, a theme already present in the Prologue.

In light of the *Temple Scroll* all three categories of interpretation need reconsideration. In the first place, although the Fourth Gospel is concerned to identify Jesus with Wisdom and the Law, as the one who displays the character of God, that in itself need not preclude him from also being portrayed in 1.51 in some sense as the replacement for Jacob/Israel. After all, in 4.12 the Samaritan woman asks plainly: 'Are you greater than our father Jacob?' In John 1.45–51 it is true that something of the traditions concerning Jacob lies behind the portrayal of Nathanael. It is Nathanael whom Jesus hails as 'an Israelite indeed in whom there is no guile!' (1.47), possibly an ironic reference to Jacob, the first to bear the name Israel but in whom there was certainly some guile (Gen. 27.35). Furthermore, the ancient popular and playful etymology of Israel as 'the one who sees God' matches John the Baptist's description of his purpose as baptizing with water so that Jesus might be revealed to Israel and Jesus' promises to Nathanael that he will '*see* greater things than these' and that he will '*see* heaven opened' (1.50–1). Perhaps the relationship between Nathanael, Jesus and the figure of Jacob is that while Nathanael is the representative Israelite, Jesus as an individual supplants the position of honour accorded Jacob himself.

Second, *Genesis Rabbah* 68.12 may be more significant than is commonly supposed nowadays. Although the actual form of the tradition presented in it cannot be dated convincingly earlier than the middle of the first millennium, it may well contain elements of traditions that are much older. For our purpose it seems significant that, while nearly all

---

27   The comments in this paragraph are based on the summary of scholarly opinions by R. E. Brown, *John I–XII*, 90–1.

the rabbinic sources simply transfer all the imagery associated with Bethel to Jerusalem, *Genesis Rabbah* 68.12, together with representing something of the interpretation of the passage to be found in the targums, speaks of the ladder first as the stairway of the temple and second as Mount Sinai, the place of the giving of the Law.

The combination of temple and Sinai in this kind of juxtaposition may be very ancient, but there could be more to the content of what was disclosed to the sleeping Jacob. To discover what that content might be we can turn to the third matter which the targums illuminate. C. Rowland has argued[28] that the targumic renderings of Genesis 28.12 are important for disclosing the content of the revelation: he suggests that *Tg. Ps.-J.* reflects the belief that the most secret things of God were hidden even from angels (*1 Enoch* 14.21; 1 Pet. 1.12); but by looking at the features of Jacob the angels can look at the features of one whose form is found on the throne of glory itself. For John 1.51 this exegetical tradition would then imply that, as Jacob, so Jesus is on the earth as the one whom the angels in heaven sought to look at, the one who embodies the mystery of God himself. It is in this way that Jesus supplants Jacob and so 1.51 at the climax of the second introduction matches 1.18 at the climax of the first: for the author of the Fourth Gospel Jesus is the one who discloses the very character of God, glory embodied in the word made flesh — that same glory is to be seen in the first sign at Cana. And this parallel between the endings of the two introductions is just the juxtaposition of Exodus 34 and the Jacob cycle which we see also in 11QT³.

For the authors of *Jubilees* and the *Temple Scroll* it is the cultic ordering of the temple and its regulations that need to be declared over against the impure Jerusalemite practice. For the author of the Fourth Gospel the Law is the grace and truth that is embodied in and disclosed by Jesus; his use of the Jacob tradition, close in his understanding also to that of the targums, gives weighty support to his notion of incarnation: in the human Jesus can be seen the image of God himself. Not surprisingly, as for the authors of *Jubilees* and the *Temple Scroll*, the combination of traditions from Exodus and Genesis leads the author of the Fourth Gospel to portray the true significance of the temple, the Sabbath, the festivals, the very nature of worship itself. So much for the two introductions to the

---

28 C. Rowland, 'John 1.51, Jewish Apocalyptic and Targumic Tradition', *NTS* 30 (1984): 498–507. Jacob traditions are prominent in several intertestamental literature, especially *Pr. Jos.* which may well come from the same school as the *Temple Scroll. Pr. Jos.*, Frag. A, speaks of Jacob as the firstborn who tabernacles among men.

Fourth Gospel and the juxtaposition of Exodus 34 and Genesis 28 at the end of each.

The other prominent Jacob tradition in the Fourth Gospel is in the narrative of the woman at the well (John 4). In the first place the dialogue between Jesus and the Samaritan woman is set at the 'city of Samaria called Sychar near the field that Jacob gave to his son Joseph. Jacob's well was there' (John 4.5–6). The use of the figure of Jacob gives some measure of legitimation to the Samaritan woman; she is no descendant of the Shechemites who raped Dinah and who were murdered by Simeon and Levi (a point that is made much of in *Jubilees*), but a descendant of Jacob who bought some land from the Shechemites before the unhappy incident took place. Then the Samaritan woman asks straightforwardly: 'Are you greater than our father Jacob, who gave us the well, and drank from it himself, and his sons, and his cattle?' (4.12).

As usual in the Fourth Gospel the meaning of the text does not only rest on the surface. Although there is no mention of Jacob purchasing or digging a well at Shechem, there are plenty of texts in which Jacob is associated with a well. The mention of the well may correspond with Jesus' phrases 'the gift of God' and 'living water' (4.10) both of which were used to describe the Torah.[29] In the *Damascus Document* (CD VI, 4–11) the well of Numbers 21.18 is identified explicitly with the Law. CD goes on to identify this law with the covenant that the faithful will keep according to Deuteronomy 7.9 (MS B); the proximity of CD to the *Temple Scroll* has already been noted, so it is not impossible, given the use of Deuteronomy 7 in 11QT^a II, 7–11, that the covenant to which it refers includes that made with Jacob at Bethel (11QT^a XXIX, 7–10). In any case in John 4 the Fourth Gospel identifies the well with Jacob. Additionally for John 4.14, as R. E. Brown has shown,[30] the best parallel is Sirach 24.21 where Wisdom claims that 'those who drink me will thirst for more'. Sirach 24.23–9 goes on to describe how the Law fills mankind with wisdom like rivers overflowing their banks. We have already noted how in this context there is explicit mention of the congregations of Jacob – as Brown says of these verses in John 4: 'In John Jesus is presented as divine wisdom and as the replacement of the Law.'[31] In light of the discussion of

---

29 See R. E. Brown, *John I–XII*, 176, 178.
30 *John I–XII*, 178; surprisingly, G. Reim, *Studien zum alttestamentlichen Hintergrund des Johannesevangeliums* (SNTSMS 22; Cambridge: Cambridge University Press, 1974), 192–3, makes no mention of this parallel.
31 *John I–XII*, 179.

these motifs in the Prologue, Brown's statement might be altered to say rather that Jesus is the Law, its meaning made explicit through being supplemented by his person; it is not so much a matter of Jesus replacing the Law. We may suggest, then, that 11QT^a is also written to disclose the true meaning of the Law.

After the Samaritan woman has perceived something of this in as much as she is able to identify Jesus as a prophet (like Moses; 4.19), the dialogue develops around the topic of worship. Since this is the principal purpose of the reworking of the Pentateuch in both *Jubilees* and the *Temple Scroll*, there need be no surprise that true worship is the most significant aspect of the Law that the Samaritan woman should grasp. The first topic in the dialogue between the woman and Jesus in this section concerns the place of worship. Intriguingly Jesus says to the woman, 'The hour is coming when neither on this mountain nor in Jerusalem will you worship the father.' 'Where then?', the reader might ask. Might some of those hearing this dialogue wish to respond by saying, 'At Bethel'? J. C. VanderKam[32] has lent his detailed support to those who see in the Jacob cycle in the *Book of Jubilees* allusions to the battles of the Maccabees against the Seleucids. J. Schwartz has taken this further with regard to Bethel.[33] He argues that before Bethel's capture and reinforcement by Bacchides (1 Macc. 9.50; *Ant.* 13.12–17), Judas Maccabee was in retreat from Jerusalem in the mountains of the Gophna region (*War* 1.45) close to Bethel. Schwartz proposes that it is these circumstances in 162 B.C.E. that provide the historical setting for the cult to be restored at Bethel which *Jubilees* 31—32 seems to stress. There are several attractive aspects to Schwartz's theory; for our immediate purpose it is worth noting that in the late second temple period there were those who still harboured notions about the cultic importance of Bethel. Some of these people, especially Levites, may have eventually found their way into the Qumran community. Whatever the case, it is clear from the archaeological evidence that no cultic centre was physically established at Bethel in the Maccabean period.[34]

The dialogue in the Fourth Gospel continues with Jesus saying, 'We worship what we know for salvation is from the Jews.' Much has been

---

32 *Textual and Historical Studies in the Book of Jubilees* (HSM, 14; Missoula: Scholars Press, 1977), 217–41.

33 'Jubilees, Bethel and the Temple of Jacob', *HUCA* 56 (1985): 63–85.

34 See J. L. Kelso, *The Excavation of Bethel (1934–1960)* (AASOR 39; Cambridge: American Schools of Oriental Research, 1968), 38–40.

written on this statement; Brown[35] favours those who see here something comparable with Psalm 76.1: 'In Judah God is known.' This comparison is significant both because Psalm 76 is an Asaph Psalm and so may justifiably be associated with Bethel,[36] and because of the Psalm's overall content with its reference to Salem, its description of God as 'more majestic than the everlasting mountains' and as 'God of Jacob'. The reference to God being greater than any mountain may be echoed in John 4.21, and the title of God as God of Jacob fits the context of John 4. Moreover, the occurrence of Salem may be relevant to how the place of John the Baptist's activity is to be understood ('At Aenon near Salim' [3.23]), since in *Jubilees* 30.1 Jacob goes up to 'Salem which is east of Shechem';[37] this seems to be the name for the land which was rightfully his, before the rape of Dinah. In this way there are several tantalizing allusions within John 3 and 4 to the Jacob traditions as represented in Psalm 76 and *Jubilees* as well as in Genesis itself. Perhaps these would amount to nothing if it were not the case that in John 4.5–6 and 12 Jacob is named explicitly. In addition it is likely that 1QS IV, 19–22 illuminates the meaning of John 4.23–4 on the nature of true worship.[38]

As Jesus is on the cross his thirst is assuaged with vinegar to fulfil the Scripture (John 19.28–9); Psalm 69, which lies behind this incident, is also referred to in 2.17. In relation to Jesus' attack on those who were selling doves in the temple, 'His disciples remembered that it was written, "Zeal for thy house will consume me"' (Ps. 69.9). There follows a reference to the 46 years that it has taken for the Herodian rebuilding of the temple. Several minor points might add up to something. First, in 11QT[a] LX, 9 there is a particular regulation to guarantee that the Levites secure their tithe from doves, which was twice the percentage that it was for booty, game and wild animals. Second, Josephus records both that the second temple was constructed by Levites aged 20 and over (*Ant.* 11.79) and that in order not to offend religious scruples Herod had been careful to have the rebuilding of the temple undertaken only by priests, those

---

35 *John I–XII*, 172.

36 See, e.g., M. D. Goulder, *The Psalms of the Sons of Korah* (JSOTSup 20; Sheffield: JSOT Press, 1982), 59–65.

37 This justifies reading MT Gen. 33.18 as Salem, although Sam. has *šlwm*.

38 According to R. Schnackenburg, 'Die "Anbetung in Geist und Wahrheit" (Joh 4, 23) im Lichte von Qumran-Texten', *BZ* 3 (1959): 88–94; O. Betz, '"To Worship God in Spirit and in Truth": Reflections on John 4, 20–26', in *Standing Before God: Studies on Prayer in Scripture and Tradition in Honor of J. M. Oesterreicher* (ed. A. Finkel and L. Frizzell; New York: Ktav, 1981), 53–72, esp. 62–5.

qualified to be in the temple precincts (15.419–21). Jesus' attack on the sellers of doves at a time when the main temple buildings were just considered complete might thus be seen as a double blow against Levites, given that some of these Levites might have considered Herod's work as near a fulfilment of their hopes as they might expect, leaving only the eschatological intervention of God himself. In addition, Psalm 69 is commonly thought to reflect the views of the pietists who earnestly desired the rebuilding of the temple after the exile; the Psalm implies their desire was misplaced and the Fourth Gospel underlines this for Herod's new building too. Lastly, it is worth noting that 11QT[a] XIV, 9–18 suggests that the purifying of the sanctuary, usually associated with the Day of Atonement, should rather be associated with the celebrations for the spring New Year in Nisan, which is, according to *Jubilees* 27.19, the time that Jacob arrived in Bethel; together with these other minor points, perhaps part of the reason for the cleansing of the temple being in the place it is in the Fourth Gospel is the result of some such calendric adjustment as well as the literary possibility that just as in the *Temple Scroll* the cleansing of the sanctuary follows the regulations for the construction of the altar, so the cleansing of the temple should precede the adjustment to the festivals that will follow later in the Gospel.

The possibility exists, therefore, that some of the members of the Johannine community were those whose fellows (perhaps Levites) may at one time have thought that their aspirations for Bethel had been realized in Jerusalem. These disciples came to recognize that their desire for the temple was misplaced; the author of the Fourth Gospel tries to show them what the Johannine church considers to be the real content of the Law given to Moses the second time he ascended the mountain. In so doing the cultic traditions associated with Jacob receive the same christological adjustment as the practice of the Sabbath and the festivals. This is not literary dependence so much as the deliberate taking over of ideas which belong together, particularly in the background of one section of the community. The ideology of the Pentateuch in the form that it is preserved in the *Temple Scroll* and *Jubilees* seems to make sense of several disparate ideas in the Fourth Gospel. It may also help account for the Fourth Gospel's stress on divine initiative; to begin in the Holy of Holies and to have a perspective of divine disclosure as at Sinai will result in the story starting with God and working out from the centre to include even the Greeks (Jn 12.20–6).

CONCLUSION

It is not possible to demonstrate that any of the authors of the New Testament books knew the *Temple Scroll*. It does appear, however, not only that there are common exegetical traditions, but also that some members of the early Christian communities came from a group whose views had earlier been expressed through such documents as the *Temple Scroll*. The hopes they may have once fostered for Bethel had proved impossible to fulfil; they had associated themselves with the Qumran community's disapproval of cultic practice in Jerusalem; perhaps they had had their hopes raised by Herod's rebuilding programme, only to have their priesthood and other characteristics of their understanding of the cult denied once again. If some of them had been retained to run the sale of offerings after the main elements of Herod's temple were complete, they may have been put in their place by Jesus. Or, later, as some of them became associated probably with either the nascent Marcan or Johannine communities, they were shown through the adaptation and adjustment of their own exegetical traditions how Jesus fulfilled all their hopes and expectations. If at any stage they had been designated 'Herodians', they would have soon wanted to lose that name!

7

Levi and the Levites in the
Dead Sea Scrolls and the New Testament

INTRODUCTION

The purpose of this chapter is to list and investigate in a preliminary fashion the references to Levi and the Levites in their various contexts in the Dead Sea Scrolls and the New Testament to see if they share common concerns, common exegetical traditions, or common elements of their own Levitical tradition.

It will soon become apparent that the literary contexts of references to Levi and the Levites share a remarkably coherent set of motifs which variously recur in the several texts. Prominent among these concerns is the association of Levi and the Levites with traditions about Jacob, particularly Jacob at Bethel. Not surprisingly there is a cultic interest behind many of the references, but commonly this interest is associated with the interpretation of the Law, considered to be a cultic activity, as much as with temple singing or hymnody.

Clearly not all the Levites were members of the *yaḥad* community, nor were the members of the *yaḥad* community all Levites, but at some time or times it seems as if certain Levites formed a major part of the movement generally, and even the Qumran community in particular. When they joined or rejoined the movement, they brought with them a set of traditions advocating their own perspective on life and, because of what we know of the redactional history of some of the texts, it is likely that they attempted to redraw the shape and practice of the community to their own ends.

The New Testament texts contain only a few references to Levi and the Levites. Often the literary contexts of such references display a set of interests akin in many ways to the particular self-understanding of the Levites which emerges from the texts found at Qumran. It seems as if at some time several early Christian communities were joined by Levites or

Levitical Qumranites who then influenced their practice and preaching, either positively or so that such preaching was constructed to show them through the use of their own traditions the significance of Jesus. In this way the New Testament can act as a source for the Judaism of which Christianity was a part.

LEVI AND THE LEVITES IN THE DEAD SEA SCROLLS

For the Dead Sea Scrolls the principal references to Levi or the Levites are in the *Rule of the Community*, the *Rule of the Congregation* (1QSa (1Q28a)), the *War Scroll*, the *Words of Moses* (1Q22 = 1QapocrMoses³?), the *Damascus Document*, 3Q7 (3QTJud?), *Testimonia* (4Q175), *Levi ar* (4Q213–14), *Narrative and Poetic Composition*ᵇ (4Q372), *Testament of Qahat ar* (4Q542), *Visions of Amram* (4Q543–49), 5Q13, and the *Temple Scroll* (11Q19 = 11QTᵃ). Some of the Qumran materials are associated with Levi either through Jacob, such as *Pseudo-Jubilees* (4Q225–26), or through Levi's immediate descendants. It is also necessary to reconsider *Pesher Habakkuk* in light of the whole discussion, since in the LXX of Bel and the Dragon Habakkuk is described as a Levite. Taken together, these texts show an interest in traditions associated with Levi in other pseudepigraphical literature: events at Shechem, association with Jacob and Joseph, and the cult at Bethel. There is a textual affinity with elements of Deuteronomy and the Books of Chronicles.

Intriguingly, the Levites occur only in the first two columns of the Cave 1 form of the *Rule of the Community* (1QS) and its Cave 4 parallels (4Q256 II, 3, 12; III, 4; 4Q257 II, 1). This opening section of 1QS is thought by some to belong with the concluding hymnic section (1QS X–XI) to the last stage of the redaction of the text;[1] were it possible to date that stage of the redaction, it might also be possible to suggest when Levites as a group became prominent in the community at Qumran. The compiler of the *Temple Scroll* has shown how Deuteronomy is to be used programmatically, even if adjusted to favour the Levites, so it is intriguing to note that it is in 1QS I–II that J. Pouilly has identified the most explicit use of Deuteronomy in 1QS.[2] 1QS was copied together with 1QSa (1Q28a) in which the sons of Levi and the Levites are also

---

1 J. Murphy-O'Connor, 'La genèse littéraire de la Règle de la Communauté', *RB* 76 (1969): 528–49; followed in most respects by J. Pouilly, *La Règle de la Communauté: son évolution littéraire* (CahRB 17; Paris: J. Gabalda, 1976), 65–84.

2 J. Pouilly, *La Règle de la Communauté*, 72–3; he notes the presence of Deut. 7.9; 27—9, especially 29.11, 18–20; and also 33.8–11.

explicitly mentioned in their executive capacity in the community (1QSa (1Q28a) I, 22; II, 1).

Particular mention of the Levites is found also in the Cave 1 version of the *War Scroll* and its fragmentary Cave 4 counterparts (4Q491–94). Whatever one makes of the structure and history of the *War Scroll* in its Cave 1 version (1QM), it may be important to note that column I is likely to give some overall clues about the final redaction of the text.[3] After what is generally considered to be a lengthy title, the first group of people to be mentioned in the scroll are the sons of Levi; they or, more straightforwardly, the Levites take a role in all the subsequent sections of the text, throughout which there is persistent use of Numbers 1—10, in which the Levites are mentioned over 40 times.[4] The Levitical material in 1QS I–II and in 1QM may be part of the explanation for the cultic and liturgical material that both those texts contain in their final redaction. Interestingly, an earlier variant of 1QM I, 2, 'The sons of Levi and the sons of Judah and Benjamin, the exiles in the desert', is to be found in 4Q372, a manuscript that survives in some 27 fragments in an Herodian hand.[5] The content of fragment 1 is in two parts: lines 1–15 describe in narrative fashion, in a pattern of sin, exile and return, the history of Joseph; lines 14–32 contain a psalm offered by Joseph, a standard lament in which he pleads for God to deliver him. The Joseph of 4Q372 is not the patriarch himself but the descendants named after him, in this case apparently, the northern tribes. The narrative of the text seems to imply that those who were responsible for casting Joseph into the lands he did not know, also provoked 'Levi, Judah and Benjamin' (4Q372 1, 14) through their words.

---

3 As P. R. Davies rightly suggests: *1QM, the War Scroll from Qumran: Its Structure and History* (Bibbia e Oriente 32; Rome: Biblical Institute Press, 1977), 113–21.

4 The Levites are mentioned in 1QM as follows: II, 2; VII, 14 (2 x), 15, 16; VIII, 9; XIII, 1; XV, 4; XVI, 7; XVIII, 5; Levi is mentioned at I, 2 and V, I.

5 See E. M. Schuller, '4Q372 1: A Text about Joseph', *RevQ* 14 (1989–90): 349–76 (4Q372 = 4QNarrative and Poetic Composition[b] in DJD 28, 165–97). The prominence of Joseph in this non-canonical narrative and psalm text is intriguing; it may be significant that Joseph occurs five times in the Psalter, four in Asaph Psalms (77.15; 78.67; 80.1; 81.5) and once in Ps. 105.17 which may belong to a Levitical redaction of the fourth book. See H. P. Nasuti, *Tradition History and the Psalms of Asaph* (SBLDS 88; Atlanta: Scholars Press, 1988); T. Korteweg, 'Joseph's Role in the Hebrew Testament of Naphtali and its Background in Post-exilic Judaism', in *Studies on the Testaments of the Twelve Patriarchs* (ed. M. de Jonge; SVTP 3; Leiden: Brill, 1975), 282–90.

Although there may be some second-century B.C.E. material preserved in the *War Scroll*, the manuscripts are all in the 'Herodian' script, apart from 4QM^c and 4QM^f which may be slightly earlier.[6] J. Duhaime, for one, has begun the painstaking task of comparing the various manuscripts of the *War Scroll* in order to discover what its recensional history may have been.[7] One point of comparison may be significant for this study. In 4QM^c there is the hint that the Levites had a status equal to that of the priests as far as the blowing of the trumpet was concerned, a function reserved solely for the priests in 1QM. Although in 1QM XVI, 7–8 (and probably in XVII, 13) the Levites join with the whole band of horn-blowers in the battle fanfare, they are not entrusted with the task of blowing any particular battle signals. 1QM VII, 12–14 describes the trumpets of summoning, of remembrance, of the fanfare, of pursuit and of withdrawal; the Levites are assigned the menial task of carrying the seven rams' horns, while the priests blow them. In 4QM^c 9–10, when the second array sorties, the Levites blow the trumpets giving the commands which correspond approximately with what can be found in 1QM VII, 12–14.[8] From this it might be deduced that 4QM^c represents the Levites in a more positive role than 1QM VII because it was a recension of the rule transmitted by Levites themselves. In the recension represented by 1QM the earlier material including 1QM VII repeats the liturgical functions of the Levites represented in Numbers,[9] while the later material including 1QM XVI and XVII allows for the Levites to have a more prominent part in the proceedings. Perhaps the actual compilation of 1QM as a whole has been influenced by another recension of the rule in which the Levites also played a more prominent part. Since 4QM^c may be the oldest manuscript version of the rule, perhaps it was brought to Qumran by those whom it represents in a more prominent way than does 1QM II–IX. The leading place of the Levites in 1QM I confirms that the final redaction of the recension of the War Rule represented by 1QM gave them a position which is not borne out by all the sections of 1QM

---

6 On the date and state of the various 4QM manuscripts, see M. Baillet, *Qumrân Grotte 4, III (4Q482–4Q520)* (DJD 7; Oxford: Clarendon Press, 1982), 12–72. See also 4Q471 (4QWar Scroll-like Text B) 1, 5, whose description of the Levites is similar to that of 1QM II, 2–3.

7 J. Duhaime, 'Etude comparative de 4QM^a fgg. 1–3 et 1QM', *RevQ* 14 (1989–90): 459–72.

8 As noted by Baillet, *Qumrân Grotte 4*, 53; cf. also 4Q285 3, 2, which also mentions the Levites with trumpets.

9 See especially Num. 1.50 and 4.15 for the Levites as porters.

itself. Here would be some evidence that probably in the mid-first century B.C.E. certain Levites became prominent in the Qumran community in such a way that older materials needed to be adjusted to take account of their position.

The basis of the Levites' status and position may be deduced from another fragmentary document, the so-called *Words of Moses* (1Q22, 1QapocrMoses^a?).[10] This is a rewritten version of the farewell of Moses in the concluding chapters of Deuteronomy, though its opening is a combination of Leviticus 1.1, Deuteronomy 1.2 and 31.12. The fragments that survive have been put together by J. T. Milik and it is clear that the first extant column is also the opening of the work. This is important for, as with 1QS and 1QM, the *Words of Moses* may present something of its particular redactional slant through the characters it names in its opening lines. According to Milik's reconstruction, Moses is commanded by God to ascend Mount Nebo with Eleazar the son of Aaron, and there told to interpret the Law which he is to disclose '[to the heads of the fa]milies of the Lev[i]tes and all the p[riests]';[11] the rest of the children of Israel are to be satisfied with the simple statement of the Law itself. This makes explicit what is only implicit in Deuteronomy 31, which is part of the opening of the text, namely that while in Deuteronomy 31.9 Moses entrusts the Law to 'the priests the sons of Levi' who are to declare it to the people every seven years, in the *Words of Moses* the Levites and priests, significantly in that order, are entrusted with the Law and its interpretation.

The way that the Levites are referred to in the *Words of Moses* as 'heads of the families of the Levites' (*r'šy 'bwt llwyym*) is the characteristic phraseology of the summary statements about the Levitical houses in 1 Chronicles 9.34 and 15.12; it also characterizes the genealogical lists of Exodus 6.14–25, in which the Levitical genealogies are the most extensive. The rewriting of Deuteronomy in the *Words of Moses* seems to be motivated out of a similar Levitical perspective.[12] But apart from

---

10 1Q22 was edited by J. T. Milik, *Qumran Cave I* (DJD 1; Oxford: Clarendon Press, 1955), 91–7; this composition used to be known by the abbreviation DM (Dires de Moïse or *dbry mšh*), but is now to be associated with 4Q375 and 4Q376.

11 1Q22 I, 3. The text then continues by elaborating on the feasts, beginning with the sabbatical year.

12 In many ways 1Q22 corresponds with the concerns of the *Temple Scroll* and its elaboration on the feasts as the correct interpretation of the Law, structurally organized on the text of Deuteronomy; see, e.g., H. Stegemann, 'The Literary Composition of the Temple Scroll and its Status at Qumran', in *Temple Scroll Studies* (ed. G. J. Brooke; JSPSup 7; Sheffield: JSOT Press, 1989), 123–48.

details of language, it is the precedence of the Levites in possessing the correct Mosaic interpretation of the Law which is of major importance. This same motif can almost certainly also be seen in *Ordinances*ᵃ (4Q159), a manuscript in a formal 'Herodian' hand, like that of *Florilegium* (4Q174, *Midrash on Eschatology* A). In the small Fragment 5, after a possible allusion to Leviticus 16.1, there is a space on line 2 before the very probable reading of 'Sons of Levi' as the start of a new sentence. Among the few words that have survived in other lines of this fragment the technical term *pesher* occurs twice (lines 1, 5), and in line 6, J. M. Allegro's restoration of '[in]terpret the Law' (*d]rwš htwrh*) is probably correct;[13] in line 4 we read 'when Moses took' (*bqht mwšh*) and in line 7, 'Moses spoke' (*dbr mwšh*). It is remarkable that in such a small fragment so many key phrases should survive, enough to enable us to see that somehow the Levites are involved in the interpretation of what Moses said. This is support for what is selected as the epitome of the function of Levi according to *Testimonia* (4Q175) 14–20. There Deuteronomy 33.8–11 is cited: 'They shall teach Jacob your ordinances and Israel your law' (cf. Neh. 8.7–8).

The purpose and perspective of these references to Levi and the Levites are tantalizingly brought together in 5Q13 which J. T. Milik has labelled 'Une règle de la secte.'[14] In this first-century C.E. manuscript whose language is similar to that of 1QS in several places, there is a meditation addressed to God which mentions creation (Frag. 1, 1–5), the sons of God (Frag. 1, 6), Enoch (Frag. 3, 2), Noah (Frag. 1, 7), Abraham (Frag. 2, 5), Jacob (Frag. 2, 6), Levi (Frag. 2, 7), the Levites (Frag. 2, 8) and the Israelites (Frag. 1, 13). In Fragment 2, 6 there is a clear mention of Jacob's dream at Bethel: 'To Jacob you made known at Bethel' (*'ly'qwb h[w]d'th bbyt 'l*).[15] This is a historical review encompassed in a liturgical framework, but a history whose salient features focus on certain figures and not others. Furthermore, in Fragment 4, 1 there is mention of the *mebaqqer*. This official features twice in the *Rule of the Community* (1QS VI, 12, 20) but many times in the Laws of the *Damascus Document* where he is associated with a priest. From the several references to the *mebaqqer*

---

13   J. M. Allegro, *Qumrân Cave 4, I (4Q158–4Q186)* (DJD 5; Oxford: Clarendon Press, 1968), 6–9.

14   M. Baillet, J. T. Milik, R. de Vaux, *Les 'Petites Grottes' de Qumrân* (DJD 3; Oxford: Clarendon Press, 1962), 181–3.

15   5Q13 2, 6 is translated by Milik as: 'A Jacob, Tu lui as fait connaître (les mystères), à Bethel.'

it seems as if he is considered to be more important than the priest;[16] perhaps he was a Levite as some have surmised.[17]

The figures of Enoch, Noah, Abraham, Jacob and Levi, together with the importance of what took place at Bethel are characteristics of other documents in which the Levites feature in a significant way. For example, Jacob occurs most obviously in the *Temple Scroll*: the redactional section of Column XXIX, 8–10 mentions 'the day of creation on which I shall create my sanctuary, establishing it for myself for all time according to the covenant which I have made with Jacob in Bethel'.[18] Although this covenant is not mentioned in Genesis, it is possible to read Leviticus 26.42 as if it refers to a specific covenant with Jacob; Leviticus 26 seems to embody much of the theological perspective of this group and is discernible as an influence behind several other texts.[19]

The *Temple Scroll* (11QT[a]) contains eight references to Levi. Two are in the phrase 'Sons of Levi' (XXII, 4; LXIII, 3) and so more properly can be considered with the other references to Levites; the remaining six all occur in the description of the gates (XXXIX, 12, 15, 16; XL, 14, 15; XLIV, 5). The gate of Levi is the central gate on the eastern wall, between Simeon and Judah. The large number of references to the gate result from the precise description of the measurements involved. The significant matter is that however the list of 12 gates is construed, in comparison with other lists of the 12 tribes, Levi can be seen in the *Temple Scroll* as preeminent; the whole scroll is compiled from a priestly, or, even more precisely, a Levitical perspective.

The Levites are mentioned in the *Temple Scroll* in several passages.[20]

---

16 As argued, for example, by M. A. Knibb, *The Qumran Community* (Cambridge Commentaries on the Writings of the Jewish and Christian World 2; Cambridge: Cambridge University Press, 1987), 118.

17 In the second edition of his *The Dead Sea Scrolls in English* (London: Penguin Books, 1968) G. Vermes has an excellent section (pp. 23–5) on the significance of the Levites, especially on the meaning of the term *maskil*, a figure whose association with various Psalms attributed to Levites supported the identification of the Guardian as a Levite; Vermes has dropped this material from his later publications and now simply reckons that the *mebaqqer* was a priest: G. Vermes, *An Introduction to the Complete Dead Sea Scrolls* (London: SCM Press, 1999), 96–7.

18 This difficult sentence is here offered in the translation of G. Vermes, *The Complete Dead Sea Scrolls in English* (London: Penguin, 1998), 200.

19 Notably CD I, 4; VI, 2; 11QT[a] LIX, 4–5, 9, 13; Ps. 106.45; Lk. 1.72–3.

20 Y. Yadin, *The Temple Scroll* (Jerusalem: Israel Exploration Society and the Shrine of the Book, 1983), 1.159–68, 349–53, 360–2 (Hebrew, 1977, 1.124–30, 284–5,

In XXI, 1 at the feast of new wine the priests drink first and then the
Levites (as is implied in 1QSa (1Q28a)), in XXIV, 11 there is a specific
reference to the burnt-offering of the Levites at the wood festival, in
XLIV, 14 there is mention of the distribution of the chambers in the walls
of the temple court which favours the Levites, in LVIII, 13 the law concerning booty is reworked so that, although the Levites still receive their
correct share, the rest is distributed more equitably, and in LX, 12 and 14
it is emphasized that the Levite from outside Jerusalem should be treated
exactly the same as his Jerusalem counterparts. Two sections in particular,
however, emphasize the Levitical perspective of the text as a whole. In
XXII, 4, 10 and 12 at the feast of the first fruits of oil and in LX, 6 in the
enumeration of Levitical dues, where particular attention is given to the
share of the Levites, it becomes clear that gifts from the altar are assigned
to the Levites, even though there is no biblical warrant for such practice.
J. Milgrom has proposed that the Levites received the shoulder, because
the foreleg of the biblical prescription for priests (Deut. 18.1–3) was
interpreted to refer to the lower part of the limb only.[21] Whatever the
case, according to the *Temple Scroll* the Levites receive a portion of the
offering. The second text of note is LVII, 12 (echoed partly in LXI, 8)
which describes how 12 of the king's advisory body of 36 are to be
Levites, along with 12 priests and 12 leaders of the people. The Levites
are to have a political as well as a cultic role.[22]

Other important Qumran material relating to Levi and the Levites is
to be found in the *Damascus Document*, in the testamentary literature
connected with Levi, Amram and Qahat, and also in 5Q13. Though
found at Qumran, there is good reason to suppose that most, if not all, of
these texts, like the *Temple Scroll* too, were composed elsewhere and represent a cultic perspective somewhat different from that of the oldest
material in 1QS. The discovery of these texts at Qumran suggests the
diversity of the movement, or even that a Levitical group, possibly not

---

276–7), comments on the Levites in 11QT[a]. For Levitical preferment in 11QT[a] see
also J. Milgrom, 'Studies in the Temple Scroll', *JBL* 97 (1978): 501–6; G. J. Brooke,
'The Temple Scroll: A Law unto Itself?', in *Law and Religion: Essays on the Place* of
Law in Israel and Early Christianity (ed. B. Lindars; Cambridge: J. Clarke, 1988),
38–9. Note also the explicit mention of Levites in 4Q365 23, 10, part of an addition
to Lev. 23.42—24.2 which corresponds with the regulations for the wood offering in
the *Temple Scroll*.
21 'The Shoulder for the Levites', in Y. Yadin, *The Temple Scroll*, 1.169–76
(Hebrew, 1.131–6).
22 This matches their quasi-executive function in 1QSa (1Q28a) I, 21; II, 1.

originally Qumranite, became influential in the movement at some point in its history.

In the *Damascus Document* Levi features twice. In CD IV, 15, after the Levites have been introduced in III, 21, Levi, the son of Jacob, is attributed with a saying concerning the three nets of Belial: fornication, wealth, and the pollution of the sanctuary. No such saying is found in precisely that way in the extant *Testament of Levi*, so there has been some scholarly speculation concerning its source.[23] In CD X, 5 (= 4Q270 6 IV, 16) there is a rule concerning the judges of the congregation, that ten should be elected, four from 'the tribe of Levi and Aaron and six from Israel'. There is nothing surprising about such a rule, but its literary context deserves some comment because CD X continues by legislating the upper age limit for judges to be 60, a ruling it justifies through an allusion to a text that is very close to *Jubilees* 23.11. *Jubilees* 22—3 contains Abraham's blessing of Jacob and notice of his death and is a pivotal text for understanding the purpose of *Jubilees* as a whole.

The Levites occur in both sections of the *Damascus Document* too. CD III, 21 contains the very significant interpretation of Ezekiel 44.15. The Hebrew text of Ezekiel is best understood as referring to one group, 'the Levitical priests, the sons of Zadok', but in the citation of Ezekiel in CD III the text is slightly adjusted so that it refers to three groups – the priests, the Levites and the sons of Zadok. The subsequent identification of these three groups implies that there were the *šby yśr'l* who departed from the land of Israel, Levites who joined them, and the elect of Israel who shall stand at the end of days. This last term could well include the remnants of the first two groups.[24] It is worth noting that the joining of the Levites is a play upon the name of Levi, the third son of Leah, through whose birth she hopes 'to be joined to Jacob'.[25]

In the Laws (CD IX–XVI) Levites are mentioned three times. In XIII, 3 in the rule for the assembly of the camps it is stated that wherever there are ten men together there must be a priest learned in the *Book of Hagu*, but that, if the priest is not expert, then a Levite is to do the

---

23 See, e.g., J. Greenfield, 'The Words of Levi Son of Jacob in Damascus Document IV, 15–19', *RevQ* 13 (1988): 319–22.

24 As proposed by P. R. Davies, *Behind the Essenes: History and Ideology in the Dead Sea Scrolls* (BJS 94; Atlanta: Scholars Press, 1987), 52–4.

25 Gen. 29.34; the same etymology with a different application is represented in *Jub.* 31.16.

interpreting.[26] The page continues by describing what occurs when a judgement has to be made involving the law of blemishes: the priest is to make the pronouncement, but the overseer shall instruct him in the exact meaning of the law *(bprwš htwrh)*. Taking the two items together it is reasonable to suppose that the overseer, since he does not make the pronouncement himself, was a Levite, though the text does not actually say this. CD XIII, 7–8 continues by outlining the functions of the overseer of the camp; his first duty is 'to instruct the many in the works of God'. The other two occurrences of Levites in the Laws of the *Damascus Document* are close together in CD XIV, 4 and 5 (= 4Q268 2, 1). In the rule for the assembly of all the camps the priests are enrolled first, the Levites second, the Israelites third and proselytes fourth. This formula is repeated for the inscription of the enrolment.

The juxtaposition in the *Damascus Document* of material concerning Levi with allusion to the *Book of Jubilees* suggests a line of tradition which is supported by other documents as well. To begin with there is the *Testament of Qahat*, an Aramaic work extant in a single copy from Cave 4 (4Q542).[27] Qahat, the son of Levi, is the speaker and he entrusts all his books to Amram his son in a manner which parallels the action of Jacob in *Jubilees* 45.15: 'And he gave all of his books and his fathers' books to Levi, his son, so that he might preserve them and renew them for his sons until this day.'[28] Of a similar testamentary genre are the seven copies of the Aramaic *Visions of Amram* of which manuscripts a (4Q543) and c (4Q545) preserve the title: 'Copy of the book of the words of visions of Amram, son of Qahat, son of Levi. All that he declared and commanded to his sons on the day of his death.'[29] There is also the *Aramaic Levi Document* variously found in six manuscripts from Cave 4; Levi[a] ar

---

26 Y. Yadin has proposed that the *Book of Hagu* may be none other than the *Temple Scroll*: *The Temple Scroll*, 1.393–94 (Hebrew, 1.301); for the history of research on the identification of this book, see Yadin's footnotes.

27 J. T. Milik, '4Q Visions de Amram et une citation d'Origène', *RB* 79 (1972): 96–7; E. Puech, 'Le testament de Qahat en araméen de la grotte 4', *RevQ* 15 (1991): 23–54; Puech's principal edition is available in DJD 31, 257–82 and references to Levi occur at 4Q542 1 I, 8; 1 I, 11; 1 II, 11.

28 Trans. O. S. Wintermute in *OTP* 2.137.

29 J. T. Milik, '4Q Visions de Amram et une citation d'Origéne', 77–92. The visions contain major elements of eschatological dualism and mention Abraham prominently. See the principal editions by E. Puech of the manuscripts containing this composition (4Q543–49) in DJD 31, 283–405. The name Levi occurs in 4Q545 1a I, 1; 4Q547 8, 2.

(4Q213) was assigned by Milik to the end of the second or beginning of the first century B.C.E.[30] In his opinion the original *Testament of Levi* was a Samaritan work 'composed in the course of the third century [B.C.E.], if not towards the end of the fourth'.[31] Of immediate interest for this study is that 4QLevi[b] ar (4Q213a) 2, 13 situates Levi's vision in Abel Mayin, a geographical location deduced from 2 Chronicles 16.4,[32] and another example of the indirect influence of the Chronicler on much of this material. Alongside these three testamentary compositions must be cited 3Q7,[33] a text which mentions the Angel of the Presence. 3Q7 6, 2 contains the single word, 'Levi'. The overall subject matter of the text corresponds with *Testament of Judah* 25.2: 'And the Lord blessed Levi; the Angel of the Presence blessed me.'

The presence of testamentary compositions amongst the Qumran library says something about the milieu in which they were passed on. However, it is as yet impossible to determine quite what the original setting of the composition was and so it is difficult to see their overall significance for our purposes, except that it seems remarkable how many of those that have survived, even if only fragmentarily, are to be associated with Levi and his descendants. In the *Testaments of the Twelve Patriarchs* the tribe of Levi assumes a preeminent place, as it does also in the *Book of Jubilees*. In *Jubilees* Isaac blesses Levi first (31.13–17), then Judah. Although a mighty prince will come from Judah (31.18–20), Levi is still the ruling tribe: the children of Levi 'shall be judges and princes and chiefs of all the descendants of Jacob's sons. They shall speak the Lord's

---

30 J. T. Milik, 'Le Testament de Lévi en araméen', *RB* 62 (1955): 389–406; *The Books of Enoch: Aramaic Fragments of Qumrân Cave 4* (Oxford: Clarendon Press, 1976), 23–4. The translated text is clearly laid out in relation to *T. Levi* in H. W. Hollander and M. de Jonge, *The Testaments of the Twelve Patriarchs: A Commentary* (SVTP 8; Leiden: Brill, 1985), 457–69; see also the principal editions of the Aramaic Levi documents by M. E. Stone and J. C. Greenfield in DJD 22, 1–72. For related compositions see also E. Puech, 'Fragments d'un apocryphe de Lévi et le personnage eschatologique. 4QtestLev[c-d](?) et 4QAJa', in *The Madrid Qumran Congress* (ed. J. Trebolle Barrera and L. Vegas Montaner; STDJ 11; Leiden: Brill; Madrid: Editorial Complutense), 449–501; and the principal editions of 4Q540–41 by Puech in DJD 31, 213–56.

31 J. T. Milik, *The Books of Enoch*, 24.

32 See H. W. Hollander and M. de Jonge, *The Testaments of the Twelve Patriarchs: A Commentary*, 133–4, for more parallels, especially between the Levi traditions and *Jubilees*.

33 M. Baillet, J. T. Milik, R. de Vaux, *Les 'Petites Grottes' de Qumrân*, p. 99; Baillet labels the very fragmentary text 'Un apocryphe mentionnant l'ange de la presence'.

word in righteousness, and dispense all his judgements in righteousness' (*Jub.* 31.15). It is no accident that fragments of the *Book of Jubilees* have been found in Caves 1, 2, 3, 4 and 11. The centrality of the figure of Jacob in the *Book of Jubilees* cannot be underestimated.[34] The many and various associations between *Jubilees* and the writings associated with Enoch have been frequently pointed out; naturally Levi is not mentioned in the latter but the overlap in cultic concerns shows that these various writings were transmitted by those with interests in common with the texts noted in this study.

One last text from the Qumran caves deserves a mention. *Pesher Habakkuk* purports to offer a demonstration that the prophecy of Habakkuk is fulfilled in the contemporary life of the community. Although there are commentaries on other prophets, albeit not explicitly on Jeremiah or Ezekiel, it may be significant to ask why Habakkuk should be singled out for such treatment. Part of the answer may lie in his Levitical associations. In *Bel and the Dragon* Habakkuk takes the imprisoned Daniel his dinner. Part of the superscription to the chapter in the LXX reads: 'From the prophecy of Habakkuk, son of Joshua of the tribe of Levi.' The Hebrew Bible tells us nothing of Habakkuk's tribe or parentage, but from this superscription we may presume that by the first century B.C.E. Habakkuk was associated by some Jews with the tribe of Levi. In the story of the Dragon Habakkuk gives Daniel pottage and bread, just as Jacob gives Esau (Gen. 25.29–34).[35] The Levitical association of Habakkuk may also account for the addition of the hymnic Chapter 3 to the actual prophecy. Given the difficulties that modern scholars have had in identifying the actual events to which *Pesher Habakkuk* seems to allude, it might be that the commentary is actually the work of those who were not familiar with the early history of the Qumran community. Perhaps *Pesher Habakkuk* represents a Levitical rewriting of the history of the community at some point after this group affiliated themselves with the Qumran Community.

---

34 On the centrality of Jacob in *Jubilees*, such as the comparison of Jacob with Adam (*Jub.* 2. 23), see J. C. Endres, *Biblical Interpretation in the Book of Jubilees* (CBQMS 18; Washington: Catholic Biblical Association of America, 1987). Jacob is mentioned as the father of Levi in 4Q225 2 II, 11 (DJD 13, 151) and 4Q226 7, 4 (DJD 13, 165) and Jacob and Levi are in sequence together in 4Q225 2 II, 12 (DJD 13, 151) and probably in 4Q226 7, 5 (DJD 13, 165).
35 The only other reference to pottage and bread together is when Elisha feeds the sons of the prophets (2 Kgs 4.38–44).

LEVI AND THE LEVITES IN THE NEW TESTAMENT

In the New Testament the references to individuals named Levi or to Levites are to be found in Mark, Luke–Acts, John, Hebrews and Revelation. Taking the relatively simpler cases first, it can be seen that the explicit mention of Levi in the list of the tribes in Revelation 7.4–8, when taken as a list of the gates of the heavenly Jerusalem, places him in the centre of the east wall of the city, which is the same as his position according to 11QT^a. The list in Revelation 7.4–8 might possibly be dependent upon that of the *Temple Scroll*.[36] In Hebrews 7 all the references to Levi and the Levites are negative as the Levitical priesthood is contrasted with that of Christ according to the order of Melchizedek but, although negative, the issues discussed in the chapter, and the language used, reflect those of the 'Levitical' texts from Qumran: tithing (Heb. 7.5–10), the reception of the Law (Heb. 7.11) and the new Law (Heb. 7.12). In addition, the contrast in Hebrews 7 is between the Levitical priesthood and that of Melchizedek, king of Salem, priest of the Most High God, a figure and terminology associated indirectly with Jesus in Luke 1.32 and 76 ('Most High'), in Luke 4.16–22 (cf. 11QMelch)[37] and possibly in John 4.23 (Salim).

In the Fourth Gospel the single explicit reference to Levites occurs at 1.19. If, as is widely accepted, John 1.1–18 are seen to form a distinct Prologue to the Gospel, then 1.19 is the first verse of what is now almost a second introduction to the Gospel.[38] The chief characteristic of this second introduction is its serial listing of christological titles, most of which are used of Jesus in the rest of the Gospel. In John 1.19–28 the

---

36 As argued by B. Thiering, 'The Date of Composition of the Temple Scroll', in G. J. Brooke (ed.), *Temple Scroll Studies*, 103–4.

37 Among those completely dissociating 11QMelch from Hebrews 7 are F. Laub, *Bekenntnis und Auslegung: Die paränetische Funktion der Christologie im Hebräerbrief* (Regensburg: F. Pustet, 1980), 38–40; D. Peterson, *Hebrews and Perfection* (SNTSMS 47; Cambridge: Cambridge University Press, 1982), 243. F. L. Horton states clearly that there is no literary dependence between the two texts, but that 11QMelch must be considered as providing much background material on the use of the Melchizedek figure in late second temple times: *The Melchizedek Tradition* (SNTSMS 30; Cambridge: Cambridge University Press, 1976), 167–70; a similar position is taken by F. Manzi, *Melchisedek e l'angelologia nell'Epistola agli Ebrei e a Qumran* (AB 136; Rome: Pontificio Istituto Biblico, 1997).

38 For more detail on this section of the Fourth Gospel see G. J. Brooke, 'The Temple Scroll and the New Testament', in G. J. Brooke (ed.), *Temple Scroll Studies*, 186–92 (Chapter 6 in this book).

titles are expressed negatively through John the Baptist's denials, in the rest of the chapter they are expressed positively: Lamb of God (Jn 1.29, 36), Man (1.30), Son of God (1.34, 49), Rabbi (1.38, 49), Messiah (1.41), He of whom Moses in the Law and also the Prophets wrote, Jesus of Nazareth, son of Joseph (1.45), King of Israel (1.49) and Son of Man (1.51). This christological compilation is organized into four days; days two and three both open with the declaration 'Behold, the Lamb of God', so structurally the opening and closing days, the first and the fourth, may have some relationship to one another. The content of the first and fourth days suggests as much too.

The first day contains John the Baptist's firm denials that he fulfils any of the roles of Christ, Elijah or the prophet. R. Bultmann has been the chief advocate of identifying the perspective of the Baptist material in the Fourth Gospel as polemic against the Baptist and his followers.[39] However, it is important not to see John 1.19–28 in too negative a fashion, for the polemic of these verses may be addressed to some element of the Johannine community, not to those outside. As such they justify the followers of the Baptist who have joined the early Christian movement, as indeed even Bultmann recognized.[40] If it is indeed the case that John was or was considered to be an Essene,[41] then the depiction of his cross-examination by the priests and Levites gives his answers a pedigree that may reflect the origin and status both of John and of some of his followers.

The fourth day (John 1.43–51) begins with Jesus calling Philip. Philip then in turn calls Nathanael by telling him that Jesus of Nazareth, son of Joseph, is the one of whom Moses and the prophets wrote. When Jesus meets Nathanael he declares him to be an Israelite in whom there is no

---

39 R. Bultmann, *Das Evangelium des Johannes* (Göttingen: Vandenhoeck & Ruprecht, 1964); *The Gospel of John: A Commentary* (Oxford: Blackwell, 1971).

40 'It is the Baptist's disciples themselves who leave their master to follow Jesus' (*The Gospel of John: A Commentary*, 84).

41 Many scholars have pointed this out, paying particular attention to the use of Isa. 40.3 in the Gospels and in 1QS VIII, 12–18; e.g., W. H. Brownlee, 'John the Baptist in the New Light of Ancient Scrolls', in *The Scrolls and the New Testament* (ed. K. Stendahl; London: SCM Press, 1958), 33–53; D. R. Schwartz, 'On Quirinius, John the Baptist, the Benedictus, Melchizedek, Qumran and Ephesus', *RevQ* 13 (1988): 635–46; H. Lichtenberger, 'The Dead Sea Scrolls and John the Baptist: Reflections on Josephus' Account of John the Baptist', in *The Dead Sea Scrolls: Forty Years of Research* (ed. D. Dimant and U. Rappaport; Jerusalem: Magnes Press, Yad Izhak Ben-Zvi; Leiden: Brill, 1992), 340–6.

guile, which seems to contrast him with Jacob. The oft-repeated verb 'see' (1.46, 47, 48, 50, 51) may be a play on the popular etymology of Israel as the 'man who saw God'. This new Jacob will also see heaven opened and the angels of God ascending and descending on the Son of Man, a motif which since Augustine has been recognized as an allusion to the ladder in Jacob's dream (Gen. 28:12).

Together the first and fourth days present a combination of ideas which can be variously seen in the Dead Sea Scrolls. There are priests and Levites encountering a figure who may have been or may have been thought to have been an Essene. Nathanael, portrayed as a second Jacob, sees Jesus, is seen by him, and is promised through the adaptation of the language of Jacob's dream that he will see even greater things. Jesus is 'son of Joseph' and the one pointed to by a right understanding of the Law and the Prophets. The author of the Fourth Gospel perhaps has the Pharisees send Levites to cross-examine John because he is concerned that some members of his community who were once Levites, perhaps among the Qumranites, be convinced that their turning to Jesus as the Christ be offered some full justification by those they would respect. There is much else in the Fourth Gospel that supports such a view, both details like the other Jacob materials in John 4 and the particular way in which the Gospel writer has Jesus replace the Temple, and also more general matters such as the extensive use of Wisdom and Wisdom traditions to offer interpretations of the Law.[42]

In Luke–Acts, the references to Levi and Levites fall into three categories. Firstly, there are the two occurrences of the proper name Levi in the genealogy of Jesus. Over against Matthew's very different genealogy, it is important to appreciate that the genealogy in Luke is best understood when arranged in a tabular form as 11 groups of seven names. This results in a periodization of time from Adam to Jesus in a picture of 11 weeks. The organization of history into 11 weeks of seven generations is to be found in *1 Enoch* 10.12, now extant in 4QEnoch[b] 1 IV, 10: Michael is there instructed to bind the Watchers for 70 generations.[43] It is difficult to determine when the binding took place, but it appears that it must be

---

42 For more detail on Wisdom and the Law in the Fourth Gospel see G. J. Brooke, 'Christ and the Law in John 7–10', in B. Lindars (ed.), *Law and Religion: Essays on the Place of Law in Israel and Early Christianity*, 102–12.

43 I owe this observation and some of the following material to R. J. Bauckham, *Jude and the Relatives of Jesus in the Early Church* (Edinburgh: T & T Clark, 1990), 315–78.

after Enoch himself has witnessed against them (*Jub.* 4.22). Enoch was known to belong to the seventh generation from Adam (*1 Enoch* 60.8; 93.3; *Jub.* 7.39; Jude 14); together with a binding of the Watchers for 70 generations, world history is thus portrayed as of 11 weeks of generations. For Luke's genealogy, as Enoch is the seventh, so Jesus is the ultimate seventy-seventh, and Jesus' only namesake in the list is not surprisingly the forty-ninth.

It is in the seventh and eleventh weeks of generations, both of which end with the name of Jesus, that the name Levi features. On both occasions it is in third place and followed by a figure named either Maththat or Matthat.[44] In the first generation, it is Enosh who is named third. In *Jubilees* 4.12 Enosh is clearly designated as the one who 'was the first to call the name of the Lord upon the earth'.[45] Although in most later rabbinic understanding Enosh is identified with the invocation of false gods,[46] the placing of a Levi twice in the same position in the Lukan genealogy suggests that for the compiler of the genealogy Enosh could be identified in a way akin to the tradition represented in *Jubilees* as the founder of worship. Thus a particular cultic eschatology seems to influence the construction of the text, a viewpoint which discloses the cultic aspect of the theological perspective of the genealogy, a concern which is matched with the Law and Wisdom tradition associated with the learned scribe of whom Enoch is the archetype.[47] All this is of a piece with what can be seen elsewhere in the Lukan hymnic materials and shows that the Lukan genealogy is not simply based on the ten weeks of the Apocalypse of Weeks (*1 Enoch* 93 [weeks 1–7] and 91.12–16 [weeks 8–10], which are now preserved in their original order in 4QEn^g ar), but combines the cultic and legal viewpoint of the Apocalypse with the periodization of *1 Enoch* 10. None of this means that Jesus was descended from the tribe of Levi; it is a theological perspective which Luke takes over from his sources and from those who were the traditors of those sources.

In the *Apocalypse of Weeks* after the tenth week 'there will be many weeks without number for ever in goodness and righteousness, and from then on sin will never again be mentioned' (*1 Enoch* 91.17). In

---

44 One wonders whether this proximity of Levi and Matthew is akin to the name change in the story of the call of Levi.

45 Trans. O. S. Wintermute, *OTP*, 2.62.

46 This is well set out by S. D. Fraade, *Enosh and his Generation: Pre-Israelite Hero and History in Postbiblical Interpretation* (SBLMS 30; Chico: Scholars Press, 1984).

47 E.g., 4QEn^e 2, 2; J. T. Milik, *The Books of Enoch*, 237.

11QMelchizedek II, 7–8 those of Melchizedek's lot may be considered to receive release and sit in judgement at the end of the tenth jubilee.[48] It has to be asked whether this tenth jubilee corresponds with the tenth of the *Apocalypse of Weeks* or with the tenth of *1 Enoch* 10.12. Perhaps it is to some extent an amalgamation of both schemes, just like the Lukan genealogy. This is confirmed by the fact that in 11QMelchizedek the events of the tenth jubilee are explained through the atonement jubilee text of Leviticus 25.9–13 juxtaposed with allusions to Isaiah 61.1–3, the very text which Jesus claims is fulfilled as he speaks in the synagogue at Nazareth (Luke 4.18–21).[49]

It is no surprise to see the name Joseph featuring more than once in the genealogy. It occurs at the end of the sixth week, with which the *Apocalypse of Weeks* identifies the fall of the temple, and at the end of the tenth week, which the *Apocalypse* associates with the judgement of the Watchers before the time of weeks without number.

It is possibly no coincidence that in Luke Jesus' ministry begins with the work and preaching of John the Baptist and then three pericopae which are linked not just redactionally by the Gospel author but also by certain elements in each of them which echo materials from the Dead Sea Scrolls. In the genealogy of Jesus the Law and the temple and those connected with them are particularly significant in its chronological arrangement; the positioning of Levi is a signal of these overall concerns. In the temptation narrative it can be convincingly argued that Luke's order depends upon Psalm 106 and its Levitical concerns.[50] In Luke 4.10–11 there is also the explicit use of Psalm 91 which is doubly significant: on the one hand, this Psalm occupies a key place in the fourth book of Psalms after the introductory Psalm 90 of Moses and, on the other

---

48 See 11QMelch as read and restored by E. Puech, 'Notes sur le manuscrit de XIQMelkîsédeq', *RevQ* 12 (1985–7): 483–513; see also the principal edition in DJD 23, 221–41. The 'Sons of Levi' are mentioned in the fragmentary 4Q247 5 (DJD 36, 189) in the so-called 4QPesher on the Apocalypse of Weeks.

49 For more detail see G. J. Brooke, *Exegesis at Qumran: 4QFlorilegium in its Jewish Context* (JSOTSup 29; Sheffield: JSOT Press, 1985), 319–23.

50 H. Swanston, 'The Lukan Temptation Narrative', *JTS* 17 (1966): 71: Ps. 106.14–15 retells Ex. 16 and Num. 11.4, 106.19–20 retells Ex. 32, 106.32–3 retells Num. 20.2–13; the events are alluded to in the same order in Luke's account of the temptations, suggesting a liturgical background under the influence of that Levitical Psalm. On the extensive use of Deuteronomy in Luke's redaction see J. Drury, *Tradition and Design in Luke's Gospel* (London: Darton, Longman & Todd, 1976), 138–64.

hand, it occurs in 11QapPs (11Q11) as part of a collection of liturgical pieces probably all to be associated with apotropaic rituals associated with the fear of possession and the need for exorcism.[51] In the synagogue at Nazareth Jesus tells the gathering that Isaiah 61.1–2 (Lk. 4.18–19) has been fulfilled and the response of the people is to ask whether he is Joseph's son. There are many other motifs too which show how the Gospel writer has modified his sources for his own purposes, but despite those redactional concerns, there seems to be enough within the three pericopae to suggest that they were originally formulated to satisfy a section of the early Christian community which may have had either Levitical or Essene connections or both.

The second item concerning a Levi in Luke involves one of the Twelve. In the Lukan parallel to Mark 2.13–17 (Lk. 5.27–32) Levi is named twice.[52] Whereas in Mark Levi sits at the place of toll, in Luke he is explicitly designated as a tax-collector, 'publican'. This might be considered of little significance except that only in Luke is there explicit mention that tax-collectors have been baptized by John the Baptist (Lk. 3.12), a point that Luke repeats later on (Lk. 7.29). Perhaps Luke is concerned for some reason to suggest that those who might identify with Levi through his patriarchal name may have been among John the Baptist's original baptisands. After Levi's conversion, it is only in Luke that it is made clear that it is Levi himself who makes a great feast for Jesus together with a crowd of tax-collectors and others.

Third, there are two texts in Luke–Acts which describe Levites. One is in the summary pericope on the life of the congregation in Jerusalem, Acts 4.32–7. Perhaps, in light of what has been said elsewhere in this catalogue of texts, it is significant that he is called Joseph; he is a Levite from Cyprus whom the apostles may have surnamed Barnabas.[53] But as well as his name and function, it is notable that the language and general

---

51 See, e.g., E. Puech, '11QPsAp[a]: un rituel d'exorcisme', *RevQ* 14 (1989–90): 377–408; 'Les deux derniers Psaumes davidiques du rituel d'exorcisme – 11QPsAp[a] IV 4–V 14', in D. Dimant and U. Rappaport (ed.), *The Dead Sea Scrolls: Forty Years of Research*, 64–89; also the principal edition in DJD 23, 181–205.

52 J. A. Fitzmyer, *The Gospel According to Luke I–IX* (AB 28; Garden City: Doubleday, 1981), 590, has noted that the reading of *Iachōbon* for Levi in several manuscripts is an obvious scribal change, influenced by Mark 3.18.

53 H. Conzelmann, *A Commentary on the Acts of the Apostles* (Hermeneia; Philadelphia: Fortress Press, 1987), 36, has noted how scholars have tried to interpret the name Barnabas appropriately, suggesting in particular that its interpretation in Acts 4.36 fits better Manaen of Acts 13.1.

content of the pericope in which he features has more similarities to the sectarian Dead Sea Scrolls than any other part of Acts.[54] The group of believers is called a company (*plēthos*) which might be considered to be a suitable counterpart to the use of *rab* and *rabbim* in the *Rule of the Community*.[55] The way in which Acts 4.33–5 describes how the company had everything in common corresponds with what can be seen of the Qumran community in 1QS I, 1–12; VI, 2–3 and 16–20, which is confirmed for the administrator of the Essene movement generally by Philo: 'He takes it and at once buys what is necessary and provides food in abundance and anything else which human life requires' (*Hypothetica* 8.11.10).[56] Acts 4.32 describes the company as of one heart and soul, a phrase which recalls Deuteronomy 6.5. This same text occurs in association with the parable of the good Samaritan, the other text in Luke–Acts to feature a Levite.

This does not seem coincidental, since both episodes illustrate the same point concerning care of the needy. In Acts the Levite provides the positive example, in Luke 10 the priest and the Levite provide the negative example. Linked to the use of Deuteronomy 6.5 is reference to Leviticus 19.18, part of the Holiness Code which is particularly significant also in the *Damascus Document*.[57] Two comments may be worthwhile. First, the *Temple Scroll* contains elaborate prescriptions for any Israelite coming into contact with any dead thing or object contaminated by a dead person. Though it was no sin to touch a corpse, the result was contamination that lasted for seven days. Since the *Temple*

---

54 Apart from Acts 4.33 which many think is a secondary interpolation. Overall it is significant that the biblical quotations in Acts 2—15 generally have more in common with biblical texts known from Qumran than with either the MT or LXX; so, e.g., J. Schmitt, 'Qumrân et la première génération judéo-chrétienne', in *Qumrân: Sa piété, sa théologie et son milieu* (ed. M. Delcor; BETL 46; Leuven: University Press, 1978), 393.

55 H.-W. Huppenbauer, 'RBYM, RWB, RB in der Sektenregel (1QS)', *TZ* 13 (1957): 136–7; J. A. Fitzmyer, 'Jewish Christianity in Acts in the Light of the Qumran Scrolls', in *Studies in Luke–Acts: Essays Presented in Honor of Paul Schubert* (ed. L. E. Keck and J. L. Martyn; London: SPCK, 1966), 245–6; reprinted in *Essays on the Semitic Background* of *the New Testament* (London: Chapman, 1971), 290–1.

56 H. Conzelmann, *A Commentary on the Acts of the Apostles*, 24, sees the information in Acts 4 as based on knowledge of the Qumran community; E. Haenchen, *The Acts of the Apostles: A Commentary* (Oxford: Blackwell, 1971), 234, on the other hand underlines the differences between Qumran and the early Church communities.

57 As pointed out by J. Murphy-O'Connor, 'A Literary Analysis of Damascus Document VI, 2–VIII, 3', *RB* 78 (1971): 210–20.

Scroll is clearly written with both a Levitical bias but also a general cultic concern, it could be that Jesus was speaking against laws which certain groups were stressing to the point where they abrogated others which were as significant and could also be deemed to come under the very Holiness Code that embodied the view of perfection for which some Jews longed. Second, the activity of the Samaritan shows that he clearly reads the neighbour of Leviticus 19.18 in the widest sense, to include all Jews and strangers as Leviticus 19.33–4 makes clear. That a lawyer should learn this lesson positively from a Samaritan and negatively from a priest and Levite, might suggest the ambience of cultic debate which Luke (and Jesus) are concerned to address.

Several similarities between Samaritan texts and the Dead Sea Scrolls have been pointed out: on the one hand, the sectarian character of the Samaritans was more apparant than real, especially after the destruction of the temple on Mount Gerizim and, on the other hand, their attitude towards some cultic matters appears remarkably similar to certain aspects of the organization and beliefs of the communities represented in the *Damascus Document* and the *Rule of the Community*.[58] Alongside these somewhat intangible parallels it must be remembered that in the Synoptic Gospels the material peculiar to Luke has many parallels with traditions that appear in the Fourth Gospel. The concern with the Samaritans is one example of this. In John 4 it is the Samaritan woman who has a lengthy dialogue with Jesus. She meets with him at Jacob's well and Jesus talks of living water; in CD VI, 4–11 the well is the Law. The *Damascus Document* goes on to identify this law with the covenant which the faithful will keep according to Deuteronomy 7. 9 (CD MS B); given the use of Deuteronomy 7 in 11QT^a II, 7–11, the covenant in the *Damascus Document* may include that made with Jacob at Bethel according to 11QT^a XXIX, 7–10.

In Mark there are no Levites, but the pericope on the call of Levi (Mk 2.13–14) serves a double duty function. It acts as an inclusion with Mark 1.16–20; between the calling of Simon, Andrew, James and John and the calling of Levi there is a sequence of healing miracles.[59] More importantly

---

58 See especially the detailed work of J. Bowman, *The Samaritan Problem: Studies in the Relationships of Samaritanism, Judaism and Early Christianity* (PTMS 4; Pittsburgh: Pickwick Press, 1975), esp. Ch. 4.

59 Levi's call is preceded in Mark by the healing of the leper; the use of Ps. 91 in an exorcistic composition at Qumran and the fact that according to Deut. 24.8 it is the Levitical priests who regulate in cases of leprosy may be significant.

for the purposes of this study the call of Levi introduces a series of disputes each of which contains several motifs with Levitical or Qumranic connections, or both, as well as with Pharisaic concerns. In the call story itself the name of Levi has caused some comment since it occurs in none of the lists of the Twelve in the New Testament and Matthew speaks solely of Matthew in the corresponding pericope identifying him as a tax-collector at another point in his Gospel. Some manuscripts attempt to solve the problem through the patronym, since in Mark 3.18 it is James, that is Jacob, who is son of Alphaeus.

The call of Levi leads directly into a discussion about table fellowship (Mk 2.15–17). This was a matter of concern to several groups within contemporary Judaism. For the Qumran community it is 1QSa (1Q28a) which speaks most clearly about it. It describes the Levites as among the men of renown in the official hierarchical organization of the community, and in describing the meal that takes place whenever ten men are gathered together, the sons of Aaron the priests come first, followed by the men of renown, including presumably the Levites. Only after them does the Messiah of Israel come and the leaders of the clans of Israel. The earlier section of 1QSa (1Q28a) defines those who are not eligible for official membership of the community; those described are the very groups with whom the Gospels portray Jesus associating.

The following pericope concerns a debate with both the Pharisees and the disciples of John the Baptist about fasting. The story has Jesus answer his questioners through the figure of the bridegroom at the wedding and the parable of the new wine not being compatible with old wine skins. Intriguingly in the whole New Testament the phrase 'new wine' occurs only here and in the parallels in Matthew and Luke. From the *Temple Scroll* (11QT^a XIX, 11–XXI, 10) we now know that some Jews observed a new wine festival at which '[the priests shall drink] first and the Levites [after them]'. Perhaps it is now possible to see how the sayings about the wedding feast and the new wine were combined; perhaps Jesus even used them together. Both are sayings about feasts. For the new wine it is a matter of stating that the feast cannot be contained in old wine skins, the containers of everyday religious practice. Jesus is challenging the religious practice of two groups by reference to that of another. The Synoptic parallels support this. In Matthew 9.15 the 'fast' of Mark 2.19 is altered to 'mourn', perhaps an allusion to the obligatory Jewish fast of mourning on the ninth of Ab. Since the feast of new wine falls on the third of Ab, the proximity of dating would help the contrast, even given the difference in calendars. Luke also contains the saying that 'no one after drinking old wine desires new, for he says, "The old is good"' (5.39). This is not a contradiction of the earlier parable, but a pointer to the fact that the new wine is not superior to the old, but appropriate for the moment. If the original festal referent had been partially obscured by Mark, it seems to have been preserved by Matthew and Luke more clearly. Perhaps Levites in the early Christian community responsible for the compilation of this series of stories about Jesus appreciated the point precisely.[60]

The sequence of disputes ends with two concerned with right practice on the Sabbath, a matter of concern to Jews generally, but known to be the subject of particular rulings by those who compiled *Jubilees* and the Laws of the *Damascus Document*. In the first (Mk 2.23–8) the dispute concerns the plucking of grain on the Sabbath. Several matters are noteworthy here. To begin with Jesus illustrates his argument by using the example of David. Y. Yadin has noted that implicitly David features in the *Temple Scroll* as an authoritative interpreter of the Law: most obviously 1 Chronicles 28.11–19 implies that the plan for building the temple (which the *Temple Scroll* may purport to be) was entrusted to David, but in other ways too David's action is taken as normative in some way, even as this may affect the Levites.[61] Second, in this pericope the high priest is named as Abiathar. In the Samuel narrative Abiathar is high priest later, in David's reign, and it is Ahimelech who was high priest at the time of the incident Jesus uses. But in 1 Chronicles 18.16 and 24.6 Ahimelech is the son of Abiathar; we may suppose that Mark preserves an understanding that reflects the tradition of Chronicles and so links Abiathar with the shewbread incident. Furthermore, with Zadok (1 Chr. 15.11), Abiathar and some Levites are addressed by David as 'The heads of the father's houses of the Levites'. Third, Yadin has proposed that the seven baskets of crumbs that are collected after the feeding of the 4,000 are a reflection of the seven baskets of bread of the Feast of Consecration or Ordination described in 11QT^a XV, 3–5, and that these seven stand for the Herodians who for him are Essenes.[62] I have argued elsewhere that this identification of loaves and people requires that something similar be said about the 5,000 and the 12 baskets of crumbs.[63] It is in the incident

60 For more detail on this see G. J. Brooke, 'The Feast of New Wine and the Question of Fasting', *ExpTim* 95 (1983–4): 175–6.

61 E.g., concerning the distribution of booty see Y. Yadin, *The Temple Scroll*, 1.358–62 (Hebrew, 1.274–7).

62 Y. Yadin, *The Temple Scroll*, 1.138–9 (Hebrew, 1.111–12).

63 G. J. Brooke, 'The Temple Scroll and the New Testament', in G. J. Brooke (ed.), *Temple Scroll Studies*, 183–5 (Chapter 6 in this book).

of David and his men eating the shewbread that the connection can be made, since David asks for five loaves and is given 12.

The second Sabbath controversy story revolves around Jesus' question concerning whether or not it is lawful to save life on the Sabbath. The subject of the healing in the controversy is the man with the withered hand. In the light of the accumulating pieces of evidence in this catalogue of texts perhaps it is not surprising that the story of a similar healing whose language comes close to this incident in Mark 3.1–6 is that of the healing of Jeroboam's hand by the altar at Bethel (1 Kgs 13.4). In 1 Kings 12 it is explicitly stated that Jeroboam's wrongdoing is the making of two idolatrous golden calves and the making of houses on high places with priests both at Bethel and at Dan who were not of the Levites; the man of God appears from Judah and the altar at Bethel is destroyed, but not before Jeroboam has tried to intervene and had his hand temporarily withered. Clearly idolatry cannot be countenanced but Jeroboam's intervention on behalf of the altar of Bethel, though presumptuous, does not result in any permanent hurt. Those who might have been in favour of an altar at Bethel might have respected the protective action of Jeroboam while decrying his idolatry. In Mark it appears that Jesus fills the role of the man of God in healing the withered hand; then, as the prophet of Bethel sees to it that the man of God is killed, so in Mark 3.6 the Pharisees and the Herodians take counsel how to destroy Jesus.

Of the Synoptics it is only in this pericope in Mark that the Herodians feature. If what has been said about the significance of the numbers of baskets of crumbs in the two feeding miracles is credible, then it is a natural Marcan phenomenon to find Pharisees and Herodians juxtaposed in this passage.[64] Overall Mark seems to have preserved a series of disputes between Jesus and the Pharisees; the series runs from the call of a Levi to the counsel of the Herodians to kill Jesus. Although in their present form they are likely to be directed at concerns in Mark's contemporary non-Palestinian Jewish–Christian dialogue, in an earlier stage the series could well reflect debates whose formulation would have interested more than just Pharisees. Those people were concerned with table fellowship, with the right celebration of the feasts, with the model of David for

---

64 On the identification of the Herodians as Essenes see C. Daniel, 'Les Hérodiens du Nouveau Testament sont-ils des Esséniens?', *RevQ* 6 (1967–9): 30–53; 'Nouveaux arguments en faveur de l'identification des Hérodiens et des Esséniens', *RevQ* 7 (1969–71): 399.

interpreting the Law, with affairs at Bethel; perhaps some of them had at some time been Herodians.

In this section of Mark as in Luke 3.1—4.30 we may have a set of traditions that contain matters of Levitical and Essene interest. Elsewhere in the New Testament, as is well known, there are many parallels with the whole corpus of the literature discovered in the Qumran caves. In the parallels mentioned here it seems as if something more specific is identifiable.

CONCLUSION

The catalogue of texts cited here is not very extensive, nor does space allow any very detailed discussion of individual pericopae. However, there is enough material here to discern common threads running through many of these passages which mention Levi or the Levites explicitly. These threads are especially a high regard for Enoch, Jacob (and Bethel), Levi and Moses, and an insistence that it is the prerogative of the Levites to interpret the Law. Links between the Enoch corpus, *Jubilees* and the *Temple Scroll* suggest that there was a common calendrical inheritance which bound the authors of this literature and which separated them from what was practised in Jerusalem in the late second temple period.

It is difficult to be precise about the history of this group of Levites who pushed their cause in the literature in which they feature. From the *Damascus Document* it seems as if they joined the movement at some time. Perhaps they did not arrive at Qumran until several decades after that community had been founded. When they came, however, they brought an extensive literature out of which they attempted to influence the copying of the Qumran community's own documents. Perhaps some had had their hopes raised by the rebuilding programme of Herod the Great, only to find that after his death, there was no room in the cultic practice of Jerusalem for them. Some may have heard John the Baptist. Some may have become members of early Christian communities and brought their concerns into early Christian preaching; perhaps their growing tendency in the first century B.C.E. towards insisting on the primacy of a Levitical Messiah[65] found a welcome hearing among early

---

65 On the wider issues of the Levitical Messiah see A. Hultgård, 'The Ideal "Levite", the Davidic Messiah, and the Saviour Priest in the Testaments of the Twelve Patriarchs', in *Ideal Figures in Ancient Judaism: Profiles and Paradigms* (ed. J. J. Collins and G. W. E. Nickelsburg; SBLSCS 12; Chico: Scholars Press, 1980), 93–110.

Christian groups, though it had to be adjusted in the way Hebrews 7 implies.

The listing of these two sets of texts one after the other discloses features that may have been characteristic of particular Levitical groups who were largely disaffected with the practice of the cult at Jerusalem. Some of them were affiliated with the movement which preserved the scrolls, perhaps especially in its Qumran form, others with some of the early Christian communities, and some possibly with both. We appear to be scratching at the surface but, even so, these textual characteristics are mutually helpful for the better understanding of all the texts concerned.[66]

---

66 This article was completed in 1989. Only a few compositions published since the general release of the remaining unpublished scrolls in 1991 have contained references to Levi or the Levites, all of which can be reconciled with the kind of analysis offered in this study. In addition to the references given in some footnotes above, in Aramaic there are 4Q245 1 I, 5 (Levi in a genealogical list of priests) and 11Q18 30, 2 (a reference to the Levites sacrificing in the New Jerusalem), and in Hebrew, 4Q281 f, 1 (a reference in an unidentified fragment to the portions assigned to the Levites with language akin to Deut. 12.12), 4Q379 1, 2 (Levi is mentioned before Reuben in a list, suggesting an emphasis on Levi) and 4Q423 5, 1a (an incidental reference to Levi in an admonition). The most significant secondary literature relating to the concerns of this study is to be found in R. C. Stallman, 'Levi and the Levites in the Dead Sea Scrolls', *JSP* 10 (1992): 163–89; R. A. Kugler, *From Patriarch to Priest: The Levi-Priestly Tradition from Aramaic Levi to Testament of Levi* (SBLEJL 9; Atlanta: Scholars Press, 1996); M. E. Stone, 'Levi', in *Encyclopedia of the Dead Sea Scrolls* (ed. L. H. Schiffman and J. C. VanderKam; New York: Oxford University Press, 2000), 485–6; R. A. Kugler, 'Priests', in *Encyclopedia of the Dead Sea Scrolls*, 688–93.

8

The *Apocryphon of Levi*[b]? and the Messianic Servant High Priest

INTRODUCTION

The texts from Qumran associated with Levi are numerous and complex and much detailed study has yet to be done before their relationships to each other and to the whole variegated history of the traditions associated with the *Testament of Levi* in particular can be adequately described.[1] The purpose of this chapter is to offer a translation in English of the two principal fragments of what has been labelled 4QApocryphon of Levi[b]? ar (4Q541) so as to draw attention to the presence in them of language from Isaiah. The passages in these two fragments seem to introduce a degree of significant evidence for the debate about the extent of the influence of the Suffering Servant (especially Isa. 52.13—53.12) on some passages in the New Testament.

Although there is no agreed list there are now several manuscripts closely associated with the traditions of the *Testament of Levi*. Much has become clearer since J. T. Milik made his presentation at the 1976 Louvain Qumran Congress. Then he spoke of numerous fragments of

---

1 It was a privilege to offer the original form of this short study in honour of Professor M. de Jonge who has contributed so much to the study both of the *Testaments of the Twelve Patriarchs* and of New Testament christology. As will become clear this study is heavily dependent upon the editorial and interpretative work of E. Puech, 'Fragments d'un apocryphe de Lévi et le personnage eschatologique: 4QTLevi[c–d](?) et 4QAJa', in *The Madrid Qumran Congress* (ed. J. Trebolle Barrera and L. Vegas Montaner; STDJ 11; Leiden: Brill; Madrid: Editorial Complutense, 1992), 449–501; and his principal edition of the same manuscripts: 'Apocryphe de Lévi', in *Qumrân Grotte 4.XXII: Textes araméens, première partie, 4Q529–549* (DJD 31; Oxford: Clarendon Press, 2001), 213–56.

five scrolls 'provenant du scriptorium qumranien' of which two, each represented by a single fragment, were of recent identification.[2]

THE QUMRAN LEVI COMPOSITIONS

The date and provenance of the *Testaments of the Twelve Patriarchs* as a whole is still under debate, but the pre-Christian date for some of the Aramaic sources which lie behind what eventually emerges as the Greek *Testament of Levi* is confirmed by the direct parallels between 1QTLevi (1Q21) Fragments 3 and 4 and the *Aramaic Levi Document* Bodleian Fragment Column a, lines 2–9 and 14–15.[3] In turn, these few lines correspond in part with Greek *T. Levi* 8.18–19, the end of the narration of the vision of the seven men who make promises about Levi's descendants. The process of editing the Cave 4 fragments associated with Levi has resulted in their editors proposing that none of the fragments from Cave 1 or Cave 4 can be clearly defined as belonging strictly speaking to a *Testament of Levi*, though some of the fragments clearly reflect some of the traditions that were subsequently to emerge in the Greek *Testament of Levi*. The fragments have now been variously assigned to the *Aramaic Levi Document* and are seen as seven early copies of the *Aramaic Levi Document* known from the Cairo Geniza.[4] 4Q213, 4Q213b, 4Q214, 4Q214a, 4Q214b all contain some correspondences with the Geniza

---

2 J. T. Milik, 'Ecrits préesséniens de Qumrân: d'Hénoch à Amram', in *Qumrân; sa piété, sa théologie et son milieu* (ed. M. Delcor; BETL 46; Gembloux: Duculot; Leuven: Leuven University Press, 1978), 95.

3 See the highlighted translation by J. C. Greenfield and M. E. Stone in H. W. Hollander and M. de Jonge, *The Testaments of the Twelve Patriarchs: A Commentary* (SVTP 8; Leiden: Brill, 1985), 460–2. For further interpretative detail, see, e.g., M. E. Stone, 'Enoch, Aramaic Levi and Sectarian Origins', *JSJ* 19 (1988): 159–70; J. C. Greenfield and M. E. Stone, 'Two Notes on the Aramaic Levi Document', in *Of Scribes and Scrolls: Studies on the Hebrew Bible, Intertestamental Judaism, and Christian Origins Presented to John Strugnell on the Occasion of his Sixtieth Birthday* (ed. H. W. Attridge, J. J. Collins and T. H. Tobin; College Theology Society Resources in Religion 5; Lanham: University Press of America, 1990), 153–61.

4 This is set out by M. E. Stone and J. C. Greenfield, 'Aramaic Levi Document', in *Qumran Cave 4.XVII: Parabiblical Texts, Part 3* (ed. J. VanderKam; DJD 22; Oxford: Clarendon Press, 1996), 1–72. This position has been accepted by H. W. Hollander and M. de Jonge, *The Testaments of the Twelve Patriarchs: A Commentary*, 21–5. Stone and Greenfield determine that the Aramaic Levi Document is extant in seven copies from Qumran, one from Cave 1 (1Q21) and six from Cave 4 (4Q213, 4Q213a, 4Q213b, 4Q214, 4Q214a, 4Q214b).

Aramaic Levi Document, sufficient in many places to permit the editors to reconstruct each manuscript cautiously; in addition, 4Q213 1 II overlaps with 4Q214a 2–3 II and 4Q214b 8. 4QLevi[b] ar (4Q213a) is important for demonstrating the antiquity of the prayer of Levi which is extant only in the Greek tradition and there only in MS e (eleventh century; Mt Athos Koutloumous 39), following *T. Levi* 2.3; it does not seem to be an integral part of the Greek *Testament of Levi*.[5]

In addition to the seven copies of the *Aramaic Levi Document*, there are two other manuscripts associated closely with Levi. 4QApocryphon of Levi[a]? ar (4Q540) and 4QApocryphon of Levi[b]? ar (4Q541) were first tentatively designated by Puech as 4QTLevi[c]? and 4QTLevi[d]?; they were previously labelled by J. Starcky as 4QAharonique A bis (4QAhA bis) and 4QAharonique A (4QAhA) respectively. Starcky had made some brief remarks about these texts in 1963 in his well-known article on Qumran messianism, but without the actual Aramaic texts it was difficult for scholars to know what to make of them.[6] To 4QApocryphon of Levi[a]? ar are assigned three fragments of which only one is extensive; the manuscript is dated palaeographically to the end of the second century B.C.E. or about 100 B.C.E. The principal fragment speaks of a little one (*z'yr'*) who seems to have endured some kind of distress (*'q'*)[7] and of whom it is predicted that he will suffer further hardship. He will leave the home of his birth and reside somewhere else, possibly at the sanctuary, whose building or rebuilding he will instigate. Puech comments that he cannot but help think of Levi and his tribe whose inheritance was not territorial, but the cult. The genre of the text is virtually impossible to define, despite several phrases which have their parallels in other testamentary and apocalyptic literature, but the numerical cipher (52?) in 1, 2, together with the hardships described may reflect a similar chronology of priesthood and what must be endured until the house of the Lord is restored anew as depicted in *Gk T. Levi* 17.8–10.[8]

---

5 See M. E. Stone and J. C. Greenfield, 'Aramaic Levi Document', ad loc. for the overlaps between the Qumran fragments and the Geniza *Aramaic Levi Document*; see Hollander and de Jonge, *The Testaments of the Twelve Patriarchs: A Commentary*, 10–17, for the description of the textual history of Greek *Testament of Levi*. K. Beyer, *Die aramäische Texte vom Toten Meer samt den Inschriften aus Palästina, dem Testament Levis aus der Kairoer Genisa, der Fastenrolle und den alten talmudischen Zitaten*, Band II (Göttingen: Vandenhoeck & Ruprecht, 2004) has retained the earlier designation of *Testament of Levi* for all the Aramaic materials, including 4Q540 and 4Q541.

6 J. Starcky, 'Les quatre étapes du messianisme à Qumrân', *RB* 70 (1963): 492.

7 A term used in *Targ. Isa.* 49.8; 50.10.

8 DJD 31, 218–20.

The principal text which Puech made available through the 1991 Madrid Qumran Congress is 4QApocryphon of Levi[b]? ar. This consists of 24 fragments, some of which are very small. In only two fragments are there complete or almost complete lines; five fragments preserve the bottom margin. It seems as if the manuscript was made up of columns with eight or nine lines each and the preservation of margins in the fragments allows the conclusion that the manuscript had at least eight or nine columns. There is a long vacat at the end of Fragment 24 which may correspond with the end of a major section or even of the whole manuscript. On palaeographic grounds Puech dates the manuscript to the end of the second century B.C.E. or about 100 B.C.E.; its writing is akin to that of 1QS, 1QIsa[a], and 4Q175 (4QTest). The Aramaic is replete with Hebraisms: notably the divine name is regularly *'l*, and in 6, 3 *mk'wbykh* appears to have been formed under the influence of *mk'b* which features in both Isaiah 53.3 and 53.4.

Since Puech has given a fully annotated version of his readings of the text, it is not necessary to repeat all his detailed work. Although there is nothing in 4QApocryphon of Levi[b]? ar that can be clearly identified as a quotation from what is later represented by the *Gk T. Levi*, it is apparent from the two principal fragments of the text as well as from other extant phrases that the text concerns a leading priest who has particular roles and who endures much, possibly being put to death. Although not a copy of the *T. Levi*, the association with some aspects of the *T. Levi* seems thoroughly appropriate, as this brief study of the two principal fragments will reveal.[9]

---

9 Other links with *T. Levi* include the following. In 4QApocryphon of Levi[a]? ar 1 II, 2 the word *t'wk*, 'error', appears as in 4QHen[c] 4, 8, and in Frags 31 and 52 of 1QTLevi; in Frag. 3, after a space, the phrase *'rw šny* may match a partially extant phrase of 1QTLevi 23, 1: *'ry šn*[. For 4QApocryphon of Levi[a]? ar 9 I, 7 with the straying of the people compare *Gk T. Levi* 4.2–4; 10.2; 14.1–2; 16.2–3 (see Puech, 'Fragments d'un apocryphe de Lévi', 455, 459, 469–70).

4QAPOCRYPHON OF LEVI[b]? AR (4Q541) 9 I, 2–7

(2)]his [wi]sdom.
And he will make expiation for all the sons of his generation;
     and he will be sent to all the sons of (3) his [peop]le (?).
His word is like a word of the heavens,
     and his teaching conforms to the will of God.
His eternal sun will shine,
     (4) and its fire will burn in all the ends of the earth.
And on the darkness it will shine;
     then the darkness will disappear (5) from the earth
     and the cloud from the dry land.
They will speak many words against him,
     and a number of (6) [fiction]s (?).
And they will invent fables against him,
     and they will speak all manner of infamies against him.
His generation evil will destroy,
     (7) [   ] will be;
And because falsehood and violence will be its setting,
     and the people will stray in his days;
     and they will be confounded.

The layout of the translation reflects Puech's proposal that the text is poetic in a way akin to *T. Levi* 18. Indeed, once it is acknowledged that the text seems to describe some future priest ('he will make expiation for all the sons of his generation and he will be sent to all the sons of his people'), then some parallels with *T. Levi* 18 are readily apparent. In 4Q541 9 I, 3–4 the images of light and fire echo several passages in the various traditions of the *T. Levi*, such as 'You will light up a bright light of knowledge in Jacob, and you will be as the sun to all the seed of Israel' (*T. Levi* 4.3)[10] and 'His star will arise in heaven, as a king, lighting up the light of knowledge as by the sun the day' (*T. Levi* 18.3).[11] Furthermore, the removal of darkness by this figure is matched in *T. Levi* 18.4 (he 'will

---

10 All translations of *Gk T. Levi* in this study are from H. W. Hollander and M. de Jonge, *The Testaments of the Twelve Patriarchs*.

11 Cf. also, '[w]ays of truth you will abandon, from all the paths of [. . .] you will be lax and you will walk in it [. . .] that d[ar]kness will come upon you' (4QLevi[a] 4, 5–7; DJD 22, 22). J. T. Milik (*The Books of Enoch*, 23–24) also restores the name Enoch in line 2; if such were the case, then perhaps some aspects of the earlier part of the

remove all darkness from under heaven') and during the priesthood of this new priest 'the Gentiles will be multiplied in knowledge upon the earth and will be enlightened through the grace of the Lord, but Israel will be diminished through ignorance and will be darkened in grief' (*T. Levi* 18.9). This seems to be a development of the thought of Isaiah 60.2–3.

Of similar substance as these parallels between 4Q541 9 I and *T. Levi* 18 is the parallel in 4Q541 9 II, 5 with *T. Levi* 8.2 which mentions 'seven men in white clothing' and the Bodleian fragment Column a, line 9: 'And those seven departed from me.' This Bodleian verse falls between what remains in 1QTLevi 3 and 4. Although 4Q541 9 II, 5 can be translated as 'seven rams', it is equally possible to translate the phrase as 'seven men'. Puech also finds an echo of the phrasing of 9 II, 7 in the Bodleian fragment Column d, lines 3–5 and 12–14 where what needs to be added to the sacrifice is described. That fits well, if the suitable subject for 4Q541 9 II, 5 is seven rams for some kind of whole burnt-offering.

As these parallels imply, the fragment of 4Q541 speaks of a priest, possibly the eschatological high priest, since his atoning function may be that of a particular Day of Atonement and his teaching and character are so brilliant and far-reaching. 4Q541 9 II, 5–7 also imply that he is the main object of vilification by those that detest him. If 4Q541 9 II, 4–7 is to be directly associated with the first column of the fragment, then its partial lines may also be understood to speak about the priest who may have had a vision,[12] and be offering a sacrifice of some sort. If the passage does indeed speak of the eschatological high priest, it is possible to construe the fragment as composed as if it is spoken by Levi to his sons concerning the future Levi.

The priestly role of teaching described in this fragment is not remarkable. However, when combined with certain phrases of other fragments, it is likely that it was a major hallmark of this priest's function. In 4Q541 2, 6–7, somebody speaks in the first person of receiving a book and speaking in riddles; there is also a vision. Furthermore, if 4Q541 Fragments 2 II, 3 and 4 I belong to the same column,[13] then the theme of

---

fragment would not be far from *Gk T. Levi* 14.1–3 which also mentions Enoch: 'heaven is purer than the earth and you are the lights of heaven as the sun and moon' (*T. Levi* 14.3).

12 This is a characteristic of *Gk T. Levi* which contains the narration of two visions: 2.3–6.2; 8.

13 As Puech convincingly proposes (DJD 31, 233–5).

wisdom becomes dominant, as also in 4Q541 7. If taken together, these fragments suggest that the wise man knows of books, parabolic speech and riddles, and has a vision in which a secret is revealed; according to 4Q541 7 the mission of the future wise man will involve wisdom in all her depths and to every extent. In 4Q541 9 the wise priest comes invested with heavenly words, teaching conformity to the will of God, and although his enemies will try to outdo his wisdom, their own verbal inventions will all be infamous lies and falsehoods. 4Q541 14 and 15 possibly mention a 'book' and 'divination' respectively.

The atoning function of this priest is clearly decribed in 4Q541 9. Here are the closest parallels with *Gk T. Levi*, especially 4.2–6 and 18.2–9, which have been mentioned above. The priest comes respelendent with light to illuminate all the sons of his people. He speaks with authority. It is important to note that this priest and the wise man of other fragments are almost certainly one and the same, as *Gk T. Levi* 2.10 suggests: the angel declares to Levi, 'You will stand near the Lord and will be his minister and will declare his mysteries to me.' The instructive and illuminating imagery of light is also a connecting point between this wise priest and the figure of the servant (Isa. 42.9; 49.6), about whom more is said below.

4QAPOCRYPHON OF LEVI[b]? AR 24 II, 2–6

2   . . .]and do not mourn in sackclo[th . . .] and do not [. . .

3   and] will redeem errors whether hi[dden . . . or] errors disclosed and the ri[ghteous] Go[d . . .

4   Search and seek and know what the dove has sought. And do not renounce him by means of exhaustion and hanging li[ke . . .

5   and a diadem/nail do not bring near to him, and you will establish for your father a name of joy and for all your brothers a proven foundation

6   you will desire {establish}. And you will see and rejoice in eternal light and you will not be from the enemy.

To understand this fragment completely satisfactorily is impossible, as the wide range of modern translations demonstrates.[14] Several features of

---

14 Puech himself has not unexpectedly changed his mind on several matters between the preliminary publication in 1992 and the principal edition in DJD 31 in 2001.

the above translation are offered tentatively. As with 4Q541 9 it is appropriate to begin by comparing some of its motifs with what is already known from Gk *T. Levi*. 4Q541 24 II, 2, 'do not mourn', can be compared with *T. Levi* 18.9: 'but Israel will be diminished through ignorance and will be darkened in grief'. With the phrase 'you will establish for your father a name of joy' can be juxtaposed the conclusion of *T. Levi* 18: 'Then Abraham and Isaac and Jacob will exult, and I, too, shall be glad, and all the saints will put on joy.' Whereas Levi in the *Gk T. Levi* talks of his joy in the first person, in 4Q541 24 II, 5 he speaks of himself in the third person. The final phrase of the fragment is difficult to translate. Evidently there is a contrast between light and something else, 'the one who hates', 'the enemy', just as there is a contrast between darkness and light, and the law of the Lord and the works of Beliar in *T. Levi* 19.1; similar contrasts can be seen in *T. Levi* 14.3–4 and 4Q213 4, 1–9, as Puech has observed.[15]

With these parallels in mind, it is possible to attempt to construe the significance of this remarkable fragment. The speaker addresses someone in the singular, instructing him to follow the example of the dove, a possible allusion to some element in the Noachic covenant, a feature which has also been thought to lie behind the appearance of the Spirit as a dove in the accounts of Jesus' baptism. The exhortation continues with two prohibitions followed by two positive statements. The prohibitions concern the treatment of one who is being punished or put to death. The first word of 4Q541 24 II, 5 is particularly difficult to interpret: it might be a defectively written *ṣyṣ'*, possibly 'diadem', part of the high priest's headgear, or it might be a term akin to the Syriac *ṣṣ'*, 'nail' or 'point'. Because the orthography in the manuscript is generally full, Puech argues against the first option and suggests that the context makes 'nail' preferable, since it could be a matter of crucifixion or torture.[16] In the exhortation there are then two statements about what the addressee will establish: joy for his father and a proven foundation for his brothers. The text ends with a formula that is almost a blessing. Since 4Q541 9 I, 7 describes how the future priest will suffer falsehood and violence, it is possible to construe 4Q541 24 as describing the violence done against

---

15 DJD 31, 256.
16 If the figure being tortured and hung (crucified?) here is indeed a future high priest, then a term involving a high priest's headgear may be suitable; the implication might then be that while he is suffering, he cannot function as a high priest.

this priest[17] and the addressee of the speech as the heir to what will happen afterwards.

THE USE OF ISAIAH IN 4Q541

Much could be said about the detailed interpretation of 4Q541 24, but the following comments, based on many of Puech's excellent observations, focus especially on the way in which allusions to Isaiah may help our understanding of the passage and the whole of the composition. For Fragment 24 the first possible link with Isaiah is in the phrase 'the ri[ghteous] Go[d . . .' (4Q541 24, 3) which echoes most clearly Isaiah 45.21: 'There is no other God besides me, a righteous God and a Saviour.'[18] The other likely link with Isaiah in this fragment is in line 6, 'and you will see light'; this corresponds with Isaiah 53.11a in 1QIsa[a] and

---

17 Since the publication of 11QT[a] LXIV, 7–13 the literature on Hebrew *tlh* and its Aramaic cognate has become extensive: J. M. Baumgarten, 'Does *TLH* in the Temple Scroll Refer to Crucifixion?', *JBL* 91 (1972): 472–81; reprinted in *Studies in Qumran Law* (SJLA 24; Leiden: Brill, 1977), 172–82; J. M. Baumgarten, 'Hanging and Treason in Qumran and Roman Law', *ErIsr* 16 (1982): 7–16; A. Dupont-Sommer, 'Observations nouvelles sur l'expression "suspendu vivant sur le bois" dans le Commentaire de Nahum (4QpNah II 8) à la lumière du Rouleau du Temple (11Q Temple Scroll LXIV 6–13', *CRAI* (1972): 709–20; J. A. Fitzmyer, 'Crucifixion in Ancient Palestine, Qumran Literature, and the New Testament', *CBQ* 40 (1978): 493–513; J. M. Ford, '"Crucify him, Crucify him" and the Temple Scroll', *ExpTim* 87 (1975–6): 275–8; D. J. Halperin, 'Crucifixion, the Nahum Pesher and the Rabbinic Penalty of Strangulation', *JJS* 32 (1981): 32–46; M. Hengel, *Crucifixion in the Ancient World and the Folly of the Message of the Cross* (London: SCM Press, 1977), 84–5; L. Merino Díez, 'La crucifixíon en la antigua literatura judía (Período Intertestamental)', *Est Ecl* 51 (1976): 5–27; L. Merino Díez, 'El suplicion de la cruz en la litertura judía intertestamental', *SBFLA* 26 (1976): 31–120; L. Rosso, 'Deuteronomio 21, 22: contributo del rotolo del tempio all valutazione di una variante medievale dei settanta', *RevQ* 9 (1977–8): 231–6; R. Vincent Saera, 'La halaká de Dt. 21, 22–23 y su interpretación en Qumrán y en Jn 19, 31–42', in *Salvación en la palabra: targum – derash – berith: homenaje al prof. A. Díez Macho* (ed. D. Munoz Léon; Madrid: Ediciones Cristianidad, 1986), 699–709; M. Wilcox, '"Upon the Tree" – Deut. 21.22–23 in the New Testament', *JBL* 96 (1977): 85–99.
18 Isa. 45.22 continues with the command 'turn to me and be saved all the ends of the earth', whose last phrase is echoed in 4Q541 9, 4. 'His eternal sun will shine, (4) and its fire will burn in all the ends of the earth' (cf. Ps. 48.11; 65.6; Isa. 26.15; 40.28; 41.5, 9).

1QIsa[b] as well as in the *Vorlage* of the LXX, adopted by the NRSV: 'Out of his anguish he shall see light.'[19] In addition, 4Q541 24 II, 4 contains the difficult phrase 'And do not renounce him (*w'l tmḥwlhy*)[20] by means of exhaustion (*šḥp'*) and hanging li[ke.' In the Hebrew Bible the rare term *šḥpt* is associated with *nkh*, 'to strike' (Deut. 28.22), which is used of God's activity towards the Servant in Isaiah 53.4, 'struck down by God'.

The use of Isaiah is confirmed in other fragments of the manuscript. We have already noted that in 4Q541 6, 3 the occurrence of *mk'wbykh* seems to be a Hebraism reflecting the use of the same term in Isaiah 53.3–4: 'a man of sorrows' (*'yš mk'bwt*), 'and he has carried our diseases' (*wmk'bynw sblm*). All this is addressed to someone in the second-person singular; perhaps this is Levi recounting to his son(s) what someone else had told him at some point. In 4Q541 10, 4, the presence of *kwr*, 'furnace', may be related to its use in Isaiah 48.10, where it is used to refer to the exile as a 'furnace of affliction' (*'ny*), whereas the metaphor is usually aplied to the trials of Israel in Egypt. The text is so fragmentary it is difficult to know what is being described.

In the more substantial Fragment 4Q541 9, it may be possible to see something of the influence of Isaiah in lines 4 and 5. The first word of line 4, *ytzh*, is probably best derived from *'zy*, 'to kindle, heat, burn', but it may be possible to read it as a Hebraism from *nzh* which regularly in Aramaic is *nd'*, 'to sprinkle', though of course for Isaiah 52.15 the verb is an old chestnut, commonly understood from an Arabic cognate meaning 'to leap'.[21] If Isaiah 52.15 lies behind the phrase here, then the implication would be that as the Servant causes many to leap, that is startles them, so the priest's fire will leap in all the corners of the earth. Some support for seeing Isaianic influence behind this phrase comes from 'all

---

19 Even in 1963 Starcky rightly resisted associating the violence endured by this eschatological high priest with that supposedly suffered by the Teacher of Righteousness ('Les quatre étapes', 492).

20 Puech has changed his original suggested reading of *w'l tmḥy lhy*, 'and don't chastise the one enfeebled', to *w'l tmḥwlhy*, 'and don't renounce', on the basis of the occurrence of *mḥl* in 4Q213 1 I, 13 and 4Q213 4, 6 (DJD 31, 254); in *Targ. Deut.* 28.22 there is a form of the verb *mḥy*, 'to smite, wound, chastise', and in *Targ. Isa.* 53.4 there is the aphel passive participle *mḥn* from *mḥy*, the same verb. If Puech's original suggestion was correct, then there would be another lexical link with the fourth Servant Song of Isaiah.

21 See Puech's remarks in DJD 31, 243; he prefers a derivation from *'zh*, but mentions the possibility of a Hebraism understood in the light of Isa. 52.15.

the corners of the earth'. The actual parallel Hebrew phrase occurs only in Psalm 65.6, a thanksgiving for harvest in which God is described as the hope of all the ends of the earth, and Isaiah 26.15, part of an eschatological psalm expressing the eventual vindication of the righteous. However, a similar Hebrew phrase (*qswt h'rṣ*) occurs in Isaiah 40.28 (God is 'the Creator of the ends of the earth'), 41.5 ('the ends of the earth tremble'), and 41.9 (Israel 'my servant' is declared to have been taken 'from the ends of the earth').[22] The similarity between 4Q541 9 II, 4–5 and Isaiah 60.2–3 has already been mentioned.

Puech's study has allowed us to see that something of these verbal associations with the servant texts of Isaiah can also be seen in 4Q540. The term in 4Q540 1, 1 used of the distress that will come upon 'the little one' is '*q*' which is used in *Targ. Isa.* 49.8 and 50.10: 'Who obeys the voice of his servant the prophet? Who does the Law in affliction?' If 4Q540 1, 5 in the same fragment is to be construed as signifying that the servant will rebuild the sanctuary, then this not only corresponds with *Gk T. Levi* 17.10, when in the fifth jubilee the priesthood will renew the house of the Lord, but also with *Targ. Isa.* 53.5 which announces that the Messiah will build the sanctuary.

All in all, this priest's activities are not only referred to with some of the phraseology associated with the Servant of Isaiah, but his career seems to mirror that of the Servant – a universal mission, light against darkness, vilification, violent suffering, sacrifice, benefits for others. The association of the priest's mission with light and the scattering of darkness mirrors the role of the Servant in Isaiah 42.6 and 49.6 (also in LXX Isaiah 51.4 and 5). In addition, the preferred reading of Isaiah 53.11 declares how after the trials the Servant will see light. The image of light associated with the Servant's mission is grounded in his role as illuminator: his teaching needs to be obeyed (Isa. 50.10), reaches the coastlands (Isa. 42.4), is from God (Isa. 50.4). *Targum Isaiah* also makes the Servant's teaching role explicit in 53.5b and 11b. As in Isaiah 50.10 the Servant's addressees remain in darkness, so do the contemporaries of the priest figure of 4Q541 9 I, 6–7. Both figures are the subject of ridicule, abuse and infamy (Isa. 50.6–8; 53.2–12); in 4Q541 this may be reflected in Fragments 6 and 10 as well as in Fragment 9. In *Targ. Isa.* 53.11–12 the role of the Servant as one who prays for sinners is underlined: 'he will pray concerning their sins', 'and he will pray concerning many sins and for him it will be forgiven the rebellious'. Although the targum makes

---

22 The phrase occurs elsewhere in the MT only in Job 28.24.

Isaiah 53 unambiguous so that it cannot speak of the death of the Servant, it retains the cultic vocation of the Servant which the Hebrew itself suggests in Isaiah 53.10 with the very difficult *'šm*. Lastly, it may be possible to construe 4Q541 24 as speaking of the death of this eschatological figure as Isaiah 53 could itself be construed, possibly even a death by crucifixion.

To appreciate the significance of all this for the New Testament it is necessary to underline the cultic role of this eschatological figure. This priest will make expiation for all the sons of his generation. Though the reference could be to any of several different kinds of sacrifice, perhaps the allusion is most likely to refer to the eschatological Day of Atonement. *Gk T. Levi* 3.5 acknowledges (as also the *Songs of the Sabbath Sacrifice* declare) that alongside the earthly service, there is a heavenly service: 'there are angels in the presence of the Lord, those who minister and make expiation to the Lord for all the sins of ignorance of the righteous'. With that in mind and with the possibility that 4Q541 9 refers to a Day of Atonement, perhaps the text speaks of the earthly counterpart to the heavenly Day of Atonement at which Melchizedek presides according to 11QMelch II, 7–8: 'And the Day of Atonement is the end of the tenth jubilee.'[23] Priestly language can also be seen at 4Q541 2 II, 4 where 'and I will bless you' is corrected by the scribe to 'and I will bless the burnt-offering of', perhaps also in 4Q541 4 II, 4 if 'your blood' is the correct understanding of the remaining letters in the line, in 4Q541 9 II, 5 when understood as 'seven rams' and in 4Q541 9 II, 7 if 'burnt-offering' should be restored there. Priestly activity also seems to be described in the rebuilding of the temple (4Q540 1, 5).

All this may be to say too much by way of interpretation, reconstruction and reading between the lines. Yet, if 4Q541 is indeed speaking of an eschatological high priest servant, we may have in this composition the earliest individualistic interpretation of the Isaianic Servant Songs in a particularly cultic direction. The stance of the *Targ. Isa.* in its particular phraseology and messianism may be directed as much against this kind of interpretation of the Servant material in Isaiah as it might be directed against any particularly Christian reading of the biblical text. At this point it is appropriate to turn to the New Testament itself.

---

23 Again, see the pioneering work of M. de Jonge: M. de Jonge and A. S. van der Woude, '11Q Melchizedek and the New Testament', *NTS* 12 (1965–6): 301–26. See now E. Puech, 'Notes sur le manuscrit de XIQMelkîsédeq', *RevQ* 12 (1985–7): 483–513; DJD 23.

THE NEW TESTAMENT: RECONSIDERING THE SUFFERING SERVANT

Although some scholars have argued forcefully for the widespread use of the Suffering Servant model either as part of Jesus' self-understanding or as part of the reflection of the earliest Christian communities or both,[24] it is now commonly argued that the Servant of Isaiah, especially 52.13— 53.12, was barely of any significance to how either Jesus or his first followers understood his death. As M. de Jonge has concluded:

> On close inspection there is little unequivocal evidence for either a close connection between Isaiah 53 and the Markan passages [Mark 10.45; 14.24] or the theory of Jesus' inspiration by this aspect of Deutero-Isaiah's teaching. More likely is the influence of the Greek translation of 53.12 on the use of the verb 'to deliver up' (*paradidōnai*) in ancient formulas, and elsewhere, in connection with Jesus' death.[25]

Or again, more recently: 'Notwithstanding J. Jeremias' careful listing of all the possible references and allusions to the texts, words, phrases and ideas found in Isa. 52.13—53.12 in the writings of the New Testament, the evidence for the use of this passage in early Christianity is slight.'[26] Enter 4Q540 and especially 4Q541.

---

24 See especially C. H. Dodd, *According to the Scriptures* (London: Nisbet, 1952), 92–6; T. W. Manson, *The Servant–Messiah: A Study in the Public Ministry of Jesus* (Cambridge: Cambridge University Press, 1953; repr. Grand Rapids: Baker, 1977); J. Jeremias, 'Pais Theo', *TDNT* 5 (1968), 677–717; J. Jeremias, *New Testament Theology* (London: SCM Press, 1971), 286–99; M. Hengel, *The Atonement: A Study of the Origins of the Doctrine in the New Testament* (London: SCM Press, 1981), 57–60 (significantly and appropriately Hengel's work is dedicated to the memory of J. Jeremias). The analysis of B. D. Chilton is more subtle and relevant: while acknowledging the relative lack of material in the New Testament concering the identification of Jesus as suffering servant, he allows for the influence of Isaianic Servant material on the New Testament authors and he posits (now apparently with some vindication) that there was a pre-Christian messianic servant (*The Glory of Israel: The Theology and Provenience of the Isaiah Targum* [JSOTSup 23; Sheffield: JSOT Press, 1983], 86–96).
25 M. de Jonge, *Christology in Context: The Earliest Christian Response to Jesus* (Philadelphia: Westminster Press, 1988), 180–1.
26 M. de Jonge, *Jesus, The Servant–Messiah* (New Haven: Yale University Press, 1991), 49.

4Q541 must now be taken into account by all future generations of scholars who wish to consider the issue. On the one hand, it now seems that there is a Jewish text whose author used the Servant passages of Isaiah to support the understanding that there was to be an eschatological priest who would suffer, possibly even that the suffering involved death, death that would lead to joyous benefits for others. M. Hengel's declaration that 'we have no clear text from pre-Christian Judaism which speaks of the vicarious suffering of the Messiah in connection with Isaiah 53'[27] may need to be qualified, as may de Jonge's own statement that 'Isaiah 52.13—53.12 is the only "suffering righteous" passage . . . and it seems not to have had much influence in Jewish circles.'[28] On the other hand, there are several texts in the New Testament which try to describe the death of Jesus, even Jesus himself, in cultic and priestly terms. If it was known within early Christian circles that the dominant individualistic understanding of the Servant texts linked them to an eschatological Levi, then, for all their suitability in many respects, the Servant passages of Isaiah, because Jesus was not a Levitical priest, may only have been of limited use to early Christian writers, or even to Jesus himself.

Despite the possibility that the Servant passages play only a limited role in the New Testament because of their dominant association in certain Jewish eschatology with the eschatological priest, nevertheless some New Testament writings reflect a concern among some authors either to use the Servant materials and redirect them to enhance the picture of Jesus, the Davidic Messiah, or to adjust other aspects of some forms of Jewish cultic practice and expectation to describe the character and effect of Jesus, especially his death. Four authors or schools of thought immediately come to mind.

First, it is clear that the letter to the Hebrews offers an elaborate description of the priesthood of Jesus. Although this is explicitly stated to be different from that of both Levi and of the angels, it is nevertheless resonant with items from earlier Jewish tradition. Jesus' high priesthood is replete with the characteristics of Aaron's priesthood – he is chosen from among mortals, he offers up prayers and supplications with loud cries and tears, he is the source of eternal salvation for all who obey him, but, above all, he is able to deal gently with the ignorant and wayward

---

27 M. Hengel, *The Atonement*, 59. Hengel dares to say without any evidence, 'At all events, a suffering Messiah did not belong to the widespread popular Messianic hope in the time of Jesus and a crucified Messiah was a real blasphemy.'

28 M. de Jonge, *Christology in Context*, 180.

since he can 'sympathize with our weaknesses' (Heb. 4.15). The background of this decription is that of the Aaronic high priest on the Day of Atonement when he fulfilled his role as no other priest could (cf. Heb. 9.11–14).

Yet Jesus was not of Levitical descent, so the author of Hebrews aligns his priesthood with that of Melchizedek. Despite the protestations of some scholars,[29] it is impossible to read this without reference to texts from Qumran.[30] Hebrews insists that Jesus is not an angel, but his priesthood is nevertheless true to what Melchizedek performs in heaven on that momentous Day of Atonement at the end of the tenth jubilee. In 4Q541 it is an eschatological Levi who completes on earth what Melchizedek acts out in heaven; true to the order of Melchizedek, for the author of Hebrews Jesus' activity is effective on earth and in heaven at the same time, once for all. Furthermore, the language of the cultic servant is adequate for the climax of the description in Hebrews 9.28: 'Christ, having been offered once to bear the sins of many' (cf. Isa. 53.12 LXX).[31]

In the Fourth Gospel certain cultic and priestly elements are obvious. Jesus is the Lamb of God who takes away the sin of the world. In the Gospel Jesus' ministry is planned around the great festivals which he effectively replaces. In light of this cultic interest and in consideration of 4Q541, perhaps it is also time to reintroduce a cultic element into some other aspects of the Fourth Gospel's portrayal of Jesus. It might be suitable to begin in Chapter 12 where there is an explicit quotation of Isaiah 53.1: 'Lord, who has believed our message, and to whom has the arm of the Lord been revealed?' Connected with Isaiah 6.9–10 (used in the Synoptic tradition to justify or explain why Jesus spoke in riddles; cf. 4Q541 3–4 I, 3–4) the Fourth Gospel explains that Isaiah had seen 'his glory' and offers as a last determined public utterance of Jesus: 'I have

---

29 For example, F. L. Horton, *The Melchizedek Tradition: A Critical Examination of the Sources to the Fifth Century AD and in the Epistle to the Hebrews* (SNTSMS 30; Cambridge: Cambridge University Press, 1976), 168: 'I have no reason to believe that Hebrews is related to the speculation about Melchizedek demonstrated in the 11Q Melchizedek'.

30 As suitably collected and analysed by P. J. Kobelski, *Melchizedek and Melchireša'* (CBQMS 10; Washington: Catholic Biblical Association of America, 1981); as acknowledged, e.g., by M. M. Bourke, 'The Epistle to the Hebrews', in *NJBC*, 392, and J. C. VanderKam, 'The Dead Sea Scrolls and Christianity', *BRev* 7/6 (1991): 46.31 4Q541 10 (*w'zl' rwḥḥ' lkwr*), with *rwḥ'* read as 'spirit', might help in understanding why Heb. 9.14 says that it was through the eternal Spirit that Christ offered himself without blemish to God.

come as light into the world, so that everyone who believes in me should not remain in darkness . . . The one who rejects me and does not receive my word has a judge; on the last day the word that I have spoken will serve as judge' (Jn 12.46, 48). An element in the themes of glory and light, so dominant in the Gospel, may be derived from the cultic figure of the servant priest who is glorified (Isa. 52.13 LXX). Might 4Q540 1, when understood as referring to the rebuilding of the temple by the future priest, help explain, together with Psalm 69, the verbal play in John 2.19 where at the cleansing of the temple Jesus declares, 'Destroy this temple, and in three days I will raise it up/rebuild it'?[32] To these matters could be added the Johannine concern with Jesus as Wisdom.

In addition to these items it is possible to understand one incident in the passion narrative of the Fourth Gospel as hinting at the high priestly status of Jesus. In the incident of the soldiers casting lots for Jesus' tunic (Jn 19.23–4) it is clear that the fact that it is seamless, of one piece from top to bottom, is significant for some reason. R. E. Brown has collected the relevant evidence.[33] *Chitōn*, 'tunic', is used of one of the garments of the high priest in Exodus 28.4 LXX and Leviticus 16.4 LXX; though the word *arraphos*, 'seamless', is not found in the LXX, Josephus (*Ant.* 3.161) describes the ankle-length tunic of the high priest as 'not composed of two pieces, to be stitched at the shoulders and the sides: it is one long woven cloth'.[34] In addition, Brown recalls Philo's interpretation of why the high priest does not rend his clothes (*himatia*): this is because the priest's garments are a visual reminder of the clothing that the Logos makes for itself in reflecting nature's unbroken mutual harmony and oneness.[35] Such motifs of unity may help explain why the soldiers in the narrative do not tear the tunic. In sum, it seems likely that the Jesus of the Fourth Gospel dies as both high priest and king.

The third New Testament work to consider is Luke–Acts. Here is a work full of cultic material. This is obvious in Luke's portrayal of Jesus as

---

32 It is possible to understand *egeirō* as 'rebuild'; cf. 1 Esd 5.44: 'Some of the heads of families, when they came to the temple of God that is in Jerusalem, vowed that, to the best of their ability, they would erect (*egeirai*) the house on its site.' Cf. 4Q541 1, 5.

33 R. E. Brown, *The Gospel according to John XIII–XXI* (AB 29A; Garden City: Doubleday, 1970), 920–1.

34 Trans. H. St. J. Thackeray, *Josephus* (LCL: London: Heinemann, 1930), IV, 393. Rev. 1.13 may also be relevant: the Greek term *podērēs* used there occurs adjectivally with *chitōn* in the description of the high priest's robe in Ex. 29.5 LXX.

35 R. E. Brown, *The Gospel according to John XIII–XXI*, 921, citing Philo, *Fug.* 108–12.

a man of prayer and in his use of the canticles, as well as his frequent setting of scenes in the temple. In the canticles the theme of light and darkness occurs (Lk. 1.79; 2.32), while the whole Nunc Dimittis is a play on passages from Isaiah 42.6, 49.6 and 52.10. According to Acts the Servant passages feature in the preaching of the early Church: in Solomon's Portico Peter in Acts 3.13 speaks of how God has glorified his servant, in Acts 8.32–3 Isaiah 53.7–8 is the passage that Philip explains to the Ethiopian eunuch, in Acts 13.47 Paul and Barnabas use Isaiah 49.6 to justify their preaching to Gentiles. More particularly it is Luke 22.37, alone of the Gospels, which cites Isaiah 53.12 as from Jesus' lips. All this is not especially extensive, as de Jonge and others have noted, but it is intriguing to note also that in Luke's genealogy of Jesus which is constructed in jubilee periods the name of Levi occurs twice.[36] It seems as if Luke's presentation of Jesus is mildly infected with a Palestinian Jewish tradition which associated the priestly Messiah with the Servant of Isaiah.

Fourth, in Mark's Gospel too there are some intriguing possibilities for supporting some earlier interpretations. At Jesus' baptism Mark's vocabulary of having the heavens rent apart is a deliberate anticipation of the rending of the veil of the temple at the moment of Jesus' death (Mk 15.38; cf. *Gk T. Levi* 10.3). Thus, according to Mark, Jesus' vocation of servanthood (Isa. 42.1; Mk 1.11) confirmed at his baptism is his vocation to die, a death which will grant access to the temple or rather, to the Holy of Holies, where only the high priest goes once a year. This vocation is ratified on two counts. First, the Spirit descends on Jesus as a dove; what this same bird has sought seems to be the object of a holy quest in 4Q541 24 II, 4. It may be that what the dove knows about concerns the chastisement and suffering of the eschatological high priest. Second, Jesus' vocation is ratified by a heavenly voice who appears to cite Psalm 2.7 and then alludes to several other passages among which are Isaiah 42.1, 4; 44.2; and Genesis 22.2, When the *locus classicus*, Mark 10.45, is put alongside these nuances in narratives which point to something of the significance of the death of Jesus according to Mark, then we may be glimpsing an understanding of Jesus not just as a prophetic martyr Servant, but as one who fulfils a cultic role as well.

---

36 On Luke's genealogy, see the incisive and detailed study of R. Bauckham, *Jude and the Relatives of Jesus in the Early Church* (Edinburgh: T & T Clark, 1990), 315–73.

CONCLUSION

In light of 4Q541 it seems that very early in Palestinian Jewish Christianity there was an attempt to use already existing traditions about the suffering of the eschatological Servant priest(-Messiah) to explain something of Jesus' purpose and mission. Because Jesus was not a Levitical priest, the use of this material was either strongly tempered with appeal to traditions which could be construed more overtly in relation to the Davidic Messiah, such as Psalm 2, or it was used by those who had a concern to handle the cultic identity of some forms of Judaism in such a way as to show how this was continued, absorbed and replaced by what God had done in the death of Jesus. The earliness of this use of Servant high priest ideology may explain why Paul can also, seemingly independently, but equally reticently, use the same Isaianic texts;[37] its persistence in a variety of forms through the first century shows that it was the tenacious expression of an aspiration worth negotiating with and refining.

---

37 Isa. 52.15 (Rom. 15.21); Isa. 53.1 (Rom. 10.16); Isa. 53.12 (Rom. 4.25); Isa. 53.12 (Rom. 8.34).

9

Luke–Acts and the Qumran Scrolls:
The Case of MMT

LUKE–ACTS AND THE SCROLLS

Since the early days of research into the meaning and significance of the Dead Sea Scrolls found at Qumran, parallels with the Gospel of Luke and the Acts of the Apostles have been pointed out frequently and in detail. It is intriguing to note that apart from the Sermon on the Mount, neither Matthew's supposed Jewishness nor Mark's early date has resulted in those Gospels having more than their fair share of parallels with the forms of Palestinian Judaism represented in the Qumran scrolls. In fact, of the Synoptics, it is the third Gospel that has featured most in discussions of literary parallels. The *locus classicus* of this distinctiveness has been the parable of the unjust steward, unique to Luke (Lk. 16.1–9), in which the term 'sons of light' (Lk. 16.8) occurs. It has been noted that this term does not occur in either the Hebrew Bible or rabbinic literature, and so may be considered in some way particular to those who preserved and composed the scrolls found at Qumran.[1]

For the Acts of the Apostles the story has been the same. Numerous

---

1 See J. A. Fitzmyer, 'The Story of the Dishonest Manager', in *Essays on the Semitic Background of the New Testament* (London: Chapman, 1971), 161–84, esp. 167–8, n. 10. Together with others Fitzmyer observes that Luke 16.8b is part of the Lukan conclusion to the story in which comment is made about Christian disciples as the children of light. The phrase also appears in Jn 12.36; Eph. 5.8; 1 Thess. 5.5. In those instances it clearly refers to Christian believers. On the phrase generally see J. A. Fitzmyer, 'Qumran and the Interpolated Paragraph in 2 Cor. 6.14—7.1', in *Essays on the Semitic Background of the New Testament*, 208–10; on the use of the phrase in 1 Thess. see most recently H.-W. Kuhn, 'The Impact of the Qumran Scrolls on the Understanding of Paul', in *The Dead Sea Scrolls: Forty Years of Research* (ed. D. Dimant and U. Rappaport; STDJ 10; Leiden: Brill, 1992), 328–9.

parallels have been noted.[2] Among the most important has been the common ownership of property by the respective communities. In the *Rule of the Community* membership of the community is by voluntary association but the surrender of property is obligatory (1QS VI, 13–23). According to Acts 4.36—5.11 it is not clear that the surrender of property was obligatory, though clearly it characterized the ideal community and was expected, as the story of Ananias and Sapphira exemplifies. Just as important as the general parallel are the technical details in common. Most significantly Acts 4.32 is the first place in Acts in which *plēthos* is used in the specific sense of the Christian congregation.[3] This terminology is remarkably close to the use of *rb* and *rbym* of the community in the *Rule of the Community*.[4] Indeed there is also some overlap in the terms *yḥd* as used in many of the texts reflecting the life and practices of the community and *koinōnia* (Acts 2.42).[5] In light of the important role played by Levites in some of the scrolls,[6] worth noting also is that the positive example provided in the matter of community of goods in Acts is the Levite Barnabas.[7]

Since the unpublished scrolls became generally available in 1991, there has been some renewed interest in parallels between the Dead Sea Scrolls and the New Testament. In several instances the study of certain fragmentary texts is in its infancy; here it is common for the New Testament evidence to be used for the better understanding of the Qumran material in itself, rather than there being any interest in drawing out the literary parallels for a better understanding of the New Testament. In many cases it has been the Gospel of Luke which has been the subject of the comparison. For example, though known before 1991, the so-called

2 Most neatly summed up by J. A. Fitzmyer in 'Jewish Christianity in Acts in Light of the Qumran Scrolls', in *Studies in Luke–Acts* (ed. L. E. Keck and J. L. Martyn; London: SPCK, 1968), 233–57.

3 See E. Haenchen, *The Acts of the Apostles: A Commentary* (Oxford: Blackwell, 1971), 230 n. 1. It is also used in this way in Acts 6.2, 5; 15.12, 30; 19.9; 21.22.

4 See especially H. W. Huppenbauer, '*rb, rwb, rbym* in der Sektenregel (1QS)', *TZ* 13 (1957): 136–7.

5 Cf. *eikon hapanta koina* (Acts 2.44) and *ēn autois panta koina* (Acts 4.32).

6 See, e.g., R. C. Stalman, 'Levi and the Levites in the Dead Sea Scrolls', *JSP* 10 (1992): 163–89.

7 For more detail see G. J. Brooke, 'Levi and the Levites in the Dead Sea Scrolls and the New Testament', in *Mogilany 1989: Papers on the Dead Sea Scrolls Volume I* (ed. Z. J. Kapera; Qumranica Mogilanensia 2; Kraków: Enigma Press, 1993), 105–29, esp. 122–3 (Chapter 7 in this book).

'Son of God' text (4Q246 = 4QApocryphon of Daniel ar) has been the cause of much debate.[8] The text is fragmentary and it is not easy to understand. The principal argument lies between those who see the Son of God and Son of the Most High as epithets used of a wicked figure and those who see the title referring to some messianic or angelic figure.[9] It is not difficult to see that those in the latter camp refer to the positive use of the title in Luke 2.30–7 to assist in their interpretation of 4Q246.[10]

Another instance of Luke playing a role in the better understanding of scrolls material concerns what a few interpreters formerly called the 'Pierced Messiah' text (4Q285 7 = 4QSefer ha-Milḥamah, Frag. 7). In this case R. H. Eisenman made the unlikely suggestion that *whmytw nśy' h'dh* should be pointed so that it was translated as 'and they will put the Prince of the Congregation to death'.[11] Because of the place of Isaiah 11.1 at the start of the disputed fragment, support for insisting that the most likely and therefore preferred pointing should produce the rendering 'and the Prince of the Congregation will kill him' included allusion to

---

8 E. Puech has published the text in full: 'Fragment d'une apocalypse en araméen (4Q246 = pseudo-Dan[d]) et le «royaume de Dieu»', *RB* 99 (1992): 98–131; DJD 22, 165–84; he relates it to other texts in *La croyance des Esséniens et la vie future; immortalité, résurrection, vie éternelle. II. Les données qumraniennes et classiques* (EB 22; Paris: Gabalda, 1993), 570–2.

9 See the convenient summary of positions on this text in F. García Martínez, 'The Eschatological Figure of 4Q246', in *Qumran and Apocalyptic: Studies on the Aramaic Texts from Qumran* (STDJ 9; Leiden: Brill, 1992), 162–79.

10 See, e.g., J. J. Collins, 'The "Son of God" Text from Qumran', in *From Jesus to John: Essays on Jesus and New Testament Christology in Honour of Marinus de Jonge* (ed. M. C. de Boer; JSNTSup 84; Sheffield: JSOT Press, 1993), 65–82: 'Luke is dependent in some way, whether directly or indirectly, on this long lost text from Qumran' (p. 66). See also J. A. Fitzmyer, 'The Aramaic "Son of God" Text from Qumran Cave 4', in *Methods of Investigation of the Dead Sea Scrolls and the Khirbet Qumran Site: Present Realities and Future Prospects* (ed. M. O. Wise, N. Golb, J. J. Collins and D. G. Pardee; Annals of the New York Academy of Sciences 722: New York: New York Academy of Sciences, 1994), 163–78, esp. 175.

11 For the media coverage of this announcement see G. Vermes, 'The Oxford Forum for Qumran Research Seminar on the Rule of War from Cave 4 (4Q285)', *JJS* 43 (1992): 85–6, esp. n. 2. Many of the most recent popular introductions to the scrolls have commented on this text unanimously arguing that it should be understood that the Prince of the Congregation is doing the killing, as does the principal edition by P. S. Alexander and G. Vermes in DJD 36, 238–41. A few voices were heard allowing the possibility of Eisenman's pointing of the Hebrew and his overall approach: e.g., J. D. Tabor, 'A Pierced or Piercing Messiah? The Verdict is Still Out', *BARev* 18 (Nov/Dec 1992): 58–9.

the use of Isaiah 11.1–5 elsewhere. Since it was claimed that 11QMelchizedek supported the interpretation of 4Q285 as describing a dying Messiah, T. H. Lim addressed the immediate problem of the most suitable reading of 11QMelch and its relation to the Gospel of Luke.[12] Even though Daniel 9.25 seems to be cited in 11QMelch II, 17–18, it is far less certain that the allusion also intended to include Daniel 9.26 with its anointed one who is cut off, since 11QMelch goes on to say how this figure saves people from Belial. It seems, however, that it is possible that 11QMelch should be viewed as providing much of the exegetical background for Luke 4.16–21 as has been widely suggested.[13] Lim goes so far as to suggest that 11QMelch provides the exegetical link between Daniel 9.25–6 and Luke 4.16–21, allowing for the early Christian development of the motif of a dying Messiah.[14]

Yet a third recent text has been better appreciated in light of the Third Gospel. The so-called 'Resurrection Text' (4Q521) has received some detailed discussion.[15] In relation to the Gospel of Luke it is 4Q521 2 II, 7–8 and 12–13 that deserve the most detailed consideration: 'For he will glorify the pious on the throne of an eternal kingdom, releasing captives, giving sight to the blind and raising up those who are bo[wed down] . . . for he will heal the wounded, give life to the dead and preach good news to the poor and he will [sat]isfy the [weak] ones and lead those who have been cast out and enrich the hungry.'[16] In Q 7.22 there is a pre-Synoptic tradition which is almost word for word in both Matthew and Luke. The

12 T. H. Lim, '11QMelch, Luke 4 and the Dying Messiah', *JJS* 43 (1992): 90–2.

13 See, e.g., G. J. Brooke, *Exegesis at Qumran: 4QFlorilegium in its Jewish Context* (JSOTSup 29; Sheffield: JSOT Press, 1985), 319–23.

14 '11QMelch, Luke 4 and the Dying Messiah', 92.

15 R. H. Eisenman, 'A Messianic Vision', *BARev* 17 (Nov/Dec 1991): 65; E. Puech, 'Une apocalypse messianique (4Q521)', *RevQ* 15 (1992): 475–522, and the principal edition in DJD 25, 1–38; R. Eisenman and M. Wise, *The Dead Sea Scrolls Uncovered* (Shaftesbury: Element Press, 1992), 19–23; G. Vermes, 'Qumran Forum Miscellanea I', *JSS* 43 (1992): 303–4; J. D. Tabor and M. O. Wise, '4Q521 "On Resurrection" and the Synoptic Gospel Tradition: A Preliminary Study', *JSP* 10 (1992): 149–62; H. Stegemann, *Die Essener, Qumran, Johannes der Täufer und Jesus* (Freiburg: Herder, 1993): 49–51, 290–1; E. Puech, *La croyance des Esséniens et la vie future; immortalité, résurrection, vie éternelle. II. Les données qumraniennes et classiques*, 627–92; J. J. Collins, 'The Works of the Messiah', *DSD* 1 (1994): 98–112; O. Betz and R. Riesner, *Jesus, Qumran and the Vatican* (London: SCM Press, 1994), 90–3; L. H. Schiffman, *Reclaiming the Dead Sea Scrolls* (Philadelphia: Jewish Publication Society, 1994), pp. 347–50.

16 Trans. J. J. Collins, 'The Works of the Messiah', 99.

disciples of John the Baptist are told by Jesus to relate to John what they have seen and heard, 'the blind receive their sight, the lame walk, the lepers are cleansed, the deaf hear, the dead are raised, the poor have good news brought to them' (Lk. 7.22). As is widely acknowledged, the first three elements of Q 7.22 are based on Isaiah 35.5–6, the fifth on Isaiah 61.1. Furthermore, the actual phrasing of the first is a direct quotation from the LXX of Isaiah 61.1b. The same rendering is used by Luke in Luke 4.18. It is this link to Luke 4 which gives the Third Gospel pre-eminence in helping determine the better understanding of 4Q521. Most notably this seems to rest in the way in which it is not necessary to assume that the anointed one referred to in 4Q521 2 II, 1 is a royal Messiah. In light of Luke's concern with prophetic elements in Jesus' ministry, particularly as he distinctively in Luke raises the widow of Nain's son,[17] the anointed one in 4Q521 might just as well refer to the eschatological prophet. At the least it can hardly be coincidental that in going beyond the biblical passages both 4Q521 and Q 7.22 refer to the raising of the dead: 'It is quite possible that the author of the Sayings source knew 4Q521; at the least he drew on a common tradition.'[18] More precisely, 'Although it is unlikely that Luke knew the Qumran text directly, it seems that he shares with its author a common set of messianic expectations.'[19]

A fourth example can be seen in the Song of Miriam (4Q365 6 II, 1–7).[20] This poorly preserved new song appears in this *Reworked Pentateuch* immediately before Exodus 15.22–6.[21] It is addressed to God as

---

17 Lk. 7.11–17. The acclamation of the crowd is 'A great prophet has arisen among us' (Lk. 7.16). This incident immediately precedes the inquiry of John's disciples. The prophetic background can be seen in 1 Kgs 17.17–24 and 2 Kgs 4.32–7.

18 J. J. Collins, 'The Works of the Messiah', 107.

19 M. O. Wise and J. Tabor, '4Q521 "On Resurrection" and the Synoptic Gospel Tradition', 161. They highlight Luke's interest in using Isaiah 61, the unique cleansing of the lepers story (Lk. 17.11–19), the raising of the widow of Nain's son (Lk. 7.11–19), and the story of the woman bent double (Lk. 13.11–16).

20 First published by S. A. White in '4Q364 and 365: A Preliminary Report', in *The Madrid Qumran Congress* (ed. J. Trebolle Barrera and L. Vegas Montaner; STDJ 11; Leiden: Brill, Madrid: Editorial Complutense, 1992), 222–4; see now the principal edition by E. Tov and S. A. White in DJD 13, 269–72.

21 The song reads:

1 you despised/you plundered . . .
2 for the triumph of (cf. Ex. 15.1) . . .
3 You are great, a saviour . . .
4 the hope of the enemy perishes and he is . . .
5 they perished in the mighty waters (cf. Ex. 15.10), the enemy . . .

saviour; together with the triumphant recollection of the military victory, there is the dramatic portrayal of a complete reversal. With 'you despised' perhaps God is portrayed as deriding the enemies of Israel; by contrast he is great. This greatness seems to be echoed in his exaltation of a feminine figure: 'and he exalted her to their heights'.[22] We may fairly presume that God is being extolled for elevating somebody of lowly status, giving her a sense of triumph.[23] The closest parallel to such phrasing can be found in the victory Song of Judith but some consideration should also be given to the Magnificat. In Luke 1.46–55 there is similarly the magnification of God as saviour and the exaltation of the lowly in the place of the powerful and rich. While it has been commonly proposed that the Magnificat may well be a slightly edited Jewish hymn,[24] perhaps from the Maccabean period, what becomes all the more striking is that the Song of Miriam, the victory Song of Judith and the Magnificat are all sung by women, commonly thought to have been a group of particular concern to Luke of all the evangelists.

All this recent activity in relation to Luke is suggestive, not only of how the New Testament has become part of the evidence for better understanding early Palestinian Judaism in all its diversity, but also for highlighting the place of Luke in preserving in its special material and in its author's handling of inherited traditions, the viewpoint of a strand of Judaism which can be found in some fragmentary scroll texts, albeit that such traditions are reoriented in light of the death and resurrection of Jesus and their meaning for everyday thought and practice in the Lukan communities.

---

6 and he exalted (cf. Ex. 15.2) her to the heights . . . you gave . . .

7 w or]king a triumph (cf. Ex. 15.1).

Some of these words and phrases are closely related to the song which Moses and the Israelites sing, but the poem is not simply a restatement of the Song of the Sea.

22 The reference to a female figure in the third person need be no problem, if the song was sung antiphonally by Miriam and the women with her. This phrase would then possibly belong to the part sung by the women.

23 For further comments on the significance of this song for women and for the New Testament see G. J. Brooke, 'Power to the Powerless: A Long-Lost Song of Miriam', *BARev* 20/3 (1994): 62–5, an expanded form of which forms Chapter 14 in this book.

24 Most notably P. Winter suggested in 1954 that both the Magnificat and the Benedictus (Lk. 1.68–79) were Maccabean Psalms: 'Magnificat and Benedictus – Maccabean Psalms', *BJRL* 37 (1954): 328–43. See also D. Flusser, 'The Magnificat, the Benedictus and the War Scroll', in *Judaism and the Origins of Christianity* (Jerusalem: Magnes Press, 1988), 126–49.

It is intriguing to note that the two significant parallels from the early years of comparison of the scrolls with Luke–Acts both fall in Lukan contexts concerning behaviour in the community, more particularly with behaviour involving money and in the case of Luke 16 also Jesus' teaching on divorce; the more recent parallels highlight overlaps in exegesis and theology rather than ethics. But, as far as what characterizes Judaism in the late second temple period, it is matters of behaviour, daily living, halakhah which are at the root of the distinctiveness of the various groups and subgroups of the time. So, as part of the overall rejuvenation of interest in the way the New Testament and the Dead Sea Scrolls might be used for their better mutual understanding, the rest of this chapter will draw out some of the similarities and differences between Luke–Acts and the halakhic text known as *Miqṣat Ma'aśê ha-Torah* (= MMT).[25]

E. Qimron has observed with some justification that 4QMMT should be seen as a pivotal text in understanding the reasons groups distinguished themselves from one another in the two-and-a-half centuries before the fall of the temple. He notes that MMT describes the opinions of three groups ('We', 'You', 'They') and that in many respects the views of these three groups might not be inappropriately linked with Essenes, Sadducees and Pharisees in some form.[26] For Qimron MMT stands at the centre of how early Judaism should be defined. For him three matters of halakhah stand at the centre of the self-definition of the various group opinions: the calendar, purity and marriage practice. As a text with such possibilities concerning group self-definition in the late second temple period, it is worth juxtaposing with Luke–Acts to see to what extent some of the concerns of Luke–Acts may be brought into focus by it. It must be underlined that this is not an attempt to argue that there is any literary dependence, but rather that some of the same issues

---

25 E. Qimron and J. Strugnell in consultation with Y. Sussmann and with contributions by Y. Sussmann and A. Yardeni, *Qumran Cave 4.V: Miqṣat Ma'aśe Ha-Torah* (DJD 10; Oxford: Clarendon Press, 1994). The composite text and English translation was reprinted in 'For This You Waited 35 Years', *BARev* 20 (Nov/Dec 1994): 56–61. An alternative English translation is available in F. García Martínez, *The Dead Sea Scrolls Translated: The Qumran Texts in English* (Leiden: Brill, 1994), 77–85. See also B. W. W. Dombrowski, *An Annotated Translation of Miqṣat Ma'aśe ha-Tôrâ (4QMMT)* (Weenzen, 1992; Weenzen/Kraków: Enigma Press, 2nd edn, 1993); B. W. W. Dombrowski, 'Miqṣat Ma'aśe ha-Tôrâ (4QMMT) in English', *The Qumran Chronicle* 4, 1/2 (1994): 28–36.

26 The same tripartite differentiation is of course found in Josephus, but is also implied in the ciphers of Judah, Ephraim and Manasseh in 4QpNah.

may be argued through in both writings, sometimes in a similar manner. In this way it is hoped that the literary achievement of Luke in his two-volume work will be clarified from yet one further direction.

MIQṢAT MA'AŚÊ HA-TORAH

MMT exists in six fragmentary copies, the oldest 'from about 75 BCE, and the youngest from about 50 CE'.[27] Enough remains to enable the reconstruction of a single composite text. As presented by Qimron and Strugnell this composite text has three parts, though they acknowledge that there may well have been other material at the start of the text.[28] In the first extant section, preserved only in 4Q394 (= 4QMMTª), there is a calendar. It lists the sabbaths and the festivals for the year: dates for the period from the second to the sixth month are preserved in five columns on two fragments, then dates for the twelfth month together with a summary formula are preserved at the start of 4Q394. It is true that the other manuscript which preserves the start of the second section, 4Q395 (= 4QMMTᵇ), has a blank space at its opening and that on this basis Strugnell has dissociated himself from his co-editor's opinion about the overall make-up of the text, but Strugnell argues his position on the basis that the calendrical material contains no polemic as is found in the second section. It could be maintained, however, that the polemic is implicit in the presentation of a calendar of 364 days in which none of the principal days of the festivals falls on a Sabbath and which mentions festivals (New Wine, New Oil) which are only found in the *Temple Scroll*.

The second section of the composite text contains 82 lines as reconstructed. After an overall brief introduction which recalls the opening words of Deuteronomy, there is discussion of 17 halakhic topics. Though there are allusions to biblical passages in many of these halakhic discussions, the order of the topics does not depend upon that of the Bible: the first eight concern sacrifices and related matters of purity (B 3–38), the

27 DJD 10, 108.
28 DJD 10, 109. For a full discussion of whether the calendrical materials are part of another manuscript, or part of 4Q394 but not to be understood as part of the same composition as MMT B + C, or are integral to MMT, see J. C. VanderKam, 'The Calendar, 4Q327, and 4Q394', in *Legal Texts and Legal Issues: Proceedings of the Second Meeting of the International Organization for Qumran Studies, Cambridge 1995, Published in Honour of Joseph M. Baumgarten* (ed. M. Bernstein, F. García Martínez and J. Kampen; STDJ 23; Leiden: Brill, 1997), 179–94; VanderKam concludes that something calendrical was indeed part of 4Q394.

other nine include six which concern the purity of Jerusalem and the temple (B 39–62; 64–74) with three short supplements, two on gifts for priests (B 62–4) and one on priestly marriage practice.

The third section is exhortatory. The language changes somewhat from the matter of fact presentation of the halakhot in the second section. However, just as that section opened with an echo of Deuteronomy, so the third section recalls the covenantal framework of Deuteronomy as it suggests that some of the blessings and curses of the Book of Moses have already been fulfilled in the days of Solomon and from the days of Jeroboam until the exile respectively (C 17–21). The third section is addressed by a first-person plural group to an individual and 'your (s.) people' (C 27).[29]

LUKE–ACTS AND MMT

Form and genre: the confirmatory instructional treatise

The first methodological factor to take into consideration is the way elements of a common form are used in both texts. Though the documents end up looking very different, MMT was first presented to the world as a letter and, as is well known, both Luke and Acts are addressed in their prefaces to Theophilus. Neither MMT nor Luke–Acts is a letter, but both are treatises of some kind.

Though still commonly talked about as a letter,[30] both of MMT's principal editors have distanced themselves from their earlier definition by insisting that clearly MMT was never intended as a personal letter, but rather as some kind of formal epistle or treatise, 'though formal descriptions of these genres are hard to make'.[31] In an Appendix to the publication of the principal edition of MMT Strugnell has distanced himself from what was written in the earlier part of the volume: 'The treatise is, at least in Hellenistic literature, a very ill-defined genre, and such a distribution of the personal pronouns [as in MMT] could be expected in many other literary contexts too. So the suggestion . . . that

---

29 The phrase 'your (s.) people' is missing from 4QMMT[f], but the term Israel is preserved at the very end of the text.

30 See, e.g., the extensive description of MMT as the 'Halakhic Letter', in L. H. Schiffman, *Reclaiming the Dead Sea Scrolls*, 83–9.

31 DJD 10, 113.

this was a treatise rather than a letter, should be withdrawn.'[32] The problem, as Strugnell perceived it, is threefold: first, the calendrical material of the first section of MMT is only present in one of the two manuscripts which preserve the part of the opening of the second section of text, thus making it possible that calendrical issues were not an integral part of the polemic of the body of the text.[33] Second, a reconstruction of the manuscript which does contain the calendrical material does not seem to allow for enough room at the start for a significant prologue to introduce the whole text. Third, the few words which preface the halakhic second section are not sufficient for introducing a treatise, but look more like an imitation of the opening of the Book of Deuteronomy which has been geared specifically to an odd collection of assorted purity rules.

For all that there are formal problems with the start of the text, the third section continues the second-person address and concludes with a phrase, *ltwb lk wlyśr'l* ('for your own welfare and that of Israel'), which is not unlike the closing formula of one of the Bar Kokhba letters, *'hwh šlwm wkl byt yśr'l* ('May there be peace (to you) and to all the House of Israel').[34] Since the second and third sections of MMT almost certainly belong together,[35] the legal material does indeed seem to have circulated in a text which had an exhortatory close with an epistolary formal element at its very end.

Since MMT exists, even today, in six copies it seems likely that it was always intended as an open circular, designed to be heard by a wide audience who might identify themselves with the 'you' of the addressee.

---

32 DJD 10, 204; Strugnell expressed the same reservations in 'MMT: Second Thoughts on a Forthcoming Edition', in *The Community of the Renewed Covenant: The Notre Dame Symposium on the Dead Sea Scrolls* (ed. E. Ulrich and J. VanderKam; Christianity and Judaism in Antiquity Series 10; Notre Dame: University of Notre Dame Press, 1994), 63.

33 Schiffman describes B 1–3 as the beginning of the letter: *Reclaiming the Dead Sea Scrolls*, 83.

34 Mur 42.7; see DJD 10, 113. For detailed discussion of the formulae used in letters of the time see P. S. Alexander, 'Epistolary Literature', in *Jewish Writings of the Second Temple Period* (ed. M. E. Stone; CRINT 2/2; Assen: Van Gorcum; Philadelphia: Fortress, 1984), 579–96, esp. 588–92.

35 The theory of R. Eisenman and M. Wise (*The Dead Sea Scrolls Uncovered* [Shaftesbury: Element Press, 1992], 196) that sections A + B and C are two separate letters has been substantially refuted by F. García Martínez, 'Dos notas sobre 4QMMT', *RevQ* 16/62 (1993): 295–7.

The author speaks consistently in the first-person plural. It is probably wrong to search for an individual author behind such a stylistic feature; whoever it is writes on behalf of a group to an audience with whom he shares much in common. His general purpose is to confirm that the two groups are much in agreement. For the particular addressee in C 28–9, this confirmation will come about through considering 'all these things', 'for we have seen that you have wisdom and knowledge of the Torah'.

Luke, distinctively of the Gospels, provides his two-part work with a prologue or preface which is echoed in the introduction of the second part. Although addressed to a particular reader, his labours are not intended for private consumption alone. Nor is his work to be considered as a letter, but more properly as a treatise of some kind directed at a certain audience. The preface to the Gospel in particular has been the subject of very extensive study, since it is widely held that to understand it would be to understand the overall purpose of the author. Some scholars have preferred to leave the generic significance of Luke 1.1–4 on a quite general level. So, for example, J. A. Fitzmyer merely underlines that the key to the prologue rests in its final phrase: 'Luke writes for Theophilus, a catechumen or neophyte, in order to give him assurance about the initial instruction that he has received.'[36] For Fitzmyer the assurance contained in the Gospel and Acts is doctrinal and didactic and does not depend upon a particular understanding of what genre of preface Luke may be attempting to imitate. More recently L. C. A. Alexander has addressed the issue of the preface most searchingly and concluded that it is to be seen in the context of 'scientific' works of the Hellenistic schools, thus suggesting that Luke–Acts should be read similarly.[37]

Now it is clear that MMT and Luke–Acts are rather different kinds of work, but both might be classed generically as treatises with a didactic element. More significantly, both appear to have been written to confirm, strengthen and assure the reader that the position they have been taught or now hold is indeed the correct or appropriate one. Both MMT and Luke–Acts are confirmatory instruction.

---

36 J. A. Fitzmyer, *The Gospel According to Luke I–IX* (AB 28; Garden City: Doubleday, 2nd edn, 1983), 301.
37 L. C. A. Alexander, *The Preface to Luke's Gospel: Literary Convention and Social Context in Luke 1.1–4 and Acts 1.1* (SNTSMS 78; Cambridge: Cambridge University Press, 1993).

Beyond the overall similarity between MMT and Luke–Acts it is interesting to note that what is planned after the meeting in Jerusalem described in Acts 15 is the writing of a letter informing the recipients of the decisions made; perhaps MMT is best understood not as a letter authored by an individual (the 'Teacher of Righteousness') but rather as the reporting of decisions perhaps taken in a council session, not unlike that in Acts 15. This would make better sense of the first-person plural pronoun used in MMT.[38]

All this has broader implications. In a previous scholarly generation it would be deemed appropriate to tease out this parallel in literary method in terms of supposing either that the author of MMT should be accounted among his literary peers in the Hellenistic world or that the outward literary form of Luke's two volumes should be considered within the parameters of Palestinian Judaism. Nowadays, such divisions are seen to be increasingly inappropriate and the real situation far more complex. This parallel in literary method should rather be seen as yet another example of how universal in the ancient Mediterranean world was the literary culture of the time.

Content: the centre of the Law

Since the overall perspective of exclusivity and rigorist interpretation of the Law is clear to see in MMT, there is little point in attempting to work through each of the halakhic statements in MMT looking for detailed parallels in Luke–Acts. However, on a general level in terms of content, three intricately related matters come to the fore in Luke–Acts through laying it side by side with MMT: the place of Jerusalem, the role of the temple, and the issue of who may worship there. This commonality is all the more surprising when it is remembered that MMT was written when the temple was very much a live institution, whereas Luke–Acts was written after the temple's demise.

In Luke–Acts Jerusalem plays a special role. 'The overarching geo-graphical perspective in Luke–Acts can be seen in the author's preoccupation with Jerusalem as the city of destiny for Jesus and the

---

38. This seems preferable to pushing the Teacher of Righteousness as the possible author of MMT on the basis of 4QpPs[a] 3–10 IV, 7–9 which describes how the Wicked Priest spied on the Teacher of Righteousness and tried to put him to death because of the precepts (*ḥwq*) and the law (*twrh*) which he had sent him. This identification is pursued in the principal edition, DJD 10, 119–20.

pivot for the salvation of mankind', says Fitzmyer.[39] The Gospel begins
and ends in Jerusalem and the city of Jerusalem may be seen as controlling individual incidents in the Gospel, such as the order of the
temptations in the temptation narrative which reach their climax in Luke
with the reference to Jerusalem, or such as the complete lack of any resurrection appearances except those in the vicinity of Jerusalem; Jerusalem
also controls whole sequences in the Gospel, such as the distinctive
journey narrative (9.51—19.27) when Jesus sets his face to go to
Jerusalem. Few would deny this central role to Jerusalem in the Gospel,
but the narrative of Acts is commonly thought of as portraying the spread
of the gospel from Jerusalem to Rome. However, even in Acts, Jerusalem
remains pivotal; not only does the narrative of Acts start in Jerusalem, but
the central narrative moment of the 'Council' is held there (Acts 15) and
Paul repeatedly gravitates back to Jerusalem (Acts 18.22; 21.15–26). In
fact the name Jerusalem features 60 times in Acts, half in Chapters 1—
14, and half spread through the remainder of the work.

Within Jerusalem it is the temple that is the focus of attention, what it
signifies in itself and how worship there is rightly ordered and practised.
For Jesus it is the place of instruction: in the infancy narrative he is found
there among the teachers, listening to them and asking questions (Lk.
2.46–9), as a foreshadowing of his later teaching ministry in the temple
(Lk. 19.47). Immediately upon entering Jerusalem the Lukan Jesus goes
to the temple not just to look around but to purge it.[40] In Acts the same
characterizes the ministry of the apostles: Peter and John in the court of
the Gentiles (Acts 3.11),[41] and the apostles generally (Acts 5.20–1, 42).
In addition the temple is, of course, the focus of prayer and worship (e.g.,
Lk. 19.45–8; Acts 3.1), the place where ritual obligations are met, particularly those involving matters of purity whether at the time of
purification (Lk. 2.22–4), after the lepers had been healed (Lk. 17.14), or
at the discharge of a vow (Acts 21.15–26).

A further matter concerning the depiction of the temple and its
worship in Luke–Acts concerns the issue of who may worship there. For
example, both Jesus' parents bring him to be presented at the temple (Lk.

---

39 *The Gospel According to Luke I–IX*, 164; Fitzmyer devotes ten pages to discussing
the geographical aspects of the Gospel, especially the central role of Jerusalem.
40 Fitzmyer notes how this echoes Mal. 3.1 with its motif of 'coming'; *The Gospel
According to Luke I–IX*, 168.
41 Josephus locates the portico in the eastern outer wall, in the court of the Gentiles
(*War* 5.185; *Ant.* 20.221).

2.2), by implication the Samaritan knows more about the significance of ritual than either the priest or the Levite (Lk. 10.29–37), the Samaritan leper, though bidden to tell the priests what had happened, is the one who returns to Jesus and prostrates himself before him (Lk. 17.11–19), the Ethiopian eunuch[42] has come to Jerusalem to worship (Acts 8.27) and Paul is falsely accused of introducing Greeks into the temple (Acts 21.28–9). It is almost as if Luke is interested in women, Samaritans, the lepers,[43] the Gentiles, not because they were marginalized socially by Jews and, by implication, by some Jewish Christians, but because they were religiously marginalized. For Luke, and for Luke's Jesus, everybody had their proper inclusive place in the worship of God.

However, there is a further implication that comparison of Luke–Acts with MMT highlights. Luke–Acts is not concerned with social and religious inclusiveness for its own sake. Such inclusiveness is according to the Law. This is shown chiefly in the way in which the charges against Paul for profaning the temple are repeatedly rehearsed. This concern with the Law is summed up by D. Juel: for Luke the 'Torah served as a pointer to the one true God in a world full of idols; it identified those who lived by it as worshippers of that God', and so Luke's 'narrative assumes that if there is a people of God, they will live by the law'.[44] Juel goes on to show how Paul's attitude to the Law is of special concern: Paul never did anything 'against the people or the customs of our fathers' (Acts 21.21) and the Jerusalem elders know that Paul has lived in observance of the Law (Acts 21.24).[45]

MMT presents a rigorist and exclusivist interpretation of the Law. The sacrificial offerings of Gentiles are prohibited; the Ammonite, the Moabite and the sexually deformed or mutilated are to be excluded from entering the congregation and from intermarriage; the blind and the deaf are legislated against; the leper cannot be readmitted until after sunset on the eighth day. The rules concerning these groups are stringent because of the holiness of Jerusalem: 'Jerusalem is the camp of holiness, and is the place which He has chosen from among all the tribes of Israel. For Jerusalem is the capital of the camps of Israel' (MMT B60–2).

---

42 Sexually mutilated; such are legislated against in MMT B39–40.

43 Lepers are legislated for in MMT B64–72.

44 D. Juel, *Luke–Acts* (London: SCM Press, 1984), 108.

45 Not all scholars read the place of the Law in Luke–Acts in this way. For a summary of various views see J. A. Fitzmyer, 'The Jewish People and the Mosaic Law in Luke–Acts', in *Luke the Theologian: Aspects of His Teaching* (London: Chapman, 1989), 175–202.

In addition to this range of sacrificial and purity regulations we noted earlier in this study that Qimron also considered marriage rules to lie at the heart of the legal self-definition of any group in late second temple Judaism. Apart from Luke 16.18 on divorce, which we discussed briefly above as pertinent to how the Law should be upheld in matters of property and marriage, it is noteworthy that the other reference to marriage law comes by implication in association with purity regulations (just as in MMT) in the decree of the apostles in Acts 15.20 which is repeated in Acts 21.25. The apostles determine to write to Gentiles who are turning to God 'to abstain only from things polluted by idols and from fornication and from whatever has been strangled and from blood'.

The term for fornication, *porneia*, corresponds with *znwt* (or *zwnh* or their verbal counterpart *znh*), technical terminology which is variously used four times in MMT. In B9 some aspect of the offering of Gentiles is 'like a woman who whored with him'. In B75 (with a minor variant in MMT[d]) Qimron and Strugnell translate the term as 'illegal marriage', with Qimron considering that MMT condemns intermarriage between priests and laity.[46] In B82 this same ruling is repeated; this time the preferred translation for *zwnwt* is 'women whom they are forbidden to marry'. In the very broken context of C5 there seems to be a general statement in the context of further marriage law which argues that '[because of] malice (*ḥms*) and the fornication (*ḥznwt*) [some] places were destroyed'. While some have seen *porneia* in Acts 15.20 as merely concerning the kinds of unchastity mentioned in Leviticus 18.6–30,[47] it seems clear from MMT that other matters in marriage practice may be involved.[48] What these may be in the case of Acts 15 requires further research.

If MMT's particular concerns in matters of cultic and marriage practice are indeed the focus for the self-definition of the group which the text represents in its first-person plural pronoun, then to discover a similar combination of cultic purity rules together with mention of

---

46 DJD 10, 55.

47 E.g., H. Conzelmann, *Acts of the Apostles* (Hermeneia; Philadelphia: Fortress Press, 1987), 119.

48 Other texts from Qumran also use *znwt* and *znh* in a range of contexts. For a recent discussion of some of these, but in relation to the Matthaean divorce pericope, see J. Kampen, 'The Matthean Divorce Texts Reexamined', *New Qumran Texts and Studies: Proceedings of the First Meeting of the International Organization for Qumran Studies, Paris 1992* (ed. G. J. Brooke with F. García Martínez; STDJ 15; Leiden: Brill, 1994), 149–67.

porneia in Acts 15 may be very significant for how Luke considered the early Christian community to be defining itself in continuity with the precepts of the Law which it was seeking to uphold, without insisting that the whole Law had to be kept by all the Gentile converts. What is taking place in MMT for the groups it is defining is also taking place in Acts 15 for the way Luke is trying to define the new heirs of the promises of God in the Law.

Method: the argument from Scripture

Discussion of the place of the Law in MMT and Luke–Acts leads us to the third area in which the juxtaposition of MMT and Luke–Acts helps us to see more clearly what is taking place in each text without insisting that there is any literary relationship between the two. In terms of the place of the Law and Scripture more broadly, it is remarkable that of all the texts in the late second temple period and just beyond which define the extent of the authoritative scriptural base with which one must grapple and from which one can argue a point, it is Luke and MMT that seem to many to share a definition. In MMT C10 the partially damaged text can be restored to read 'so that you may study (carefully) the book of Moses and the books of the Prophets and (the writings of) David'. This corresponds most closely of contemporary literature with Luke 24.44: 'everything written about me in the law of Moses, the prophets, and the psalms must be fulfilled'.[49]

The place of scripture in Luke–Acts has commonly been understood in terms of the model of the fulfilment of prophecy, with the Prophets and Psalms playing an obvious role in the two works. On this basis it is argued that Luke presents the ministry, death and resurrection of Jesus as the fulfilment of prophecy so that with him or after him there is a new period of history. We have already noted that Luke does not seem to

---

49 J. C. VanderKam (*The Dead Sea Scrolls Today* [London: SPCK, 1994], 142–57) has provided a comprehensive collection of references in relation to information on the extent and character of the 'canon' at Qumran. On whether MMT really refers to a tripartite canon there has been much debate; many prefer to see a reference to just two sets of authoritative Scriptures, with the second set being further defined and extended; see, e.g., E. Ulrich, 'The Non-attestation of a Tripartite Canon in 4QMMT', *CBQ* 65 (2003): 202–14. Part of the further definition of the 'prophets' may include the Psalms and other works; see the more detailed comments in Chapter 4, n. 6.

propose that what is new is discontinuous with the past, so the periodization of history with Jesus as the middle of Lukan time should not be pressed too far. The apostolic decree in Acts shows that what is happening, at least in the scheme of Luke–Acts, is not something entirely new. Furthermore we should note that the Law still has a part to play, even if for most Gentile Christians that is rather minimal. Thus it is not entirely appropriate for the use of Scripture in Luke–Acts to be subsumed in the prophecy–fulfilment model. For Luke Jesus is, among other things, a Law-abiding, Jerusalem-oriented prophet; he is concerned with restoration rather than innovation.

If for Luke–Acts an awareness of the three divisions of the canon mentioned explicitly in Luke 24.44 enables the modern reader to appreciate the continuing significance of the Law in the Lukan scheme, it is pertinent to ask conversely of MMT where the place of prophets and of David lies. For the individual halakhot in section B the reference point is predominantly matters in the Torah, especially Leviticus, Numbers (15 and 19) and Deuteronomy (23); there is little, if any, appeal to the Prophets[50] or to the Psalms. However, in section C (with the help of some restoration) it is clear that the author links adherence to the particular interpretation of the Law which is advocated in MMT B to historical experiences as these are narrated in the former prophets: '[the blessings have (already) befallen in . . .] in the days of Solomon the son of David. And the curses [that] have (already) befallen from the days of Jeroboam the son of Nebat and up to when Jerusalem and Zedekiah King of Judah went into captivity' (C18–19). The exhortation of MMT is grounded in the recollection of the past which demonstrates that some of the blessings and curses presented in the Torah have already been fulfilled. Thus simply articulating the Law is not sufficient; its particular application has to be justified from as broad a perspective as possible. Part of that perspective is the example of David, known not just from the histories but also from his Psalms; he is the example of the righteous man who was delivered and, most importantly, forgiven (C25–6). The interpretation of Law in MMT, like the Law itself, is thus offered as a gift not a threat.

Within Scripture itself this justification for adhering to a particular interpretation of the Law is presented most explicitly in the so-called

---

50 Qimron and Strugnell (DJD 10, 55) prefer to see the words from Jer. 2.3 in MMT B76 as a general reference to Scripture as a whole which declares Israel to be holy. Since there is an introductory formula, it may be preferable to see it as an explicit citation.

Deuteronomistic History. The precepts of Deuteronomic theology are the criteria applied to each ruler in turn. It is not surprising then that Strugnell should have noted in particular the place of Deuteronomy in the overall structure of MMT B and C. As MMT B is introduced with words which echo Deuteronomy 1.1, so C focuses on how blessing and curse (echoing Deut. 27—8) are to be fulfilled especially as the end time is upon the reader. In a less explicit fashion parts of Deuteronomy have been seen to be instructive for appreciating some of the compositional elements in Luke, especially Luke 9.51—18.14 which is entirely made up of non-Marcan material,[51] or even ideas behind the composition of the whole of Luke–Acts.[52] In these ways the Book of Deuteronomy appears schematically influential in both works, as in several others of the time.

A final point can be made which is not distinctive of what MMT and Luke–Acts may share, but is common to the scrolls and the New Testament in general. The attitude to Scripture is displayed through the formulae which introduce quotations of it. In MMT there are several such formulae: *š' ktwb* (B27 introducing a form of Lev. 17.3), *'p ktwb* (B66 introducing a paraphrase of Lev. 14.8), *kt]wb š-* (B70 introducing a paraphrase of Num. 15.30), *kšktwb* (B76 probably introducing Jer. 2.3), *ktwb š-* (B77 introducing a paraphrase of Lev. 19.19), *ktwb bspr mwšh š-* (C6 introducing a paraphrase of Deut. 7.26), *bspr ktwb* (C11 with no further text preserved), *ktwb š-* (C12 introducing a paraphrase of Deut. 31.29), *kt[wb* (C12 introducing a paraphrase of Deut. 30.1–3), *[ktwb bspr] mwšh wbs[pry hnby'y]m š-* (C17 with little text extant), *šktwb bs[pr mw]šh* (C21 closing a general statement). The formulae all concern writing, probably because formulae with terms for speaking are used to represent the opinions of the author and his group. In MMT there is no instance of an introductory formula not introducing a scriptural text or paraphrase, though specific books are only mentioned in the exhortatory section. There thus appears a clear demarcation between Scripture and

---

51 See, e.g., C. F. Evans, *Saint Luke* (TPI New Testament Commentaries; London: SCM; Philadelphia: Trinity Press International, 1990), 34–7.

52 So, e.g., R. Morgenthaler has described the composition of the whole of Luke–Acts in terms of the 'law of duality', the literary pattern of the two-volume work being the working out of the principle that true testimony must be established by the mouth of at least two witnesses (Deut. 19.15): *Die lukanische Geschichtsschreibung als Zeugnis: Gestalt und Gehalt der Kunst des Lukas* (Zurich: Zwingli Verlag, 1949), Vol. 2, 8.

the author's own or his group's own interpretations, which is also the case for Luke–Acts and the whole New Testament.

CONCLUSION

There can be little question of any literary dependence of Luke–Acts on a text like MMT, but by putting the two texts side by side in this brief fashion several aspects of each have been highlighted. Both have some generic features in common as being treatises with the aim of instruction that confirms views with which the recipient is already sympathetically familiar. Both place considerable importance on Jerusalem and the temple as the locus for defining their own stances on issues; such definitions involve matters of purity, particularly as these may concern who may participate in the appropriate way in the worship of God. Sexual laws or marriage practice is also a community marker, though again both texts take very different lines. Both texts argue on a similar scriptural basis, a seemingly trite observation which is of value in seeing that MMT is not just legal prescription for its own sake and Luke–Acts is not tied exclusively to the prophecy–fulfilment model of the use of Scripture, but has a continuing place for the Law. With many of the issues in common, it is nevertheless all the easier to see that the answers proposed in each writing are poles apart. While the author of MMT looks for the day when temple practice will be pure, Luke comes to realize that it not only can be, but has to be done without, though its significance abides. While MMT is rigidly exclusivist, Luke–Acts is inclusivist. In light of a text like MMT the literary achievement of the author of Luke–Acts may be seen a little more clearly; at the least we can see that his literary concerns cannot be entirely divorced from the issues around in the Palestinian Judaism of his day.

10

The *Commentary on Genesis A*
and the New Testament

INTRODUCTION

The aim of this chapter is to identify and discuss some of the parallels between 4Q252 (*Commentary on Genesis A*) and the New Testament writings. I am not concerned to argue that some sections of the New Testament show direct literary dependence upon the Dead Sea Scrolls, but to describe some of the exegetical concerns of the compiler of 4Q252 and to place them alongside various phrases and pericopae in the New Testament to draw out the similarities and differences for the better mutual understanding of both sets of literature.

A brief general description of the manuscript of 4Q252 is appropriate.[1] Six fragments have been assigned to 4Q252. On the right-hand edge of Fragment 1 there is evidence of a thong used to tie the rolled-up manuscript. Thus Fragment 1 preserves the opening column of the manuscript. All six extant fragments taken together preserve parts of six columns of writing. Since the margins are preserved between Columns I and II, II and III, III and IV, and V and VI, and since there is no evidence of stitching impressed on Columns IV or V, it is most likely that all six columns were written on one single piece of leather. Furthermore, because of mirror-writing preserved on the reverse of Fragment 1, it is possible to calculate precisely how tightly rolled the manuscript was; it is very unlikely that it contained any text beyond that of Column VI.[2]

---

1 The Hebrew text and an English translation are available in DJD 22, 185–207. Fragment 1 was published in a preliminary form by T. H. Lim, 'The Chronology of the Flood Story in a Qumran Text (4Q252)', *JJS* 43 (1992): 289–90; Column V was published by J. M. Allegro in 'Further Messianic References in Qumran Literature', *JBL* 75 (1956): 174–5 + Plate I.
2 A more detailed description of the physical remains of the manuscript can be found in G. J. Brooke, 'The Genre of 4Q252: from Poetry to Pesher', *DSD* 1 (1994): 161–5.

It is generally the top part of the manuscript that has been preserved: the top of Columns I, II and III on Fragment 1, the top of Columns III and IV on Fragment 5, and the top of Columns V and VI on Fragment 6. Column I also extends to the bottom margin; the column is 22 lines long.

This six-column work covers topics from Genesis 6—49 and the sequence of the scriptural text is used for ordering the material. There is a series of exegetical pericopae, though no one method of interpretation is consistently used and the pericopae are often introduced abruptly. So, for example, in 4Q252 I, 1 the possessive ending of *qṣm*[3] in I, 1[4] has no obvious antecedent.[5] The overall concern of the central sections of exegesis in the text is the right of a certain group to inherit and possess the land which was God's gift to the patriarchs. This is preceded by a section in which the flood is shown to have lasted for exactly 364 days, thus providing a foundational description of the calendar used by the text's compiler. The central sections are followed by two pericopae concerned with 'the latter days', namely the eschatological fulfilment of the curses of Amalek and the blessings of Jacob.

THE CONTENTS OF 4Q252 AND THE NEW TESTAMENT

The chronology of the flood

4Q252 I, 1–II, 5 contain a chronicle of the flood which is already the subject of several studies.[6] The surface of the text describes the duration of the flood and the dates of some of the key events during it. There is no

---

3 The term seems to require its standard biblical meaning of 'end', but it may be ambiguous, since in other Qumran texts it clearly means 'time' or 'period', most obviously in 4Q180 on which see the detailed study of D. Dimant, 'The "Pesher on the Periods" (4Q180) and 4Q181', *IOS* 9 (1979): 77–102.

4 Unless otherwise indicated, all references are to column and line on the basis that the six fragments of 4Q252 can be suitably reconstructed into six consecutive columns.

5 T. H. Lim considers that 'the antecedent of "their end" is "all flesh"' and refers to Gen. 6.13: 'The Chronology of the Flood Story in a Qumran Text (4Q252)', 291. An antecedent is supplied in the translation of Eisenman and Wise: 'in the 480th [year] of Noah's life their (Wicked humanity) end came for Noah' (*The Dead Sea Scrolls Uncovered* [Shaftesbury: Element Books, 1992], 88).

6 T. H. Lim, 'The Chronology of the Flood Story in a Qumran Text (4Q252)', *JJS* 43 (1992): 288–98; R. H. Eisenman and M. O. Wise, *The Dead Sea Scrolls*

extraneous narrative: nothing describing the construction of the ark or the process of entering it, and nothing is said of the effects of the flood. The content of most of the verses of Genesis which are cited concerns the dates when various events occurred. In fact only a few verses with chronological information are excluded. Overall the concern is to show that the flood lasted for exactly 364 days, the basic solar year. Within the year various dates are mentioned which when set against the solar calendar as it can be reconstructed, for instance, as lying behind the festival section of the *Temple Scroll*, shows that none of the dated events in the flood story takes place on a Sabbath or on the principal days of a festival. Two theological points are thus being made. On the one hand, the judgement inflicted through the flood reflects the way the universe is organized. On the other hand, within the solar year, all that happens to Noah and his family happens at times other than the Sabbaths and the principal days of festivals. Thus Noah and his family reflect God's favouring them by keeping his times and seasons. In this respect the concern is not unlike the *Book of Jubilees* in which the chronology of the flood is the exemplary basis for the author's major apology for observing a 364-day calendar and all that it implies (*Jub.* 6.32–8).

Noah, the flood and the ark are types of righteous obedience, judgement and salvation as can be seen from their widespread use and adaptation in many texts from the second temple period and later.[7] There appear to be two matters which variously recur in the New Testament. The first is calendrical. It is not appropriate here to engage in the continuing debate about whether differences between the solar calendar (which also knows of the phases of the moon) and the lunar calendar (which intercalates according to the solar year) can account for the differences between the chronologies of the Synoptics and the Fourth Gospel. However, one feature of 4Q252 is particularly striking: 4Q252 is the only pre-Christian Jewish text yet known which is concerned to date by the days of the week. Thus interposed into the regular descriptions of dates according to the year of Noah's life and the day of the month, the commentator (or his source) places references to the days of the week.

Uncovered, 77–79; U. Glessmer, 'Antike und moderne Auslegungen des Sintflutberichtes Gen. 6–8 und der Qumran-Pesher 4Q252', *Forschungsstelle Judentum Theologische Fakultät Leipzig* 6 (1993): 3–79; H. Jacobson, '4Q252: Addenda', *JJS* 44 (1993): 118–20; T. H. Lim, 'Notes on 4Q252 fr. 1, cols. i–ii', *JJS* 44 (1993): 121–6.
7 See the material collected together by J. P. Lewis, *A Study of the Interpretation of Noah and the Flood in Jewish and Christian Literature* (Leiden: Brill, 1968).

Indeed that *šbt* should so clearly mean 'week' is a post-biblical use of the term, common in Mishnaic Hebrew.[8] The third day of the week is referred to in I, 8, the fourth day in I, 9 and 11–12, the fifth day in I, 7 and 9, and the sixth day in I, 10. In addition to the obvious absence of the seventh day whose rest is not broken by any person, object or event in the narrative, it is notable how frequently things take place on the first day of the week (I, 4, 13, 17, 19; II, 2, 3).

The flood begins on the first day of the week (2nd month/17th day), and so after one complete year the earth is dried up and Noah exits from the ark (2/17). During the year of the flood, the moment when Noah has real evidence that the flood is decreasing, when he sees the tops of the mountains, is also the first day of the week (11/10), as also the are the days on which he sends out the dove (11/17, 11/24, 12/1). The only day of the week that is mentioned in the New Testament, perhaps for similar reasons of emphasis, is the first day of the week (Matt. 28.1; Mk 16.2, 9; Lk. 24.1; Jn 20.1, 19; Acts 20.7; 1 Cor. 16.2). The way that the resurrection of Jesus is dated so uniformly and so explicitly in the tradition and that event remembered in the cultic activities of the early churches, with the first day of the week being a day of resurrection (resuscitation) also for Eutychus (Acts 20.9–10), may rest in part in an exegetical tradition which recalled the way of salvation in the narrative of the flood, alongside which could be placed other biblical traditions such as the sign of Jonah (Matt. 12.39–41; Lk. 11.29–32), which may itself be linked with the flood through a pun on the name of Jonah.[9] The appearance of the Spirit descending like a dove at Jesus' baptism, together with the reference to 'forty days and forty nights' (Gen. 7.12) in the temptation pericope has also led many to observe Noah typology in the narrative of the baptism

---

8 It has been suggested that *šbt* in texts like Gen. 29.27–8, Lev. 23.15 and 25.8 should be translated as 'week' but it is not necessary from the context to do so, nor is there any Old Testament text which refers to the individual days of the week in this way.

9 Hence the difficulty in interpreting the equivalent Aramaic term in 4Q541 24, 4: 'Scrute et recherche et connais ce qu'a demandé la colombe (*ywn'*)' (E. Puech, 'Fragments d'un apocryphe de Lévi et le personnage eschatologique. 4QTestLévi^c–d(?) et 4QAJa', in *The Madrid Qumran Congress: Proceedings of the International Congress on the Dead Sea Scrolls, Madrid 18–21 March 1991* [ed. J. Trebolle Barrera and L. Vegas Montaner; STDJ 11.2; Leiden: Brill/Madrid: Editorial Complutense, 1992], 475–6); 'Cherche et demande et sache ce que demande l'agitateur' (DJD 31, 253); in his DJD version Puech understands the form to come from the use of a Hebraism with the root *ynh*, 'to oppress'.

and temptation of Jesus. Just as the stress on the first day of the week in the New Testament might illuminate the emphasis on it in 4Q252, so the association of this scheme of dating with the salvific events of the flood narrative might illuminate some aspects of various elements in the New Testament.

The second matter which the flood pericope in 4Q252 helps to illustrate concerns exhortation. Noah and the flood are used to illustrate the way people will be behaving when the Son of Man comes in Matthew 24.37–9 and Luke 17.26–7.[10] Exactly as in the days of Noah the human manner will be unrepentant carelessness. The counterpart to this is the righteousness of Noah himself.[11] In Hebrews 11 Noah is an example of obedient faith; through his respect for God's warning and the building of the ark, the author of Hebrews states that Noah condemned (*katekrinen*) the world. Commentators generally gloss over the phrase but it may now help us to a better understanding of the preposition in 4Q252 I, 1: 'their end came for Noah (*b' qṣm lnwḥ*)'. Noah's action allows the execution of judgement to take place; he condemns the world. The exhortatory use in 1 and 2 Peter is well known. In 1 Peter 3.20–2 the flood and the deliverance of eight people through its waters is the type of baptism, its antitype (*antitupos*, 1 Pet. 3.21). But for the author of this section of 1 Peter the significance of flood and baptism concerns 'a good conscience, through the resurrection of Jesus'. The link between the eight people being saved and the day of new creation and resurrection is made explicit by Justin,[12] but to the exegetical process might now be added the importance of the first day of the week in the Noah chronology of 4Q252. In 2 Peter 2.4–10 Noah features again in a longer moral exhortation. The examples of judgement are the fallen angels, the ancient world (except Noah and seven others) and Sodom and Gomorrah (except Lot); the chief sins are depraved lust and the despising of authority. Since 4Q252 I, 2 contains a use of Genesis 6.3, it is likely that the compiler intended to refer

---

10 A Q saying, like the Jonah allusion already mentioned; surprisingly in his comprehensive survey, *A Study on the Interpretation of the Flood in Jewish and Christian Literature*, J. P. Lewis makes no mention of this saying.

11 Noah is righteous according to Philo, *Confusion* 105; *Giants* 3, 5; *Migration* 125; *Names* 189; *Posterity* 48, 173, 174; *2 Enoch* 34.3; Justin, *Dial.* 138; *Apos. Con.* 8.12.22; etc.

12 *Dial.* 138.1. Early Christians connected the symbolism of the number 8 with the eighth day: *Barn.* 15.9; Justin, *Dial.* 24.1; 41.4; 138.1. See R. Bauckham, *Jude, 2 Peter* (Word Biblical Commentary 50; Milton Keynes: Word, 1986), 250 on 'eighth' in 2 Pet. 2.5.

implicitly to the fallen angels. The chronology of the flood is based on the premise that humanity, apart from Noah and his family, continues for only 120 years after the sons of God cohabited with the daughters of humankind. Indeed sexual depravity is a major feature of the implied exhortation of 4Q252: in addition to the hints of fallen angels and humankind in the time of Noah, mention is made of the curse of Canaan (for Ham's uncovering of Noah's nakedness; II, 5–7), the utter destruction of Sodom and Gomorrah (III, 1–6), the destruction of Amalek (IV, 1–2) and Reuben's sleeping with Bilhah (IV, 3–7). 4Q252 provides another example of a similar list of negative examples; the existence of such lists may account for some of the differences between the exhortations of 2 Peter 2.4–10 and Jude 5–8 on which it may partially depend.[13] For 4Q252 the closest exhortatory passage is in the *Damascus Document* II, 14–III, 18; this concerns those who go astray, particularly 'with eyes of whoredom' (CD II, 16).

Noah to Abraham

The next subsection of text, 4Q252 II, 5–8, begins with Noah and ends with Abraham. The last clause of this unit of text, 'He gave the land to Abraham his friend', deserves some consideration in relation to James 2.23. The clause is a truncated paraphrase of 2 Chronicles 20.7, but notably the designation of Abraham as friend of God is retained. Together with 2 Chronicles 20.7 Abraham is named as the friend of God only in Isaiah 41.8 in the rest of the Hebrew Bible,[14] but there is no mention of the gift of the land in the Isaianic context; rather, the concern is with the offspring of Abraham, the choice or election of Jacob/Israel. For 4Q252 the most significant parallel is in the same exhortatory part of the *Damascus Document* that has already been mentioned (CD II,

---

13 Jude 5–8 lists the angels and Sodom and Gomorrah; it does not mention Noah and his generation. On various matters to do with how 4Q252 handles sexual misde-meanours see I. Fröhlich, 'Themes, Structure and Genre of Pesher Genesis', *JQR* 85 (1994–5): 81–90; I. Fröhlich, '"Narrative Exegesis" in the Dead Sea Scrolls', in *Biblical Perspectives: Early Use and Interpretation of the Bible in Light of the Dead Sea Scrolls* (ed. M. E. Stone and E. G. Chazon; STDJ 28; Leiden: Brill, 1998), 81–99.

14 In addition to the passages discussed here, Abraham is the friend of God in early Jewish literature in *Pr. Azar.* 12; *Jub.* 19.9; *Apoc. Abr.* 9.6; 10.5; *Test. Abr.* A 1.6; 2.3, 6; 8.2, 4; 15.12; 16.5, 9; B 13.1; in early Christian literature in *1 Clem.* 10.1; 17.2; Tertullian, *Adv. Jud.* 2.7; Irenaeus, *Adv. Haer.* 4.14.4, 16.2; and in Islam in the Quran, *sura* 4.124.

15–III, 2): 'Abraham (*'brhm*) . . . was accounted a friend (*wy'l 'whb*) through his keeping of the commandments of God' (CD III, 2).[15] The broader context of the exhortation concerns who will possess the land and who are the rightful heirs of Abraham.

James 2.23 is the only place in the New Testament where Abraham is designated 'friend of God (*philos theou*)'.[16] In James this designation is associated chiefly with Abraham's willingness to offer Isaac on the altar (Jas 2.21), though it is an explanatory gloss on the citation of Genesis 15.6. The label is not linked to the gift of the land (2 Chr. 20.7) nor to the election of Jacob/Israel (Isa. 41.8). Since the LXX uses *philos* in neither Isaiah 41.8 nor 2 Chronicles 20.7, it is likely that the epithet in James was derived from neither, but from some reworking of the Abraham cycle of Genesis in early Jewish literature. The similarity to the immediate context of CD III, 2 and the occurrence of the designation in Greek-speaking Judaism, especially Philo,[17] may well suggest that James is simply 'echoing a familiar description of Abraham which ultimately has a scriptural background'.[18]

Of significance in the juxtaposition of James and 4Q252 is the broader context. In 4Q252 Abraham is designated friend in relation to the gift of the land; the passages from the Abraham cycle which survive in 4Q252 suggest this is worked out through the reworking of the story of Abram's entry into the land (Gen. 15.9, 17 reworked in 4Q252 II, 8–13,

---

15 Cf. *Jub.* 19.9: 'And he said not a single word regarding the rumour in the land how that God had said he would give it to him and to his seed after him, and he begged a place there to bury his dead; for he was found faithful, and was recorded on the heavenly tablets as the friend of God' (trans. R. H. Charles, *APOT* 2.41). Cf. Philo, *Sobriety* 55–6.

16 Ironically, for all that R. Eisenman is very concerned to show the links between the Letter of James and the 'sectarian' scrolls in order to support his theory that James is the Teacher of Righteousness (*James the Just in the Habakkuk Pesher* [SPB 35; Leiden: Brill, 1986]), in *The Dead Sea Scrolls Uncovered* no mention is made of this most explicit parallel between Jas 2.23 and 4Q252; though, of course, the parallel need give no support to his theory.

17 M. Dibelius and H. Greeven, *James: A Commentary on the Epistle of James* (Hermeneia; Philadelphia: Fortress Press, 1976), 172–3, juxtapose several passages in Philo to suggest that Philo understood Gen. 15.6 to imply that Abraham deserved the title 'friend of God'. They also consider whether the title was given to Abraham only as a reward after death or during his lifetime, and argue that Philo, at least, understood it as a title belonging to Abraham during his lifetime.

18 S. Laws, *A Commentary on the Epistle of James* (BNTC; London: Black, 1980), 136–7.

which, like the flood, is given a precise chronology), through its purification in the destruction of Sodom and Gomorrah (III, 1–6), and through
his willingness to offer Isaac (Gen. 22.10–12 reworked in 4Q252 III,
6–9). In the Letter of James it is the offering of Isaac that is singled out as
the explanation for why Abraham's faith was reckoned to him as righteousness. The two passages, Genesis 15.1–6 and 22.1–19, are alone the
places where Abraham's offspring are numbered by the stars. The
promise of offspring in Genesis 15, which Abraham believes, is fulfilled
in Genesis 22 when Abraham is told that his offspring will be as
numerous as the stars because of his obedience, with the implication,
because of the replay of the same motif in Genesis 26.4, that Isaac is to be
the offspring through whom the promise is carried towards fulfilment.
The argument in James fits with the exegetical tendency in 4Q252,
though the emphasis in the former is on faith brought to completion by
works and in the latter on the gift of the land and its implications.

Abram chronology

As a bridging section it is the third poetic half-line ('a land he gave to
Abraham his friend', 4Q252 II, 8) which forms the background for the
next section of text. The compiler moves to describe certain dates concerning Abram. The text becomes increasingly fragmentary, but it seems
likely that its intention is to clarify the chronology of Abram's entry into
the land (II, 13), and thus to provide the chronological framework for
the demonstration of how God himself keeps his promises. It is the entry
to the land which was probably expounded in more detail in Column II.
4Q252 II, 11 appears to paraphrase Genesis 15.9 in which God
commands Abram to bring him various animals. These animals belong
to a covenant ritual. In the context of other community writings from
Qumran, it is possible to suggest that the narrative of Genesis 12—15 is
being rehearsed here because the commentator implicitly recognizes that
it is not necessarily the case that all who claim some physical descent
from Abraham are heirs to the promise made to him. In the section of the
Damascus Document to which reference has already been made it is clear
that the community of its author considered itself to be the only true
Israel returned from the exile. Other residents in the land were illegitimate claimants. Thus 4Q252, and its immediate textual counterparts,
provides evidence of disputes within early Judaism concerning who
could lay claim to the promises given to Abraham.

The early Christian communities variously joined in this debate. So in

Matthew 3.9 and Luke 3.8 John the Baptist is represented as proclaiming: 'Do not presume to say to yourselves, "We have Abraham as our ancestor"'; in Matthew 8.11–12 in response to the centurion's faith Jesus declares that many will come from east and west to eat with Abraham, Isaac and Jacob while the heirs of the kingdom will be thrown into the outer darkness, a saying that is used in a different context in Luke 13.28–9. A similar point is made in the parable of the rich man and Lazarus (Lk. 16.19–31); there is no automatic right of association with Abraham. Similarly Luke has Jesus declare that the repentant Zacchaeus is indeed a 'son of Abraham' (Lk. 19.9). Those rehearsing the Magnificat or Benedictus in primarily a Gentile context make similar claims to be heirs of Abraham (Lk. 1.55, 73). John 8 plays out the motif with ferocity: 'If you were Abraham's children, you would be doing what Abraham did' (Jn 8.39). Stephen's speech in Acts 7 is a declaration that some Jews have betrayed their inheritance.

Most explicitly it is Paul who tries to argue through the issue concerning who are the rightful heirs of Abraham. In Romans 4 he appeals to the righteousness of Abraham which was his before ever he was circumcised; thus, 'if it is the adherents of the law who are to be the heirs, faith is null and the promise is void' (Rom. 4.14). The argument in Galatians is more layered. As part of the overall concern to show that 'those who believe are the descendants of Abraham' (Gal. 3.7), Paul uses the motif of blessing and curse which is displayed climactically in 3.13–14.[19] This juxtaposition of blessing and curse is thematically present in 4Q252, both explicitly and implicitly: explicitly Canaan is cursed (II, 6), the sons of Noah are blessed (II, 7), Isaac passes on the blessing of Abraham (III, 13) and Jacob utters blessings (IV, 3); implicitly humankind at the time of the flood is cursed, Abraham is blessed, and the denial of a blessing for Esau is worked out in the destruction of Amalek. But alongside this general similarity, which is widely recognized as integral to the structure of Genesis itself,[20] Paul shows an interest in the exegetical concern with

---

19 H. D. Betz ('Galatians', *IDBSup* 353; expanded in *Galatians* [Hermeneia; Philadelphia: Fortress Press, 1979]) has even argued that 'in carrying a conditional curse and blessing (1.8–9; 6.16), Galatians functions as a "magical" letter, confronting the addressees once again with the choice between salvation and condemnation; depending on what they will choose, curse or blessing will automatically be activated'.

20 Cf. D. J. A. Clines, *The Theme of the Pentateuch* (JSOTSup 10; Sheffield: JSOT Press, 1978), 29: 'The theme of the Pentateuch is the partial fulfilment – which implies also the partial non-fulfilment – of the promise to or blessing of the

the dating of the promise to Abraham. In light of 4Q252 it is no longer appropriate to say that 'for the apostle's argument the length of the period has, of course, no significance, save that the longer the covenant had been in force, the more impressive is his statement'.[21] The text of 4Q252 is sadly fragmentary just at the place where its compiler attempts to sort out the confusion over the dates of the covenant with Abraham and the entry into the land, a confusion which involves the duration of the exodus. Some manuscripts of LXX Exodus 12.40 declare that the 430 years included both the time of the exodus and the time that the patriarchs were in Canaan.[22] Thus it seems as if Paul is siding with an exegetical tradition which measured Israel's history from the time when the covenant promise was made to Abraham. His concern is clear; the giving of the Law pales in significance in comparison with the promise to Abraham. As already mentioned, 4Q252 implies that the chronology of the date of the entry into the land of Canaan is important because it belongs in an exegetical framework which is concerned to justify one group's claim to the inheritance of Abraham over against that of others.

Sodom and Gomorrah

4Q252 III, 2–6 contains somewhat fragmentary material concerning Sodom and Gomorrah. The text seems to present an abbreviation and adaptation of Genesis 18.23–33. While the MT may be construed as that Abraham was bargaining for a minimum number of righteous which would save Sodom, 4Q252 seems to imply that he was bargaining for both Sodom and Gomorrah, since Gomorrah is a feasible restoration at the end of III, 2, mentioned in association with 'this city' (III, 3). The end of III, 3 and the start of III, 4 probably contain a reworked form of the final divine answer: the sole surviving word at the end of line 3, *ṣdyqym*, 'righteous ones', occurs in the answer to Abraham concerning

---

patriarchs. The promise or blessing is both the divine initiative in a world where human initiatives always lead to disaster, and a re-affirmation of the primal divine intentions for man.'

21 E. W. Burton, *A Critical and Exegetical Commentary on the Epistle to the Galatians* (ICC; Edinburgh: T & T Clark, 1921), 184.

22 This is not simply a matter of Greek vs. Hebrew witnesses for Ex. 12.40, since the Samaritan Pentateuch agrees with LXX[B] in reading 435 years for the duration of residence in Canaan and Egypt, whereas LXX[A] reads 430. The concern in 4Q252 II, 9 with the duration of Abraham's stay in Haran (five years) implies that its compiler is also working with the chronological difficulties from the perspective of Ex. 12.40.

the 50 but *'nwky l' 'šḥyt*, 'I will not destroy', part of which survives at the start of line 4, is an emphatic form of the Lord's answer to Abraham in Genesis 18.28, 31 and 32. The presentation of the Genesis pericope also involves phraseology from Deuteronomy 13 and possibly elsewhere.[23]

As has been shown in detail by J. Loader,[24] the Sodom and Gomorrah pericope has an extensive history in Jewish literature of the second temple period to which 4Q252 now needs to be added. Sodom and Gomorrah also occur in several places in the New Testament. In Matthew 10.15 (and Lk. 10.12;[25] Sodom only) the saying is preserved in which Jesus declares that it will be more tolerable for Sodom and Gomorrah on the day of judgement than for any city which rejects those who carry the message brought by the disciples.[26] The stress here is on hospitality and the reception of those bearing the gospel message. The motif of the need to receive the message is the point of Matthew 11.23–4 (Sodom only) in which Capernaum is compared unfavourably with Sodom. None of these concerns is apparent in 4Q252. In Luke 17.22–37 Jesus declares to his disciples that on the day that the Son of Man is revealed people will be behaving just as in the time of Noah or Lot. The note that 'it rained fire and sulphur from heaven and destroyed all of them', probably depends straightforwardly on Genesis 19.25, though the totality of destruction is the hallmark of Deuteronomy 13 (in the version in 11QTᵃ) and Deuteronomy 20. It is living without care that seems to be the problem, rather than any particular sexual immorality.

---

23 The pericope alludes to the law concerning the idolatrous city in Deut. 13.13–19, as pointed out by M. Bernstein, '4Q252: From Re-Written Bible to Biblical Commentary', *JJS* 45 (1994): 15. Deut. 20.10–18, part of the rules for war, may also be in mind.

24 J. A. Loader, *A Tale of Two Cities: Sodom and Gomorrah in the Old Testament, early Jewish and early Christian Traditions* (Contributions to Biblical Exegesis and Theology 1; Kampen: Kok, 1990). Loader makes reference to texts found at Qumran only within the context of his discussion of the New Testament. He suggests that the absence of the Sodom and Gomorrah motif from Qumran texts such as 1QapGen and CD may have been the result of the site at Qumran being so relatively close to the site of Sodom and Gomorrah. But Loader should have noted texts such as 4Q180 II, 1–10 (as in D. Dimant, 'The "Pesher on the Periods" (4Q180) and 4Q181', *IOS* 9 [1979]: 82–4) and the 'fire of brimstone' (*'š gwpryt*) used for divine chastisement according to 1QpHab X, 5.

25 Lk. 9.51–6 contains a similar set of motifs concerning inhospitality, but without mentioning Sodom or Gomorrah.

26 Loader (*A Tale of Two Cities*, 120) points out how the injunction in Heb. 13.2 concerning hospitality recalls Genesis 18—19.

Whereas in 4Q252 the stress seems to be on the possession of the land with a subsidiary motif of election, in Romans 9—11 the land plays no part but the discussion is all of election. In Romans 9.27–9 Paul uses Isaiah 10.22, which alludes to the children of Israel being numbered like the sand of the sea, and then he cites Isaiah 1.9 (LXX). In the Isaianic context it is a matter of there being survivors for Israel, in contrast with Sodom and Gomorrah. Paul argues that the destruction of Sodom and Gomorrah implies that many of the people of Israel may be destroyed and that the only way that the promise of God can be fulfilled is if the Gentiles are included within the remnant of Israel. The use and reuse of Sodom and Gomorrah from Isaiah to Paul in terms of election makes more sense now that 4Q252 offers us something of a similar approach.

However, it is with Jude 7 and 2 Peter 2.6, which may be dependent upon Jude, that the concern is with sexual lust and immorality. Here we seem to come closer to the handling of the whole Genesis tradition in 4Q252. The possession of the land can be put in jeopardy by sexual mis-behaviour and the land must be purified from such abuses for the inheritance to be sure.[27] Disobedience involving sexual depravity results in the severest punishment on the day of judgement. The varying cata-logue of typological offenders in both texts is not dissimilar from that of 4Q252, though it is closer to CD II, 16–III, 12. The nature of the sexual immorality is open to dispute.

The binding of Isaac

The end 4Q252 III, 6 can only be understood as citing Genesis 22.10 and the subsequent partial phrases can all be matched with phrases from verses 10–12. The awkwardness of the presentation of the Genesis pericope in effectively starting with Abraham's hand being ready for killing Isaac and the way in which what survives of the retelling of the story in 4Q252 is almost word for word the text of Genesis itself make it difficult to see what may have been the compiler's chief concern in pre-senting the extract from the story. Perhaps he was interested in the way Isaac was spared so that God's promise that Abraham's seed would possess

---

27 Cf. 4Q180 II in which there is mention of 'to inherit . . . land' preceding a section on Sodom and Gomorrah: see D. Dimant, 'The "Pesher on the Periods" (4Q180) and 4Q181', 82–5. Dimant points out how the text speaks of Mount Zion and Mount Moriah which are probably to be identified, a possibility implied in the next pericope of 4Q252 concerning the binding of Isaac.

the land could be fulfilled or perhaps he was interested in the purity of Jerusalem (cf. 2 Chr. 3.1).

The binding of Isaac is seen to lie behind the use of the term 'beloved' in the New Testament. As J. D. G. Dunn states, 'It may just be possible that the use of "beloved" in [Mark] 1.11 and 9.7 was intended to recall the offering up of Isaac (Gen. 22.2, 12, 16), for the Aqedah (the binding of Isaac) certainly played a significant role in subsequent Jewish and Christian theology and may already have been a subject of meditation at the time Mark wrote his Gospel.'[28] Although much can be said of the background of many New Testament passages in relation to the early Jewish exegetical treatment of the binding of Isaac, in association with the Suffering Servant of Isaiah 53,[29] not enough survives in 4Q252 to make a comparison possible, beyond what has already been said in relation to the Letter of James concerning the juxtaposition of the binding of Isaac and Abraham being designated 'friend of God'. Nothing in the New Testament juxtaposes the Sodom and Gomorrah story and the binding of Isaac in the abrupt way in which the two stories are put together in 4Q252.

Isaac's blessing of Jacob

4Q252 Fragment 4 hangs loose, but is probably suitably placed in Column III. The mention of El Shaddai suggests that it is Isaac's blessing of Jacob with which the text is concerned; only there in Genesis (28.1–5) does the appropriate combination of words occur. The blessing has two parts, the promise that he will be fruitful and numerous, and the promise of the land. As with the story of the binding of Isaac, not enough of the tradition survives in 4Q252 for us to be sure of the interest of the compiler. However, it seems likely that once again the concern of the blessing with the possession of the land, the land that God gave to Abraham (Gen. 28.4; cf. 4Q252 II, 8), is once again to the forefront. In the whole New Testament only Hebrews 11.20 is particularly concerned to focus on Isaac's blessing of Jacob, but Esau is included as well.

---

28 J. D. G. Dunn, *Christology in the Making* (London: SCM Press, 1980), 48.
29 See especially G. Vermes, *Scripture and Tradition in Judaism* (SPB 4; Leiden: Brill, 2nd edn, 1983), 193–227; also P. R. Davies and B. D. Chilton, 'The Aqedah: A Revised Tradition History', *CBQ* 40 (1978): 514–46.

Amalek

The material on Amalek in 4Q252 Column IV is among the most intriguing in the scroll. The Amalekites may be mentioned for several reasons. Primarily their annihilation will be a feature of the promised eschatological rest for those who possess the land. Their destruction, when put alongside that of Noah's generation, Sodom and Gomorrah, and Canaan is part of the purification of the land from the pollution of sexual misbehaviour. The blotting out of the offspring of Esau emphasizes that the inheritance belongs to Jacob and his descendants. There is no explicit use in the New Testament of the traditions concerning Amalek, either in their biblical form or in the shape of later exegesis.

The blessings of Jacob

After the brief mention of Amalek there is a vacat which is followed by a title: *brkwt y'qwb*, 'blessings of Jacob'. Immediately after the title there is the quotation of Genesis 49.3, the blessing of Reuben, which is all represented.[30] The interpretation begins after a further vacat with the introductory formula *pšrw*, 'its interpretation is'. The interpretation itself states that by this blessing Jacob reproved Reuben for sleeping with Bilhah his concubine.

Next follows the blessing of Judah, published for the first time in 1956,[31] which has received much comment.[32] The many discussions of this section of text now need some revision in light of the rest of 4Q252. What has not yet been noticed is the way that 4Q252 V, 2 reflects Jeremiah 33.17 (*l' ykrt ldwd 'yš yšb 'l ks' byt yśr'l*).[33] Again the wider context in Jeremiah is significant:

---

30 There is no textual or versional support for the omission of any words.

31 J. M. Allegro, 'Further Messianic References in Qumran Literature', *JBL* 75 (1956): 174–6.

32 See especially D. R. Schwartz, 'The Messianic Departure from Judah (4QPatriarchal Blessings)', *TZ* 37 (1981): 257–66, and the literature cited there.

33 Cf. Gen. 49.10 in the Palestinian Targum: 'I will liken thee, my son Jehuda, to a whelp, the young of a lion; for from the killing of Joseph my son thou didst uplift thy soul, and from the judgment of Tamar thou wast free. He dwelleth quietly and in strength, as a lion; and as an old lion when he reposeth, who may stir him up? *Kings shall not cease, nor rulers, from the house of Jehuda* (italics mine), nor *sapherim* teaching the law from his seed, till the time that the King, the *Meshiha*, shall come, the youngest of his sons' (trans. J. W. Etheridge, *The Targums of Onkelos and Jonathan ben Uzziel on the Pentateuch with the Fragments of the Jerusalem Targum* [New York: Ktav, reprinted 1968], 330–1).

In those days and at that time I will cause a righteous Branch
to spring up for David; and he shall execute justice and righteousness in the land. In those days Jerusalem will be saved
and Judah will live in safety. And this is the name by which it
will be called: 'The Lord is our righteousness.' For thus says
the Lord: David shall never lack a man to sit on the throne of
the house of Israel, and the levitical priests shall never lack a
man in my presence to offer burnt-offerings, to make grain
offerings, and to make sacrifices for all time. (Jer. 33.15–18)

The Davidic Branch shall execute justice and righteousness in the land.
The Jeremiah passage continues with mention of the covenant whose
sure character is established as securely as the day and the night come at
their appointed times. Jeremiah 33.22 is a reworking of Genesis
22.17–18, a passage of Genesis which might well have been referred to in
4Q252 III. Since Judah is sometimes used as a designation of the community and the 'men of the community' are explicitly referred to in
4Q252 V, 5, it is likely that the interpretation of Genesis 49.10 should be
understood in close proximity with other community texts. For this
reason it is probable that the Interpreter of the Law featured in V, 5.
Thus, although the *Meḥoqeq* is explicitly identified with the covenant of
kingship, it is quite appropriate to associate the overall significance of the
exegesis with the interpretation of Numbers 21 in CD VI, 2–11.

The Shoot (Branch) of David derives from Zechariah 3.8 and 6.12
which is reused in Jeremiah 23.5–6 and 33.15–16 of the future Davidic
king who will be accompanied by the Levites. The motif is associated
with Isaiah 11.1 most explicitly in 4QpIsaᵃ 8–10 and 4Q285, with
2 Samuel 7.11 in 4Q174 1–3, 10–12, and with Genesis 49.10 in 4Q252
V, 1–4. The messianic significance of the similar title in Isaiah 11.1 is also
juxtaposed with motifs from Genesis 49.9–10 in Revelation 5.5, though
the particular significance of the designation in its context in Revelation
is unclear; it designates the one who has conquered and so is qualified to
open the scroll and its seven seals and the kingship belongs to the saints
from every tribe and language and people and nation whom the Lamb
has ransomed (cf. 'For to him [the Shoot of David] and his seed has been
given a covenant of the kingship of his people for everlasting generations'
4Q252 V, 4). Isaiah 11.1 is quoted with the full force of its universal
implications in the LXX in Romans 15.12 and may lie behind the
unknown quotation in Matthew 2.23. Another bunch of images is
grouped together in Revelation 22.16. The cultic milieu of some of the

exegetical traditions represented in Revelation may account for why the title that is associated with cultic functionaries, Levites, is most explicitly used only in that book.

4Q252 AS A WHOLE

When 4Q252 is taken as a whole, it is easy to see that its surviving pericopae follow the order of Genesis. There are some matters from Genesis which do not seem to be mentioned, such as the Joseph cycle.[34] What remains provides exegetical clarification of passages involving Noah (and his sons), Abraham, Isaac and Jacob. This selective exegetical clarification highlights certain passages which are of continuing significance for the text's compiler in some way.

Most obviously this continuing significance may be seen to rest in the way that most of the pericopae involve blessings and curses. The flood remains typologically threatening, as does the narrative of the destruction of Sodom and Gomorrah, cities of Canaan. God's purposes are demonstrated through Noah's curse of Canaan, through the exclusion of Japhet, through the persistence with which the Amalekites are pursued to their destruction. Abraham's blessing, thoroughly justified by his offering of his beloved son, is passed on by Isaac to Jacob. Jacob's blessing is clarified, particularly in relation to the 'men of the community'. Although the pericope on the binding of Isaac may be best understood in terms of the promise of offspring, it is the promise of the land which is foremost in the text's discussion of the blessings and curses of eschatological significance.[35] The curse of Canaan, the exclusivity of the tents of Shem, the chronology of Abraham's entry, the destruction of Sodom and Gomorrah, Isaac's transmission of the blessing to Jacob, the ultimate annihilation of the Amalekites – all concern the promise of the land. All that remains of 4Q252 seems to suggest that its compiler considered

---

34 Largely absent from the New Testament too, except in Stephen's speech in Acts 7.
35 On the significance of the land in the Qumran texts see M. O. Wise, 'The Temple Scroll and the Teacher of Righteousness', in *Mogilany 1989 Papers on the Dead Sea Scrolls offered in Memory of Jean Carmignac: Part II The Teacher of Righteousness, Literary Studies* (Qumranica Mogilanensia 3; ed. Z. J. Kapera; Kraków, 1991), 136–47, and R. L. Wilken, *The Land Called Holy: Palestine in Christian History and Thought* (New Haven: Yale University Press, 1992), 1–45, especially nn. 33–48. Cf. H. Stegemann, '"Das Land" in der Tempelrolle und in anderen Texten aus den Qumranfunden', in *Das Land Israel in biblischer Zeit (Jerusalem Symposium 1981)* (ed. G. Strecker; Göttingen: Vandenhoeck & Ruprecht, 1983), 154–71.

himself and his audience as those with the right credentials to take up the promise of the land. Most especially the inheritance of the promised land belongs to those who are not involved in any kind of sexual misdemeanour. The activities of the Watchers cause the flood, Canaan is cursed for the uncovering of Noah's nakedness, Sodom and Gomorrah receive their due reward (there are not sufficient righteous people), the Amalekites are proverbially sexually loose, and Reuben is reproved and permanently displaced for his sexual misbehaviour. This exegetical slant is also strikingly applied in the exhortations of the *Damascus Document*.

By contrast, the same passages of Genesis, when used in the New Testament, are not referred to the land. The blessing of Abraham and the divine promise to him is discussed by Paul solely in terms of its universal significance as the basis for the inclusion of Gentiles within God's purposes with the concomitant need to demonstrate the limits of the significance of the Law given to Moses. Attention is thus directed not at the land but at the meaning of Abraham's offspring and the promise that Abraham will be the father of many nations. The Gospels also variously reflect the challenge of the early Christian communities to the definition of the fatherhood of Abraham.

Nevertheless in several exegetical details there are some overlaps between 4Q252 and the New Testament. Some matters are calendrical and chronistic. The terminology used in 4Q252 of the days of the week is a striking precursor of the New Testament's reference to the first day of the week. The concern with the chronology of the entry of Abraham into the land is to be found in both.

Some matters concern the reapplication of scriptural epithets. 4Q252 provides us with one more example of a text in which Abraham is called God's friend; the use of the epithet in James 2.23 is associated with the binding of Isaac, a pericope also of interest to the compiler of 4Q252. The messianic designation of the future Davidic king as the shoot is variously reflected in association with other scriptural passages in some New Testament texts; again, whereas in 4Q252 the context of the interpretation of Genesis 49.10 implies that the benefits of the messianic rule will be restricted only to the members of the community, the scroll that the lion of Judah will open contains the names of a universally gathered reconstituted Israel.

In addition, there is typological exegesis in both. It is striking that in the Gospels the sayings concerning Noah and the flood and Sodom and Gomorrah all belong exclusively to Matthew and Luke. Their typological application certainly involves judgement, but in several cases we have noted that the concern is with the reception of the gospel message brought by the disciples rather than with the destruction of evildoers. However, in 2 Peter and Jude the use of the types is closer to what can be seen as a major subsidiary theme in 4Q252, namely, sexual misdemeanour: Noah's generation and the inhabitants of Sodom and Gomorrah are the types of careless living and sexual immorality. Furthermore, eventually it may be possible to see how the very abrupt introduction of the binding of Isaac can be best explained in light of the context of 4Q252; is it envisaged as the key atoning sacrifice for the purification of the land? The typological use of the sacrifice of Isaac as the voluntary self-offering which has atoning effect is probably hinted at in several New Testament passages as a whole variety of early Jewish exegetical traditions are applied, especially by Paul, to the death of Jesus to aid in the understanding of it as being 'according to the Scriptures'.

The presentation of extracts of Genesis in 4Q252 does not radically alter the understanding of any particular pericope in the New Testament, but it does provide one more significant strand in the tapestry of early Palestinian Jewish eschatological exegesis which provides the backdrop for much from Scripture and its contemporary interpretation that is represented in the New Testament writings.

11

From Qumran to Corinth: Embroidered Allusions to Women's Authority

INTRODUCTION

This chapter has its origin in noticing that the phrase *ky 'yn l'mwt rwqmh btwk h'dh* in 4Q270 (4QD^e) 7 I, 14 seems to defy literal translation. This is most especially because *rwqmh*, or similar words from the root *rqm*, is attested in Hebrew from biblical contexts right up to its reuse in modern Hebrew as referring to something variegated, of mixed colours, usually something embroidered or woven.[1]

This consistency is attested in the Qumran literature too. The term occurs eight times in the Cave 4 copies of the *Songs of the Sabbath Sacrifice*.[2] In 4Q402 2, 3 the context is very broken but there seems to be a description of the Holy of Holies; C. Newsom translates the word as 'brocade'. In 4Q403 1 II, 1 Newsom translates the phrase *rwqmt rwḥ qwdš qwdš'ym* as 'the mingled colours of a spirit of holiest holiness' and notes for the term *rwqmh* here that 'although often rendered as "embroidery," the word refers to variegated colour, usually in garments or other fabrics, but also in decorative stone and metalwork (see 1 Chr. 29.2; 1QM V, 6)'.[3]

---

1 Jastrow, 2.1497 (and with the extended meaning in rabbinic literature based on Ps. 139.15 of 'to form the limbs of an embryo'); BDB, 955; KBL, 909–10. For modern Hebrew cf., e.g., A. Zilkha, *Modern Hebrew–English Dictionary* (New Haven: Yale University Press, 1989), 265.

2 C. Newsom, 'Shirot 'Olat HaShabbat', in *Qumran Cave 4.VI: Poetical and Liturgical Texts, Part 1* (DJD 11; Oxford: Clarendon Press, 1998), 225, notes that 'the form *rwqmh* (biblical Hebrew *rqmh*) is an example in the fem. of the preference in Qumran Hebrew for *qutl* forms over *qitl*'. See E. Qimron, *The Hebrew of the Dead Sea Scrolls* (HSM 29; Atlanta: Scholars Press, 1985), §100.31 and §330.1.

3 Newsom, 'Shirot 'Olat HaShabbat', 281, 283. The importance of 1 Chronicles 29 for the language of the Sabbath Songs is highlighted by J. R. Davila, 'The Macrocosmic Temple, Scriptural Exegesis, and the Songs of the Sabbath Sacrifice', *DSD* 9 (2002): 1–19.

She reckons that in the broken context of the line there is a description of the appearance of the throne of glory and its attendant spirits. In 4Q405 14–15 I, 3 the term appears as *rwqmwtm*, 'probably the *nomen rectum* in a construct chain',[4] to be translated as 'their many-coloured'; in line 6 the term occurs in the phrase *m'śy rwqmwt pl' bdny 'lwhym ḥyym*, 'work of wondrous mingled colours, figures of living god-like being'.[5] In 4Q405 15 II–16, 4 the broken start of the line reads *bdbyr pnw rwqmwt*, 'in the shrine of His presence, the mingled colours['.[6] The text goes on to describe things engraved and the figures of god-like beings. 4Q405 19, 3–6 reads as follows:

> [3]The workmanship of the spi[rits] of the wondrous firmament (is) [4]brightly blended, [spi]rits of the knowledge of truth[and]righteousness in the holy of [ho]lies, [the im]ages of living god-like beings, images of [5]luminous spirits. A[l]l their [workmanship] (is of) h[oly] wondrous mosaic, [spirits] of mingled colours,[fi]gures of the shapes of god-like beings, engraved [6]round about their [gl]orious brickwork, glorious images of the b[ric]kwork of splendour and majes[ty.][7]

The subject matter of this eleventh Sabbath Song is the divine throne chariot and its attendants. The four figures of the merkabah are apparently engraved on the throne.[8] 4Q405 20 II—21–22, 10–11 reads: 'And there is a [ra]diant substance with glorious mingled colours (*brwqmt*), wondrously hued, brightly blended, the spirits of living godlike beings which move continuously with the glory of [the] wondrous chariots'.[9] And 4Q405 23 II, 7 has: 'In their wondrous stations are spirits (clothed with garments of) mingled colours, like woven work, engraved with figures of splendour.'[10]

---

4   Newsom, 'Shirot 'Olat HaShabbat', 332.
5   Newsom, 'Shirot 'Olat HaShabbat', 331.
6   Newsom, 'Shirot 'Olat HaShabbat', 335.
7   Newsom, 'Shirot 'Olat HaShabbat', 341.
8   Newsom ('Shirot 'Olat HaShabbat', 340) also draws attention to J. M. Baumgarten's observation that the *Zohar* describes the four creatures as engraved on the throne using the term *mrqm'* among others: J. M. Baumgarten, 'The Qumran Sabbath Shirot and Rabbinic Merkabah Traditions', *RevQ* 13 (1988): 204.
9   Newsom, 'Shirot 'Olat HaShabbat', 347.
10 Newsom, 'Shirot 'Olat HaShabbat', 362.

In a general vein Newsom comments as follows:

> The appearance of angelic beings is described several times in the *Shirot* in language which borrows from the Priestly writer's description of the garments of the priesthood and of the tabernacle hangings . . . Although the noun *rwqmh* is not used by the Priestly writer, the phrase *m'śh rqm* occurs frequently in descriptions of the workmanship of the screens in the tent of meeting and of the high priest's sash (Exod. 26.36; 27.16; 28.39; etc.). In 1QM VII 11 *m'śh rqm* is rendered by the phrase *ṣwrt ryqmh m'śh ḥwšb*. It is difficult to find a suitable English equivalent for the phrase *m'śy rwqmh*. It designates a multicoloured weave in fabrics or garments but can also be applied to the multicoloured appearance of other substances or products (see 1QM V 6, 9, 14).[11]

The suitable rendering of the phraseology of the War Rule (*'bdny rwqmh*) is indeed something like 'many colored ornaments' as J. Duhaime, for one, has put forward.[12] The term also occurs in 4Q161 7–10 III, 24 (*wbgdy ryqmwt*, 'garments of variegated stu[ff]'),[13] 4Q179 1 II, 12 (*wmśy tlkt wrwqmh*, 'and silk, purple and variegated stuff'),[14] and probably in 4Q462 1, 5 (*rwqmh*, 'embroidered robe').[15]

---

11 Newsom, 'Shirot 'Olat HaShabbat', 225–6.

12 J. Duhaime, 'War Scroll (1QM, 1Q33)', in *The Dead Sea Scrolls, Hebrew, Aramaic, and Greek Texts with English Translations, Volume 2: Damascus Document, War Scroll, and Related Documents* (ed. J. H. Charlesworth; Princeton Theological Seminary Dead Sea Scrolls Project 2; Tübingen: Mohr Siebeck; Louisville: Westminster John Knox, 1995), 107–9.

13 M. P. Horgan, *Pesharim: Qumran Interpretations of Biblical Books* (CBQMS 8; Washington: Catholic Biblical Association of America, 1979), 76.

14 J. Strugnell, 'Notes en marge du volume V des "Discoveries in the Judaean Desert of Jordan"', *RevQ* 7 (1969–71): 163–276, esp. 251.

15 M. Smith, '4QNarrative C', in *Qumran Cave 4.XIV: Parabiblical Texts, Part 2* (ed. J. VanderKam; DJD 19; Oxford: Clarendon Press, 1995), 198–200; Smith comments extensively on the word in Qumran usage and he notes the possible alternative reading of *ryqmh*, which he translates as 'empty-handed'. In a similar manner F. García Martínez and E. J. C. Tigchelaar, *The Dead Sea Scrolls Study Edition* (2nd edn; Leiden: Brill; Grand Rapids: Eerdmans, 2000), 2.940–1, prefer to read *ryqmh*, 'empty-handed'.

In addition to these uses of the word in the non-biblical manuscripts found at Qumran, J. F. Elwolde has drawn attention to the *plene* spelling of *rwqmty* in the presentation of Psalm 139.15 (MT: *l' nkḥd 'ṣmy mmk 'šr 'śyty bstr rqmty bthtywt 'rṣ*) in 11QPs[a] to argue that the word was probably understood by the copyist as a noun, not a verb as in the MT.[16] For this interpretation Elwolde argues from three angles. First, the lack of a *waw* in the first syllable of the verbal form *'śyty* within Psalm 139.15 as presented in 11QPs[a17] strongly suggests that it was not understood as *pu'al* (as in MT) but as *qal*. As such *'śyty* would no longer be in strict parallelism with *rwqmty*, so other ways of understanding the latter could be entertained in addition to seeing it as a *pu'al* verbal form. Second, taking it as a noun is supported by the Greek rendering of the Psalm in which *rqmty* is translated as *hē hypostasis mou*, 'my substance'. Third, such an understanding may have resulted from the scrutiny of morphologically similar forms of the word in other biblical texts such as Ezekiel 16.18 and 26.16, and Psalm 45.15, in all of which it is clearly a noun.

On the basis of such comparisons Elwolde proposes that in certain contexts the noun had an extended symbolic meaning. Thus in Ezekiel 26.16 the 'embroidered garments' (*bgdy rqmtm*) which the princes of the sea take off as they lament for Tyre are symbolic of the status of the princes; they are 'the garments of their status'. For Elwolde in Psalm 45.15 it is 'by acts of authority' (*lrqmwt*) that the princess is brought to the king, the plural signifying something qualitative, such as the 'joy' of the next verse. More probable is Elwolde's understanding of Ezekiel 17.3, a description of Nebuchadnezzar as an eagle, in which the Greek rendering of *hrqmh* is *to hēgēma*, 'leadership'. Elwolde thus finds a meaning for *rwqmh* of 'authority, leadership, status': 'the semantic processes underlying this development are probably to do with metonymy of expensive clothing/covering and the power represented by it'.[18]

---

16 J. F. Elwolde, '*Rwqmh* in the Damascus Document and Ps. 139.15', in *Diggers at the Well: Proceedings of a Third International Symposium on the Hebrew of the Dead Sea Scrolls and Ben Sira* (ed. T. Muraoka and J. F. Elwolde; STDJ 36; Leiden: Brill, 2000), 65–83.

17 Ps. 139.15 in 11QPs[a] XX, 6–7 reads as follows: *lw' nkḥd 'ṣby mmkh 'šr 'śyty bstr rwqmty bthtywt 'rṣ*.

18 Elwolde, '*Rwqmh* in the Damascus Document and Ps. 139.15', 72; Elwolde also comments that a sense of the root *rgm* as 'speak with authority', which is unattested in the Hebrew of the Bible may have assisted the semantic development.

From all this information concerning the appearance of the term in contemporary texts which could indeed have been known to the scribes of the first-century copies of the *Damascus Document*, if not to the passage's original author, what is to be made of the strange occurrence of *rwqmh* in 4Q270? In addition to the basic meanings which the noun carries in its various contexts in the Songs of the Sabbath Sacrifice and the War Rule, it is important to note that the term occurs in contexts which seem to develop the language of the priestly writer concerning various cultic items, and that part of the development is a kind of linguistic transfer to spiritual beings who are associated with the multicoloured character of the heavenly shrine. Furthermore, as Elwolde has indicated, the term's semantic development by metonymy seems to be present in the Hebrew Bible as becomes apparent by considering the Greek renderings of Psalm 139.15 and Ezekiel 17.3.

4Q270 7 I, 13–15 AND ITS VARIOUS INTERPRETATIONS

4Q270 7 I, 13–15 reads as follows:

13   *'šr ylw]n 'l 'bwt*
14 [*yšlḥ*] *šmn h'dh wl' yšwb* [*w'm*] *'l h'mwt wn'nš 'šr*[*t*] *ymym ky 'yn l'm*[*w*]*t rwqmh btwk*
15 [*h'dh*]

As Elwolde has pointed out,[19] there have been several attempts in recent years to translate this pair of sentences, since the text became widely known through the reconstruction work of B.-Z. Wacholder and M. Abegg,[20] and more explicitly in the preliminary editorial work of J. M. Baumgarten.[21]

---

19 Elwolde, '*Rwqmh* in the Damascus Document and Ps. 139.15', 74–7.
20 B. Z. Wacholder and M. G. Abegg, *A Preliminary Edition of the Unpublished Dead Sea Scrolls: The Hebrew and Aramaic Texts from Cave Four, Fascicle 1* (Washington: Biblical Archaeology Society, 1991), 46; listed as 4QD^e Frag. 11, Col. 1, lines 13–15.
21 J. M. Baumgarten, 'The Cave 4 Versions of the Qumran Penal Code', *JJS* 43 (1992): 270. Baumgarten also referred briefly to this passage in 'The Qumran Cave 4 Fragments of the Damascus Document', in *Biblical Archaeology Today, 1990: Proceedings of the Second International Congress on Biblical Archaeology* (Jerusalem: Israel Exploration Society, The Israel Academy of Sciences and Humanities, 1993), 396.

Baumgarten's first published translation of the passage reads as follows:

> One who murmurs against the Fathers shall be [sent forth] from the congregation and shall not return. If (he murmurs) against the Mothers he is to be penalized for ten days, for the Mothers do not have authority (?) within the [congregation].[22]

Baumgarten's capitalization of the terms Fathers and Mothers results from his considering them to be 'honorific titles applied to senior members of the community, apparently akin to the Brothers and Sisters mentioned in 4Q502'.[23]

The earliest attempt at rendering the passage in a popular translation of the scrolls was made by F. García Martínez in his 1992 Spanish translation:

> . . .] sobre los padres, [saldrá] de la congregación y no retornará [más. Pero si es] sobre las madres, será castigado diez días porque no hay para las madres mezcla (?) en medio de [de (sic) la congregación.[24]

His view on how the text might be handled has remained similar in his subsequent renderings into English which have gone through several editions:

>] about the fathers, [shall leave] the congregation and not come back [again. But if it is] about mothers, he shall be punished for ten days because for mothers there is no mingling (?) in the midst of [the congregation . . .][25]

---

22 Baumgarten adds a note that the translation, 'authority', is suggested by the context; he also refers to other uses of *rwqmh* in the scrolls.

23 Baumgarten, 'The Cave 4 Versions of the Qumran Penal Code', 271.

24 F. García Martínez, *Textos de Qumrán* (Madrid: Editorial Trotta, 1992), 115 (as 4Q270 11 I, 13–15).

25 F. García Martínez, *The Dead Sea Scrolls Translated: The Qumran Texts in English* (Leiden: Brill, 1994), 66 (as part of 4Q270 11 I, 13–15); repeated identically in the second edition (Leiden: Brill; Grand Rapids: Eerdmans, 1996), 66; and with E. J. C. Tigchelaar in *The Dead Sea Scrolls Study Edition, Volume 1 (1Q1–4Q273)* (Leiden: Brill; Grand Rapids: Eerdmans, 2000), 617 (as 4Q270 7 I, 13–15).

He focuses on the notion of variegation in the root and tentatively proposes to render the term as 'mingling',[26] implying that since the mothers do not have the same place in the congregation as the fathers, the term must refer to the way in which the mothers are effectively excluded from the deliberations of the congregation and therefore an offence against them is deemed far less serious than one against the fathers. J. Maier was the next scholar to publish a translation of the difficult passage:

] gegen die Väter, [dann gehe er hinaus] aus der Gemeinde und kehre nicht [wieder; und wenn] gegen die Mütter, [dann wird er be]straft zeh[n] Tage, denn den Mütt[er]n geziemt keine Einordnung (*rwqmh*) innerhalb [der Gemeinde.[27]

Maier comments that *rwqmh* 'Wohl von *rqm* abgeleiteter terminus technicus für eine feste Anordnung'.[28] He understands *rwqmh* as some kind of technical term for 'order' but does not explain from where he obtains such a sense for the root *rqm*. His translation takes seriously the implication of the differences in the punishment meted out for the two offences and so he takes the term as reflecting some kind of status or relative position, so that the mothers have no suitable place or order in the congregation.

Next to offer a slightly revised rendering of the problematic term was J. M. Baumgarten, the scholar responsible for the *editio princeps* of the Cave 4 fragments of the *Damascus Document*.

One who murmur]s against the fathers [shall be expelled] from the congregation and not return; [if] it is against the mothers, he shall be penalized for ten days, since the mothers do not have authoritative status (?) within [the congregation.[29]

26 Elwolde ('*Rwqmh* in the Damascus Document and Ps. 139.15', 74) notes how the English version somewhat inappropriately changes a straightforward noun ('mezcla' ['mixture']) into a gerundive ('mingling').

27 J. Maier, *Die Qumran-Essener: Die Texte vom Toten Meer, Band II: Die Texte der Höhle 4* (Uni-Taschenbücher 1863; Munich: Ernst Reinhardt, 1995), 229 (as 4Q270 11 I, 13–15).

28 *Die Qumran-Essener*, 22, n. 345.

29 J. M. Baumgarten, *Qumran Cave 4.XIII: The Damascus Document (4Q266–273)* (DJD 18; Oxford: Clarendon Press, 1996), 164.

Although he has altered the translation of *rwqmh* from 'authority' to 'authoritative status', as in his preliminary study of the regulation, Baumgarten comments on the problematic word as follows: 'The translation of *rwqmh* is suggested by the context. In 4QShirShabb and 11QShirShabb the word is used for embroidered figures, and in 4Q405 the phrase *rwqmt kbwd* occurs, but there is no apparent etymological connection with the sense required here.'[30]

In 1996 a fresh collection of English translations was issued. E. M. Cook was responsible for the relevant passage of the *Damascus Document* under consideration here. He rendered the passage as follows:

> Whoever speaks] against the fathers, [he must leave] the congregation and never return; [but if] against the mothers, he must suffer reduced rations ten days, for the mothers have no such esteem within [the congregation.[31]

Like Maier, Cook has reckoned that the passage has to do with the relative importance of fathers and mothers in the congregation and so he gives the term *rwqmh* the extended meaning of 'esteem', though that seems only indirectly connected with anything variegated, multi-coloured or woven.

In the fifth edition of his well-known translation, G. Vermes offered the following rendering of the passage:

> [If he has murmured] against the Fathers, he shall leave and shall not return [again (cf. 1QS VII, 17). But if he has murmured] against the Mothers, he shall do penance for ten days. For the Mothers have no *rwqmh* (distinction?) within [the Congregation.[32]

Of all the translators considered so far, he seems the most willing to display the difficulty that the term *rwqmh* causes. He leaves the Hebrew term in his translation and offers an interpretation in parentheses. His interpretation supposes like Baumgarten and others that the phrase has

---

30 *Qumran Cave 4.XIII: The Damascus Document*, 166.
31 M. Wise, M. Abegg, E. Cook, *The Dead Sea Scrolls: A New Translation* (San Francisco: HarperCollins, 1996), 73 (as 4Q270 11 I, 13–15).
32 G. Vermes, *The Complete Dead Sea Scrolls in English* (London: Penguin, 1998), 152.

to do with the value put on the status of the mothers in the congregation and he suggests that they have no distinction within it.

In 1997 C. Hempel also offered a version of the rule:

> [He who murmu]rs against the fathers [shall be sent away] from the congregation and not return; [if it is] against the mothers [he shall be pu]nished te[n] days for the m[o]thers have no *rwqmh* in the midst of [the congregation].[33]

Somewhat like Vermes, Hempel declines to translate the term and she comments in an extensive note that none of the previous translations known to her seems entirely satisfactory. 'Baumgarten's translation seems too harsh on the position of women as portrayed in this offence. Clearly women and men are not treated as equals in our passage. Nevertheless, the mere presence of a penalty for "murmuring against the mothers of the congregation" implies that they *do* have some authority.'[34] In a not dissimilar vein E. M. Schuller translates the phrase as 'for the mothers do not have *rwqmah* (?) within the [congregation]', and notes that the phrase has not yet been explained in a convincing manner.[35]

J. Elwolde's proposal offers substantial support to Baumgarten's rendering of the text. He has argued in detail that an extended meaning of *rwqmh* as 'authority, leadership, status' was known at least to the Greek translators of the Psalms and Ezekiel and at Qumran. He has concluded that in the community referred to in 4Q270 'women members in some sense "didn't count"'. A murmurer against the mothers is fined for (just) ten days, for mothers have no "essential being", "authority" or "status" in the midst of the community, that is to say they "count for nothing" or "have no (intrinsic) right to be" there'.[36]

Elwolde also reports on three other suggestions for *rwqmh*. T. Muraoka has noted that the Greek term *hypostasis* can also have the

33 C. Hempel, 'The Penal Code Reconsidered', in *Legal Texts and Legal Issues: Proceedings of the Second Meeting of the International Organization for Qumran Studies, Cambridge 1995, Published in Honour of Joseph M. Baumgarten* (ed. M. Bernstein, F. García Martínez and J. Kampen; STDJ 23; Leiden: Brill, 1997), 348.

34 Hempel, 'The Penal Code Reconsidered', 347, n. 54.

35 E. M. Schuller, 'Women in the Dead Sea Scrolls', in *The Dead Sea Scrolls After Fifty Years: A Comprehensive Assessment* (ed. P. W. Flint and J. C. VanderKam; Leiden: Brill, 1999), 2:129.

36 Elwolde, '*Rwqmh* in the Damascus Document and Ps. 139.15', 73.

204   SCROLLS ILLUMINATE THEIR NT COUNTERPARTS

sense of 'wealth, substance, property'.[37] Elwolde rightly reckons that this meaning is not appropriate for Psalm 139.15, but might fit Ezekiel 17.3. If it is allowed at all as a rendering of *rwqmh*, then on that basis 4Q270 would concern the rights the mothers lacked because they did not contribute any property to the congregation in their own right. Overall this particular understanding is problematic because elsewhere in the community texts little or nothing is suggested about any link between rights or status in the congregation and the property that is handed over or contributed.

E. Qimron also made a proposal in reaction to Elwolde's presentation.[38] He suggested that the underlying semantics of *rqmh* concern things being connected or related and that in 4Q270 *rwqmh* would mean 'connection, relationship'. This would imply that the mothers were not connected with the congregation in any way. However, the fact that there is some punishment for murmuring against the mothers strongly suggests that there is some kind of connection with the community. Indeed, it is hard to accept that mothers had no connection with the community given the various roles women play in some of the community compositions found in the Qumran caves.

The third proposal noted by Elwolde was made by V. A. Hurowitz and has been presented in a separate short study.[39] Hurowitz has suggested that the term has nothing to do with embroidery but is a Hebrew form or phonetic variant of the Akkadian term *rugummû* which, he argues, is widely attested in legal contexts meaning 'legal claim'. He has noted that it appears in the formulation *rugummâ (la) rašê* and *rugummâ (ul) îši*, 'to have (no) legal claim' or 'there is (no) legal claim' which appears to be similar to the idiom of the Qumran usage in 4Q270, *'yn l- rwqmh*. Hurowitz has suggested that the Akkadian term entered Hebrew by way of Aramaic as **rwgmh* and metamorphized ever so slightly either in general or on a one time basis into *rwqmh*. The less severe punishment for one who murmurs against the mothers comes about because the mothers have 'no legal claim' or 'right to reparation' against the offender. Though this idiomatic argument is intriguing, it does not entirely satisfy

---

37 LSJ 1895b; Elwolde, '*Rwqmh* in the Damascus Document and Ps. 139.15', 76–7.

38 Elwolde, '*Rwqmh* in the Damascus Document and Ps. 139.15', 77.

39 Elwolde, '*Rwqmh* in the Damascus Document and Ps. 139.15', 77; V. A. Hurowitz, '*Rwqmh* in Damascus Document 4QDᵉ (4Q270) 7 i 14', *DSD* 9 (2002): 34–7.

on two counts: on the one hand, it does not explain why, if there is no legal claim, the offender should be punished at all and, on the other, it does not negate the notion that, even if it belongs within a much earlier technical legal idiom, *rwqmh* was nevertheless understood in this first-century B.C.E. context as referring to something which by metonymy could mean 'authority'.

All these various attempts at rendering this problematic phrase try to take into account the immediate context in which the same offence committed against the fathers in the congregation is treated very differently from when it is committed against the mothers. 'Mothers' appears to be a label that designates an office of some sort described in terms of fictive kinship and so it is not a straightforward matter of patriarchal discrimination, but one which presupposes that in a particular institutional setting 'Mothers' are inferior to 'Fathers'. The identification of mothers as holding some kind of office supports the view that we are dealing with matters of relative authority or status whatever the precise meaning of *rwqmh*.

The broader context also helps a little. The sentences which we are discussing are part of a list of rules which may be termed 'the laws of the many' (*mšpṭ hrbym*). The three rules which precede the one we are discussing are, first, that anyone who despises these laws shall be expelled; second, that anyone who breaches the law by taking food that is not his own must return it to the man from whom he took it; and third, that anyone who commits fornication with his wife shall be expelled. This ruling which immediately precedes the law on fathers and mothers is best understood, it seems to me, in terms of 1QSa (1Q28a) I, 9–11. That passage shows that a man may not have intercourse with a woman until he is 20 years old, 'when he knows good and evil'. Then she (his wife) shall be received to give witness against him about the rulings of the Law (*mšpṭwt htwrh*). One must assume that it was acknowledged that the woman, presumably the wife, is the only one who can testify whether her husband has committed fornication with her, whatever that may involve.[40] In this matter at least, the woman's testimony is both necessary and acceptable; 1QSa (1Q28a) appears to be precise and explicit about the exceptional and limited case in which a wife's testimony is acceptable. If that may help to explain the rule immediately preceding the one about murmuring against fathers and mothers, then it may be no surprise that

---

40 See the various comments by Schuller, 'Women in the Dead Sea Scrolls', 2:126–27, 133–34.

the rule makes it clear that in fact the mothers have only slender authority or limited status within the congregation.

It should be noted that as in 1QSa (1Q28a) the key term in 4Q270 which defines the group is congregation (*'dh*) not community (*yḥd*). It is pertinent for the purposes of this chapter to recall that the *Rule of the Congregation* also contains a brief delimitation of the congregation, particularly as it is understood as an assembly (*qhl*):

> And any man who is afflicted with any one of the human uncleannesses shall not enter into the congregation (*qhl*) of these. And anyone who is afflicted with these so as not to take his stand among the congregation (*'dh*): And any who is afflicted in his flesh, crippled in the legs or the hands, lame or blind or deaf or dumb, or if he is stricken with a blemish in his flesh visible to the eyes; or a tottering old man who cannot maintain himself among the congregation (*'dh*); these may not enter to take their stand among the congregation of the men of renown, for holy angels are in their council.[41]

In sum, the rule concerning an offence against fathers and mothers justifies different punishments on the basis that the mothers do not have *rwqmh* in the midst of the congregation (*'dh*). Other texts found in the Qumran caves, as well as biblical material, show that *rwqmh* does indeed mean something variegated, multicoloured, especially woven or embroidered material, though other objects, especially cultic ones, may be so described. It might be reasonable to suppose that the limitation of the status of the mothers in the congregation is reflected in the fact that they are not permitted to wear a mark of authority in the congregation. Perhaps that sign is particularly something cultic, possibly a piece of embroidered cloth associated with priestly status. The presence of angels also prevents various groups of people from taking a full place in the congregation.

Let us conclude this section by posing a question: if Paul were to have translated *rwqmh* in this passage of the *Damascus Document* into Greek, might he have found it appropriate to have used the term *exousia*? If so, then we should turn to 1 Corinthians 11 to help us appreciate Baum-

---

41 Trans. L. H. Schiffman, *The Eschatological Community of the Dead Sea Scrolls: A Study of the Rule of the Congregation* (SBLMS 38; Atlanta: Scholars Press, 1989), 37–8.

garten's translation of 4Q270 7 I, 14: 'since the mothers do not have authoritative status (?) within the congregation'.

AUTHORITY IN 1 CORINTHIANS 11.10

I have just tentatively suggested that the use of the term *exousia* in 1 Corinthians 11.10 may help the better understanding of a particular congregational rule in 4Q270, but it may well be the case that the two passages are mutually illuminating. 4Q270, for all that we do not understand it well, may assist in the better interpretation of 1 Corinthians.

Dozens of articles and chapters in books have been penned on the perplexing passage in 1 Corinthians 11 concerning the relative status of men and women in the worshipping community.[42] It would be foolhardy to think that a short paper can solve all the issues, but I will briefly make a few comments on two matters. The first is a matter of detail. What is the most suitable way of understanding and interpreting the word *exousia* in this context? The second is a more general issue. In insisting on women having their heads covered, is it possible to determine whether Paul was encouraging the observance of Jewish or Greek customary practice?

It is clear from any dictionary article on the word *exousia* that its meaning, determined by multiple uses, has to do essentially with authority and power.[43] For the New Testament, W. Foerster proposes that the term's role is based on three foundations: it denotes power which decides rather than physical power, it is power in a legally ordered whole, and so also it may denote power as exercised in a community, the hallmark of which may be its freedom, its empowerment.[44] But even Foerster writes a special section on 1 Corinthians 11.10 in which he argues, on the basis of the immediate context, that the term relates to veiling[45] from the standpoint of the relation of woman to man and that it refers to the moral obligation of the woman, not to any kind of constraint. The veil is thus a

---

42 For much recent bibliography see especially W. E. Mills, *1 Corinthians* (Bibliographies for Biblical Research New Testament Series 7; Lewiston: Mellen Biblical Press, 1996), 57–63.

43 BDAG 277–8; with a special paragraph on 1 Cor. 11.10 seeing the word as referring either to power exercised by women to protect themselves from 'the amorous glances of certain angels' or as referring to a symbol of womanly dignity.

44 W. Foerster, *TDNT* 2.566.

45 The substitution of *kalumma* for *exousia* in references to 1 Cor. 11.10 from Irenaeus onwards are helpfully listed by J. Winandy, 'Un curieux *casus pendens*: 1 Corinthiens 11.10 et son interprétation', *NTS* 38 (1992): 621–2.

sign of woman's subordination to man and *exousia* is to be understood by metonymy. This is indeed the majority opinion among ancient and modern interpreters, even though it attributes a passive sense[46] to *exousia* and requires in the wider context an understanding of *kephalē* which does not seem lexically defensible.[47]

While it is clear that the wider context of the passage requires that what is at stake in 1 Corinthians 11.10 is indeed a matter of the relative status of men and women in the worshipping community, it is possible to understand that the authority taken by a woman here is not that granted through her supposed subordination to her husband, but rather it has to do with her relative empowerment as a woman.[48] As Paul anticipates his views of natural law (1 Cor. 11.13–15) and customary behaviour,[49] especially in other churches (1 Cor. 11.16), he weaves

---

46 The problem of the resultant passive sense is highlighted by G. D. Fee, *The First Epistle to the Corinthians* (NICNT; Grand Rapids: Eerdmans, 1987), 519–20.

47 This majority opinion comes about partly because it is assumed Paul is reflecting a hierarchical view standard in late antiquity (e.g., J. Ziesler, *Pauline Christianity* [Oxford: Oxford University Press, 1983], 116) and partly because of the understanding of Paul's use of the term 'head' in the preceding context; although several commentators (e.g., J. Murphy-O'Connor, 'Sex and Logic in 1 Corinthians 11.2–16', *CBQ* 42 [1980]: 491–3) have seen the term as indicating only that woman is entirely derived from man as her 'source', many still seem to prefer to understand the term 'head' metaphorically in terms of authority: see, e.g., W. Grudem, 'Does kephalē ["Head"] Mean "Source" or "Authority" in Greek Literature? A Survey of 2,336 Examples', *TJ* 6 (1985): 38–59; also the rebuttal by R. S. Cervin *TJ* 10 (1989): 85–112; and the response by W. Grudem, *TJ* 11 (1990): 3–72; cf. also J. A. Fitzmyer, 'Another Look at KEFALH in 1 Corinthians 11.3', *NTS* 35 (1989): 503–11.

48 This may be reinforced through noting the doubling of the argument: as a man 'naturally' has a shaved head, so he should not cover it further, and as a woman naturally has a head covered with long hair, so she should repeat and reinforce the natural effect by covering her head again. After the presentation of this paper L. H. Schiffman drew my attention to the use of this passage of 1 Cor. in some modern Jewish communities where women's double head covering is an issue.

49 Namely, that for women to have shaved heads was a mark of shame, perhaps associated with female slaves or prostitutes. His disarming question in 1 Cor. 11.13 ('Judge for yourselves: is it proper for a woman to pray to God with her head uncovered [*akatakalupton*]?') strongly suggests that he was aware that it was customary in the Graeco-Roman world for praying women to have covered heads (cf. the texts cited in BDAG 29). On the other hand, Winandy, 'Un curieux *casus pendens*: 1 Corinthiens 11.10 et son interprétation', 621–9, suggests that Paul was amicably constructing an argument to help justify what was already being practised in the Corinthian church, a practice which seemed to go against standard conventions.

together a theological perspective on the differing roles of man and woman in relation to 'glory', so that what a woman wears on her head empowers her to take her place in the cultic activity of the local church,[50] or at least shows that she is in charge of her own prophetic practice.[51] Despite the difficulty for this interpretation caused by the apparent overall argument of both the immediate and wider context (cf. 1 Cor. 14.33–6), some scholars have thus seen this cryptic verse as reflecting Paul's overall presupposition (cf. Gal. 3.28) that in the community of believers who are in Christ, the standard distinctions between men and women are both overcome through a kind of realized eschatology but also maintained[52] as the cosmic dimensions of God's victory in Christ are worked through.[53] The sign of that is not that everyone ends up looking the same, but that for Paul women's authority is to be marked by customary decorum, either with a veil or with braided hair tied up.[54] Paul might

---

50 See, e.g., M. D. Hooker, 'Authority on Her Head: An Examination of I Cor. XI.10', *NTS* 10 (1963–4): 410–16; followed recently by J. D. G. Dunn, *The Theology of Paul the Apostle* (Grand Rapids: Eerdmans, 1998), 590. Murphy-O'Connor argues that Paul is concerned to show on the one hand that the men and women are different as both the created order and convention show, but also that in dressing her hair as a woman, it becomes a symbol of the authority she enjoys ('Sex and Logic in 1 Corinthians 11.2–16', 497–8).

51 As argued, e.g., by D. R. Hall, 'A Problem of Authority', *ExpTim* 102 (1990): 39–42: 'Paul's purpose would seem to be to establish the right of a woman prophet to do what she wished with her own head – i.e., in this context, to keep it covered' (p. 40). Cf. also Fee, *The First Epistle to the Corinthians*, 520: 'For this reason the woman ought to have the freedom over her head to do as she wishes.'

52 This tension in the passage is highlighted by, e.g., P. Perkins, *Ministering in the Pauline Churches* (New York: Paulist, 1982), 58–9.

53 This has led some scholars to infer that Paul is arguing against a Corinthian interpretation of Gen. 1 which was inhibiting his view that Christ alone was the image of God and which was being used to permit women to behave in the same way as men; see, e.g., A. C. Wire, *The Corinthian Women Prophets: A Reconstruction through Paul's Rhetoric* (Minneapolis: Fortress Press, 1990), 122–8.

54 The customary practice of women being covered, especially in the presence of angels, may be seen all the more clearly through consideration of the instruction of the man from heaven to Aseneth: 'Remove the veil from your head, and for what purpose did you do this? For you are a chaste virgin today, and your head is like that of a young man' (*Jos. Asen.* 15.1 [*OTP* 2.225–6]). The divinely delivered Thecla also puts on men's attire (*Acts Paul* 43). However, the jury is still out on what may have constituted customary practice more locally in Corinth for women participating in worship; there is some evidence that in mystery cult worship Greek women put aside their veils and loosened their hair, so Paul may have been wanting to support

also be dealing with the complicating factor of women of various social statuses being present in the Corinthian church;[55] some of the wealthier ones in particular could have long since, even in their pre-Christian lives, lost any sense of necessary subordination.[56]

Within the context of the relative status of men and women, it is what may be worn by the woman that empowers her; without *rwqmh*, by extension, the mother (even despite her technical official role) in the Damascus congregation has no significant empowered place, without *exousia* on her head, for Paul, the Corinthian Christian woman should be unable to take her place in the worshipping community. It is clear that neither *rwqmh* nor *exousia* means 'veil', but that the former from the side of its use for variegated embroidery seems to acquire the extended meaning of 'authority', the other from its use as a term for authority acquires the extended meaning denoting also what signifies that authority, namely, what covers the head, for most interpreters a 'veil', but for others simply the hair properly bound up.[57]

---

alternative custom to distinguish Christian worship from other local options. See Wire, *The Corinthian Women Prophets*, 220–3 (Appendix 8). On the general significance of the veil in the pre-Islamic Near East, especially as denoting the woman as an appurtenance, see K. van der Toorn, 'The Significance of the Veil in the Ancient Near East', in *Pomegranates and Golden Bells: Studies in Biblical, Jewish, and Near Eastern Ritual, Law, and Literature in Honor of Jacob Milgrom* (ed. D. P. Wright, D. N. Freedman and A. Hurvitz; Winona Lake: Eisenbrauns, 1995), 327–39.

55 See, e.g., W. A. Meeks, *The First Urban Christians: The Social World of the Apostle Paul* (New Haven: Yale University Press, 1983), 70–1.

56 Because of the ways in which the social diversity of their members are overcome, G. Theissen describes the kind of social ethos that emerged in churches like that at Corinth as 'love-patriarchalism': *The Social Setting of Pauline Christianity: Essays on Corinth* (Minneapolis: Fortress Press, 1982; Edinburgh: T & T Clark, 1990), 106–8. It should, of course, be added that the adoption and adaptation of social conventions in a particular form in a church like Corinth does not establish timeless principles for how all later generations of Christians should behave: see, e.g., M. Langley, *Equal Woman: A Christian Feminist Perspective* (Basingstoke: Marshalls, 1983), 51–2. Also note the comment by M. D. Hooker, 'Paul', in *The Oxford Companion to Christian Thought* (ed. A. Hastings, A. Mason and H. Pyper; Oxford: Oxford University Press, 2000), 521–4, quotation from 523–4: 'It is an irony of history that Paul's writings so quickly became "canonical"; that the man who protested that his converts must not subject themselves to the Law had his work turned into "law" and treated as binding on later generations . . . his teaching about women dressing in a comely way when leading church worship was regarded as authoritative for centuries, even though it was largely based on social convention at the time (1 Cor. 11.2–16).'

57 E.g., Murphy-O'Connor, 'Sex and Logic in 1 Corinthians 11.2–16', 488–90.

Several scholars have tried to explain further Paul's use of *exousia* with this extended meaning by suggesting that he had a Hebrew or Aramaic word in mind as he constructed his sentence.[58] The proposal which has most often been followed by those who take this line is that developed by G. Kittel.[59] Paul's use of *exousia* rests on an Aramaic *šlṭwnyh* which is once used in the sense of veil,[60] and that the underlying stem *šlṭ*, meaning 'to conceal', has been linked with the very similar *šlṭ*, 'to rule', to produce *exousia* either as a mistranslation or as a popular etymology.[61] An alternative has been proposed by G. Schwarz; he prefers to understand *exousia* as representing *ḥwmr*.[62] Yet another alternative has been put forward by P. J. Tomson: he suggests that the Hebrew word lying behind *exousia* is its direct counterpart *ršwt*, 'power, authority, control'.[63] Like many others, Tomson maintains that the veil is a sign of woman's subordination to man.

A corollary of how *exousia* is understood concerns the interpretation of the clause mentioning angels. Again, more than a few options have been proposed here. Although the proposal that the Greek refers to human messengers has been supported by some interpreters since

---

58 See, e.g., A. Jirku, 'Die Macht auf dem Haupte (I Kor. 11.10)', *NKZ* 32 (1921): 710–11; M. Ginsburger, 'Le gloire et l'autorité de la femme dans I Cor. 11.1–10', *RHPR* 12 (1932): 245–8.

59 G. Kittel, 'Die "Macht" auf dem Haupt [I Cor. xi.10]', *Rabbinica* (Arbeiten zur Vorgeschichte des Christentums 1/3; Leipzig: Hinrichs, 1920), 17–31.

60 *Y. Šabb.* 6.8b: 'headband', but literally, 'authority', commenting on Isa. 3.18.

61 Apparently without knowledge of Kittel's proposal Ginsburger suggested the same in 'Le gloire et l'autorité de la femme dans I Cor. 11.1–10', 248. This interpretation is adopted by J. A. Fitzmyer, 'A Feature of Qumran Angelology and the Angels of 1 Cor. 11.10', in *Essays on the Semitic Background of the New Testament* (London: Chapman, 1971; Missoula: Scholars Press, 1974), 194. Fitzmyer's very influential study first appeared in *NTS* 4 (1957–8): 48–58; it was reprinted in *Paul and Qumran* (ed. J. Murphy-O'Connor; London: Chapman, 1968), 31–47; in *Essays on the Semitic Background of the New Testament*, 187–204; and again in *The Semitic Background of the New Testament* (The Biblical Resources Series; Grand Rapids: Eerdmans; Livonia: Dove Booksellers, 1997), 187–204 (+ Appendix, 292).

62 G. Schwarz, 'exousian echein epi tēs kephalēs? (1. Korinther 11 10)', *ZNW* 70 (1979): 249. Schwarz follows J. Levy in understanding this as meaning both 'power' and 'head-covering, veil'; for *ḥwmr* I and II, Jastrow, 435–6, gives 'great importance' and 'joint, knot, bead, amulet'.

63 P. J. Tomson, *Paul and the Jewish Law: Halakha in the Letters of the Apostle to the Gentiles* (CRINT 3/1; Assen: Van Gorcum; Minneapolis: Fortress Press, 1990), 135–6, 147, n. 283.

antiquity,[64] the majority take the angels as heavenly creatures, though it is not their example that should be followed, as some have maintained. Tomson belongs to the influential subset within this group from Tertullian onwards who understand that they are those angels who might be tempted to seduce and rape the women, unless they are reminded in a suitable way that the women are under protective authority[65] and are not available.[66] On this understanding the *exousia* becomes a quasi-magical item whose authority is prophylactic; woman's natural frailty is protected from evil spirits.[67] Some scholars suggest that, without appealing directly to Genesis 6, Paul is endorsing conventional behaviour because he acknowledges that for the time being the world is under the control of spiritual powers, here designated as angels.[68]

More commentators support the opinion that the angels referred to by Paul are good and the veil is thus either a mark of respect for their presence; or, in light of 1QM VII, 4–6, 1QSa (1Q28a) II, 3–11, and 4Q266 8 I, 7–9, a way of guaranteeing that there are no bodily defects

64 More recently by A. Padgett, 'Paul on Women in the Church. The Contradictions of Coiffure in 1 Corinthians 11.2–16', *JSNT* 20 (1984): 81; supported by J. Murphy-O'Connor, '1 Corinthians 11.2–16 Once Again', *CBQ* 50 (1988): 271–2, and Winandy, 'Un curieux *casus pendens*: 1 Corinthiens 11.10 et son interprétation', 628.

65 H. Conzelmann, *1 Corinthians: A Commentary on the First Epistle to the Corinthians* (Hermeneia; Philadelphia: Fortress, 1975), 189, concludes that 'we can get no further than to presume that the head covering represents a protective power', 'a compensation for the natural weakness of woman over against cosmic power'.

66 See, e.g., J. Meier, 'On the Veiling of Hermeneutics (1 Cor. 11.2–16)', *CBQ* 40 (1978): 220–1; J. D. G. Dunn, *Christology in the Making* (London: SCM, 1980), 323, n. 108. This line has been followed from the Qumran perspective by H. Stegemann, *The Library of Qumran: On the Essenes, Qumran, John the Baptist, and Jesus* (Leiden: Brill; Grand Rapids: Eerdmans, 1998), 95: he understands the angels in 1 Cor. 11.10 in a negative way.

67 This interpretation is unlikely, not only because Paul makes very little elsewhere of the fallen angels, but also because in the immediate context Paul gives no hint that he is referring to the protection of women from an angelic sexual attack. Wire argues against seeing the angels as likely rapists in *The Corinthian Women Prophets* (p. 121), but seems to have changed her mind subsequently: 'Paul seems to be projecting male sexual desire on the angelic host, threatening cosmic idolatry and immorality if the women do not cover their heads "on account of the angels"' ('1 Corinthians', in *Searching the Scriptures: A Feminist Commentary* [ed. E. Schüssler Fiorenza; London: SCM, 1995], 2:179).

68 See, e.g., D. E. H. Whiteley, *The Theology of St. Paul* (2nd ed.; Oxford: Blackwell, 1974), 26.

(including a woman's shaved head) which might undermine the purity of the worshipping community which includes angels;[69] or a matter of the woman being covered to prevent the angels from the misplaced worship of man whose glory she represents.[70] All three of those possibilities could result from Paul attempting to refute a view among the women in the church at Corinth that they could now be like angels in prayer and prophecy; Paul puts angelic tongues in their proper place in 1 Corinthians 13.1. More intriguingly in light of the Qumran parallels adduced earlier in this study, whereas the presence of angels restricted membership of the congregation there, for Paul women can indeed take their place in the worshipping community, even in the presence of angels, providing they do so with their heads covered.[71]

In light of the discussion above let us pose the question the other way round: if Paul were to have translated *exousia* in 1 Corinthians 11 into Hebrew, might he have found it appropriate to have used the term *rwqmh*?

Part of the answer to such a question may lie in how one understands the degrees of Jewishness possible for Paul in Corinth. Various proposals have been put forward. Many of the strongest belong to the time when, despite a wealth of evidence to the contrary, Judaism and Hellenism were thought of as mutually exclusive. Finds, such as those in the caves at and near Qumran, have contributed greatly to breaking down this crude dichotomy. Even in the 1950s Fitzmyer in using the Qumran evidence to argue for a particular understanding of the angels in 1 Corinthians 11.10

---

69 As argued by Fitzmyer, 'A Feature of Qumran Angelology and the Angels of 1 Cor. 11.10'; a similar view was proposed independently by H. J. Cadbury, 'A Qumran Parallel to Paul', *HTR* 51 (1958): 1–2. For a more nuanced description of what the scrolls may say about worship with the angels, see E. Chazon, 'Liturgical Communion with the Angels at Qumran', in *Sapiential, Liturgical and Poetical Texts from Qumran: Proceedings of the Third Meeting of the International Organization for Qumran Studies, Oslo 1998, Published in Memory of Maurice Baillet* (ed. D. K. Falk, F. García Martínez and E. M. Schuller; STDJ 35; Leiden: Brill, 2000), 95–105; she argues that 'human praise is *like* but not *equal* to angelic praise' (p. 105).

70 Thus Paul distinguishes humans from God, even though they reflect the divine glory, and seems to distance himself from those contemporary stories which describe the angelic worship of Adam because he reflects God's glory: see especially *L.A.E.* 13–17.

71 Murphy-O'Connor comments: 'In Paul's view women had full authority to act as they were doing, but they needed to convey their new status to the angels who watched for breaches of Law. The guardians of an outmoded tradition had to be shown that things had changed' ('Sex and Logic in 1 Corinthians 11.2–16', 497).

was dismantling the polarity, though he discretely disclaimed any knowledge of how a view present in some scrolls found at Qumran might also be found in Paul's letter to the Corinthian church. I would side with Fitzmyer and argue that Paul's Jewish background and his appreciation of the Jewishness of at least a small part of the Corinthian congregation in combination with his understanding of much Jewish and non-Jewish custom with regard to the dress of women outside the home and particularly in worship settings should permit us to use information from the Qumran scrolls to illuminate what Paul may have meant when he wrote to the Corinthians. This is not to draw a single simple line of direct literary influence from one group to another, but so to conceive the cultural map of the Eastern Mediterranean world at the turn of the era that the use of literary topoi in two distinct contexts which share many similarities is deemed entirely justifiable. Similarly, with due care not to suggest any direct historical connection between the two, it is legitimate to use the language and argument of 1 Corinthians 11.10 to illuminate how best the strange phraseology of the *Damascus Document* should be understood.

CONCLUSION

This brief study has argued that in certain details the *Damascus Document* and 1 Corinthians may be mutually illuminating.

For 4Q270 7 I, 13–15 it is reasonable to suppose that the limitation of the status of the mothers in the congregation comes about because they are not permitted to wear a mark of authority in the congregation. Perhaps that sign is particularly something cultic, a piece of embroidered cloth associated with priestly status. Comparison with the use and significance of *exousia* 1 Corinthians 11.10 suggests that Baumgarten and others are entirely justified in understanding *rwqmh* in an extended sense as implying authority.

For understanding the argument in 1 Corinthians 11.10 it is reasonable to suppose that the authority a woman must wear on her head, whether a veil or braided hair bound up, enables her to participate in the praying community in her proper place so that the worshipping angels are not compromised by any kind of unnaturalness. Comparison with 4Q270 suggests that Paul's use of the word *exousia*, though unexpected by the modern reader, might not have been particularly unusual. What is worn by a woman, in this case 'on her head', is a sign of (her) authority.

PART THREE

THE SCROLLS AND THE GOSPELS: MUTUAL ILLUMINATION OF PARTICULAR PASSAGES

12

The Wisdom of Matthew's Beatitudes

INTRODUCTION

L'Abbé Jean Carmignac died in October 1986 after a long and productive pastoral and scholarly career, the hallmark of which was his enthusiastic establishing of the *Revue de Qumrân* which he edited with consummate skill for nearly 30 years. Until 1994 the *Revue de Qumrân* was the only journal devoted solely to the study of the Dead Sea Scrolls and from time to time previously unpublished scrolls have appeared among its articles. In honour of Jean Carmignac the new editorial body published a memorial volume of the journal[1] and there were several contributions in it which contained previously unpublished fragments of scrolls. One of these hitherto unpublished fragments features in the contribution by Emile Puech of the Ecole Biblique as part of a larger argument for the improved reading and reconstruction of the well-known *Hymn Scroll* (1QHª).[2] It is with this new fragment, labelled 4QBeatitudes, that this study is concerned, especially in as much as it may shed new light upon the beatitudes in Matthew's Gospel.

4QBEATITUDES

The existence of this fragment of 4QBeatitudes was first notified by l'Abbé Jean Starcky in 1954; subsequently in the *Revue Biblique* he commented that it contained a set of macarisms but was not to be identified with similar passages in *1 Enoch*.[3] It is part of an 'Herodian' manuscript;

---

1 *Mémorial Jean Carmignac: Etudes Qumrâniennes, RevQ* 13 (1988).
2 'Un hymne essénien en partie retrouvé et les Béatitudes: 1QHª V 12–VI 18 (= col. XIII–XIV 7) et 4QBéat.,' *RevQ* 13 (1988): 59–88.
3 *CRAI* (1954): 408; 'Le travail d'édition des fragments manuscrits de Qumrân', *RB* 63 (1956): 67.

in his preliminary publication Puech actually says it is dated to the Herodian period, but one must not confuse the designation of palaeographical types with actual historical periods, although there is some correspondence. We are probably dealing with a manuscript that comes from some time between 50 B.C.E. and 50 C.E. Puech did not publish a photograph of this fragment in the *Mémorial Jean Carmignac*, so the following revised translation into English is based on his subsequent edition of the Hebrew text in which several manuscript pieces are put together to make a fragment with the remains of three columns, the set of beatitudes belonging in the first six lines of Column 2.[4] Though the Hebrew appears in continuous lines, the actual spaces in the manuscript enable the text to be laid out stichometrically.

Blessed is the man who speaks the truth (?)] (1) with a pure heart,
    and does not slander with his tongue. (space)
Blessed are those who hold fast to her statutes,
    and do not take hold of (2) the ways of iniquity. (space)
Blessed are those who rejoice in her,
    and do not utter in the ways of foolishness. (space)
Blessed are those who seek her (3) with pure hands,
    and do not search for her with a deceitful heart. (space)
Blessed is the man who has attained Wisdom. (space)
    He walks (4) in the Law of the Most High,
    and prepares his heart for her ways. (space)
And he controls himself by her instructions,
    and always takes pleasure in her corrections,
        (5) and does not forsake her in the afflictions of tes[ting.] (space)
And in the time of oppression he does not abandon her,
    and does not forget her [in the days of] dread,
        (6) and in the submission of his soul does not reject [her. (space?)]

---

4 The transcription published by Puech in 'Un hymne essénien en partie retrouvé et les Béatitudes', 85, was used for the original of this article published in 1989; the translation offered here has been revised slightly in light of the official publication by Puech of all 50 extant fragments of 5Q525 in DJD 25, 115–78. Several pieces of manuscript are joined to form Frag. 2 which contains the remains of three columns of writing with the beatitudes forming the first six lines of Col. 2 ; a further fragment, Frag. 3, also comes from Col. 2. Thus the beatitudes are technically designated as 4Q525 2–3 II, 1–6: Frags 2–3, Col. II, lines 1–6.

PUECH'S USE OF 4QBEATITUDES

Before turning directly to the comparison with the beatitudes in the Gospels, it is pertinent to consider how Puech uses this text in his reading of the Qumran *Hodayot* scroll (*Thanksgiving Hymns*). Puech's overall argument concerns the reordering of the columns of the *Hodayot* scroll. Part of his argument for the reordering of the *Hodayot* Scroll depends on his improved reading of the text itself. For his Column VI (= old 1QHᵃ XIV) Puech proposes to reconstruct the text so that it contains a long blessing in which the term 'blessed are those' or 'happy are those' is not repeated. To justify his restoration he appeals to 4QBeatitudes as the most obvious parallel among the scrolls themselves.

Puech's reconstruction of Column VI is most readily accessible in English in the version by F. García Martínez and E. J. C. Tigchelaar as 1QHᵃ VI, 2–7:[5]

> (2) Fortunate,] the men of truth and those chosen by jus[tice, those probing] (3) the mind and those searching for wisdom, those bui[lding . . . those who l]ove compassion and the poor in spirit, those refined (4) by poverty and those purified in the crucible [. . . those who cont]rol themselves until the time of your judgments (5) and those alert for your salvation. And you [. . .] and you have strengthened your statutes [through their hands] to make (6) judgment on the world and to give as an inheritance all [. . .] holy for everlasting generations. And all (7) foundations of their deeds with pleas[ure . . .] the men of your vision. (space)

Here, rather than actual spaces between phrases in the manuscript, it is the use of the conjunction that enables the text to be presented sticho-metrically. Each line has two elements, such as 'those probing the mind'

---

5 'Un hymne essénien en partie retrouvé et les Béatitudes,' 66–8. On p. 88 Puech records H. Stegemann's disagreement with him concerning the restoration of the text as a macarism, but he defends his proposals on the basis of the large amount of common vocabulary between 4QBeat (4Q525) and 1QH VI. The English version given here is that of by F. García Martínez and E. J. C. Tigchelaar, *The Dead Sea Scrolls Study Edition* (Leiden: Brill; Grand Rapids: Eerdmans, 2000), 1.152–53; it is slightly altered to show the poetic character of the section and the precise verbal parallels with 4QBeatitudes. Note also that García Martínez and Tigchelaar preserve Puech's macarism, but renumber his lines 13–18 as 2–7.

and 'those searching for wisdom' which are joined by the conjunction; the following pair is then introduced without it. This composition is thus similar to 4QBeatitudes whose first part is a set of four couplets, but in 4QBeatitudes each couplet has a positive phrase followed by a negative one.

There are also some obvious parallels between the content of this passage of the *Thanksgiving Hymns* and the language of 4QBeatitudes. Three topics occur in both texts:

1 'seeking' either insight or Wisdom (1QH^a VI, 3; 4QBeat 2–3 II, 2);
2 'being pure' or 'purified in the crucible' (1QH^a VI, 4; 4QBeat 2–3 II, 3, 5);
3 'those who control themselves/he who controls himself' (1QH^a VI, 5; 4QBeat 2–3 II, 4).

In addition, in the prose passage that immediately follows the extended blessing of 1QH^a VI, 2–5, 'statutes' (1QH^a VI, 5) and 'hand' (1QH^a VI, 5) both occur, as also in 4QBeatitudes (4QBeat 2–3 II, 1, 3).

There is a further similarity too, though it is not an exact verbal correspondence. In 4QBeatitudes 6 we read, 'in the submission of his soul' (*b'nwt npšw*). Puech compares this with a passage in the Qumran *Rule of the Community* (1QS III, 8–9): 'and it is through the submission of his soul (*b'nwt npšw*) to all the statutes of God that his flesh shall be purified'.[6] This line is part of a passage concerned with initiation into the covenant of the community at the end of the probationary period. The same context probably lies behind the phrase 'poor in spirit (*'nwy rwh*)' in 1QH^a VI, 3, for it occurs elsewhere in Qumran literature in the *War Scroll* (1QM XIV, 7) in a hymn which recalls the covenant to which the community has been called: 'Blessed be the God of Israel who keeps mercy towards his covenant . . . Among the poor in spirit (*'nwy rwh*) [there is power] over the hard of heart, and by the perfect of way all the nations of wickedness have come to an end.' The same phrase is echoed in the *Rule of the Community* (1QS IV, 2–6): 'These are their ways in the world: to enlighten the heart of man, to make level before him all the ways of righteousness and of truth, and to instil into his heart reverence

6 Trans. M. A. Knibb, *The Qumran Community* (Cambridge Commentaries on the Writings of the Jewish and Christian World; Cambridge: Cambridge University Press, 1987), 91; Knibb also comments on the significance of this passage in relation to initiation into the community.

for the precepts of God, a spirit of humility (*rwḥ 'nwh*) . . . The visitation of all those who walk in it will be healing.' In both these passages (1QM XIV, 7; 1QS IV, 3) not only is there recollection of the way into which the community member was initiated, but also that recollection is given an eschatological significance. The occurrence of the same phrase in Matthew 5.3 and of a similar phrase in 4QBeatitudes 2–3 II, 6, both explicitly beatitudes (or macarisms),[7] may be significant for how the Matthaean Beatitudes as a whole are to be understood. At least Puech's reconstruction of 1QH[a] VI, 3–4 gives us the most ancient attestation of the phrase 'poor in spirit' in a macarism.

In sum, because of the several parallels in content, Puech seems to be justified in reconstructing 1QH[a] VI, 2–5 as a series of beatitudes of which only the first would have been introduced with the technical formula 'Blessed are those'.[8] Some of the terminology of both 1QH[a] VI, 2–7 and 4QBeatitudes is also present in other passages in the sectarian scrolls. These are concerned, either directly or indirectly, with initiation and its significance from an eschatological perspective.

4QBEATITUDES AND MATTHEW'S BEATITUDES

Structure

1. The initial blessing of 4QBeatitudes has to be reconstructed. Because 'heart' and 'tongue' are singular, the whole couplet is likely to have contained macarisms in the singular. Since it is not uncommon in the initial phrase for 'Blessed' to be omitted from the second macarism of a pair, Puech observes that 4QBeatitudes can be considered as having the same overall structure as the Matthaean Beatitudes: 8 + 1. It could be, however, if we follow the careful use of spacing in the manuscript, that we should rather talk of a structure of 4 + 1. The difference between 8 + 1 and 4 + 1 may just be a matter of poetics; the overall parallel in structure between the two passages remains striking whatever mathematical figures are used. I will assume a pattern of 8 + 1 in the following remarks.

---

7 The term 'macarism' is used by scholars to distinguish this kind of wisdom blessing from the more explicit cultic blessing or benediction.

8 The term 'blessed' commonly introduces two clauses without being repeated for the second (e.g., Ps. 1.1); some texts have longer constructions which may be considered to stand under the initial 'blessed' (e.g., Ps. 84.5–7 [Heb. 6–8]). Sir. 25.7–11 contains a series of ten with only two introductory 'blesseds'.

2. In both Matthew and 4QBeatitudes the first and the eighth beatitude have common ingredients. In Matthew the first and eighth end with the same clause, 'For theirs is the kingdom of heaven' (Matt. 5.3, 10). In 4QBeatitudes the heart is mentioned in both. 4QBeatitudes' inclusio is also reinforced by its overall references to parts of the body: the 'heart' and 'tongue' of 4QBeat 2–3 II, 1 and 2 are matched by the 'hand' and 'heart' of 4QBeat 2–3 II, 7 and 8.

3. It is often noted by commentators that the Matthaean Beatitudes may contain some four-line stanzas. Matthew 5.3 and 5 may have belonged together so that 'inheriting the land' matches and interprets 'the kingdom of heaven'.[9] Matthew 5.7 and 9 perhaps originally belonged together, each ending with a passive verb.[10] Although the spaces in the manuscript make us construe the first eight beatitudes in 4QBeatitudes as a set of four couplets, their content suggests that they may be understood as two stanzas of four lines each. In the second stanza, three of the four half-lines contain reference to 'her', that is, Wisdom: in the first four the reference is rather to 'her statutes'. In this way Law and Wisdom are juxtaposed and identified with one another.

4. The four pairs of macarisms in 4QBeatitudes are clearly constructed as opposites, so that 1, 3, 5 and 7 are positive, 2, 4, 6 and 8 are negative. Likewise it has been noticed that at least the central six macarisms in Matthew (Matt. 5.4–9) also contain alternating opposites: the meek, the merciful and the peacemakers can only have their particular characteristics in a social context: those who mourn, who hunger, and who are pure in heart do not need such a social setting.[11]

5. The ninth element in both develops what precedes it. In Matthew the ninth beatitude is a development of what is described briefly in the eighth concerning persecution. In 4QBeatitudes the ninth beatitude describes the one who has obtained wisdom, the natural development from the description in beatitudes 7 and 8 of those who seek and search for her.

6. In a somewhat different way Matthew's ninth blessing is distinctive in being the only one in the series in the second-person plural, but

---

9 See, e.g., D. Hill, *The Gospel of Matthew* (NCB; London: Marshall, Morgan and Scott, 1972), 112.

10 See, e.g., M. Black, *An Aramaic Approach to the Gospels and Acts* (3rd edn; Oxford: Oxford University Press, 1967), 156–7.

11 As pointed out by A. Kodjak, *A Structural Analysis of the Sermon on the Mount* (Religion and Reason 34; Berlin, 1986), 54.

attached to the previous eight through the content of the eighth. The ninth element in 4QBeatitudes is in the singular, attached to the eighth through antithetical parallelism, but matching the first and second in number. In fact, Matthew's ninth beatitude may also be connected with the first through the eighth, 'heaven' being mentioned in all three.

7. In 4QBeatitudes the ninth blessing has an overall introduction: 'Blessed is the man who has obtained wisdom.' The spaces in the manuscript may suggest that this introduction was at one time an independent unit; in 4QBeatitudes it has been expanded and interpreted. The expansion contains eight phrases which can be subdivided either according to content into two sets of four – first, four positive ones, second, four negative or, following the spacing of the manuscript, into an initial couplet and then two triplets. It is interesting that the ninth of Matthew's Beatitudes seems to contain three negative elements in the macarism ('revile', 'persecute', 'speak evil against') followed by two commands ('rejoice and be glad') which share a dependent clause and then a phrase containing a comparison with the prophets which is presumably meant to be positive and encouraging for the audience. As a whole then Matthew 5.11–12 may be construed as two triplets:

> Blessed are you when men revile you
> and persecute and speak falsely against you
> all evil on my account.

> Rejoice and be glad,
> for your reward is great in heaven,
> for so they persecuted the prophets before you.

When considered from the point of view of a possible Semitic original, these two triplets have a balancing rhythm of 3/3/2, 2/3/3. The two triplets in the ninth beatitude of 4QBeatitudes may be considered as having the not dissimilar rhythmic pattern of 2/3/3, 3/3/3. Luke's parallel, however, has four elements of vilification, including 'hate', and so matches the pattern of four positive and four negative verbs in 4QBeat 2–3 II, 4–6; Luke 6.22–3 are also widely regarded as more likely to reflect a Semitic original than Matthew 5.11–12. When construed as such, their rhythm is 3/3/3, 3/3/4. Luke 6.22 preserves a 'son of man' which Matthew seems to turn into a personal pronoun (as is the case also in Matt. 16.21; cf. Lk. 9.22) which suggests he may have retained a text altogether more original than Matthew's. But 4QBeatitudes now allows for Matthew's text to be recognized as just as Semitic. It may no longer be possible to propose which is the more original; rather, both may reflect something Semitic but under the influence of a slightly varying tradition. Here is a further argument for those who would deny that Luke depended directly on Matthew or vice versa.[12]

Content

1. 4QBeatitudes clearly contains some eschatological language, even though its macarisms are principally an exhortation to live according to Wisdom who is the Law of the Most High. It is in its ninth beatitude that the eschatology becomes most explicit with mention of affliction, testing and the days of dread. The ninth Matthaean beatitude is also highly eschatological, but so are also the second halves of each in the initial series of eight. It might be that this permits the conclusion that Matthew is taking further what has already begun in earlier traditions, namely, the adaptation of Wisdom formulas by expanding them with explicitly eschatological concerns.

2. 4QBeat 2–3 II, 1 is restored on the basis of Psalm 15.2–3: 'He who speaks truth in his heart, who does not slander with his tongue.' A similar motif is found in several texts, notably Psalm 37.29–31: 'The righteous shall possess the land, and dwell upon it for ever. The mouth of the right-eous utters wisdom, and his tongue speaks justice. The law of his God is in his heart.' The several parallels between these verses and 4QBeatitudes need not be spelled out; what is more important is the use of the same Psalm (vs. 11) in Matthew 5.5, 'the meek shall possess the land/earth', part of which is repeated in Psalm 37.29, just cited.

3. In Matthew 5.6 the satisfaction given those who hunger and thirst after righteousness may also echo Psalm 37. Verses 18–19 read: 'The Lord knows the days of the perfect, and their inheritance will abide for ever; they shall not be put to shame in time of evil, and in the days of famine they shall be satisfied.' In the light of Psalm 37 the righteousness to which Matthew 5—6 refers may be construed in terms of having the law in one's heart and practising it.[13] This is implied also in 4QBeatitudes in its mention of the 'statutes' and of 'the law of the Most High'.

12 E.g., C. M. Tuckett, 'The Beatitudes: A Source-Critical Study', *NovT* 25 (1983): 193–207.

13 F. M. Cross considers Lk. 6.21 to represent Jesus referring to Ps. 37.11 in terms of the eschatological banquet, as is also implied in 4QpPs[a] II, 10–11: *The Ancient Library of Qumran and Modern Biblical Studies* (New York: Doubleday, 1958), 67.

4. The metaphor of hunger and thirst implies earnest desire for right-eousness. So in Sirach 24.19–21 those who 'desire' Wisdom will 'hunger' and 'thirst' for more. The hunger and thirst of Matthew 5.6 can thus be matched in the search for Wisdom of the seventh beatitude of 4QBeati-tudes. Since 'for righteousness' sake' in Matthew 5.10 is substituted with 'for my sake' in the ninth beatitude, we may also assume that the right-eousness of Matthew 5.6 can be personified: while those inspired by 4QBeatitudes will search for Wisdom, those struck by the Matthaean Beatitudes will seek for Jesus. Puech also notes that the two verbs for search used in 4QBeat 2–3 II, 2–3 are found in parallel in Psalm 78.34, a section of the Psalm which portrays Israel as behaving in a way precisely opposite to that recommended in 4QBeatitudes.

5. For 'pure in heart' in Matthew 5.8 we now have the same phrase in 4QBeat 2–3 II, 1 (*lb thwr*). The significance of this is that the phrase now clearly occurs in a macarism; we need no longer suppose that the phrase in Matthew 5.8 represents a mistranslation of an Aramaic original as M. Black has ingeniously proposed.[14] Most commentators have been satisfied with referring to Psalm 24.4 to illuminate the meaning of the Matthaean beatitude. 4QBeatitudes now makes that reference all the more pertinent, since both it and Psalm 24 are concerned with a pure 'heart' and clean 'hands' (4QBeat 2–3 II, 1 [*lb thwr*], 3 [*bwr kpym*]; Ps. 24.4 [*nqy kpym wbr lbb*]), with not swearing 'deceitfully' (4QBeat 2–3 II, 3; Ps. 24.4), with 'seeking' (4QBeat 2–3 II, 2; Ps. 24.6), and with 'submission of his soul' and 'not lifting up his soul' (4QBeat 2–3 II, 6; Ps. 24.4). Ps. 51.10 (Heb. 51.12) is also relevant since it actually contains the phrase 'pure in heart' exactly as in 4QBeat 2–3 II, 1.

6. There are several comments that need to be made about the paral-lels in content between the ninth beatitude in 4QBeatitudes and Matthew 5.11–12. With the phrase 'takes pleasure in her corrections' (4QBeat 2–3 II, 4) Puech compares 1QH[a] IX.10, 'in my trial I have found pleasure'. In commenting on that passage in 1QH[a] S. Holm-Nielsen observes that a similar thought is to be found in 1 Peter 4.12–13.[15] 1 Peter 4.12–13 reads: 'Beloved, do not be surprised at the fiery ordeal which comes upon you to prove you, as though something strange were

---

14 *An Aramaic Approach to the Gospels and Acts*, 158, n. 2.
15 *Hodayot: Psalms from Qumran* (Aarhus: Universitetsvorlaget, 1960), 161; he also compares *2 Bar.* 52.6. M. D. Goulder reckons that 1 Pet. 4.12–14 is written with Matt. 5.11–12 in mind: *Midrash and Lection in Matthew* (London: SPCK, 1974), 255–6.

happening to you. But rejoice in so far as you share Christ's sufferings, that you may also rejoice and be glad (*charēte agalliōmenoi*; cf. Matt. 5.12) when his glory is revealed.' In light of 4QBeat 2–3 II, 5–6 we should also add 1 Peter 4.14: 'If you are reproached for the name of Christ, you are blessed [*makarioi*].' Here then are several echoes of Matthew's ninth beatitude, which is structurally in the same position as the material this mirrors in 4QBeatitudes and which is concerned with joy in suffering 'for my sake'. Also of significance is that the first pair of macarisms in 4QBeatitudes is about truthful speech, not slandering; the ninth beatitude in Matthew is about persecution brought about especially through reviling and the uttering of all manner of evil.

The phrase 'for my sake' occurs five times in Matthew (5.11; 10.18, 39; 16.25; 19.29); in all these cases the Gospel speaks of the dangers of persecution through which the disciples will earn their spurs.[16] With the necessary affliction that the wise man endures according to 4QBeatitudes Puech compares Isaiah 48.10. Because we should also have one eye on Matthew 5 and even 1 Peter, the whole of Isaiah 48.9–11, part of an oracle that refers to what Israel endured in the exile, is worth citing: 'For my name's sake I defer my anger, for the sake of my praise I restrain it for you, that I may not cut you off. Behold I have refined you, but not like silver; I have tried you in the furnace of affliction. For my own sake, for my own sake, I do it, for how should my name be profaned? My glory I will not give to another.'[17] The interpretation given Psalm 37.11 (Matt. 5.5) in 4QpPs[a] II, 10–11 also concerns testing: 'The interpretation concerns the congregation of the poor ones, who will accept the appointed time of affliction, and they will be delivered from all the traps of Belial. But afterwards they will delight in . . . '[18]

7. The persecution described in Matthew 5.10–12 is the result of the disciple living up to his calling. In that connection we have already noted that with 4QBeat 2–3 II, 6, 'in the affliction of his soul', must be compared 1QS III, 8, 'the humble submission of his soul', a text that belongs in the context of initiation.

---

16 As is pointed out by P. S. Minear, *Matthew: The Teacher's Gospel* (London: Darton, Longman & Todd, 1984), 47.

17 The LXX uses *heneken* in Isa. 48.9–11, as does Matt. 5.11.

18 Trans. M. P. Horgan, *Pesharim: Qumran Interpretations of Biblical Books* (CBQMS 8; Washington: Catholic Biblical Association of America, 1979), 196. A similar thought of the righteous enduring persecution can also be found in 4QFlorilegium III, 18–IV, 4 citing Dan. 12.10 and 11.32; cf. 1QS I, 17–18; 4QpPs[a] II, 19; CD XX, 27.

Genre

In his preliminary publication Puech described 4QBeatitudes simply as a wisdom text containing macarisms. He noted in passing that the text is not so much eschatological teaching as an exhortation to live according to the Law of God. Two matters deserve extra comment under this heading in relation to the parallels between 4QBeatitudes and Matthew 5. First, although eschatology is not consistently prominent in 4QBeatitudes, it is present, so both 4QBeatitudes and Matthew 5.3–12 may be defined as Wisdom material that has been adapted so as to give it an eschatological perspective. In 4QBeatitudes this is implicit in the matter of trial and correction that the blessed endure; in Matthew 5.11–12 the persecution is linked to reward in heaven so that the text has an eschatological motif, even if it has to be read into the text from Matthew 24.3–14, 34–7. There is eschatology in the 'reward' clause of each of Matthew's beatitudes too. As Wisdom material adapted eschatologically, both 4QBeatitudes, and more especially Matthew 5.3–12, are exhortations; not so much the presentation of the right way to behave in the end times, but the description of the way of integrity which is not afraid of death and which is already to be seen among those obedient disciples whose lives anticipate the coming of the kingdom.

Second, it is commonly supposed that there are two kinds of macarism: sapiential and apocalyptic. The sapiential kind may occur either as a reinforcement of the view that wealth, health and good reputation reflect God's blessing, or as a challenge to such a view, sometimes called 'the macarism of the wise man', in which blessing comes rather to those who keep the Law, to the poor, etc.[19] Some macariarns can be delivered with considerable satire (*1 Enoch* 103.5–6: 'Blessed are the sinners . . .'). Since the Matthaean Beatitudes do not seem to be straightforwardly sapiential, they are commonly considered to be apocalyptic. So K. Koch, for example, aligns them with the macarisms that occur in Jewish apocalyptic, such as *2 Enoch* 52.1–16, and those of the Book of Revelation, such as Revelation 14.13–14.[20] It seems, however, that 4QBeatitudes enable us to see that the Matthaean Beatitudes are a more subtle combination of elements: Wisdom materials, particularly in the

19 See, e.g., H.-D. Betz, *Essays on the Sermon on the Mount* (Philadelphia: Fortress Press, 1985), 25 and 32–3.

20 K. Koch, *The Growth of the Biblical Tradition: the Form-Critical Method* (London: A. & C. Black, 1969), 7.

macarisms proper, eschatological adaptations in the 'reward' clauses, with some of the language of apocalyptic, such as 'seeing God', that belongs not just to the expression of those suffering persecution but to the language of initiation.

Theological motifs

1. Because of the appearance of Wisdom in the ninth element of 4QBeatitudes, it is appropriate to make some remarks here on the Matthaean concern to identify Jesus with Wisdom. With reference to the sayings that follow immediately after the beatitudes D. Hill, among others, mentions that in rabbinic metaphorical use 'salt' chiefly denotes Wisdom;[21] light is a common metaphor for the Law.[22] In Sirach 24.23–7 we read about Wisdom: 'All this is the book of the covenant of the Most High God, the law which Moses commanded us . . . It makes instruction shine forth like light.' Wisdom and Law are now here back to back in 4QBeat 2–3 II, 3–4. Perhaps such a tradition explains the position of the salt and light sayings in the Sermon on the Mount: the disciples are to be true to the wisdom and law disclosed by Jesus in his summary teaching, and perhaps even in his person.

M. J. Suggs has proposed that Matthew 5.11–16 belong together as a three-part commissioning: 5.11–12 are the blessing, 5.13–15 the naming, 5.16 is the commission proper.[23] Suggs suggests that this is matched in part in Matthew 23.33–6 where the Wisdom–Christ figure sends out his wise men and prophets to persecution. Because it is for their view of the Law and Wisdom that the disciples will be persecuted, it is imperative that Matthew clarifies the relationship between Jesus and the Law; this he does in the very next verses (Matt. 5.17–20). The association of Wisdom and Law in 4QBeatitudes helps us see more clearly the probable reasons behind the organization of this part of the Sermon on

---

21 D. Hill, *The Gospel of Matthew*, 115. W. Nauck describes how salt can represent both Wisdom and the way of the wise disciple: 'Salt as a Metaphor in Instructions for Discipleship', *ST* 6 (1952): 165–78, esp. 169–70.

22 G. Vermes, 'The Torah is a Light', *VT* 8 (1958): 436–8; cf. *T. Levi* 14.4; *Exod. Rab.* 36.3. M. J. Suggs connects light with both the Law and those who teach it (*2 Bar.* 77.13–16) and notes that the Qumran Psalms scroll describes David as wise and a light who spoke through prophecy (11QPs[a] XXVII, 2–11): *Wisdom, Christology and Law in Matthew's Gospel* (Cambridge: Harvard University Press, 1970), 124–5. Light and wisdom are associated in Eph. 5.8–15.

23 M. J. Suggs, *Wisdom, Christology and Law in Matthew's Gospel*, 121–2.

the Mount: the reminder of the blessedness of the initiate (5.3–10) is then made operative through a commissioning (5.11–16). In 4QBeatitudes it is Wisdom who corrects and instructs, though the text is careful to say that the testing and refining is not instigated by her. The corresponding time of persecution in Matthew 5.10–12 which is to be endured 'for my sake' echoes the justification associated with suffering and persecution in several Wisdom traditions involving persecution. Most notable among these traditions is 4 Maccabees which contains the stories of Eleazar who refuses to transgress the Law (4 Macc. 4–7) and the mother and her seven sons, all of whom are martyred for their obedience to the Law (4 Macc. 8–17). In the introduction to the book the writer describes all the eight martyrs of his story as blessed (4 Macc. 1.10). Furthermore, Eleazar alone is twice described as blessed (*makarios*): 'O blessed old man and of much grey hair and of law-abiding life, whom the faithful seal of death has perfected' (4 Macc. 7.15; cf. Matt. 5.48) and 'He knows that it is blessed to endure any suffering for the sake of virtue' (4 Macc. 7.22). Also the fourth brother describes the deaths of the first three as blessed (4 Macc. 10.15) and the narrator says the same of the death of the sixth brother (4 Macc. 12.1). These martyrs die for the sake of the Law, for the sake of virtue, for the sake of God, etc.[24] In Matthew Jesus is represented as aligning his disciples with just such a tradition of righteous suffering. Moreover, just as Matthew 5.11–12 may be a *Q saying, so in other 'Q' passages the motif of the persecution of the prophets and the wise men is repeated (Matt. 23.34–6 // Lk. 11.49–51; Matt. 23.37–9; Lk. 13.34–5).[25] The persecution of the followers of righteousness is not just an affair of Matthaean concern, but may well go back through 'Q' to Jesus himself.

The many parallels in the Matthaean Beatitudes with wisdom literature need not be listed here; indeed, some have already been mentioned. More important than those parallels is Matthew's overall interest in other parts of the Gospel to identify Jesus with Wisdom herself. The most well-known example of this occurs in Matthew 11.28–30 in which Jesus addresses his audience like Wisdom: 'come to me, all who labour and are heavy laden, and I will give you rest. Take my yoke upon you and learn

---

24 For virtue: 4 Macc. 1.8; 7.22; 11.2; for the Law: 4 Macc. 6.27; for God: 4 Macc. 10.20; 16.19, 21, 25; 17.20; for religion/piety: 4 Macc. 9.30; 13.12, 27; 15.12; 16.13, 17; 17.7; 18.3. However, nowhere in 4 Maccabees is the preposition *heneken*, 'for the sake of' (Matt. 5.11), used, as it is in the LXX in Isa. 48.9–11.

25 C. M. Tuckett, 'The Beatitudes: A Source-Critical Study', 206.

from me.' This is widely acknowledged to echo Wisdom's invitation in Sirach 51.23–7: 'Draw near to me, you who are untaught, and lodge in my school . . . Put your neck under the yoke, and let your souls receive instruction . . . See with your eyes that I have laboured little and found for myself much rest.'[26] This saying is only in Matthew, but there are several which have parallels in Luke but for which the differences between Matthew and Luke can be explained in part by Matthew's concern to identify Jesus with Wisdom, whereas Luke merely wishes to present Jesus as Wisdom's agent or messenger.[27] The juxtaposition of 4QBeatitudes and Matthew 5.10–12 suggests this too: in the former Wisdom requires obedience and endurance in times of trial, in the latter such endurance is for 'my name's sake'. As A. Kodjak puts it for Matthew, 'While Christ utters the Beatitudes, He is also the content of his utterance and thus communicates or reveals Himself to the audience.'[28] Luke's Beatitudes do not show such overt connection with Wisdom or with Palestinian Wisdom traditions.

2. Another theological motif of the Sermon on the Mount which may now be given some attention is its Lord's Prayer and how this may be echoed or anticipated literarily in the Beatitudes. Sometimes it has been noted that Matthew 5.7, 'Blessed are the merciful, for they shall obtain mercy', echoes the approach of Jesus in the Lord's Prayer, 'forgive . . . as we forgive', which Matthew makes quite explicit in his comment on the prayer in 6.14–15.[29] But perhaps more attention should he paid to the ninth beatitude. The evil that comes in the false speech of the persecutors may be an example of the work of the evil one. The term 'evil' is certainly ambiguous in Matthew 5.37 as it is in Matthew 6.13. 4QBeatitudes now adds to this view of persecution the wider terminology of trial which we have noted is also echoed in 1 Peter 4.12–14. This might explain the eschatological urgency in the parallelism of the last two petitions of the

---

26 See, e.g., W. C. Allen, *A Critical and Exegetical Commentary on the Gospel according to St Matthew* (ICC; Edinburgh: T & T Clark, 1907), 123–4; M. J. Suggs, *Wisdom, Christology and Law in Matthew's Gospel*, 99–106.

27 E.g., Lk. 7.35 // Matt. 11.19; Lk. 11.49 // Matt. 23.34; Lk. 13.34–5 // Matt. 23.37–9. See the christological discussion of these passages in J. D. G. Dunn, *Christology in the Making: An Inquiry into the Origins of the Doctrine of the Incarnation* (London: SCM Press, 1980), 197–206.

28 A. Kodjak, *A Structural Analysis of the Sermon on the Mount*, 68.

29 E.g., C. Gore, *The Sermon on the Mount: A Practical Exposition* (London, 1896), 38–9; D. Hill, *The Gospel of Matthew*, 112–13.

Matthaean Lord's Prayer, particularly since in 4QFlorilegium this time of trial is associated explicitly with Belial.[30]

Furthermore, although the prayer's doxology is not widely attested, it too may not be simply a neat liturgical extra adapted from 1 Chronicles 29.11–13, but rather an expression of the same eschatological hope that is discernible in the ninth beatitude. In 1 Peter 4.14, after reference to the trials to be endured, some manuscripts read 'you are blessed because the spirit of glory and of God rests upon you', others read 'you are blessed because the spirit of glory and of power and of God rests upon you'. The hint of the doxology of the Lord's Prayer does not seem coincidental. It could well be that Matthew 5.11–12 is a literary anticipation of the Lord's Prayer; to pray that prayer is to stand under the risk of persecution 'for my sake'.

3. Before 4QBeatitudes was published certain parallels between the Matthaean Beatitudes and the writings from Qumran had been noted. Most obviously the use of Psalm 37.11 in Matthew 5.5, cited above, was put next to the interpretation of the same text in 4QpPsᵃ.[31] But even before the *Psalms Commentary* (4QpPsᵃ) was published K. Schubert proposed that many elements in the Sermon on the Mount appear to represent a dialogue with or polemic against ideas to be found in the scrolls.[32] He identified those Jews who said you must hate your enemies (Matt. 5.43) with the Essenes on the basis of some passages like 'Love everyone whom God has elected and hate everyone whom he has rejected' (1QS I, 4). Schubert also supposed that the first beatitude might have been written with Essenes in mind; they called themselves 'the poor' (1QpHab XII, 3, 6, 10) and Jesus may originally have meant that the poor in spirit were those who were voluntarily poor, poor by will, a feature of Qumran Essene life as far as 1QS and Josephus jointly testify. In Matthew 5.12 Schubert reckoned that the words of Jesus must be taken to mean that the disciples stand in the line of Prophets (presumably those of earlier epochs); but also within the saying may be a polemic against certain Essenes who considered themselves as prophets as some of

30 4QFlor IV, 1–2: 'That is the time of refining/trial which is coming (upon the house of) Judah to complete [. . .] of Belial.'

31 F. M. Cross, *The Ancient Library of Qumran and Modern Biblical Studies*, 61–2; K. Stendahl, 'Matthew', in *Peake's Commentary on the Bible* (ed. M. Black and H. H. Rowley; London: Nelson, 1962), 775.

32 K. Schubert, 'The Sermon on the Mount and the Qumran Texts', in *The Scrolls and the New Testament* (ed. K. Stendahl; London: SCM Press, 1958), 118–28.

the scrolls might suggest and as Josephus agrees.[33] To stand in line with the prophets is to understand and apply the Law as Jesus proclaims it, not as the Essenes interpreted and practised it.

The publication of 4QBeatitudes now indeed suggests that the first, third, sixth, eighth and ninth Matthaean Beatitudes may be interacting with Essene understanding, but not necessarily on the level of overt polemic against it. Rather, Jesus or, more likely, Matthew (or the community of 'Q'), uses a common fund of Palestinian Wisdom texts to put over his eschatological exhortation. As in 4QBeatitudes Matthew's exhortation challenges the socially acceptable 'blessedness' of wealth, health and fame by offering a different set of values based on the interpretation of the Law. Some of the Jewish Christians in Matthew's community may have been Essenes at some time; the echo of their writings and value system may be an attempt to show how they are to find their place in the community. Thus Matthew's Beatitudes are pastorally invigorating as well as being anti-Essene polemic.

4. The fifth beatitude in 4QBeatitudes raises a particular problem. This approves of swearing by Wisdom. However, many scholars would suppose that the radical rejection of oaths in Matthew 5.33–7 is a point where Jesus' teaching is represented as coming close to that of the Essenes.[34] Josephus describes how any word of the Essenes 'has more force than an oath; they refrain from swearing for they say that one who is not believed unless he call upon the divinity is already condemned in advance'.[35] Josephus also mentions oaths that the initiate must make before becoming a full member of the community; he lists 12 of them.[36] Formal swearing of oaths by the initiate is also defined in the *Rule of the Community* (1QS V, 7–11); such an undertaking involves walking according to God's will, separation from all the people of falsehood who walk in the way of wickedness and who do not seek his statutes. All this

---

33 1QpHab VII, 3–5; Josephus, *War* 2.159; *Ant.* 15.373–9. G. Stanton, among others, argues that the opposition envisaged in Matt. 5.11–12 is that of the scribes and Pharisees: 'The Gospel of Matthew and Judaism', *BJRL* 66 (1984), 267–8.
34 E.g., D. Hill, The Gospel of Matthew, 126.
35 *War* 2.135.
36 *War* 2.137–42. The *Damascus Document* (CD IX, 8–12; XV, 1–5; XVI, 6–12) and the *Temple Scroll* (11QT[a] LIII, 9–LIV, 5) describe the practice of making oaths more extensively; perhaps they come from an earlier, even pre-Qumran, period in the life of the community, or reflect life among Essenes not actually living at Qumran; see T. S. Beall, *Josephus' Description of the Essenes Illustrated by the Dead Sea Scrolls* (SNTMS 58; Cambridge: Cambridge University Press, 1988), 68–70.

implies that oaths are an important part of initiation, but that speaking with oaths is an unnecessary part of the Essene's living according to the right interpretation of the Law. The proximity of much of the language of these initiatory oaths to that of 4QBeatitudes implies that it too is a reminder of Essene initation and that the oath referred to in 4QBeat 2–3 II, 2 is an allusion to the oath of the initiate to live according to Wisdom, which is the right interpretation of the Law.

To return to the Sermon on the Mount with that in mind is to face once again the question of the significance of the Beatitudes at the start of the Sermon. It might be that 4QBeatitudes give us some further evidence that Matthew's Beatitudes are to be read in light of the initiation performed when new members joined the community. Such may be confirmed from the wider use of macarisms in the Hellenistic world. H.-D. Betz has argued convincingly that eschatological judgement passed proleptically is a feature of macarisms in several different kinds of text, the earliest example of which may be in the *Homeric Hymn to Demeter*: 'Happy is he among men upon earth who has seen these mysteries; but he who is uninitiate has no part in them; never has a lot of like good things once he is dead, down in the darkness and gloom.'[37] The macarism is addressed to those who have been initiated into the Eleusian mysteries. Within the Jewish tradition Betz points to 4 Ezra 8.46–54 and *2 Enoch* 42.6–14 and 52.1–15, texts which speak of the initiation of the seer, and of the reader who follows him, into the affairs of the world to come. The macarisms of both 4QBeatitudes and Matthew 5.3–12 recall the values into which the community member has been initiated in order to encourage perseverance in the face of opposition and to confirm a particular worldview which does not straightforwardly endorse religious piety and human well-being in this life. It is not surprising that the Matthaean Beatitudes are a source of inspiration to Christians suffering persecution and political deprivation.

CONCLUSION

It goes without saying that the publication of 4QBeatitudes should act as a corrective influence on those who assign all the differences between Matthew's and Luke's Beatitudes to the creative genius of Matthew. Although there is no need to argue for literary dependence of Matthew upon 4QBeatitudes, their similarities in structure, content, genre and

37 Cited in H.-D. Betz, *Essays on the Sermon on the Mount*, 26–7.

theology suggest that in presenting the teaching of Jesus in the way he does Matthew is standing firmly in line with the developing Wisdom traditions of some section of first-century Palestinian Judaism and Jewish Christianity ('Q'). Matthew was a scribe who sought to bring out of his treasure what is new and what is old.

Much in his Beatitudes rests firmly in the old. Among these matters may be his use of this literary form to remind his audience of their initiation and its significance for how one views the world, and his concern to show that right behaviour depends first upon obedience. Most of the language is traditional too, recognizably echoing the Wisdom literature and certain common features of Jewish eschatology.

Yet much in Matthew's Beatitudes is new. His particular connections between the beatitudes and the prayer of the disciples shows strikingly how prayer facilitates endurance. His particular eschatological stress, pronounced in the distinctive *hoti* clauses of each macarism, anticipate the verdict of the last judgement for the believer. But above all his use of Wisdom traditions shows that for him the Wisdom of the Beatitudes is none other than Jesus himself.[38]

---

38 See also E. Puech, '4Q525 et les péricopes des Béatitudes in Ben Sira et Matthieu', *RB* 98 (1991): 80–106; H.-J. Fabry, 'Der makarismus: Mehr als nur eine Weisheitliche Lehrform: Gedanken zu den neu-edierten Text 4Q525', in *Alttestamentliche Glaube und Biblische Theologie: Festschrift für Horst Dietrich Preuß zum 65. Geburtstag* (ed. J. Hausmann and H.-J. Zobel; Stuttgart: Kohlhammer, 1992); E. Puech, 'The Collection of Beatitudes in Hebrew and in Greek (4Q525 1–4 and Mt 5, 3–12)', in *Early Christianity in Context: Monuments and Documents* (ed. F. Manns and E. Alliata; Jerusalem: Franciscan Printing Press, 1993), 353–68; C. A. Evans, 'Jesus and the Dead Sea Scrolls from Qumran Cave 4', in *Eschatology, Messianism, and the Dead Sea Scrolls* (ed. C. A. Evans and P. W. Flint; Studies in the Dead Sea Scrolls and Related Literature; Grand Rapids: Eerdmans, 1997), 91–100; J. C. R. de Roo, 'Is 4Q525 a Qumran Sectarian Document?', in *The Scrolls and the Scriptures: Qumran Fifty Years After* (ed. S. E. Porter and C. A. Evans; JSPSup 26; Roehampton Institute London Papers 3; Sheffield: Sheffield Academic Press, 1997), 338–67.

13

4Q500 1 and the Use of Scripture in the Parable of the Vineyard

INTRODUCTION

Seven fragments have been assigned to the papyrus manuscript 4Q500.[1] Of these seven fragments six are very small and have preserved on each of them only two or three letters. Fragment 1 is more substantial, with parts of seven lines of writing preserved. The purpose of this study is to set 4Q500 Fragment 1 alongside the parable of the vineyard[2] (Matt. 21.33–45; Mk 12.1–12; Lk. 20.9–18) to suggest that it may now provide both more suitable and more contemporary Jewish information for the better understanding of the parable than the Jewish materials commonly adduced by New Testament commentators.

4Q500 1

M. Baillet thought either that some fragments of 4Q500 might be wrongly assigned to 4Q502 or that all the fragments which he had assigned to 4Q500 might be better assigned to 4Q502.[3] In the end the height of the letters and the distance between the lines persuaded him that the fragments of 4Q500 should probably be treated separately. 4Q500 1 is a cream-coloured papyrus fragment with some strands of its

---

1 M. Baillet, *Qumrân Grotte 4 III (4Q482–4Q520)* (DJD 7; Oxford: Clarendon Press, 1982), 78–9 and plate XXVII.

2 Perhaps more commonly known as the parable of the wicked husbandmen, or the parable of the wicked tenants, or just as the parable of the tenants. However, because this study will highlight the significance of the vineyard in particular, the parable will be known throughout as the parable of the vineyard.

3 Baillet labelled 4Q502 'Rituel de marriage' (DJD 7, 81–105), though it may be nothing of the sort; see J. M. Baumgarten, '4Q502: Marriage or Golden Age Ritual?', *JJS* 34 (1983): 125–35.

fibre of a slightly more reddish hue. Its black ink is easily legible and its handwriting is dated palaeographically by Baillet to the first half of the first century B.C.E.

4Q500 1 contains the remains of seven lines as follows:

1   ]° [
2   *bk*] *'ykh ynṣw w*° [ ]° [ ]° [
3   ]*yqb tyrwš*ᵏ*kh* [*b*]*nwy b'bny*[
4   ] *lš'r mrwm hqwdš* [
5   ]*mt 'kh wplgy kbwdkh b*[
6   ]° *kpwt š'šw'ykh* ° [
7   *k*]*rmkh*⁴   [

1   ] . . . [
2   ] may your [mulb]erry trees blossom and . . . [
3   ] your winepress [bu]ilt with stones [
4   ] to the gate of the holy height [
5   ] your planting and the streams of your glory . . . [
6   ] . . . the branches of your delights . . . [
7   ] your [vine]yard.   [

Perhaps because he associated 4Q500 with the more extensive 4Q502 Baillet entitled 4Q500 'Bénédiction'. In a detailed and incisive study of 4Q500 1, J. M. Baumgarten has clarified that the blessing is clearly addressed to God; more precisely, he has convincingly placed the fragment within Jewish exegetical tradition concerning the vineyard, a tradition in which the image is variously linked with the temple and the garden of Eden.⁵

As Baumgarten has implied, the most suitable way to discover the significance of the fragment is to identify the scriptural passages which its language seems to reflect. Lines 1 and 7 can be discounted: line 1 has the merest traces of letters and line 7 a restoration based on how the rest of

---

4 Based on the restoration proposed by J. M. Baumgarten, '4Q500 and the Ancient Conception of the Lord's Vineyard', *JSS* 40 (1989): 2: [*wkr*]*mkh*. In fact the ink traces at the start of the line are entirely compatible with *reš*, although a few other letters might fit equally well.

5 '4Q500 and the Ancient Conception of the Lord's Vineyard', *JJS* 40 (1989): 1–6. F. García Martínez catalogues 4Q500 with poetic texts as one of several 'other compositions': *The Dead Sea Scrolls Translated* (Leiden: Brill, 1994), 402; in his translation he renumbers lines 2–7 as 1–6.

the fragment is suitably understood. Line 2 contains a form of *nṣṣ*, 'sparkle, blossom'. This word occurs only three times in the Hebrew Bible. In two of these (Song 6.11; 7.13 [ET 7.12]) it is a matter of the 'pomegranates blooming' in parallel with the 'vines budding'.[6] In the third (Qoh. 12.5) it is the almond that blossoms. These associations strongly suggest that Baillet is correct to propose restoring the first partially extant word in the line as from *bk*,[7] commonly rendered as 'mulberry tree'. This is another infrequent word in scriptural texts. It occurs in 2 Samuel 5.23–4 (// 1 Chr. 14.15) where the rustling of its leaves becomes the sign for David to attack the Philistines. Its only other occurrence which, as Baumgarten points out, is more significant for appreciating 4Q500 1 is in Psalm 84.7 (ET 84.6):

> Happy are those whose strength is in you,
>> in whose heart are the highways to Zion.
> As they go through the valley of Baca they make it a place of springs;
>> the early rain also covers it with pools.

This Psalm in praise of God for dwelling in Zion associates the pilgrim's approach to the temple through the valley of Baca, the mulberry valley, with the welling up of water.

Line 3 speaks of the winepress for the new wine; both words are common and occur together in Proverbs 3.10, Hosea 9.2 and Joel 2.24, in idiomatic contexts of blessing or barrenness. There is also a winepress in the vineyard of Isaiah 5.2. The winepress in 4Q500 1, 3 is built with stones of some kind. That the association in particular with Isaiah 5 is not fanciful is confirmed by the fragment's line 6; there 'the branches of your delight', *kpwt šʿšwʿykh*, echo the phrase 'his delightful plant', *nṭʿ šʿšwʿyw*, of Isaiah 5.7 which is identified as the people of Judah.[8] Both Wisdom (Prov. 8.30–1) and various aspects of the Law (Ps. 119.24, 77, 92, 143, 174) are described as the Lord's delight; otherwise the term is used in the Hebrew Bible only in the taunt of Ephraim in Jeremiah 31.20, and in Isaiah 5.7. Given the presence of the winepress in line 3 and the most probable restoration of *krm* in line 7, it is most likely that the use of *šʿšwʿ* completes a triplet of allusions to Isaiah 5.1–7, the song of the vineyard.

---

6 The language of the Song of Songs seems also to lie behind the description of Wisdom in 4Q525 3 III, 5 (*wnṣny ʾrgmwn*); cf. Song 2.12; 3.10.

7 The suffix in the full restoration is misprinted in Baumgarten's study as *bk] ʾybh*.

8 See Baumgarten, '4Q500 and the Lord's Vineyard', 1–2.

In line 4 the phrase 'the gate of the holy height' is not to be found in Isaiah 5, but a very similar expression occurs in Psalm 102.20: the Lord looks down from his holy height to see the earth and hear the groans of the people, especially those who pray in Zion. If the phrase in 4Q500 1 refers to heaven, then perhaps the whole fragment describes something of what it is like there.[9] On the other hand, the holy height could simply be a reference to Jerusalem, especially the temple mount, whose delights mirror those of the heavenly abode.

Line 5's 'your planting' (*mṭ'kh*) may reflect the use of *nṭ'* in Isaiah 5.7, but is itself used of the people in Isaiah 60.21 and 61.3. Those restored from exile will be 'the Lord's planting'. Furthermore, in both these verses the planting is linked with the glorification (root *p'r*) of God. The phrase 'the streams of your glory', 'your glorious streams', could be addressed to Zion, though it is more likely that it is God himself who is addressed. The scriptural background of the phrase may lie in various places. According to Psalm 65.10 the river of God (*plg 'lhym*) is full of water so that the earth may be watered. Or again Psalm 46.5 describes a river whose streams make glad the city of God (*nhr plgyw yśmḥw 'yr 'lhym*), the holy habitation of the Most High. Isaiah 32.2 speaks of streams of water in Zion (*plgy mym bṣywn*). Ezekiel 47.1–12 confirms that there is much water flowing from below the threshold of the temple, though nowhere in the Ezekiel material is *plg* used of these streams.[10]

For Baumgarten the likely combination of ideas lying behind 4Q500 is confirmed in two treatments of Isaiah 5 in Jewish tradition. In *Targum Pseudo-Jonathan* Isaiah 5.2 is rendered as *wbnyt mqdšy bynyhwn w'p mdbḥy yhbyt lkpr' 'l ḥṭ'yhwn*, 'And I built my sanctuary among them and also my altar I gave as atonement for their sins.' This text is often cited in studies on the parable of the vineyard. It seems as if it is clear that the

---

9 Baumgarten ('4Q500 and the Lord's Vineyard', 3) compares this with the description of heaven on earth in *1 Enoch* 24—6, which includes mountains, fragrant trees, precious stones and streams.

10 The plural form of *plg* in 4Q500 1, 5 supports setting the term against a scriptural background rather than seeing its use as reflecting the technical terminology of 4QpNah 3–4 IV, 1 and CD XX, 22, though that terminology may itself have roots in similar scriptural texts, rather than Gen. 10.25 alone, because of its association with matters to do with the temple and Jerusalem. On the technical phrase *byt plg* see R. T. White, 'The House of Peleg in the Dead Sea Scrolls', in *A Tribute to Geza Vermes: Essays on Jewish and Christian Literature and History* (ed. P. R. Davies and R.T. White; JSOTSup 100; Sheffield: JSOT Press, 1990), 67–98; that study now needs reworking in light of all the occurrences of the root *plg* in the scrolls.

tower of the Isaianic allegory refers to the sanctuary and the winepress to the altar, the blood from which may be envisaged as flowing like wine out from the temple. This understanding seems to be further reflected in *Tosefta Sukkah* 3.15, *wybn mgdl btwkw zh hykl yqb ḥsb bh zh mzbḥ wgm yqb ḥsb bw zh ḥšyt*, 'and he built a tower in its midst, this refers to the temple; he dug a winepress in it, this refers to the altar; and also he dug a winepress in it, this refers to the channel'. The winepress has a double referent: the altar and the channel in which the sacrificial blood flows away. The beneficial qualities of the blood-flow may lie behind the picture of the rivers of living water emanating from the threshold in Ezekiel 47.

The association of the tower in the vineyard with the sanctuary in Jerusalem may also be seen in *1 Enoch* 89.50, the description of the building of the Solomonic temple: 'And that house became large and broad, and for those sheep; and that house was low, but the tower was raised up and high; and the Lord of the sheep stood on that tower, and they spread a full table before him.' This provides for an early attestation of the sanctuary being considered as a tower, but there is nothing explicit in this Enoch passage which might link it more precisely with the Isaianic vineyard.[11]

4Q500, therefore, almost certainly uses the Isaiah 5 vineyard material in interpretative association with a description of the temple, either heavenly or, more probably, earthly, which is the suitable place for the people (Isaiah's own interpretation) to bless God (possibly the genre of 4Q500). The overall suggestion of this study is that perhaps in 4Q500 1 we possess not just a link between the vineyard text of Isaiah 5 and its interpretative use in Jewish exegesis of the second century C.E. and later, but that the combination of motifs in 4Q500 1 provides the opportunity for the better appreciation of the parable of the vineyard in which several of the same motifs occur in association with yet other scriptural material. Before passing to the parable itself, it is worth drawing out some other ideas about the temple and the community which are to be found in the texts found at Qumran and which may also be illuminated by what Baumgarten has observed in 4Q500 1.

---

11 Baumgarten, '4Q500 and the Lord's Vineyard', 3, citing D. Dimant, 'Jerusalem and the Temple in the Vision of the Beasts (*1 Enoch* 85–90) in the Light of the Views of the Sect from the Desert of Judaea', *Shnaton* 5–6 (1983): 177–93.

SOME OTHER QUMRAN TEXTS

The pleasant planting

That Isaiah's own interpretation of the vineyard as the house of Judah is in view in 4Q500 seems clear from the use of the pleasant planting motif (*nṭʿ šʿšwʿyw*) from Isaiah 5.7 in 4Q500 1, 5–6 (*mṭʿkh . . . šʿšwʿykh*). In several texts from Qumran the terms for planting (*mṭʿ*, *mṭʿt*) are used and in some instances their referent is the community there, or some precursor of it. It is not necessary to rehearse all the references,[12] but recollection of a couple might be suggestive for the developing argument of this study.

The metaphor of planting, both *mṭʿ* and *mṭʿt*, is most explicit in the *Hodayot*. For example, 1QH^a XVI, 4–8.[13] '[I give you thanks, Lord,] because you have set me in the source of streams in a dry land, in the spring of water in a parched land, in the canals which water a garden [of delights in the middle of the desert,] [so that] a plantation (*mṭʿ*) of cypresses and elms [may grow,] together with cedars, for your glory. Trees of life in the secret source, hidden among the trees of water. They must make a shoot grow in the everlasting plantation (*mṭʿt*), to take root before it grows.'[14] Or again, 1QH^a XVI, 20: 'But the plantation (*mṭʿ*) of fruit [. . .] eternal [. . .] for the glorious garden (*ʿdn*) and will [bear fruit always.] By my hand you have opened their spring with channels [of water] [putting them in] straight lines, correctly, the planting (*mṭʿ*) of their trees with the plumbline of the sun, so that [. . .] with foliage of glory (*kbwd*).'[15] The planting demands an allegorical interpretation in relation to the community for which the poet presents himself as responsible.

In addition to these key poetic passages in 1QH^a, the image of

---

12 Cf. E. Qimron, 'The Language', *Qumran Cave 4.V: Miqṣat Maʿaśe Ha-Torah* (DJD 10; E. Qimron and J. Strugnell; Oxford: Clarendon Press, 1994), §3.5.2.20 on MMT B 62: 'The word *mṭʿt* occurs ten times in QH: twice in 1QS, four times in 1QH^a and once each in 4Q418 81 13, 4Q423 2 7, 4QD^e and CD. In MH it is found in three passages in the *Tosefta: Šebiʿit* 1.1, 3; *Kilʾayim* 3.3. BH uses instead the masculine synonym *mṭʿ*, a form somewhat less frequent in QH (it appears four times in 1QH^a col. 8, and twice in *DJD* 7). It is not used in MH.'
13 The column numbers for 1QH^a follow the definitive reordering as represented in E. Puech, 'Quelques aspects de la restauration du Rouleau des Hymnes (1QH)', *JJS* 39 (1988): 38–55.
14 Trans. F. García Martínez, *The Dead Sea Scrolls Translated*, 345.
15 Trans. F. García Martínez, *The Dead Sea Scrolls Translated*, 346.

planting is used in the *Damascus Document* just once (CD I, 7): 'He visited them and caused a root of planting (*mṭ't*) to spring from Israel and from Aaron to possess his land and to grow fat on the good things of his earth.'[16] Here there is an indirect quotation of Isaiah 60.21.[17] Elsewhere in CD a *Book of Jubilees* is cited as an authority and so it is no surprise to discover the image there also in a key opening section on repentance and restoration (*Jub.* 1.16–18): 'And with all my heart and with all my soul I shall transplant them as a righteous plant. And they will be a blessing and not a curse. And they will be the head and not the tail. And I shall build my sanctuary in their midst and I shall dwell with them and I shall be their God and they shall be my people truly and rightly and I shall not forsake them, and I shall not be alienated from them because I am the Lord their God.'[18]

This may be partially echoed in the *Rule of the Community*, 1QS VIII, 4–8: 'When these are in Israel, the Council of the Community shall be established in truth. It shall be an Everlasting Plantation (*mṭ't*), a House of Holiness for Israel, an Assembly of Supreme Holiness for Aaron . . . It shall be that tried wall, that *precious corner-stone*, whose foundations shall neither rock nor sway in their place (Isa. xxviii, 16).'[19]

In addition to the motif of planting which is most obvious in the *Hodayot*, the motif of delight or pleasantness[20] also occurs there six times; 1QH[a] XV, 21; XVII, 8, 13, 32; XVIII, 31; XIX, 7. 1QH[a] XVIII, 30–2 reads as follows: 'My heart rejoices in your covenant and your truth delights (*tš'š'*) my soul. I flourish like an iris, my heart opens to an ever-lasting spring, my support is an elevated refuge (*m'wz mrwm*).'[21]

The house and sanctuary

As the quotation from the *Rule of the Community* (1QS VIII, 4–8) makes clear, the community is portrayed as a plant in association with other

---

16   Partially preserved in 4QD[a] (4Q266) 2, 11–12 and 4QD[c] (4Q268) 1, 14–15.

17   On the inversions, explanatory substitution, and the Qere/Ketiv in the allusion, see C. Rabin, *The Zadokite Documents* (Oxford: Clarendon Press, 2nd edn, 1958), 3.

18   Cf. *Jub.* 7.34; 21.24; *1 Enoch* 10.16 (linked with planting vines for plenty); 84.6; 93.2; *Ps. Sol.* 14.3.

19   Trans. G. Vermes, *The Complete Dead Sea Scrolls in English* (London: Penguin Books, 1998), 109. Cf. 1QS XI, 8.

20   Root *š'* as in 4Q500 1 6.

21   Trans. F. García Martínez, *The Dead Sea Scrolls Translated*, 352.

metaphors, the most prominent of which is that of the house.[22] This is a metaphor with at least a double meaning, for it implies some connection especially with the house of Aaron, and thus denotes the priestly status of the community; also it is a dwelling place where atonement is worked out, and thus it portrays the continuity of the community with the sanctuary and its cultic practice.

As is well known, this metaphor of the house is treated in an even more complicated fashion in 4Q174 where 2 Samuel 7.10–14 is exegeted, first, to refer to the sanctuary in several guises, namely the Solomonic and the future eschatological temple of which the community itself seems to be an anticipation, and then, second, the house is played upon to refer to the Davidic house and the expectation of one who will arise to save Israel.[23]

The understanding of the community as an anticipation of the eschatological sanctuary is based in a phrase which has provoked much scholarly discussion but which is particularly significant for the purposes of this present study: *mqdš ʾdm*. In light of recent studies it seems that the phrase has two principal aspects which need to be held together for its full significance to be grasped.[24] On the one hand, the phrase seems to mean 'sanctuary of men';[25] that is, the community is a sanctuary in which

---

22 The association between planting and house is made not just in the *Rule of the Community* but probably also in 4Q174 in which the root *nt'* is used as the catchword to link the quotations from 2 Sam. 7.10 and Ex. 15.7; see G. J. Brooke, *Exegesis at Qumran: 4QFlorilegium in its Jewish Context* (JSOTSup 29; Sheffield: JSOT Press, 1985), 178.

23 See esp. B. Gärtner, *The Temple and the Community in Qumran and the New Testament* (SNTSMS 1; Cambridge: Cambridge University Press, 1965), 30–42; R. J. McKelvey, *The New Temple: The Church in the New Testament* (London: Oxford University Press, 1969), 46–53; G. J. Brooke, *Exegesis at Qumran*, 178–93; A. Steudel, *Der Midrasch zur Eschatologie aus der Qumrangemeinde (4QMidrEschat*[a.b]*)* (STDJ 13; Leiden: Brill, 1994), 41–6, 161–9.

24 Not considered in detail here are the possibilities that *mqdš ʾdm* refers to a 'manmade sanctuary' over against the temple not made with human hands, or that it refers to a 'sanctuary amongst men': on these understandings see Brooke, *Exegesis at Qumran*, 184–5.

25 See Brooke, *Exegesis at Qumran*, 184–93 ('sanctuary of men'); D. Dimant, '4QFlorilegium and the Idea of the Community as Temple', in *Hellenica et Judaica: Hommage à Valentin Nikiprowetzky z' l* (ed. A. Caquot, M. Hadas-Lebel, J. Riaud; Leuven: Peeters, 1986), 165–89 ('temple of men'); A. Steudel, *Der Midrasch zur Eschatologie aus der Qumrangemeinde (4QMidrEschat*[a.b]*)*, 31 ('Heiligtum von Menschen').

the offerings will be the *m'śy twdh*, 'works of thanksgiving', a play upon the phrase *m'śy twdh*.[26] On the other hand, more recently, and presented in opposition to the understanding of 'sanctuary of men', M. Wise has taken the phrase more at face value and rendered it as 'Temple of Adam'.[27] For Wise the phrase expresses the hope for the restitution of some ideal cultic place where God will be present and where there is suitable obedience in the offering of sacrifices. In support of his understanding Wise cites CD III, 12–IV, 4. The text describes the community as the heirs of the covenant: 'But God in his wondrous mysteries atoned for their evil and forgave their sin. He built for them "*a sure house in Israel*," (2 Sam. 7.16) whose like has never existed from ancient times until now. Those who hold to it will possess long life and all the glory of Adam' (CD III, 18–20).[28] Within the slightly broader context of CD, which is speaking about the proper practice of the cult in the eschatological period, it seems as if that proper practice is to be equated with the glory of Adam in an *Urzeit–Endzeit* typology and notice of its location juxtaposes, in an interpretative fashion, the eschatological sanctuary with Eden.[29] The association of the sanctuary with Eden, especially through the motif of water, has also been highlighted above in relation to 4Q500.

This second understanding of *mqdś 'dm* is assisted by reference to two

---

26 The reading *m'śy twdh* originally tentatively proposed by J. Strugnell, 'Notes en marge du Volume V des «Discoveries in the Judaean Desert of Jordan»', *RevQ* 7 (1969–71): 221, has been firmly supported by Brooke, *Exegesis at Qumran*, 108; E. Puech, *La croyance des Esséniens en la vie future: immortalité, résurrection, vie éternelle?* (EB 22; Paris: J. Gabalda, 1993), 578; H.-W. Kuhn, 'Die Bedeutung der Qumrantexte für das Verständnis des Galaterbriefes: aus der Münchener Projekt Qumran und das Neue Testament', in *New Qumran Texts and Studies:Proceedings of the First Meeting of the International Organization for Qumran Studies, Paris 1992* (ed. G. J. Brooke with F. García Martínez; STDJ 15; Leiden: Brill, 1994), 205–6; A. Steudel, *Der Midrasch zur Eschatologie aus der Qumrangemeinde (4QMidrEschat*[a.b]*)*, 44. Several scholars still prefer to read *m'śy twrh*, including D. Dimant, '*4QFlorilegium* and the Idea of the Community as Temple', 169, who admits working solely from the photograph.

27 '4QFlorilegium and the Temple of Adam', *RevQ* 15 (1991): 103–32; reprinted in a revised form as 'That Which Has Been is That Which Shall Be: 4QFlorilegium and the *mqdś 'dm*', in *Thunder in Gemini and Other Essays on the History, Language and Literature of Second Temple Palestine* (JSPSup 15; Sheffield: JSOT Press, 1994), 152–85.

28 Trans. M. Wise, *Thunder in Gemini*, 176.

29 *Jub.* 3.9–12 associates Eden with the Holy of Holies; see Wise, *Thunder in Gemini*, 179, n. 78.

passages in 4Q171, 4QpPs[a]. On Psalm 37.18–19 the interpreter
comments: 'those who have returned to the wilderness, who will live for a
thousand generations in prosperity. To them belongs all the inheritance
of Adam, and to their progeny, forever.'[30] On Psalm 37.22 the commentary is, 'Its meaning concerns the Congregation of the Poor, [to wh]om
belongs all the inheritance of the Great [Ones; for] they shall inherit the
high mountain of Isra[el, and] shall delight [in] his holy [moun]tain.'[31]
This is an important text. To begin with it clarifies an element in what is
to be inherited. To jump ahead a little, let us recall that one of the principal understandings of the parable of the vineyard concerns the matter of
inheritance, which is explicitly mentioned in Mark 12.7 and parallels.
The inheritance of Adam is further defined in terms of the inheritance of
the high mountain (*mrwm*) of Israel, the mountain of his holiness
(*qwdšw*). If these two parallel phrases, 'high mountain' and 'his holy
mountain', are reduced to their principal elements, a phrase not unlike
that preserved in 4Q500 results; the vineyard in 4Q500 signifies
metaphorically the holy height (*mrwm hqwdš*).

Another aspect of the importance of the *pesher* on Psalm 37.22
deserves attention too. The phrase 'the high mountain of Israel' occurs
only three times in the Hebrew Bible, all in Ezekiel: 17.23, 20.40 and
34.14. Ezekiel 17.22–3 is a messianic allegory: 'Thus says the Lord God:
I myself will take a sprig from the lofty top of a cedar; I will set it out. I
will break off a tender one from the topmost of its young twigs; I myself
will plant it on a high and lofty mountain. On the mountain height of
Israel I will plant it, in order that it may produce boughs and bear fruit
and become a noble cedar.' Ezekiel 20.40 is part of the vision of the
restoration of Zion. Again *qdš* and *mrwm* are juxtaposed. 'For on my
holy mountain, the mountain height of Israel, says the Lord God, there
are all the house of Israel, all of them, shall serve me in the land; there I
will accept them, and there I will require your contributions and the
choicest of your gifts, with all your sacred things.' Ezekiel 34.14 is part of
the picture of God as the true shepherd: 'I will feed them with good
pasture, and the mountain heights of Israel shall be their pasture.' This
holy mountain of God is described most completely in Ezekiel 28.11–19
where it is explicitly associated with Eden.[32] Thus, it is clear that in

---

30 Trans. M. Wise, *Thunder in Gemini*, 180.

31 Trans. M. Wise, *Thunder in Gemini*, 181.

32 Yet other texts found at Qumran, but not necessarily sectarian in any narrow
sense, show something of how a worshipping community can conceive of itself as
participating with the angels in the worship of heaven. So the *Songs of the Sabbath*

4Q171 it is not accidental that Psalm 37.18–19 is interpreted in relation to the inheritance of Adam and Psalm 37.22 is interpreted with regard to the inheritance of the high mountain. The scriptural antecedents in Ezekiel in particular point to the exegetical connection between the two: the high mountain of Israel is the Eden where the glory of Adam will be restored.

With all this in mind, it is surely the case that the understandings of *mqdš 'dm*, as referring to a community anticipating the eschatological sanctuary and as referring to an Adamic sanctuary of Eden restored, should not be seen as mutually exclusive. This has already been suggested in part by E. Puech who comments on his translation of *mqdš 'dm* as 'un sanctuaire d'Homme' as follows: 'Nous rendons *'dm* par "Homme", comme une allusion au premier homme, Adam, mais en préservant l'intention de l'auteur de signifier le type de sanctuaire que le fidèle doit bâtir = un temple d'hommes (de justes).'[33] Thus the phrase *mqdš 'dm* can mean both 'a sanctuary of men' and 'a sanctuary of Adam', and Wise's insights concerning the Edenic connections of the imagery can be integrated with those of the high mountain within the understanding of the vineyard of Isaiah 5; that vineyard is interpreted in Isaiah itself as being the people of Judah, though we can see in 4Q500 that the vineyard is also the temple, with Edenic overtones.[34] All these associations are confirmed yet further by the motif of water in 4Q500 5, 'your glorious streams'. The intriguing glory of these streams may match the glory of Adam, the glory of God

---

Sacrifice speak of what is happening in the lofty heavens, using language similar to that which Ezekiel has used of the earthly sanctuary on the high mount in Jerusalem. Something of this can be seen for example in the fragmentary 4Q400 1 I, 20–II, 2:

20 [g]od[like] elim, priests of the lofty heavens (*mrwmy rwm*) who [draw] near
21 [ ] ... [ ] ... [ ] ... [pr]aises of
1   your lofty kingdom (*rwm mlkwt*[*kh*]) [
2   the heights (*mrwmym*) [

33 *La croyance des Esséniens en la vie future: immortalité, résurrection, vie éternelle?* 2.578, n. 33.
34 Another text, 4Q265, also assists in this understanding, as Puech points out: *La croyance des Esséniens en la vie future: immortalité, résurrection, vie éternelle?* 2.578, n. 33. For more detail on the relevant part see now J. M. Baumgarten, 'Purification after Childbirth and the Sacred Garden in 4Q265 and Jubilees', in *New Qumran Texts and Studies: Proceedings of the First Meeting of the International Organization for Qumran Studies, Paris 1992* (ed. G. J. Brooke with F. García Martínez; STDJ 15; Leiden: Brill, 1994), 1–10, esp. p. 6: 'What may certainly be deduced from the etiological explanation found in *Jubilees* and in 4Q265 is the concept of the primeval garden as a prototype of the sanctuary'.

himself, which belongs both in the sanctuary and in Eden as is implied in
CD III, 19–20. Also, as already mentioned, streams belonging to God
are found especially in Psalm 46.5: 'there is a river the streams whereof
make glad the city of God, the holiest dwelling place of the Most High'.
Baumgarten proposes that an 'eschatological reflex' of this can be found
in Joel 4.18: 'A spring shall issue forth from the house of the Lord which
will water the valley of Shittim.'[35]

4Q500 1 thus seems to stand at a highly potent metaphorical inter-
change. In just a few words there are hints of the vineyard which is the
chosen people of God, there are hints that the vineyard was associated
with Jerusalem,[36] and with the sanctuary in particular. And the traditions
about the sanctuary link it with two theological perspectives, one in
which the earthly mirrors the heavenly, the other an *Urzeit–Endzeit*
typology which involves the eschatological sanctuary being described in
terms of the garden of Eden. Through other closely related Qumran texts
these ideological motifs are variously reinforced or expanded. And in all
of them, the chosen community is involved, either as the heirs of divine
promises or as the sanctuary of men/Adam, as a holy house for Aaron.

THE PARABLE OF THE VINEYARD

In light of all that has now been said through the focus of 4Q500 1 we
can turn to the parable of the vineyard. The whole pericope (Matt.
21.33–45; Mk 12.1–12; Luke 20.9–18)[37] is usually divided into three
sections: the parable proper with its narrative conclusion in terms of

---

35 '4Q500 and the Lord's Vineyard', 3. In later texts these associations are continued: cf. Rashi on Ps. 46.5; *2 Enoch* 8.5; *Masseket Kelim*; *Hekhalot Rabbati* 8.4.

36 Probably confirmed by 4QpIsa[b] II, 6–7, 10 taking Isa. 5.11–14, 24–5 as speaking
against scoffers in Jerusalem.

37 Apart from the triple tradition the parable is also known in the Gospel of
Thomas 65—66: 'He said, "There was a good man who owned a vineyard. He leased
it to tenant farmers so that they might work it and he might collect the produce from
them. He sent his servant so that the tenants might give him the produce of the
vineyard. They seized the servant and beat him, all but killing him. The servant went
back and told his master. The master said, 'Perhaps they did not recognize him.' He
sent another servant. The tenants beat this one as well. Then the owner sent his son
and said, 'Perhaps they will show respect to my son.' Because the tenants knew that it
was the heir to the vineyard, they seized him and killed him. Let him who has ears
hear." Jesus said, "Show me the stone which the builders have rejected. That one is
the cornerstone."' Trans. T. O. Lambdin, 'The Gospel of Thomas (II, 2)', in *The Nag
Hammadi Library in English* (ed. J. M. Robinson; Leiden: Brill, 1977), 125–6.

audience reaction (Mk 12.1–8, 12 //), the logion of Jesus in the form of a question (Mk 12.9a) which either he answers for himself or is answered by his audience, and the proof-text from Psalm 118.22–3. Since the narrative conclusion comes after the logion and proof-text in all three Gospels, it is clear that the three elements are understood to belong together and should be interpreted together. Even in the Gospel of Thomas, which lacks any narrative framework, the parable and the proof-text follow one after the other.[38] The parable has generated a vast secondary literature; it is not necessary to rehearse it all in detail but to highlight certain questions and issues concerning the use of Scripture in the parable which may have light shed upon them from what we have discerned in 4Q500 1.

Allegory

Much in the history of scholarship on this parable (and of course on the parables as a whole) has been a concern to define it generically. For this text in particular the debate has been about the place of allegory in the teaching of Jesus and the New Testament more generally. The problem may be posed on the one hand by asking, in light of the other parables which are attributed to Jesus, whether this one also deserves the label 'parable', as it is explicitly designated in Mark 12.12 and Luke 20.19. On the other hand, it is important to ask whether the presence of allegorization, as in the mention of the 'beloved son' (Mk 12.6; Lk. 20.13), should be seen primarily as characteristic of early Christian understanding, having little or nothing to do with Jesus himself. Two issues thus emerged: could the modern definition of the genre of parable be broad enough to include the kind of allegory which is found in the parable of

---

38 The proposal that the Gospel of Thomas represents the earliest form of the parable because it does not contain the allusion to Isa. 5, Christological hints (Mk 12.6), the concluding question, and because it has only a traditional threefold sending, has been supposed among others by R. McL. Wilson, *Studies in the Gospel of Thomas* (London: Mowbray, 1960), 101–2; J. D. Crossan, 'The Parable of the Wicked Husbandmen', *JBL* 90 (1971): 456–67; J. E. and R. E. Newell, 'The Parable of the Wicked Tenants', *NovT* 14 (1972): 226–7. For opposition to the priority of the form in Thomas see the discussion and works cited by K. Snodgrass, *The Parable of the Wicked Tenants: An Inquiry into Parable Interpretation* (WUNT 27; Tübingen: J. C. B. Mohr, 1983), 52–4, and his earlier article 'The Parable of the Wicked Husbandmen: Is the Gospel of Thomas Version the Original?', *NTS* 21 (1974): 142–4. To this writer, on balance, the form in Thomas seems secondary.

the vineyard, and could such a sub-genre be attributable to Palestinian Judaism of the time of Jesus, and to Jesus himself?

Until the modern period the allegorical views of the earliest Christian commentators were widely accepted as normative for the understanding of the parable.[39] As is often recalled, it was A. Jülicher who first challenged the allegorical understanding of parables, at least in so far as he insisted that those which were authentic to Jesus had no allegorical characteristics.[40] In this vein some scholars have attempted to understand the authentic tradition in the parable which might be traced back to Jesus by peeling away the layers of allegory which were perceived as secondary. For example, C. H. Dodd[41] is clear that the quotation of Psalm 118 is a later addition to an original story which reflects a first-century Palestinian situation of an absentee landlord and which in general terms is a 'prediction' by Jesus himself of his impending death; J. Jeremias[42] removes the secondary allegorization introduced in the Markan and Matthaean accounts under the influence of the reference to the vineyard of Isaiah 5, and in seeing the Lukan form as more original, suggests that the parable is another presentation of the concern of Jesus 'to justify the offer of the gospel to the poor'.

Despite being very aware of the problem posed by those approaches which are based on negative assumptions about the significance of allegorization, in his extensive study of the parable K. Snodgrass himself stands firmly on the shoulders of those earlier scholars. He proposes that it is indeed possible to discover an original parabolic story by comparing the four accounts of the parable, the three in the Synoptic Gospels and the one in the Gospel of Thomas. Determining the content of such an original story depends both on literary critical decisions but also on producing a story which is coherently credible. For Snodgrass this means that Jewish parallels both need to be and can be adduced for proposing what might make a suitable original. As a result, not unlike Jülicher, Dodd and Jeremias, Snodgrass concludes that an original parable of the vineyard was focused on one point, namely the issue of election; even

---

39 Snodgrass, *The Parable of the Wicked Tenants*, 3, n. 1, refers briefly to the early Christian allegorical interpretations of the parable and cites the overviews of ancient interpretation in R. Silva, 'La parabola de los renteros homicidas', *Compostellanum* 15 (1970): 322–6, and J. Gnilka, *Das Evangelium nach Markus* (Zurich: Benzinger Verlag, 1979), 2.149–50.

40 *Die Gleichnisreden Jesu* (Freiburg: J.C.B. Mohr, 1888–9), 1.65–85.

41 *The Parables of the Kingdom* (London: Nisbet, 1935), 124–32.

42 *Rediscovering the Parables* (London: SCM, 1966), 57–63.

more recently this single point approach is attested in the application of socio-rhetorical criticism to the parable by J. D. Hester.[43]

The problem with these approaches is that they do not sufficiently allow for the possibility that the original parable, if that is ever knowable, could have contained more than one point, even if only because more than one scriptural passage may have been in mind as it was told and rehearsed and, quite possibly, more than one kind of hearer was known to be in the audience and in need of being addressed. These criticisms have been neatly made by several recent interpreters and are presented well by C. L. Blomberg.[44] In the parable of the vineyard in whatever canonical form we read it, we are dealing with mixed metaphors, all gloriously intermingled. Also problematic, as is epitomized in the lengthy study of M. Hengel,[45] is the way interpreters have been determined to anchor their reconstructed originals in the realities of daily life in first-century Palestine rather than in the scriptural allusions which are clear in the extant narratives. Over against those assumptions, the working basis of this study is that the parable of the vineyard can be allowed to stand as an allegory in some form and its basis in scriptural allusion should not be sidestepped in the quest for some supposedly more original and more credible form of the story.

The vineyard

Quite apart from what any original form of the parable may have looked like, it is clear in the triple tradition that it is an allegory, not least because of the dependence of its phraseology, at least in large part, on LXX Isaiah 5.1–7. This is most explicit in Mark and Matthew which both include the details of the hedge, the winepress and the tower. But, though Luke omits those details, he clearly is aware of the scriptural allusion, since he alone gives the distinctive question by the landlord in Luke 20.13, 'What

---

43 'Socio-Rhetorical Criticism and the Parable of the Tenants', *JSNT* 45 (1992): 27–57. Hester peels away 'allegorical accretions' to discover a parable which is about the relationship of the Jewish farmer to the land. 'This relationship is explored within the theo-political theme of "inheritance"' (p. 57).

44 *Interpreting the Parables* (Leicester: Apollos, 1990), 29–69; his analysis has as part of its agenda a concern to attribute as much as possible to the historical Jesus.

45 M. Hengel, 'Das Gleichnis von den Weingärtnern Mc 12 1–12 im Lichte der Zenonpapyri und der rabbinischen Gleichnisse', *ZNW* 59 (1968): 1–39.

shall I do?', echoing the *ti poiēsō* of LXX Isaiah 5.4.[46] Because of Luke and because Isaiah 5 offers its own interpretation of the vineyard as the people of Judah, many modern interpreters have not allowed the tower and winepress any significance. The problem has been exacerbated by an over-literal perspective often based in the difficulty supposedly made by the parable itself, for though the vineyard might be the land of the people, it is clear that the son is cast out of it, by which is understood that Jesus was cast out of Jerusalem. So Snodgrass, for example, denies that the vineyard could be either Israel or Jerusalem.[47] He prefers to see it, in line with Isaiah, as designating the elect of God and all the privileges that go with that election. What is then passed on to others in the terms of the parable is this privilege of election.

Because of the desire to interpret the parable as an original single point story, few scholars have taken Jewish uses of Isaiah 5 seriously into account in interpreting the details of the parable as it stands. Those who have are shown by Snodgrass to be somewhat mutually contradictory. For example, if one follows Isaiah 5 itself, then the vineyard represents the house of Israel in which are planted the people of Judah (Isa. 5.7); but such identification makes little sense of the subsequent casting out of the son (Mk 12.8), particularly in the Matthaean form in which the expulsion precedes the killing, indicating that Matthew understood the vineyard to be Jerusalem. In any case Snodgrass asks how Israel can be taken away and given to others.[48] However, if contemporary Jewish understanding of the vineyard as Jerusalem or as its cult is allowed some credence, especially since the date of a fragment like 4Q500 1 cannot be gainsaid, then the conclusions of several scholars that the parable is primarily about Israel in miniature, that is Jerusalem, its temple and its cult,

---

46 Hester is wrong to say that in Luke there is no theme from Isaiah: 'Socio-Rhetorical Criticism and the Parable of the Tenants', 32. On the extent of the influence of LXX Isa. 5.1–7 in Mark 12.1–9 see J. S. Kloppenborg Verbin, 'Egyptian Viticultural Practices and the Citation of Isa. 5.1–7 in Mark 12.1–9', *NovT* 44 (2002): 134–59 ('Mark agrees with the LXX, but never with the MT *against* the LXX', 159); C. A. Evans, 'How Septuagintal is Isa. 5.1–7 in Mark 12.1–9?', *NovT* 45 (2003): 105–10 ('Although a degree of septuagintalism cannot be denied, there is in fact agreement with the Hebrew, the presence of non-septuagintal elements, and important points of coherence with Jewish interpretive traditions', 105).

47 *The Parable of the Wicked Tenants*, 74–6.

48 *The Parable of the Wicked Tenants*, 74.

fits very well.[49] In relation to this D. Juel has especially stressed the relevance of *Targum Pseudo-Jonathan* Isaiah 5.2 in linking the vineyard to Jerusalem and the tower to the temple.[50] Even more particularly, C. A. Evans has argued persuasively that in early Jewish interpretation the association of Isaiah 5.1–7 not only with the temple but also with its destruction justifies understanding the parable of the vineyard as juridical, as designed to force its audience into self-condemnation, as is made explicit in Mark 12.12.[51] For Evans the identification of the vineyard and its constituent parts in relation to the temple facilitates taking the quotation of Psalm 118.22–3 integrally with the rest of the parable, an observation to be discussed further below.

It can be argued that because Luke can do without the hedge, the winepress and the tower, the need to understand the vineyard as signifying a particular place is greatly reduced, especially if the simplicity of the form of the parable in the Gospel of Thomas is counted in favour of seeing Luke as in some way preserving an early form of the parable. But, quite apart from the likelihood that Gospel of Thomas 65 is itself a secondary simplification, Luke's knowledge of Mark and his decision to omit certain features may also suggest that these items are significant for something in the Markan and Matthaean forms of the story. As such it seems more likely that the vineyard is Jerusalem, Israel in miniature, the tower is the sanctuary and the winepress the altar and its drainage system which can take on various eschatological significances. The servants who come are universally recognized as prophets. Now some prophets spoke especially about cultic matters and right worship, so their mission could fit with the cultic understanding of Isaiah 5, though once again it is not necessary to press every detail. The inheritance, as we have noted in relation to Qumran texts, may also relate to temple practice, either in itself or as the purpose of the gift of the land to Israel in the first place.

---

49 Snodgrass, *The Parable of the Wicked Husbandmen*, 74, n. 10, cites several scholars who have variously taken this line, notably E. Lohmeyer, 'Das Gleichnis von der bösen Weingärtnern (Mk 12, 1–12)', *ZST* 18 (1941): 274–5; P. Carrington, *According to Mark* (Cambridge: Cambridge University Press, 1960), 251; R. H. Gundry, *The Use of the Old Testament in St. Matthew's Gospel* (Leiden: Brill, 1967), 44. More recently, C. Evans has made similar proposals, though he is keenly aware that the Jewish evidence he cites may all be later than the synoptic material: 'On the Vineyard Parables of Isaiah 5 and Mark 12', *BZ* 28 (1984): 82–6.

50 *Messiah and Temple: The Trial of Jesus in the Gospel of Mark* (SBLDS 31; Missoula: Scholars Press, 1977), 136–7.

51 'On the Vineyard Parables of Isaiah 5 and Mark 12', 83.

Election

Since Snodgrass and, more recently, Hester have both come to the conclusion from different perspectives that election and inheritance dominate the parable, both in its written form in the triple tradition and in what may be reconstructed as an earlier and more original form, it is important to comment more closely on the character and content of that election.

For Snodgrass this status of election involves 'the law, the promises, and the working of God in the past and present, or as the vineyard is interpreted in Matthew 21.43, the kingdom of God. That which is taken and given to others is the special relationship to God which results from being his elect, or in short, election itself.'[52] There is no mention here of anything to do with the temple or cultic practice and its significance. The use of the Isaiah vineyard material is important for introducing the theme of special relationship, but for Snodgrass it is only introductory and the significance of its details should not be pressed. It functions solely as a symbol for the chosen possession of God, which is how Snodgrass sees the role of the vineyard in many biblical passages.[53] For the purposes of his own interpretation Snodgrass thus jumps directly from a collection of biblical uses of the vineyard to the use of the vineyard in the parable; at this stage in his presentation he omits any reference to contemporary Jewish understandings of the vineyard and its component elements.

Hester is only really concerned with what may be supposed to be an original form of the parable. In this he sees inheritance as 'the central, generative theme',[54] a theme which can be fully appreciated only when set against the background of first-century absentee landlords. As such it is not the intention of the parable's speaker to portray the owner as a sympathetic figure; most certainly he should not be understood allegorically as God. Rather the story of the parable revolves around the tenants who in the economic framework of the times are the impoverished farmers of property once their own but which is now owned by an absentee. Thus as the story runs they are threatened not only with the loss of their livelihood, but also with the loss of their land itself. The coming of the son in

---

52 *The Parable of the Wicked Tenants*, 76.
53 He refers particularly to Ps. 80.9–20; 2 Kgs 19.30; Isa. 3.14; 27.2; 37.31; Jer. 6.9; Hos. 14.6–9.
54 'Socio-Rhetorical Criticism and the Parable of the Tenants', 34.

the story introduces a focus on inheritance; the tenant farmers see what was once their land being passed on to somebody else's heir. In this light the key question, as Hester sees it, is 'Whose land is it really?' With the death of the legal heir, the answer in the story is that the land is the proper inheritance of the tenant farmers. For Hester the vineyard is merely a term for land; scriptural traditions and early Jewish exegesis play no part in how the details of the stories might be understood.

If we resist the need to reconstruct a form of the story behind that in the triple tradition and accept the parable of the vineyard as allegory, in that its details self-evidently correspond with particular people, places or things, then the exposition of the likely significance of those details becomes imperative. In place of Snodgrass's status of election or Hester's attention to the inheritance of the land, I would restore as significant in the allegory the figure of the vineyard and, for Mark and Matthew, the various items in the use of Isaiah 5, Isaiah 5, that is, as taken and handled in contemporary Palestinian Jewish texts such as 4Q500. Thus the parable of the vineyard is about how the leaders of Judaism have abused their privileged role in Jerusalem and its temple, the centre of the worship of God. It is the significance of all of that which will be passed to others. It is around these matters that the issues of election and inheritance are to be understood.

The use of Psalm 118

The attention of scholarship to peeling away what are seen as later accretions and its concern with identifying the single point which underlines the meaning of a reconstructed parable have had repercussions for how the whole pericope has been viewed. Parables as single point stories are defined as discrete entities. It is generally assumed that any sayings outside the story line of the parable proper are likely to be secondary accretions from the oral transmission and missionary use of the stories in the early churches. Despite its attestation in the triple tradition and the Gospel of Thomas, for the parable of the vineyard this has meant that the citation of Psalm 118.22–3 has been widely considered to be a later addition to the parable and its judgement saying, an opinion justified in particular by the popularity of the Psalm verses as proof-texts in other passages in the New Testament.[55]

---

55 See Snodgrass, *The Parable of the Wicked Tenants*, 95.

Now the rediscovery of Jewish parallels both in general in terms of form and structure, and also in particular in relation to this motif of the vineyard which is leased out, has led some scholars to place the citation of Psalm 118 back as an integral part of the parable. As with the scriptural argument that forms the framework for the example story of the Good Samaritan, so in the case of the parable of the vineyard it is argued that the closing scriptural citation rounds out the teaching of the parable as an integral part of the whole which thus needs to be redefined as a pericope. Jewish methodology is then cited to explain how the citation of Psalm 118 is suitable for the earlier story.[56] Together with several others, Snodgrass considers that the Psalm citation belongs together with the parable through a standard wordplay involving *bn* and *'bn*.[57] This paronomasia can indeed be found in Exodus 28.9–10 and Joshua 4.6–7; and possibly in Lamentations 4.1–2[58] and Zechariah 9.16. Nor is there any major problem with the change from Hebrew to Aramaic, since there is ample evidence in relation to proper names to show the use of *bn* in Aramaic texts and *br* in Hebrew ones,[59] as well as a delightful account in Josephus (*War* 5.272) of how the warning used to be given in Jerusalem when a stone was being catapulted into the city by the Romans: the shout would go up 'the son is coming' (*ho huios erchetai*).[60]

Although wordplays may be part of how scriptural passages are linked and understood, the more widely recognized way for citations to be joined to an exegetical argument or story is through catchword association. In the case of the parable of the vineyard, unless one supposes a biblical text to be responsible for the phrase 'beloved son' (Mark, Luke),[61]

---

56 See E. E. Ellis, 'New Directions in Form Criticism', in *Jesus Christus in Historie und Theologie: Festschrift für H. Conzelmann* (ed. G. Strecker; Tübingen: J. C. B. Mohr, 1975), 299–315; E. E. Ellis, 'How the New Testament Uses the Old', in *New Testament Interpretation: Essays on Principles and Methods* (ed. I. H. Marshall; Exeter: Paternoster Press, 1977), 205.

57 *The Parable of the Wicked Tenants*, 95–106 and esp. 113–18.

58 In Lam. 4.1–2 the possible wordplay involves *'bny qds* being interpreted figuratively as *bny sywn*; this juxtaposition may be important for the purposes of this study in associating the sanctuary and Zion.

59 Cf. DJD 2, Nos 22, 29, 30, 36 (Hebrew texts with *br*); Nos 23, 74 (Aramaic texts with *bn*).

60 For discussion see Snodgrass, *The Parable of the Wicked Tenants*, 115–16.

61 Matt. 21.37 has only 'his son'. For a detailed study of Matthew's particular redactional interests in relation to this formulation see J. D. Kingsbury, 'The Parable of the Wicked Husbandmen and the Secret of Jesus' Divine Sonship in Matthew: Some Literary-Critical Observations', *JBL* 105 (1986): 643–55.

which has indeed been suggested (Gen. 22.2; Judg. 11.34; Tob. 3.10), then the explicit biblical text for the Psalm verse to be linked with is Isaiah 5.1–2. The two texts can indeed be linked through the motif of building with stones. Mark and Matthew have a form of Isaiah 5.1 long enough to include that the man built a tower; Psalm 118.22 speaks of the builders who rejected the stone. For the parable of the vineyard E. E. Ellis suggests the links between Isaiah 5.1–2 and Psalm 118 are the motifs first of the stone, reflected in the former's use of *sql* (LXX *hecharakōsa*) and the latter's use of *'bn* (LXX *lithon*), and second of building with *bnh* (LXX *oikodomein*) used in Isaiah 5.2 and Psalm 118.22.[62] The first of these looks a little weak, though possible. Yet it could be part of a wider association between the two verses based on a knowledge of Isaiah 5 in another form. This form may now be hinted at in 4Q500 1, for in line 3 the wine-press is described as built with stones (*bnwy b'bny*[). Is there a much more involved wordplay at work in the parable with its opening and closing quotations, a wordplay based on *'bn, bnh*, and possibly *bn*?[63] 4Q500 may allow us to see that the interconnectedness of the various elements in the parable of the vineyard, in its biblical surround (Isa. 5.1–2 and Ps. 118.22–3) and in the story proper, may be more complex and appropriate than hitherto supposed. The whole pericope, consisting of story, logion and proof-text, has an integrity which puts the burden of proof that it contains secondary accretions firmly on those who are looking for an 'originally' simple story with a single point.

The context

The treatment of parables as isolated pericopae is commonly further justified in part on the basis of the way in which the evangelists have grouped parables together in collections. It can be readily admitted that no wise teacher would ever have spoken so many parables together at one time as feature in Matthew 13. But such an observation should not force the conclusion that the evangelists always placed parables out of narrative

---

62 'How the New Testament Uses the Old', 205.

63 Isa. 5.1 speaks of the vineyard as *bn šmn*. Perhaps too, the motif of the beloved may further bind the various elements of the passage together: Isa. 5.1 (. . . *lydydy šyrt dwdy* . . . ; LXX . . . *tō ēgapēmenō asma tou agapētou* . . .); Gen. 22.2 (*yhydk*; LXX *ton agapēton*); Mk 12.6 and Lk. 20.13 (*agapēton*). On the problems of *dwdy* in Isa. 5.1 see J. A. Emerton, 'The Translation of Isaiah 5,1', in *The Scriptures and the Scrolls: Studies in Honour of A. S. van der Woude on the Occasion of his 65th Birthday* (ed. F. García Martínez, A. Hilhorst, C. J. Labuschagne; VTSup 49; Leiden: Brill, 1992), 18–30.

(or even historical) context. So the question remains as to whether the context of the parable of the vineyard aids its better understanding.

In light of what has been suggested about the role of Jerusalem, the temple and its altar in understanding the symbolism of the vineyard and its structures, and in light of the likelihood that the quotation of Psalm 118 is an integral part of the 'original', the answer to the question concerning the suitability of the parable to its context must be affirmative. In Mark (and Luke) Jesus is addressing chief priests, scribes and elders in the temple; in Matthew he is again in the temple apparently talking to the chief priests and elders (Matt. 21.23), but gets a reaction from the chief priests and Pharisees. The narrative context sets the parable in the temple.

The temple context is a suitable setting for the pericope's use of scripture from start to finish. Attention to the temple setting may also make suitable sense of a particular difference between Mark and the other two Synoptic Gospels. In Mark the son is killed before being cast out of the vineyard. Since the winepress is linked with the altar in some Jewish tradition, the fact that Mark has the son killed before he is cast out of the vineyard might enhance the cultic aspect of the son's death;[64] Matthew and Luke, 'knowing what really happened', put it all in the correct order so that the son's death (the crucifixion) takes place outside the vineyard.

The Jesus tradition?

Since there is no hint in the parable that the vineyard or its tower are yet destroyed, the parable with its integral use of Psalm 118 probably belongs in the pre-70 layer of early Christian tradition. How far back does it all go? Could it be that this temple material in a temple context goes back to shocking teaching suitably remembered with minor adjustments?[65] In other words, here may be genuine features of the teaching of Jesus himself, most especially his particular use of Scripture.[66]

---

64 Especially if the 'beloved' motif (Mark and Luke only) recalls Isaac and the aqedah.
65 J. Blank has provided the most extensive study that argues against associating the parable directly with Jesus. His argument depends chiefly upon seeing the motif of 'the sending of the son' as a post-Easter product, even though its immediate context of the sending of the slaves, the prophets, may be based on Jer. 7.25–8. However, it should be noted that Blank considers the parable, largely in its Marcan form, to belong in the very earliest layers of Palestinian Jewish Christian tradition: 'Die Sendung des Sohnes: zur christologischen Bedeutung des Gleichnisses von den bösen Winzern Mk 12, 1–12', in *Neues Testament und Kirche: für Rudolf Schnackenburg* (ed. J. Gnilka; Freiburg: Herder, 1974), 11–41.
66 Identification with Jesus' own teaching seems preferable to associating the

Although many scholars have thought that the kernel of the single point parable could go back to Jesus, even with the motif of the sending of the son,[67] only a minority of scholars has held to the view that almost all the parable with its allegorical features and its secondary use of Psalm 118 may go back to Jesus. Their opinions are exemplified in V. Taylor's classic commentary on Mark in which it is argued that although there may be one or two later features in the pericope, the way in which the son is aligned with the 'slaves' whom the owner sends to the vineyard with no mention of resurrection is hardly in tune with the early church concern to heighten the difference between Jesus and his predecessors. Furthermore, 'the fundamental idea of the parable contains nothing which contradicts the teaching of Jesus'.[68] Those who discern either an allusion to the temple in the parable or recognize the coherence of the overall use of scripture in the pericope, or both, tend towards concluding that in large measure the material goes back to Jesus himself. Thus C. A. Evans underlines some Semitic features in the Marcan version of the parable in his analysis of the parable in which he proposes that the parable picks up on the juridical function of Isaiah 5.1–7 itself in relation to the temple.[69] Or again, on the basis of paying attention to the overall uses of Scripture in the parable (in its Matthaean form) C. Blomberg concludes that 'the entire passage holds together as a coherent unit of thought, and that there is no reason not to ascribe this unity to Jesus' original teaching'.[70] 4Q500

---

parable with the teaching of John the Baptist to his disciples about the son, which was then taken over into the Jesus tradition, as suggested by J. C. O'Neill, 'The Source of the Parables of the Bridegroom and the Wicked Husbandmen', *JTS* 39 (1988): 485–9. O'Neill considered only one item, the issue of Jesus' self-designation as son; he paid no attention to the overall structure of the parable and its wider narrative context.

67 J. E. and R. R. Newell are among recent students of the parable who see no christological point in the sending of the son; for them it is a feature of the point Jesus is trying to make about absentee landlords in his own day: 'The Parable of the Wicked Tenants', 236.

68 *The Gospel According to St. Mark* (London: Macmillan, 2nd edn, 1966), 472. Some redaction critics have rather stressed the difference between Jesus and his predecessors; see, e.g., in relation to Luke, D. L. Bock, *Proclamation from Prophecy and Pattern: Lucan Old Testament Christology* (JSNTSup 12; Sheffield: JSOT Press, 1987), 126–7. Bock is unclear about how much of the parable goes back to Jesus and how much is an early church composition.

69 'On the Vineyard Parables of Isaiah 5 and Mark 12', 85, esp. n. 18; see also his reiteration of some of these features in 'How Septuagintal is Isa. 5.1–7 in Mark 12.1–9?', *NovT* 45 (2003): 105–10.

70 *Interpreting the Parables*, 251.

and its Qumran counterparts do not provide the sources which Jesus or others used, but they show what exegetical traditions were current in Palestine at the time of Jesus.

OTHER NEW TESTAMENT TRADITIONS

Hebrews 13.6–16

Two passages in other New Testament writings may go some way towards underlining the temple interpretation given the parable of the vineyard here in light of 4Q500 1. The first is Hebrews 13.6–16. Not only is Psalm 118.6 used in Hebrews 13.6 but also the elaboration of the argument in the verses that follow (Heb. 13.10–16) concerns the altar that Christians have, the motif of what happens inside the sanctuary and outside the camp (Heb. 13.11–12), an intricate juxtaposition of ideas reflecting the two angles which also feature in the Synoptic tradition of the parable of the vineyard. Mark speaks of the death inside (perhaps because of the location of the altar there), whereas Matthew and Luke locate the death outside the vineyard.

It is also worth noting the way the argument develops in Hebrews 13.10–14. The places referred to are as follows: the altar (v. 10), the tent (v. 10), the sanctuary (v. 11), the camp (v. 11), the city gate (v. 12), outside the camp (v. 13), no lasting city here (v. 14), city to come (v. 14). Thus the author argues that Jesus' death as sacrifice is to be of continual temporal and spatial significance, so the geographical locations are not mutually exclusive, what actually took place outside the camp is made sense of by what happens on the altar. Those who would read the motifs of the parable of the vineyard very strictly, as if the people of Judah, Jerusalem and the temple must all be read into the imagery of the parable, if at all, without any overlap, in the light of this passage in Hebrews might be able to see that the city and the sanctuary are interchangeable; the meaning of what takes place outside is informed by what normally takes place inside.

A further note on the exhortation of Hebrews 13 may not be out of place. This concerns what is looked for (Heb. 13.14). The hope for 'the city that is to come' seems to match the inheritance of the vineyard as city in the parable and the promised inheritance described in 4QpPsᵃ: 'they shall inherit the high mountain of Israel and shall delight in his holy mountain'. As has been noted above, this *Psalms Commentary* belongs together with a group of other texts, including 4Q500 1, whose motifs in relation to the temple are mutually illuminating.

1 Peter 2.4–10

In an exhortatory context that is not dissimilar to that of Hebrews 13, 1 Peter 2.4–10 recalls many of the images discussed in this study: the spiritual house, the people as priests, the rejected stone. The juxtaposition of ideas in the passage is all too familiar. As with the parable of the vineyard, so the Qumran texts may help the better understanding of the passage. It is necessary only to recall 1QS VIII, 4–8, as cited in an earlier part of this study. The use of Isaiah 28.16 and the metaphorical adaptation of cultic motifs for the better understanding of the believing community and its purposes is clear both in the *Rule of the Community* and in 1 Peter.

Also to be noticed in 1 Peter 2 is the use of Isaiah 8.14–15: 'A stone that makes them stumble, and a rock that makes them fall.' The catchword between Psalm 118.22 and Isaiah 8.14–15 in 1 Peter 2.7–8 is evidently 'stone'. In this section of 1 Peter there is no occurrence of the term 'son'. This may support the view that the principal catchword association in the parable is between Isaiah 5.1–2 and Psalm 118.22–3, through their common motif of 'building', rather than between Psalm 118.22–3 and the 'sending of the son' through a play on words involving *'bn* and *bn*.

Isaiah 8.14 features also in Romans 9.32–3, together with Hosea 2.23, as in 1 Peter 2.10; and, of course, it features in a secondary fashion in Matthew 21.44 and Luke 20.18. Isaiah 8.12–13 is alluded to at 1 Peter 3.14–15. Thus, although the parallel associations in Romans suggest we have an early Christian set of proof-texts, it may also be that we should look behind such combinations to other uses of Isaiah 8.[71] Of note is the use in 4Q174 of Isaiah 8.11 of those who turn away from the way of the people, who do not walk in the counsel of the wicked, an exegesis which follows immediately after the elaborate interpretation of 'house' in the previous section of the manuscript: house as temple, as sanctuary, as human sanctuary or temple of Adam, as the Davidic line. In other words, we have come full circle, in as much as in 1 Peter we find a set of scriptural passages playing a key role in linking the community addressed with the temple and its significance as can also be seen in some texts from Qumran among which can now be placed 4Q500 1.

There is no use of Isaiah 5 in 1 Peter, but the use of Psalm 118 in association with other Isaianic texts, together with the metaphorical transfer

---

71 Also earlier associations of Isa. 8 with Isa. 28; see Snodgrass, *The Parable of the Wicked Tenants*, 98, n. 11.

of the cultic significance of the community, all come together to support the probability that the most suitable way of reading the parable of the vineyard as a whole is through the same perspective, that of the adaptation of allusions to the temple city, the temple, and its significance.

CONCLUSION

In its few extant phrases 4Q500 1 seems to offer a glimpse of the handling of Isaiah 5 which expounds its temple significance. When set alongside the parable of the vineyard, particularly its use of scripture, several matters become clearer. The allegorical character of the parable should not be downplayed as secondary and insignificant. The vineyard should not be understood solely in terms of real-life situations in first-century Palestine, but in light of the scriptural allusion which rests behind its use as that was understood in contemporary Jewish texts, such as 4Q500; the vineyard is Israel in miniature, Jerusalem and its temple and all that takes place upon the altar. The motif of election is significant, not in terms of Christian displacement of Israel, but in terms of who may participate in the cult, in the right worship of God. It is the authorities in the temple who are undermined, challenged and displaced, not Israel as a whole. The proof-text from Psalm 118 is remarkably coherent with the opening parts of the parable, so much so that it can be deemed an integral part of the pericope (as the use of *bnh* in 4Q500 helps us see). The literary context of the parable is thoroughly suitable to its use of Scripture; Jesus is portrayed as in the temple, challenging those in charge. Indeed the historical context portrayed suggests that the use of Scripture in the pericope as a whole is not the result of the creative work of the early Church, but goes back to Jesus himself, to a Jesus who even taught in the temple.

14

Qumran: The Cradle of the Christ?

INTRODUCTION

There are three main ways in which the similarities between some of the Dead Sea Scrolls from Qumran and some of the writings of the New Testament can be explained. The first two can be stated very directly and in so doing their probable shortcomings are all the more obvious. Some have maintained, much to the delight of the media, that what was taking place at Qumran was the cradle from which early Christianity was born and a very few have baldly argued that Jesus himself was either wholly or in part both brought up in and lived as a member of the movement of which the Qumran community was the headquarters. Ernest Renan's oft-quoted statement that Christianity is an Essenism which has largely succeeded[1] is made specific through a reading of the Qumran scrolls. A combination of ignoring some problematic details and of exercising overly vivid imaginations has resulted in a hybrid Jesus less credible than ever.

Yet others have insisted that the differences are so great between what we can learn from the scrolls of the community which collected them and the early Christian records of Jesus and the movement he founded that there can be no way of drawing a relationship between them. On the one hand, the key characteristics of Qumran Essenism are priestly purity, a determined protection of sacred space, hardline legal interpretation, all produced by a group which is the product of the educated urban elite, principally from Jerusalem. On the other hand, Jesus is from a lower middle-class small town family whose ministry shows him to have an affinity with country folk. His table fellowship is open and notably scandalous. Although he seems to gravitate towards Jerusalem, he does so not

---

1 J. E. Renan, *Histoire du peuple d'Isräel* (Paris: Calman, 1891), 5.70.

out of concern to support its institutions, but on the basis of some eschatological fervour which, as Josephus and others have let us see for a very
long time, was all too common in Palestine at the time. The Qumran
scrolls can only add minimally to the general picture; they cannot help us
in any detailed way to appreciate better the historical or other concerns of
the New Testament authors.

The third way of relating the evidence of the scrolls to the evidence of
the New Testament about Jesus is more difficult to characterize as it takes
many forms and is often presented in a nuanced way.[2] The similarities
between the two bodies of approximately contemporary literature
cannot be reduced to identity, but neither can the differences force us to
dismiss them as insignificant. Something has to be said, for example,
about how in the whole of Jewish literature between the Bible and the
Mishnah, it is only in 4Q521 and the Jesus saying in the double tradition
(Q) of Luke and Matthew that Isaiah 61.1–2 is expanded with a statement about the raising of the dead.[3] 'He will heal the wounded, and
revive the dead and bring good news to the poor' says 4Q521; 'the dead
are raised, the poor have good news brought to them' echoes Luke (Q)
7.22 as Jesus answers the disciples of John the Baptist concerning
himself. Whether we conclude that Jesus must have known of this tradition directly from a Qumran source[4] or that it was mediated to him some
other how, the details of the similarities are too great to be brushed aside.

SOME RESONANCES BETWEEN THE DEAD SEA
SCROLLS AND THE GOSPEL BIRTH NARRATIVES

In this short chapter I wish to look briefly at four items from the Qumran
scrolls which have resonances with the birth of Jesus and its associated
narratives. The discussion will show some of the varying ways in which
the third way of trying to relate the Dead Sea Scrolls and the New Testament literature may be suitably undertaken.

---

2 As, e.g., in J. H. Charlesworth and W. P. Weaver (eds), *The Dead Sea Scrolls and the
Christian Faith: In Celebration of the Jubilee Year of the Discovery of Qumran Cave 1*
(Harrisburg: Trinity Press International; London: SCM Press, 1998).

3 4Q521 is commonly known as the *Messianic Apocalypse* and is available in English
in G. Vermes, *The Complete Dead Sea Scrolls in English* (London: Penguin Books,
1998), 391–2.

4 J. J. Collins, 'The Works of the Messiah', *DSD* 1 (1994): 107, comments on this
parallel that 'It is quite possible that the author of the Sayings source knew 4Q521;
at the least he drew on a common tradition.'

Son of God and Son of the Most High

The first item is not unlike the parallel between 4Q521 and Luke (Q) 7.22. 4Q246 is officially labelled an Aramaic Apocryphon of Daniel.[5] A single substantial fragment (14 x 9 cms) of this first-century B.C.E. manuscript survives; it comes from the end of a sheet of leather. The first column of nine lines is extant only at its left side; the second column is completely preserved, but the text must have continued on to another column on a further sheet of leather. From the broken context of the first column it seems as if an interpreter, possibly Daniel, comes before a king to explain a vision which the king has seen. In addition to the kings of Assyria and Egypt, the interpreter describes another royal figure who clearly belongs to the future. The line is broken but the surviving words can be translated as '. . . great he will be called and by his name will he be surnamed'. At the top of the second column the interpreter declares: 'He will be called the Son of God and the Son of the Most High they will name him.' The text continues by describing the rule of the kings as a time of great turmoil when peoples and provinces destroy one another. This violence is followed by an epoch when the people of God will arise and there will be peace. The eternal kingdom which ensues is characterized by truth and righteousness. It is difficult to determine whether or not the last king of the three mentioned, the Son of God and the Son of the Most High, is the king of God's people during this time.

The difficulties in making sense of the text have provoked a wide range of scholarly interpretations. Some have suggested that all three kings are to be viewed negatively and that the last is an antichrist or an actual ruler of Judea who was viewed in a very poor light by the author of the composition since he has taken the titles Son of God and Son of the Most High unlawfully. Others have argued that the third king is to be associated with the people of God in a positive way and that he is to be understood as either a messianic figure or a guardian archangel who fights on Israel's behalf.[6]

---

5 4Q246 has been published in its official edition by E. Puech, '4QApocryphe de Daniel ar', in *Qumran Cave 4.XVII: Parabiblical Texts, Part 3* (ed. G. J. Brooke, et al.; DJD 22; Oxford: Clarendon Press, 1996), 165–84. It is readily available in English in G. Vermes, *The Complete Dead Sea Scrolls in English*, 576–7.
6 A summary of the various views can be found in J. J. Collins, *The Scepter and the Star: The Messiahs of the Dead Sea Scrolls and Other Ancient Literature* (New York: Doubleday, 1995), 154–72.

Whatever the case with the correct understanding of 4Q246, four striking parallels with Luke 1.32–5 emerge. In Luke Gabriel's message to Mary is divided into two parts. Together with other details, in Luke 1.30–3 he describes the one who will be named Jesus, who will be great, called Son of the Most High, whose kingdom will have no end. In the second part of the message (Lk. 1.35–7), in answer to Mary's question 'How can this be?' Gabriel states that the Holy Spirit will come upon her and the power of the Most High will overshadow her so that the child will be holy and called Son of God. According to Luke Jesus will be great, he is to be Son of the Most High, to have an eternal kingdom, and to be called Son of God.

When one or two of the same motifs occur in two different passages, it is necessary to exercise caution. When the same four items occur in a few lines in one text and in as many verses in another, some kind of explanation is called for. It is clear that the language of various Danielic traditions is reflected in both 4Q246 and Luke 1.32–7. Most especially there are echoes of Daniel 2.44: 'And in the days of those kings the God of heaven will set up a kingdom that shall never be destroyed, nor shall this kingdom be left to another people. It shall crush all these kingdoms and bring them to an end, and it shall stand forever.' Daniel 7.27 also comes to mind: 'The kingship and dominion and the greatness of the kingdoms under the whole heaven shall be given to the people of the holy ones of the Most High; their kingdom shall be an everlasting kingdom, and all dominions shall serve and obey them.'

While it is possible that both 4Q246 and Luke 1 are independent meditations on Danielic promises, it seems preferable to consider seriously that Luke 1 was dependent upon some such tradition as is found in 4Q246 and that whoever compiled Gabriel's message to Mary understood the third king mentioned in 4Q246 in a positive way as the individual personification of the eschatological rule of the people of God. There are no explicit hints that the third king in 4Q246 has Davidic features, but the author of Luke 1 provided them to complete his positive reading of his source: 'the Lord God will give to him the throne of his ancestor David' (Lk. 1.32). The parallel between 4Q246 and Luke 1.32–7 indicates to the modern interpreter that the description of the birth and naming of Jesus is one way of reading a polyvalent Jewish tradition.

The woman in travail

The second item is a piece of narrative poetry. One of the first manu-scripts to come to light from Cave 1 is a copy of a set of *Thanksgiving Hymns* (in Hebrew, *Hodayot*). It is widely and very suitably supposed that one of the leading figures in the community at some point wrote several of these hymns as reflections upon his own experiences. These poems have an autobiographical feel to them. Detailed studies of stylistic consis-tency and vocabulary usage suggest that even if the poems cannot be attributed directly to the community's Teacher of Righteousness, at least they form a coherent body of verse almost certainly authored by a single person.

In what is now designated as Column XI of the *Thanksgiving Hymn* scroll there is a poem which is so tightly expressed that it is extremely dif-ficult to translate. Almost every phrase is replete with double meanings.

> I am in distress, like a woman in labor with her firstborn
> when her travail begins, when the mouth of her womb pulses
> with agony, when the firstborn of the woman writhes within
> her. Surely children come forth through the breakers of
> death, and she who gives a man birth suffers agonies!
>   Yet through the breakers of death she delivers a male child,
> and through hellish agonies bursts forth from the bearer's
> womb: a Wonderful Counsellor with His mighty power!
>   But when the man comes safely through the breakers, they
> all rush upon his bearer: grievous agonies strike those giving
> birth, terrors come to their mothers. When he is born, the
> travails all turn back on the bearer's womb.[7]

The author likens his psychological and possibly also his physical suffer-ings to a woman giving birth. And when the male firstborn child is safely delivered, the poet continues to belabour his point and his agonies continue in the afterbirth. The one born is the Wonderful Mighty Coun-sellor, words that are borrowed from Isaiah 9.6: 'For a child has been born for us, a son given to us; authority rests upon his shoulders; and he is named Wonderful Counsellor, Mighty God, Everlasting Father, Prince of Peace.' Isaiah speaks of a coming king who will occupy the throne of

---

7 This effective translation is by M. O. Wise, *The First Messiah: Investigating the Savior Before Christ* (San Francisco: HarperSanFrancisco, 1999), 105.

David. The Qumran poet noticeably stops short of referring to God in his allusion to Isaiah 9.6 or of developing the royal imagery with reference to a kingly Messiah. Since it is clear that the poet likens himself to the woman in travail, I am inclined to believe that the child born is representative of the community for which the poet considered himself as a parent.[8] The messianic language of Isaiah thus has a corporate significance.

Three small matters seem to confirm this view. First, the term used for the one delivered is *geber*, 'man', a Hebrew word used exclusively of human offspring; so the offspring must be considered fully human. Second, there is a delightful possibility in the phrase 'Wonderful Counsellor with his mighty power' of reading the two consonants translated usually as the preposition 'with' ('*im*) as the noun 'people' ('*am*); the 'Wonderful Counsellor is a people of mighty power'. This double entendre would support a corporate reading of the figure. Third, in another Qumran sectarian composition, the so-called *Eschatological Midrash* (4Q174), an interpretation of Psalm 2 identifies the anointed one of the Psalm with the chosen ones of Israel, namely the community members. Thus what was taken as a messianic passage in the late second temple period was also capable of being understood corporately with reference to a select community.

In light of all this we may propose that the poetic birth narrative of 1QH^a XI urges upon those who reflect on the birth of Jesus to be on the lookout for corporate meanings in the texts, so that his birth is conceived as the birth of all people. Furthermore, as a contemporary literary trope the ongoing agony of the one who gives birth is easily discernible in the one whose soul shall also be pierced (Lk. 2.35) or who flees into the wilderness before the dragon (Rev. 12.5–6). Any actual birth of a messianic community is simply the delivery of the divine muse which once found the mind of the Qumran teacher most fertile and conceived there a whole community.

Begetting the Messiah

The third item concerns eschatological hope. There are two appendices to the Cave 1 version of the *Rule of the Community* (1QS). The first is a two-column rule book for the last days (1QSa (1Q28a)) which has

---

8 An idea first put forward by W. H. Brownlee, 'Messianic Motifs of Qumran and the New Testament', *NTS* 3 (1956–7): 12–30.

become known either as the *Rule of the Congregation* or occasionally as the *Messianic Rule*. The closing section of this rule book describes what happens at meals when there are at least ten men gathered together. The manuscript is somewhat damaged with some pieces missing altogether and others barely legible. In places the opening of this final unit of the *Messianic Rule* is both damaged and difficult to read. The part which concerns us for the birth of Jesus is in the title to the section: 'This is the assembly of famous men, [those summoned to] the gathering of the community council, when [God] begets the Messiah with them.'⁹ G. Vermes translates the same significant phrase as 'When God engenders (the Priest-) Messiah' and comments that the reading of *yôlîd*, 'engenders' or 'begets', is confirmed by computer image enhancement.¹⁰ M. Wise notes the difficulty in the reading here and alongside 'when [God] has fa[th]ered(?) the Messiah' also offers 'when the Messiah has been revealed' based on a recent proposal by E. Puech who has detected elements of a supralinear letter which adjusts the final contentious word of the line.¹¹

This manuscript is regularly dated to the first quarter of the first century B.C.E. It raises the question whether a Jewish text of that time really speaks of God begetting the Messiah. Sadly the leather is badly darkened at the end of the line just where the crucial word occurs and the beginning of the next line where one would expect to find the subject of that verb mentioned is missing. Thus, if the subject of the verb at the end of the line was God, then sadly he is a deus abscondita. Perhaps not surprisingly, several Jewish scholars tend to prefer alternative readings and restorations here, such as that by J. Licht, taken up by L. H. Schiffman: 'when [at the end] (of days) the messiah [shall assemble] with them'.¹² Some other scholars have offered alternative suggestions too, such as 'when the Messiah has been revealed', as has already been mentioned. The majority, however, from the first attempts to be sure about the reading which was published in the official edition of the manuscript in 1955 until the most recent edition of the Hebrew text by F. García

9 This is the translation of F. García Martínez, *The Dead Sea Scrolls Translated* (Leiden: Brill, 2nd edn., 1996), 127.
10 G. Vermes, *The Complete Dead Sea Scrolls in English*, 159.
11 M. Wise's two alternative translations are in M. Wise, M. Abegg and E. Cook, *The Dead Sea Scrolls: A New Translation* (New York: HarperCollins Publishers, 1996), 147. The alternative proposal is by E. Puech, 'Préséance sacerdotale et Messie-Roi dans la Règle de la Congrégation (1QSa (1Q28a) ii 11–22)', *RevQ* 16 (1994): 351–66.
12 L. H. Schiffman, *The Eschatological Community of the Dead Sea Scrolls* (Atlanta: Scholars Press, 1989), 54, n. 6.

Martínez in 1997, have dared to read *yôlîd*, 'begets' or 'engenders', and have understood the passage to be about the divine parenting of the Messiah.[13]

Given such a reading, it would be unwise to think that this Jewish text from about 100 B.C.E. was referring to a virgin birth. Rather, in line with a biblical text such as 2 Samuel 7.14, the text can be considered as endorsing a particularly intimate relationship between God and the anointed king. What are the implications for the New Testament birth narratives of this reading and understanding of the *Rule of the Congregation* II, 11–12? Of primary importance must be the way in which metaphor takes priority over literalness. If the Qumran text expresses no concern for how the divine parenthood of the Messiah came about, it is because the assumption must be that he had good Jewish parents and was fully human; no contemporary Jewish texts would suggest otherwise. In Luke and Matthew, therefore, the priority of metaphor has been mis-placed and a proof-text from the Greek translation of Isaiah 7.14 introduced. That proof-text has ever since held the doctrine of the full humanity of Jesus to ransom.

Praising God's greatness

The fourth item helps us to see that those who reflected on the birth of Jesus recognized that something of the creative strength of God was at work in what had taken place. Several of the scrolls from Qumran contain compositions which are slightly reworked forms of the biblical books as we know them today. It is clear that before each book of the Bible had a fixed text form, those who viewed them as authoritative copied them not in the idolatrous fashion which is worship of the letter without recognition of the meaning, but rather as writings which were of continuing living signifi-cance to be ever improved in minor ways so that God's purposes for Israel contained in them could be heard all the more readily in each successive generation. One of these reworked biblical paraphrases is known to Qumran scholars as the *Reworked Pentateuch*. This survives in several copies; it is the one labelled 4Q365 which concerns us here.

---

13 The official edition of the manuscript was produced by D. Barthélemy in D. Barthélemy and J. T. Milik (eds), *Qumran Cave I* (DJD 1; Oxford: Clarendon Press, 1955), 117. The recent edition by F. García Martínez is in F. García Martínez and E. J. C. Tigchelaar, *The Dead Sea Scrolls Study Edition*, Vol. 1 *1Q1-4Q273* (Leiden: Brill, 1997), 102.

The so-called *Reworked Pentateuch* follows what is now contained in the traditional text of the Hebrew Bible very closely for the most part. However, from time to time there are some significant differences from what is now accepted as canonical by Jews and most Christians alike. At Exodus 15 the manuscript is poorly preserved, but enough survives for us to know that before Exodus 15.22–6, which is represented almost as in the traditional Hebrew Bible, there was a narrative poem. Sadly the damage to the manuscript only allows us to read a few opening words on each line. What is preserved reads as follows:

> you despised (?) [
> for the majesty of [
> You are great, a deliverer (?) [
> the hope of the enemy has perished, and he is for[gotten] (or:
>   has cea[sed])
> they perished in the mighty waters, the enemy (or 'enemies') [
> Extol the one who raises up, [a r]ansom . . . you gave (?) [
> [the one who do]es gloriously [[14]

In these tantalizing lines, there seems to be preserved the song which Miriam sang as the counterpart to that which Moses and the male Israelites had sung after safely crossing the sea (Ex. 15.1–18). In the Bible as we have it, Miriam is given the opening verse of the Song of the Sea to sing. Exodus 15.1 is repeated by her almost verbatim in Exodus 15.21. It is as if she then goes on to repeat the whole song in imitation of Moses and the men, as their faithful echo. In this *Reworked Pentateuch* composition, rather than being a mere echo, she seems to have her own song to sing. A few of the words which survive, such as 'mighty waters' (cf. Ex. 15.10), suitably take up the motifs of the Song of the Sea, but overall Miriam's song is different, a distinctive song for a woman.[15]

The surviving text is frustratingly fragmentary, but two motifs are striking. First, Miriam addresses God directly as great, a deliverer. The

---

14 This is the translation in the principal edition of the manuscript by E. Tov and S. White in *Qumran Cave 4.VIII: Parabiblical Texts, Part I* (ed. H. Attridge et al.; DJD 13; Oxford: Clarendon Press, 1994), 270; for a slightly different rendering see Chapter 15 in this book.

15 This fragmentary song has not been commented upon in any great detail, but see G. J. Brooke, 'Power to the Powerless: A Long-Lost Song of Miriam', *BARev* 20/3 (May–June 1994): 62–5, a longer form of which is produced as Chapter 15 in this book.

address 'You are great' might at first sight seem a common way for a psalmist to call upon God, but the phrase is surprisingly rare. Its exact equivalent is to be found only in Psalm 86.10, part of a prayer for deliverance from personal enemies, and in the Book of Judith 16.13. Judith 16.1–17 is a victory song which Judith sings after the divine defeat of Holofernes and the Babylonian army through her powerless agency: 'The Lord almighty has foiled them by the hand of a woman' (Jud. 16.5). The second noteworthy motif in the new Song of Miriam is how the sixth line contains a reference to exaltation. It seems as if the phrase exhorts the hearer to extol God who raises somebody up. What the original context contained can only be guessed at. Perhaps there was a reference to the way God had raised up a downtrodden and nearly defeated Israel. For our purposes it is this very activity of God which exemplifies his greatness. The very same combination of motifs is found in the victory song of another Mary in Luke 1.46–55: 'My soul magnifies the Lord . . . He has lifted up the lowly.'

Some modern commentators might wish to propose that this new Song of Miriam was very old and had long been part of the narrative of Exodus before some scribe dared to replace it with the opening verse of the male chorus. I suspect the song is secondary. It seems to be another example of the kind of victory songs which are attributed to women in the late second temple period. Indeed it could well be a second-century B.C.E. composition, like the song in Judith 16. Some have argued that Mary's Magnificat is the adaptation of a Jewish victory song from the Maccabean period.[16] If so, then all three songs would be roughly contemporary. In these songs we can see clearly that it is permissible for women to sing of the victorious greatness of God, to admit their frailty in all things and to acknowledge forcefully that it is God alone who raises up the lowly.

---

16 For some general comments on how the Benedictus (Lk. 2.68–79) may similarly reflect the language of some of the Dead Sea Scrolls see R. E. Brown, *A Coming Christ in Advent: Essays on the Gospel Narratives Preparing for the Birth of Jesus (Matthew 1 and Luke 1)* (Collegeville: The Liturgical Press, 1988), 51.

CONCLUSION

The Qumran texts show us what was conceivable in Judaism at the time. Our four texts make significant contributions to the better appreciation of the Gospel birth narratives. In light of 4Q246 we can see that the stories of the birth of Jesus were but one or more ways of reading polyvalent Jewish tradition. On the basis of the *Thanksgiving Hymn* we note that the narrative allows for a corporate understanding so that it is legitimate to consider that all people can receive their identity through this one illegitimate birth. The *Rule of the Congregation* shows that it is not scandalous to talk of divine parenthood providing that metaphor takes priority over literal explanation. The Song of Miriam shows us that some aspects of God's power are most readily visible when sung about by a woman. Thus the manuscripts from Qumran provide us with several of the planks that make up the cradle of the Christ. But much of its overall structure and the baby it cradles are strictly speaking from another carpenter's shop altogether.

15

Songs of Revolution:
The Song of Miriam and its Counterparts

INTRODUCTION

Among the Dead Sea Scrolls made available in 1991 were four manuscripts which contain large sections of the Pentateuch in a reworked form.[1] A manuscript like these four has been known about for a long time and it is probably a fifth example of the same genre, though not a copy of the same composition.[2] These manuscripts can be dated with reasonable certainty in the second or early first century B.C.E.; indeed one of them was part of an extensive carbon 14 examination.[3]

Many of the variants contained in these *Reworked Pentateuch* manuscripts are little more than stylistic improvements or minor changes in spelling which do not affect the meaning. In many places they seem to correspond with what has long been known in the Samaritan Pentateuch. However, in some places the manuscripts contain more extensive material which is not to be found in the Pentateuch as it is preserved in the Masoretic Text as represented in modern Hebrew Bibles or in any

---

1 These MSS are numbered 4Q364, 365, 366 and 367. E. Tov and S. A. White Crawford have been responsible for editing them: E. Tov and S. White, 'Reworked Pentateuch', in *Qumran Cave 4.VIII: Parabiblical Texts, Part I* (ed. H. Attridge et al.; DJD 13; Oxford: Clarendon Press, 1994), 187–351.

2 4Q158 was published by J. M. Allegro in *Qumrân Cave 4: I (4Q158–4Q186)* (DJD 5; Oxford: Clarendon Press, 1968), 1–6. On this manuscript see also M. Segal '4QReworked Pentateuch or 4QPentateuch?', in *The Dead Sea Scrolls Fifty Years after their Discovery: Proceedings of the Jerusalem Congress, July 20–25, 1997* (ed. L. H. Schiffman, E. Tov and J. C. VanderKam; Jerusalem: Israel Exploration Society and the Shrine of the Book, Israel Museum, 2000), 391–9; G. J. Brooke, '4Q158: Reworked Pentateuch[a] or Reworked Pentateuch A?', *DSD* 8 (2001): 219–41.

3 G. Bonani, M. Broshi, I. Carmi, S. Ivy, J. Strugnell, W. Wölfi, 'Radiocarbon Dating of the Dead Sea Scrolls', *Atiqot* 20 (July 1991): 27–32; the article is well summarized by H. Shanks, 'Carbon-14 Tests Substantiate Scroll Dates', *BARev* 17 (1991): 72.

other version. In some ways the passing on of the text of the Pentateuch is not unlike the handling of the tradition to be found in the *Temple Scroll.*

THE SONG OF MIRIAM

The section of 4Q365 (*Reworked Pentateuch*[c]) which sparked this study occurs in Fragment 6a, Column II.[4] In Column I there are remains of Exodus 14.12–21 and 15.16–21. Column II consists for the most part of the beginnings of fifteen fragmentary lines. Lines 8–14 can be reconstructed from Exodus 15.22–6 which they represent for the most part in a way not unknown from other texts and versions. Lines 1–7, therefore, contain a text which breaks the sequence of Exodus 15 in the manuscript. The extant beginnings of lines 1–7 each contain only a very few words, but enough for us to know that the section contains a poetic piece, addressed to God as saviour. Although the full context is missing the surviving words may be translated as follows:

1   you despised[5] [
2   for the triumph of [
3   You are great, the saviour of [
4   the hope of the enemy perishes and he is for[gotten
5   they perished in the mighty waters, the enemy [
6   and exalt the one who raises up, [a r]ansom . . . you gave (?)[
7   wo]rking a triumph [

Some of these words and phrases are closely related to the song which Moses and the Israelites sing, but the poem is not simply a restatement of the Song of the Sea. The text of Exodus as it stands in the witnesses to date can be understood to imply that when Miriam sings, she simply repeats the Song of the Sea; the narrator merely provides an opening verse to indicate this. What we now have in 4Q365 is the Song of Miriam,[6] evidence that in one tradition at least Miriam had her own song which matched that of Moses but was not the same.[7]

---

4 DJD 13, 269–72.
5 The perennial problem of the great similarity of *waw* and *yod* in many of the Qumran manuscripts means that the letters could be read as *bzyt*, 'you despised' (from *bzh*) or as *bzut*, 'you plundered' (from *bzz*).
6 This is the designation of J. Strugnell.
7 On the status of Miriam in the late second temple period see, e.g., the way Pseudo-Philo describes her as the recipient of divine revelation (*L.A.B.* 9.9–10), no doubt building on her description as prophet in Ex. 15.20.

The matching can be seen most clearly in the words and phrases which are picked up in these lines from the earlier song. So the phrase 'in the mighty waters' in line 5 is an imitation of Exodus 15.10 ('they sank like lead *in the mighty waters*'). The word translated here as 'triumph' in lines 2 and 7 is used verbally in Exodus 15.1 ('for he has *triumph*ed gloriously'). Perhaps the use of the motif of exaltation is also taken from the Song of the Sea: 'And I will *exalt* him' (Ex. 15.2). The matching occurs also in the way that God is addressed in the second person in line 3 (and probably also line 1), as he is in Exodus 15.11–17.[8]

However, what is remarkable about these few fragmentary lines is the implication that together with the triumphant recollection of the military victory, there is the dramatic portrayal of a complete reversal. There are only tantalizing hints of this. Two items involve God. First, in line 1 it may be possible to understand the extant letters as 'you despised'; perhaps here God derides the enemies of Israel. Second, in line 3 God is extolled as 'great, a saviour'. In contrast, probably with those who have been defeated, God's greatness is affirmed, as well as his role as saviour. Then, in line 6, after the repetition of the mighty military victory, this greatness seems to be echoed in some kind of exaltation: 'and exalt the one who raises up'.[9] We may fairly presume that God is being extolled for elevating somebody of lowly status, giving him or her a sense of triumph. The military victory is thus accompanied by a reversal of some kind, quite possibly for Miriam.

To make so much out of so few and fragmentary lines might seem injudicious. But the most obvious parallels to the possibilities of these phrases contain something of the same themes that it is tempting to see in this Song of Miriam. There appear to be two strands of tradition where similar combinations feature: songs attributed to Jewish women and songs preserved in the *War Scroll* from Qumran.

---

8 Ps. 93, which celebrates divine kingship (cf. Ex. 15.18), has the two motifs of triumphant majesty (Ps. 93.1) and mighty waters (Ps. 93.4), clearly echoing Ex. 15 like this new poem.

9 It is also possible to translate the phrase (*wrwmmnh lmrwmm*) as 'and he exalted her to the heights'. The change in the verb from the second to the third person in such a proposal is problematic, but the reference to a female figure in the third person need be no problem. If the song was sung antiphonally by Miriam and the women with her, then this phrase would possibly belong to the part sung by the women.

SONGS OF WOMEN

Speaking of God as great is common enough. Various Psalms, including now 4Q372 1, 29,[10] acknowledge the greatness of God, but in the third person. Psalm 48.1 declares 'Great is the Lord and greatly to be praised'; Psalm 96.4 echoes the same phrasing, 'For great is the Lord, and greatly to be praised.' The second-person address is only to be found in the Bible in traditions associated with David. In Psalm 86.10 the same wording as 4Q365 6 II, 3 occurs: 'For *you are great* and do wondrous things.' The Psalm is an individual plea for deliverance, a term which occurs in verse 13. The overall context of the acclamation of God's greatness is the affirmation of his uniqueness ('there is none like you among the gods') which all the nations shall come to recognize. In 2 Samuel 7.22 David acknowledges in a very similar fashion the greatness of God as he prays: 'You are great, O Lord God; for there is no one like you.'

The closest verbal parallel to the brief address 'You are great' together with a thoroughly suitable context comes in the hymn of Judith 16 at verse 13: 'I will sing to my God a new song: O Lord, *you are great* and glorious, wonderful in strength, invincible.' It is likely that two aspects of Judith's song of praise are significant for our better understanding of the Song of Miriam in 4Q365. To begin with, although there are parallels with other biblical texts too,[11] Judith 16 is commonly associated with the Song of the Sea in Exodus 15. So, for example, P. W. Skehan has tried to make out that Judith 16 is in fact an interpretative replay of Exodus 15.[12] And T. Craven has made explicit their similarities in terms of function, form and content.[13]

---

10 'For a God great, holy, mighty and majestic, awesome and marvellous' (DJD 28, 170). See E. M. Schuller, 'The Psalm of 4Q372 1 Within the Context of Second Temple Prayer', *CBQ* 54 (1992): 68 and 72–5, where she analyses the list of epithets in relation to other similar traditions.

11 Most notably with the Song of Deborah in Judges 5: see, e.g., S. A. White, 'In the Steps of Jael and Deborah: Judith as Heroine', in *'No One Spoke Ill of Her': Essays on Judith* (ed. J. C. VanderKam; SBLEJL 2; Atlanta: Scholars Press, 1992), 5–16.

12 P. W. Skehan, 'The Hand of Judith', *CBQ* 25 (1963): 94–110. Notable among the overlaps which Skehan notes are: (1) 'The Lord crushes wars' (Ex. 15.3 LXX), 'The Lord is a God who crushes wars' (Jud. 16.2); (2) the use of *dunamis* for army in both (Ex. 15.4; Jud. 16.3); (3) 'I will draw my sword' (Ex. 15.9), 'to draw his sword' (Jud. 16.4); (4) 'Your right hand' (Ex. 15.6 2x), 'by the hand of woman' (Jud. 16.5); (5) 'the mountain of your inheritance' (Ex. 15.17); 'my hill country' (Jud. 16.4).

13 T. Craven, *Artistry and Faith in the Book of Judith* (SBLDS 70; Chico: Scholars Press, 1983), 111–12.

In various places in Jewish tradition Judith is associated with Hannukah,[14] but also with the Exodus.[15] The link with Hannukah in particular is not inappropriate, not only for the obvious ways in which the story of Judith parallels that of Judas Maccabee, but because the themes of the weak against the mighty and of the few against the many are replayed in both stories. But with Judith, because she is a woman, these themes become the focus of reversals of an unexpectedly forceful kind.[16] Whereas the men of Bethulia have not known how to respond, Judith, a woman alone, has stood against the Assyrian: 'the Lord Almighty has foiled them by the hand of a woman, for their mighty one did not fall by the hands of the young men . . . the sons of Titans . . . or tall giants; but Judith daughter of Merari with the beauty of her countenance undid him.' The oppressed and weak are victorious with the Lord on their side.

The point is not just that God rescues his feeble people, but that those who supposedly are strong among his people and should be able to protect them, or at least attempt to do so, are put down through God foiling the enemies of the people 'by the hand of a woman'. The Song of Judith is thus revolutionary in a twofold way. Not only does it show that God protects the weak, but that he protects the weak through the weak. Here is a text that gets at the mighty oppressor outside, but also at those who would dominate inside the community. Perhaps it is not surprising that when Judith was being enacted in sixteenth-century Germany, the defiant hymn of God's greatness *Ein feste Burg* was sung as the play reached its climax.

The combined motifs of the greatness of God and the elevation of the weak are presented most obviously in the New Testament's Magnificat (Lk. 1.46–55). Though modelled in part on the Song of Hannah (a similar song also associated with a woman), the thought of the Magnificat is yet more revolutionary, for whereas the Song of Hannah looks for divine action as a possible present reality, the Magnificat portrays the

---

14 See M. S. Enslin and S. Zeitlin, *The Book of Judith* (Leiden: Brill, 1972), 26.

15 In a number of Passover Haggadot Judith is connected with the Exodus story: see, e.g., the illustration from the 1526 *Prague Haggadah* in *Encyclopaedia Judaica*, Vol. 7, Col. 1088.

16 These have been brought out strikingly by A.-J. Levine, 'Sacrifice and Salvation: Otherness and Domestication in the Book of Judith,' in *'No One Spoke Ill of Her': Essays on Judith* (ed. J. C. VanderKam; SBLEJL 2; Atlanta: Scholars Press, 1992), 17–30.

reversal as accomplished for those who identify with its message. There is
no safety for the mighty or the rich who might sing such a song.

The following are among the motifs which the Magnificat shares with
the fragmentary Song of Miriam. Both acknowledge the greatness of
God. Though this is not as direct a parallel as can be found between
4Q365 6 II, 3 and Judith 16.13, the two texts echo one another in the
parallelism of Luke 1.46b–47a: 'My soul makes *great* the Lord, and my
spirit rejoices in God *my saviour.*' While it is difficult to be clear who is
being elevated in the Song of Miriam, the motif is echoed in Luke 1.52:
'He has put down the mighty from their thrones and has *exalted* the
weak.'[17] There is also a possible parallel between the phrase '*he has done
powerfully* with his arm' (Lk. 1.51) and the distinctive '*he has done tri-
umphantly*' of 4Q365 6 II, 7.[18] Furthermore, if the first word preserved in
the extant line 1 is read as 'you plundered' (*bzwt*), then there may be an
indirect parallel with the action of God in Luke 1.51: 'He has scattered
the proud in the thoughts of their hearts.' On one occasion the LXX
renders the Hebrew 'plunder' (*bzz*) with the same Greek term as is used
in the Magnificat here (*diaskorpizō*), so the two terms have some overlap
of nuance.

Some have seen the Magnificat as a pre-Lukan composition which
Luke or his source has used for his own purposes. Most notably P. Winter
suggested in 1954 that both the Magnificat and the Benedictus (Lk.
1.68–79) were Maccabean psalms.[19] More recently D. Flusser attempted
to show how both hymns may reflect a common source which is also
reflected in the Qumran *War Scroll*, which we also discuss below.[20]
Whatever the details, there is considerable weight behind seeing the
Magnificat as reflecting pre-Christian hymnic terminology and the discovery and publication of the Song of Miriam, for all its fragmentariness,
is further support for this idea. If so, that which lies behind the

---

17 Lk. 1.52 makes into a general proposition what is applied to Mary alone in Lk.
1.48; the root *tapeinō* is used in both cases. The LXX commonly uses *hupsoun* to
render forms of *rmm*.

18 Lk. 1.51 reads *epoiēsen kratos*; the LXX uses *kratos* to translate *g'wt* in Ps. 89.10.
The LXX renders the related term *g'wh* with *megaloprepeia* or *megaloprepēs*; Lk. 1.49
has 'the Mighty One has done great things for me', *epoiēsen moi megala ho dunatos*.

19 P. Winter, 'Magnificat and Benedictus – Maccabean Psalms', *BJRL* 37 (1954):
328–43.

20 D. Flusser, 'The Magnificat, the Benedictus and the War Scroll', in *Judaism and
the Origins of Christianity* (Jerusalem: Magnes Press, 1988), 126–49.

Magnificat, even the whole poem itself, the Song of Judith and the Song of Miriam all present us with three variations on a theme.

It is remarkable how these songs have been associated with women. One cannot but wonder whether their revolutionary celebration of God's victory for the weak through the weak is linked with various leading women in order to reduce the force of its message. In the case of the Song of Miriam, we are faced with several literary problems. First of all we have to decide what is the right way to understand the Exodus narrative: did Miriam simply lead Moses and the Israelites in singing the Song of the Sea, or did she sing something separately? Then, if we decide she sang something separately, what did she sing? Was it a repetition of the Song of the Sea or something else which has an opening verse like the previous Song? If in this text of 4Q365 Miriam had her own song, how far back may such an association go? At what point was this new song edited in to or excluded from the tradition of Exodus? Was it only the compiler of this *Reworked Pentateuch* who knew of a floating liturgical tradition which had echoes of the Song of the Sea, and placed it suitably with Miriam as the lead singer?

The questions are real. Several scholars have noticed the textual problems in this part of Exodus. Some have even thought that the Song of the Sea should really be associated with Miriam and that only if the surface of the Hebrew narrative is misconstrued is it given to Moses. According to this theory, argued most recently by J. G. Janzen,[21] the Song is what Moses and the Israelites sang in response to Miriam's lead, which is implied by the masculine pronouns in Exodus 15.21 ('sang to *them*: Sing [masc. pl.]'). It is only attributed to Moses because of the order of the narrative and it seemed appropriate for him to get all the good tunes. Additionally it is remarkable how among the few characters who are named in the narrative of the Book of Exodus are the two midwives, Shiphrah and Puah (Ex. 1.15), who in disobeying the Pharaoh are responsible for delivering the people, a deliverance which eventually leads to the climactic Exodus.[22] From the point of view of the construction of the narrative of Exodus 1—15, it would be apt to have Miriam singing the song of salvation. Now 4Q365 implies that in one tradition

---

21 J. G. Janzen, 'Song of Moses, Song of Miriam: Who is Seconding Whom?', *CBQ* 54 (1992): 211–20. See also P. Trible, 'Bringing Miriam Out of the Shadows', *BARev* 5 (1989).

22 I owe this observation to T. Dennis; Janzen makes a similar comment in 'Song of Moses, Song of Miriam: Who is Seconding Whom?', 219.

the narrative of Exodus was taken as it stands and Miriam given a separate song to balance that assigned Moses and the Israelites.

THE *WAR SCROLL*

In addition to these songs variously linked with women, there are two sections in the Qumran *War Scroll* (1QM XI and XIV) which echo the same motifs. These two sections are replete with stock biblical phraseology, especially from the prophets, so the following comments are not concerned with any claim of literary dependence of these hymnic sections upon the Song of Miriam. Rather, the intention of drawing out the similarities of genre and content is to aid in the better understanding of both texts, each in its own right.

The first passage is part of a recital of how God's victory has been assured from of old. He defeated Goliath and the Philistines through the hand of David (XI, 1–3), he had other victories in the past too (XI, 3–4), he will defeat the hordes of Belial just as he defeated Pharaoh and his chariots (XI, 7–11), and he will defeat the Kittim (XI, 11–17). In the last two sections there are some items which overlap with the concerns of the Song of Miriam. Whereas the Song of Miriam seems to speak of the way the enemy has lost hope (line 4), 1QM XI, 9 speaks of how in the battle God opens 'a door of *hope* (Hos. 2.17) for the despondent heart'. That hope rests in the victory over the enemy which is as assured as the defeat of Pharaoh and his charioteers: 'You will do to them *as to Pharaoh and as to the captains of his chariots in the Red Sea*' (1QM XI, 9–10).

These two parallels are then followed by a set of poetic phrases describing how God works through the 'poor' and those of 'beaten spirit'. God abandons 'into the hands of the poor the enemies from all the lands, and by the hand of those bent in the dust You will make low the mighty of the peoples'. The text then becomes somewhat fragmentary, but in this humbling of the mighty somebody (probably God himself) is magnified and sanctified. The powerful are brought low by God's action through those who are lowly. Though the text is not explicit, there is obviously an implied reversal of status for the poor and downtrodden. Perhaps, just as these phrases seem to echo items of the Song of Hannah and also the Magnificat where such reversal is extolled, so there could be echoes here of the theme of exaltation which is hinted at in the extant line 6 in the Song of Miriam.

The second section of the *War Scroll* which has some close affinity with the remains of the Song of Miriam is the Hymn of Victory of 1QM

XIV, 4–17. Not only is the overall genre of victory song the same, but once again there are particular motifs which seem to correspond. The opening of the hymn is a blessing of God as the one who keeps his covenant and the appointed times of *salvation*. This matches the description of God as *saviour* in the Song of Miriam. The poem continues by describing how God has *raised up* the despondent and the dumb, the humble in spirit and the perfect of way.

While the enemies of 1QM XI might be thought of solely as consisting of foreign powers who are effectively at the beck and call of Belial, in 1QM XIV the enemy is not specifically identified: it is all those who think themselves mighty, swift, honoured, all with such empty existence. The passage is lyrically forceful:

(10) You have raised up (11) the fallen by your strength,
but the exalted in stature You have cut down . . .
And for all their mighty men there is no deliverer,
and for their swift men there is no escape.
And their honoured men (12) You will reward with *shame*,
and all their creatures of vanity You have turned to nothing.
But we, Your holy people, by Your true deeds will praise Your name
(13) and by your mighty deeds we will *exalt* always . . .

The italicized words are the possible points of direct parallelism with the Song of Miriam. If in line 1 of that song there is the use of the verb 'to despise' (*bzh*), then this is matched by the way that those full of self-esteem are rewarded with 'shame' (*bwz*). The vocabulary of exaltation is also present in both places, though whereas in the Song of Miriam it appears that God is doing the raising up, in 1QM XIV, 13 those who sing the hymn are exalting God.

Taking up the hints of those who have considered that the Magnificat and Benedictus may be pre-Christian hymns, D. Flusser has shown how this section of the *War Scroll* has many affinities with those two poems.[23]

---

23 'The Magnificat, The Benedictus and the War Scroll', in *Judaism and the Origins of Christianity* (Jerusalem: Magnes Press, 1988), 134–43. Links between the Magnificat and Benedictus and the *Hodayot* from Qumran have recently been proposed by M. P. Horgan and P. J. Kobelski in 'The Hodayot (1QH) and New Testament Poetry', in *To Touch the Text: Biblical and Related Studies in Honor of Joseph A. Fitzmyer, S.J.* (ed. M. P. Horgan and P. J. Kobelski; New York: Crossroad, 1989), 179–93.

He proposes that all three may depend on a common source whose basic components would include the very sections which comparison with the new Song of Miriam now suggests. At this point the two traditions seem to overlap, those of the victory songs associated with women, and those of the victory songs in the *War Scroll*.

CONCLUSION: SONGS OF REVOLUTION

As with many sections of the scrolls from Qumran, the Song of Miriam is frustratingly fragmentary. And yet enough remains to allow us to propose that the song took up some of the themes of the Song of the Sea, just as Judith's victory song does, and interlaced those motifs with a perspective which suggests that God's victory is often shame for the proud, the arrogant and the mighty, victory that is brought about surprisingly through the weak and downtrodden. In an eschatological context in which the mighty in Israel might be considered to be the enemy just as much as any foreign power, these motifs become revolutionary.

Perhaps it is not surprising that these songs are to be found associated with women or in a composition like the *War Scroll*. By their survival in such places we can see that those keen on supporting the social status quo could marginalize the threat of such poems. This seems to be true if these texts are viewed with an eye on the political context of second temple period Palestine and the emerging stability of the text of the Torah which supported such status quo – hence the Song of Miriam did not survive in the text which eventually became authoritative. It seems to be the case also, if one considers the social structures within the emerging communities of the early Church, especially those for whom Luke's infancy narrative would have had immediate significance – the well-to-do in that community would undermine themselves every time they read the Magnificat. In either case the message is that God's victory is assured, often through the agency of the weak, and the reversal it entails might just topple those who thought they were most secure by being on the winning side.

16

4Q252 and the 153 Fish of John 21.11[1]

INTRODUCTION

The principal edition of 4Q252, *Commentary on Genesis A*, was published in 1996.[2] In a paper published in the same year I tried to draw out some of the ways in which 4Q252 might help with the better understanding of some items in the New Testament, especially where there was a common use of passages from Genesis.[3] There was no attempt in that paper to suggest any kind of literary dependence of the New Testament authors upon this Genesis commentary, but rather the juxtaposition of 4Q252 and various New Testament passages was undertaken to show something of the extent of shared exegetical concerns. The same is the case in this study in which a further intriguing item is explored. I will juxtapose two texts, 4Q252 and John 21.11, to try to illuminate the possible

---

1 It was a privilege to have been asked to contribute this short study in honour of Professor Hartmut Stegemann whose knowledge of the fragmentary Dead Sea Scrolls has been inspiring and whose attempts at placing them in a broader context have been exhilarating.

2 G. J. Brooke, '252. 4QCommentary on Genesis A', in *Qumran Cave 4.XVII: Parabiblical Texts, Part 3* (ed. G. J. Brooke et al. in consultation with J. C. VanderKam; DJD 22; Oxford: Clarendon Press, 1996), 185–207. A bibliography of studies which have appeared since the complete manuscript of 4Q252 has been available is presented on p. 185 of the principal edition. For H. Stegemann's own brief comments on 4Q252 see H. Stegemann, *Die Essener, Qumran, Johannes der Täufer und Jesus: Ein Sachbuch* (Spektrum Band 4249; Freiburg: Herder, 1993), 170–2; in English as H. Stegemann, *The Library of Qumran: On the Essenes, Qumran, John the Baptist, and Jesus* (Grand Rapids: Eerdmans; Leiden: Brill, 1998), 121–2.

3 G. J. Brooke, '4Q252 et le Nouveau Testament', *Le déchirement: Juifs et chrétiens au premier siècle* (ed. D. Marguerat; Le Monde de la Bible 32; Geneva: Labor et Fides, 1996), 221–42; an English version of this paper is Chapter 10 in this book.

meaning of the latter which has been a veritable interpretative crux from the earliest times through to the modern period.

4Q252 I, 8–10

4Q252, *Commentary on Genesis A*, is a selective commentary on various passages of Genesis from Genesis 6 to 49. Several attempts have been made to discern whether or not there is a common theme in the passages of Genesis upon which comment is made;[4] none has been entirely successful. The lack of success derives not just from the fragmentary state of much of the six columns of the manuscript, but also from the bewildering array of genres in which the commentary is presented: there is rewritten Bible, some interpretation of the plain sense of the scriptural text, some poetic material, some halakhic exegesis, as well as *pesher* proper.[5]

It is with some of the detail of the opening pericope of 4Q252 that this study is concerned. After an introductory paraphrase of Genesis 6.3a which provides the overall chronological framework in relation to Noah's life, the opening section of the commentary is a rewritten form of Genesis 7.10—8.18. In the paraphrase the commentator's concerns become apparent: the commentary is intended to elucidate the precise chronology of the year of the flood. The narrative of Genesis is presented with all the material cut out which is extraneous to that purpose. So, for example, there is no mention of the building of the ark and whereas Noah's age is mentioned in both Genesis 7.6 and 7.11, the commentator uses the second occurrence alone. Likewise, the 40 days mentioned in Genesis 7.17 are redundant in the overall scheme of producing a flood that lasted for exactly one year, so they are omitted.

The overall chronological concern of this retelling of the flood story is an emphasis on the view that Noah and his entourage were in the ark for exactly 'a complete year of three hundred and sixty-four days' (4Q252 II, 2–3). The following dates occur in the reworked narrative:

---

4 See especially G. J. Brooke, 'The Thematic Content of 4Q252', *JQR* 85 (1994–5): 33–59; I. Fröhlich, 'Themes, Structure and Genre of Pesher Genesis', *JQR* 85 (1994–5): 81–90; I. Fröhlich, '"Narrative Exegesis" in the Dead Sea Scrolls', in *Biblical Perspectives: Early Use and Interpretation of the Bible in Light of the Dead Sea Scrolls* (ed. M. E. Stone and E. G. Chazon; STDJ 28; Leiden: Brill, 1998), 81–99.

5 On the variety of interpretative genres see G. J. Brooke, 'The Genre of 4Q252: From Poetry to Pesher', *DSD* 1 (1994): 160–79. A particularly significant study of the exegetical issues in 4Q252 is M. J. Bernstein, '4Q252: From Re-Written Bible to Biblical Commentary', *JJS* 45 (1994): 1–27.

Reference	Event	Date	Day of the week
1.3–4	Start of flood	17/2	First
1.5–7	End of forty days of rain	26/3	Fifth
1.7–8	End of 150 days flooding	14/7	Third
1.8–9	Waters decrease	15–16/7	Fourth and Fifth
1.10	Ark rests on Mount Hurarat	17/7	Sixth
1.11–12	Tops of mountains appear	1/10	Fourth
1.12–13	Noah opens the window	10/11	First
1.14–17	Dove returns second time	24/11	First
1.17–20	Dove sent forth again	1/12	First
1.20–22	Waters dry up	1/1	Fourth
2.1–2	Noah leaves the ark	17/2	First

The relative paucity of dating information in the narrative of Genesis itself allows for the commentator to date precisely a long list of events during the year. The manifold implications of this commentary for the history of the text of Genesis and for the dating of the flood in other retellings of the same story need not detain us here.[6] The primary concern of this study is to note that the commentator is clearly aware that in relation to the 364-day calendar that is being used, the 150 days of Genesis 8.3b does not cover the five months between the start of the flood (17/2; Gen. 7.11) and the ark coming to rest on Mount Ararat (17/7; Gen. 8.4). In addition to five standard months of 30 days each, during that period two quarter days would have fallen, at the ends of the third and sixth months respectively.[7] Thus the commentary cleverly

---

6 See especially T. Lim, 'The Chronology of the Flood Story in a Qumran Text (4Q252)', *JJS* 43 (1992): 288–98; U. Glessmer, 'Antike und moderne Auslegungen des Sintflutberichtes Gen. 6–8 und der Qumran-Pesher 4Q252', *Theologische Fakultät Leipzig: Forschungstelle Judentum* (Mitteilungen und Beiträge 6: Leipzig: Thomas Verlag, 1993): 30–9; R. S. Hendel, '4Q252 and the Flood Chronology of Genesis 7–8: A Text-Critical Solution', *DSD* 2 (1995): 72–9; M. A. Zipor, 'The Flood Chronology: Too Many an Accident', *DSD* 4 (1997): 207–10.

7 J. M. Baumgarten has argued that the author of *Jubilees* knew of the problem concerning the two-day discrepancy and so studiously avoided the date on which the ark is said to have landed on the mountains of Ararat ('The Calendars of the Book of Jubilees and the Temple Scroll', *VT* 37 [1987]: 76). However, the context in *Jubilees* only concerns the quarter days, the days of remembrance, which the author is concerned to associate with the flood narrative. The calendrical problems concerning the chronology of the flood with particular reference to *Jubilees* are highlighted by J. M. Baumgarten, *Studies in Qumran Law* (SJLA 24; Leiden: Brill, 1977), 108–9.

inserts a period of two days when the waters decrease slightly so that the ark can become grounded on the mountains of Ararat on the seventeenth of the seventh month which is the hundred and fifty-third day after the start of the flood.

The text of the *Genesis Commentary* is remarkably terse. With respect to the grounding on the mountains of Ararat it reads simply as follows:

> *And the waters swelled upon the earth for one hundred and fifty days* (Gen. 7.24), until the fourteenth day *in the seventh month* (Gen. 8.4a) on the third day of the week. And at the end of *one hundred and fifty days the waters decreased* (Gen. 8.3b) for two days, the fourth day and the fifth day, and on the sixth day *the ark came to rest on the mountains of Hurarat; i[t was the] seventeenth [da]y in the seventh month* (Gen. 8.4). *And the waters continued to decrease until the [te]nth month* (Gen. 8.5a), its *first* day, the fourth day of the week *the tops of the mountians appeared* (Gen. 8.5b). (4Q252 I, 7–12)[8]

Apart from the additions which clarify the datings and which especially relate the dates to the days of the week, there is no further exegetical comment. However, although the commentator remains silent, four matters can be briefly highlighted. To begin with, it is clear that the ark comes to land on the hundred and fifty-third day after the flood began. In this calendrical scheme, the number 153 can be seen to be associated with the security that accompanies the beginning of the end of the flood. This invests the number 153 with a significance not readily perceived before. Second, in the biblical account (Gen. 8.4) the ark comes to rest on the seventeenth day of the seventh month. There is thus a correlation between the hundred and fifty-third day from the start of the flood and the seventeenth day of a month, between 153 and 17. There is also the number of the month, the number 7. Third, it may be significant that the two days which are added to the 150 correspond with the first and second days of Sukkoth. The waters cease to swell on the earth on the eve of Sukkoth itself (14/7), nothing happens on the first two days of the feast as the waters decrease further (15–16/7) and the ark suitably comes to rest on the seventeenth of the seventh month, the eve of the Sabbath (18/7) that falls within the octave of Sukkoth. The association of the

---

8 The words set in italics correspond closely with the MT Hebrew of Genesis.

beginning of the end of the flood with Sukkoth may indicate some exegetical matters that should be made explicit. Fourth, as with the rest of the events in the flood narrative, nothing takes place on a Sabbath; the waters, the ark and Noah himself take no initiative on the seventh day. As the complete list above shows, the first day of the week is especially prominent in the story and is mentioned explicitly five times in the commentary, but the seventh day is never mentioned.

4Q252 I, 8–10 AND JOHN 21.11

Although the number 153 does not occur in the text of 4Q252, it is clear that the ark comes to rest on Mount Ararat on the hundred and fifty-third day after the start of the flood, on the seventeenth of the seventh month. The question now arises whether this new information concerning the possible significance of the number 153 can be used to improve the understanding of the appearance of the same number in John 21.11: 'So Simon Peter went aboard and hauled the net ashore, full of large fish, a hundred and fifty-three of them; and though there were so many, the net was not torn.'

Several modern commentators have been determined not to become embroiled in speculation concerning the number of the fish. Some have suggested that 153 was the number of fish actually caught that day.[9] Others have acknowledged that for the number to have been recorded at all, it probably has some symbolic or allegorical significance: 'Why the multitude of believers is represented exactly through the number 153 does not allow of a satisfactory explanation; nevertheless it must have an allegorical meaning, since it is not a round number.'[10] However, in light of 4Q252 I, 8–10, aspects of several of the proposals for understanding the significance of the number seem to become more feasible.

This exploration for meaning begins with a twofold observation. On the one hand, it should be recalled that according to 4Q252 it is Noah and his family who are brought to safety on the hundred and fifty-third

9 E.g., J. H. Bernard, *A Critical and Exegetical Commentary on the Gospel According to St. John* (ICC; Edinburgh: T & T Clark, 1928), 699–700.

10 R. Bultmann, *The Gospel of John: A Commentary* (ET Oxford: Blackwell, 1971), 709. Cf. B. Lindars' view: 'None of the solutions is really convincing. They all require that the number should be regarded as code-language . . . The number naturally arouses curiosity, but the story still makes its point clearly enough without any solution to the problem' (*The Gospel of John* [NCB; London: Marshall, Morgan & Scott, 1972], 631).

day; on the other hand, there is widespread agreement among commentators on the Fourth Gospel that the overall purpose of the story of the
miraculous fish in John 21 is to recall that Peter has a specific role as a
leader of the fisherfolk, those who are committed to bring people from all
the nations in the world to membership of the Church. The call of Peter
(and others) in the Synoptic tradition makes this plain: 'Follow me and I
will make you fish for people' (Mk 1.17; Matt. 4.19; cf. Lk. 5.10). Membership of the Church is marked by baptism. In light of this twofold
observation it is worth recalling that Noah and his family are linked typologically with baptism in the Petrine tradition in the New Testament.
The typology is expressed most fully in 1 Peter 3.20–1: 'God waited
patiently in the days of Noah, during the building of the ark, in which a
few, that is, eight persons were saved through water. And baptism which
this prefigured now saves you . . . as an appeal to God for a good conscience, through the resurrection of Jesus Christ.'[11] Not surprisingly
several commentators on John 21 have been inclined to read the 153 fish
as symbolic of those brought into the Church and the water as representing baptism.[12]

The 153 fish may symbolize the totality and range of the disciples'
catch (cf. Matt. 13.47). This interpretation is usually associated with
Jerome.[13] In his comments on Ezekiel 47.6–12 Jerome states that 'writers
on the nature and properties of animals, who have learned "fishing" in
either Latin or Greek (one of whom is the most learned poet Oppianus
Cilix), say there are one hundred fifty-three species of fish'.[14] R. M. Grant
has assessed Oppian's list in detail and has correctly noted that it is very
difficult to reckon his total as 153: 'No one who did not have the number
153 already in mind could approach Oppian's work and count the

---

11 The same motif of Noah and his family being saved is present in 2 Pet. 2.5.

12 P. Niewalda, *Sakramentenssymbolik im Johannesevangelium?* (Limburg: Lahn,
1958), 83; R. E. Brown, 'The Johannine Sacramentary', in *New Testament Essays*
(London: Geoffrey Chapman, 1967), 73–4. Strangely the most recent comprehen-
sive discussion of water and baptism in the Fourth Gospel omits any consideration of
John 21: L. P. Jones, *The Symbol of Water in the Gospel of John* (JSNTSup 145;
Sheffield: Sheffield Academic Press, 1997).

13 As pointed out, among many others, by F.-M. Braun, 'Quatre "signes" johan-
nique de l'unité chrétienne', *NTS* 9 (1962–3): 153; having cited Jerome, Braun
concludes 'en toute hypothèse, l'intention de l'auteur était de signifier la conversion
du genre humain'.

14 *PL* 25.474C; trans. R. M. Grant, 'One Hundred Fifty-Three Large Fish (John
21.11)', *HTR* 42 (1949): 273.

species of fish, especially since Oppian himself declares them uncount-able and does not list them in any systematic way.'[15] Thus it is most likely that Jerome has interpreted Greek zoology by way of the Gospel and so done some creative counting. Grant himself follows Augustine and suggests that for the author of John 21 the number's significance may rest in it being the total of the numbers one to seventeen, and that seventeen is the sum of seven and ten, two numbers widely held to be important,[16] but he notes especially that the Gospel writer stresses only the size of the catch.

The possible association of the number 153 with a baptismal typo-logical understanding of Noah and his family coming to safety on the hundred and fifty-third day after the start of the flood may receive some slight confirmation from the way in which this safe arrival seems to be associated with the Feast of Sukkoth. According to the 364-day calendar which lies behind the rewriting of the flood narrative in 4Q252 the waters cease swelling on the eve of Sukkoth and after two further days the ark touches ground on the eve of the Sabbath which falls in the octave of Sukkoth. In the Fourth Gospel, Sukkoth forms the background to the narrative of John 7.1—8.59 and beyond. In addition to the theme of light which runs through that section of the Gospel and may reflect some form of the lighting of lamps in the temple during the festival, the theme of water is also present. In particular the saying in John 7.37–8 concern-ing living waters is capable of being understood as an interpretation of several aspects of the Feast of Sukkoth, and one of these can be its associa-tion with baptism. In a characteristically balanced way, R. E. Brown concluded that 'nevertheless, we are not averse to seeing a broad sacra-mental symbolism here in the sense that this passage of John would have led the early Christian readers to think of Baptism, much as in ch. iv'.[17]

Without being explicit 4Q252 links the number 153 with the Feast of Sukkoth. The details of temple practice during the festival in the 200 years before its destruction is not clearly known, but later tradition asso-ciates a particular water rite with the festival. In addition, one intriguing tradition may point to another aspect of how the polyvalent symbolism of the number 153 can be understood. In the *Tosefta* there is a passage

---

15 R. M. Grant, 'One Hundred Fifty-Three Large Fish', 273.

16 Cf. *M. 'Abot* 5.1–11; Philo, *Decalogue* 26; *Creation* 99–104.

17 R. E. Brown, *The Gospel according to John I–XII* (AB 29; Garden City: Double-day, 1966), 329.

which has led commentators to link the phrase 'rivers of living waters' (Jn 7.38) with Zechariah 14.8 and Ezekiel 47.2:[18]

> Why is it called 'the Water Gate'? Because through it they bring a flask of water for the water libation on the Festival. R. Eliezer ben Jacob says, 'Through it the water comes out [on the south side]' (Ezek. 47.2). 'This teaches that they flow outward like the water of a flask.' 'And they are destined to flow down from below the south end of the threshold of the Temple, [south of the altar]' (Ezek. 47.1) . . . And it says, 'On that day waters will go forth from Jerusalem' (Zech. 14.8) (*t. Sukk.* 3.3–8).[19]

Since John 7 and 8 are clearly set at the Feast of Sukkoth, it is likely that in the Johannine tradition there was an awareness that Ezekiel 47 was one of several scriptural passages which could be effectively used in relation to Sukkoth.[20]

Mention of the association of Ezekiel 47 and Sukkoth brings us to another aspect of the number 153 in John 21.11. Various attempts have been made to suggest that as with the number 666 in Revelation 13.18[21] so the number 153 should be seen to reflect a proper name; the sum of the numerical value of its letters would total 153. Since 153 is the sum of the numbers one to 17, it is important that any solution should also be able to make a suggestion to explain the number 17. The most persuasive proposal concerning both numbers is that of J. A. Emerton who has noted that the story of the fishes in John 21 has commonly been seen as partly dependent upon Ezekiel 47, especially verse 10.[22] 'People will

---

18 It is important to recall that Jerome's comments on the 153 fish of Jn 21.11 come in his commentary on Ezek. 47.

19 Trans. J. Neusner, *The Tosefta Translated from the Hebrew: Second Division, Moed (The Order of Appointed Times)* (New York: Ktav, 1981), 218–19.

20 As is supported by C. H. Dodd, *The Interpretation of the Fourth Gospel* (Cambridge: Cambridge University Press, 1954), 349–50.

21 The transcription of Nero which gives the value of 666 is attested in an Aramaic scroll from Murabbaʿat: 'Reconnaissance de dette, en araméen', *Les grottes de Murabbaʿat* (ed. P. Benoit, J. T. Milik, R. de Vaux; DJD 2; Oxford: Clarendon Press, 1961), 101; see D. R. Hillers, 'Revelation 13.18 and the Scrolls from Murabbaʿat', *BASOR* 170 (1963): 65. On some of the many suggestions for the *gematria* in Rev. 13.18 see J. Massyngberde Ford, *Revelation* (AB 38; Garden City, NY: Doubleday, 1975), 215–17, 225–7.

22 J. A. Emerton, 'The Hundred and Fifty-Three Fishes in John XXI.11', *JTS* 9 (1958): 86–9. Emerton notes that Ezek. 47.10 may also lie behind John 7.38.

stand fishing beside the sea from En-gedi to En-eglaim; it will be a place for the spreading of nets; its fish will be of a great many kinds, like the fish of the Great Sea' (Ezek. 47.10). Emerton has shown that 153 is the value of (En-)eglaim (' = 70; g = 3; l = 30; y = 10; m = 40) and that the value of (En-)gedi is 17 (g = 3; d = 4; y = 10). He has noted that the prefix 'yn 'may not be significant since it means "spring" and is not necessarily to be thought of as an essential part of the proper names'.[23] The strength of Emerton's suggestion lies in the way that proper names representing both 153 and 17 are found in a single verse, a verse which is part of a passage that for several reasons has otherwise been seen as a possible backdrop for elements in John 21.1–14.

Emerton's proposal received further support from P. R. Ackroyd who noted that in Greek there are many different spellings for the two proper names concerned. However, he discovered two which provided the right numerical total so that the *gematria* based on Ezekiel 47.10 can work in Greek too: *eggadi* (33) and *agalleim* (120) when put together make 153.[24] Emerton himself questioned the value of Ackroyd's observations, rightly insisting that the *gematria* really works well only in Hebrew.[25] Additional support has been provided by P. Trudinger who has argued that the wider context of Ezekiel 47 as a depiction of the age to come should also be taken into account. In such light the commission to the disciples and the later churches to be fishers of people is the beginning of the age to come which has been inaugurated by the death and resurrection of Jesus, whereby ancient prophecy is fulfilled.[26] Emerton's ability to give proper names with numerical values for both 17 and 153 makes his proposal preferable to others, quite apart from the further supportive suggestions in this essay.[27] Even the fact that the places in Ezekiel 47.10 are both to be

---

23 'The Hundred and Fifty-Three Fishes in John XXI.11', 88.

24 P. R. Ackroyd, 'The 153 Fishes in John XXI.11 – a Further Note', *JTS* 10 (1959): 94. Ackroyd specified that he had derived *ēggadi* from MS 449 and *agalleim* from MSS 49, 90 and 764; that the spellings he has used to produce the correct total come from different manuscripts 'does not, in view of the great variety of spelling attested, seem of any great moment'.

25 J. A. Emerton, 'Some New Testament Notes', *JTS* 11 (1960): 335–6.

26 P. Trudinger, 'The 153 Fishes: a Response and a Further Suggestion', *ExpTim* 102 (1990–1): 11–12.

27 Emerton's *gematria* is thus to be preferred to the many other proposals, including the following: H. Kruse who proposed both *qhl h'hbh*, 'congregation of love' and *bny h'lhym*, 'children of God', preferring the former ('Magni Pisces Centum Quinqua-ginta Tres', *VD* 38 [1960]: 137–48); N. J. McEleney who suggested allocating numerical values to the letters of the alphabet in reverse from which the letters *ichth*

found at the Dead Sea rather than the Sea of Galilee is also not insurmountable in light of the tradition in *Tosefta Sukkah* 3.9 in which the waters referred to in Ezekiel 47.8 flow into the Sea of Tiberias.[28]

The presence of both 17 and 153 in the *gematria* of the proper names in Ezekiel 47.10 is remarkable. Perhaps all this particular playing with numbers receives conclusive further support from 4Q252. We have already noted that in 4Q252 day 153, the first day of safety, occurs in Sukkoth, the festival with which Ezekiel 47 is traditionally associated. It should be noted, moreover, that according to the 364-day calendar the hundred and fifty-third day from the start of the flood is also explicitly stated to be the seventeenth day of the seventh month. Thus in the calendar of the flood as represented in 4Q252 the numbers 153 and 17 can be understood as occurring together. Some may view this as simply a very remarkable coincidence. There is no evidence that the author of 4Q252 had Ezekiel 47 in mind in this part of the commentary, though the geographical locations here being discussed are very close to Qumran. However, even if the *Genesis Commentary* makes no apparent use of Ezekiel 47, in having the numbers 153 and 17 coincide, it seems as if the commentator was aware of the numerology which saw them as mathematically and therefore symbolically connected.

While the place names in Ezekiel 47.10 may account for the numbers 153 and 17, the number seven also occurs in 4Q252 as the number of the month in which both the hundred and fifty-third day and the seventeenth day coincide. The number seven is not found explicitly in John 21, though it could be understood as one of the significant constituent elements of the number 17. However, it is often pointed out that

---

total 153 ('153 Great Fishes [John 21, 11] – Gematriacal Atbash', *Bib* 58 [1977]: 411–17); J. A. Romeo who used Jn 1.12 and 11.52 to support *bny h'lhym* ('Gematria and John 21.11 – The Children of God', *JBL* 97 [1978]: 263–4); K. Cardwell who has proposed ĒMERA, 'day' (ĒMER = 153 + A = 1), counting both the 153 mentioned explicitly and the one already on the fire, and pointing out that Justin, Clement of Alexandria and Hippolytus all call Jesus 'day' which may be an ancient title of the Logos (cf. Philo, *Alleg. Interp.* 1.20) ('The Fish on the Fire: Jn 21.9', *ExpTim* 102 [1990–1]: 12–14). See further suggestions as laid out by R. Bultmann, *The Gospel of John: A Commentary*, 709, n. 2.

28 As pointed out in support of Emerton's thesis by B. Grigsby, 'Gematria and John 21[11] – Another Look at Ezekiel 47[10]', *ExpTim* 95 (1983–4): 178. The label Sea of Tiberias is used only in Jn 6.1 and 21.1 in the whole New Testament; perhaps the use of the name reflects the phraseology of an ancient exegetical traditional based in Ezek. 47.

according to John 21.2 there are seven disciples engaged in fishing. Might this be an attempt to represent in the story something which could correspond numerically to the number of the month in which days 153 and 17 coincide?

In relation to John 21.11 it has often been pointed out that 153 is the sum of the numbers one to 17, a triangular number.[29] It seems as if the first to notice this for John 21.11 was Augustine.[30] Although 'we know of no speculation or established symbolism related to the number 153 in early thought',[31] the pre-Christian symbolic or philosophical use of numbers is generally associated by commentators with the Pythagoreans. For knowledge of this among Jews, the fragmentary remains of the writings of the second-century B.C.E. Alexandrian Jewish philosopher Aristobulus are generally cited,[32] especially his notes on the Sabbath in which he discusses the power of the numeral seven in a Pythagorean way, though without actually mentioning Pythagoras in what survives.[33] At this juncture then we may recall one last piece in the puzzle, namely that in his discussion of why the Essenes were excused from taking the oath of loyalty to Herod, Josephus compares them with the Pythagoreans: 'Among those spared from being forced to do this were also those we call Essenes, a group which employs the same daily regime as was revealed to

---

29 C. K. Barrett has argued that 153 must be symbolic and has concluded that 'we are left with the observation that 153 is a triangular number and = 1 + 2 + 3 . . . + 17. 17 itself is the sum of 7 and 10, both numbers which even separately are indicative of completeness and perfection. The fish then represent the full total of the catholic and apostolic Church' (*The Gospel According to St John* [London: SPCK, 1955], 484); the last sentence of this quotation is removed in the second edition. Cf. the scepticism of E. Haenchen: 'It contributes nothing to our understanding to say that 153 is the triangular number of 17' (*John 2: A Commentary on the Gospel of John Chapters 7–21* [Hermeneia; Philadelphia: Fortress Press, 1984], 224).
30 Especially *Tract. in Joh.* 122.8; see the summary of several relevant passages in Augustine's writings by H. Kruse, 'Magna Pisces Centum Quinquaginta Tres', 135–6.
31 As is correctly pointed out by R. E. Brown, *The Gospel According to John*, 2.1075.
32 For detail and bibliography on Aristobulus, see E. Schürer, *The History of the Jewish People in the Age of Jesus Christ* III/1 (ed. G. Vermes, F. Millar, M. Goodman; Edinburgh: T & T Clark, 1986), 579–87.
33 See, especially, M. Hengel, *Judaism and Hellenism: Studies in their Encounter in Palestine during the Early Hellenistic Period* (London: SCM Press, 1974; based on the 1973 German edn), 1.166–7; an English translation of the fragments of Aristobulus is provided by A. Y. Collins, 'Aristobulus', in *The Old Testament Pseudepigrapha* (ed. J. H. Charlesworth; London: Darton, Longman & Todd, 1985) 2.837–42.

the Greeks by Pythagoras' (*Ant.* 15.371).[34] It is almost certainly not the case that the Essenes modelled themselves on the Pythagoreans, but rather that for Josephus some aspects of their self-contained organization and outlook resembled those of the Pythagoreans.[35] Perhaps among such similarities some concern with number also prompted the comparison, and if the Qumran community was Essene in some form, then such a similarity could be found there too.

In sum, according to 4Q252 the ark comes to rest on the mountain on the hundred and fifty-third day after the start of the flood, a day which is also the seventeenth of the seventh month and the eve of the Sabbath which occurs in the octave of Sukkoth. This information encourages a fresh review of the various interpretations of the 153 fish of John 21.11. The background knowledge provided by 4Q252 enables us to see that a combination of several views may be most appropriate. In light of the use of Noah typology elsewhere, the catch may be understood to have baptismal echoes. The link with Sukkoth and the calendrical combination of 153 and 17 in 4Q252 is supportive of the exegesis of the numbers in association with Ezekiel 47, especially by *gematria* on the proper names En-gedi and En-eglaim in Ezekiel 47.10. The numerology involved may be indicative of one of the characteristics of the Essenes (and, therefore, probably of the writings of the Qumran community) which could have caused Josephus to have associated them with the Pythagoreans.

THE IMPLICATIONS FOR JOHN 21

The disclosure of the combination of 153 and 17 in 4Q252 in relation to the flood story and the bringing to safety of Noah and his family during the Feast of Sukkoth has several implications for the better reading of John 21. These cannot be treated in any exhaustive fashion here.

In the first place, the interpretation of the number 153 offered here, which in fact combines elements of several views offered over the

---

34 G. Vermes and M. D. Goodman, *The Essenes According to the Classical Sources* (Sheffield: JSOT Press, 1989), 51.

35 The most sober assessment of the way in which the juxtaposition of Essenes and Pythagoreans should be viewed is provided by M. Hengel, *Judaism and Hellenism*, 1. 243–7. On the similar use by the Essenes and the Pythagoreans of physiognomy as a means of controlling admission to their conventicles see P. S. Alexander, 'Physiognomy, Initiation, and Rank in the Qumran Community', in *Geschichte – Tradition – Reflexion: Festschrift für Martin Hengel zum 70. Geburtstag*, Band I, *Judentum* (ed. P. Schäfer; Tübingen: J. C. B. Mohr [Paul Siebeck], 1996), 392.

centuries seems to rule out three ways of reading the number 153. It seems inappropriate to suppose that the number was intended to be used openly by readers for their own allegorical interpretations.[36] It also seems unlikely that the number is intended simply to represent a very large number as one reading of John 21.11b might imply: 'though there were so many, the net was not torn'. Furthermore, although the number is not self-evidently symbolic, there is more than enough evidence gathered during centuries of reflection to suggest that it is not the number produced from the recollection of eye-witness testimony. Erring on the side of caution, it is this last view which R. E. Brown himself endorses.[37] The number 153 in John 21.11 is symbolic.

In second place, the appearance of a compatible tradition using Noah and the flood in a clearly Petrine tradition underlines the peculiarly Petrine character of John 21.[38] The chapter is largely constituted from three pericopae, one involving the miraculous catch of fish, the second the definition of Peter's role as shepherd, and the third the destinies of Peter and the Beloved Disciple. The invitation to martyrdom is entirely compatible with the role of the shepherd as that is described in John 10, but it is particularly appropriate in light of the suffering made explicit in the traditions of 1 Peter, suffering which is to be experienced by community members. In addition to wishing to preserve additional resurrection stories, this Petrine context of impending persecution could provide part of the motivation for including these particular ones in John 21, when, apparently, there are so many stories to choose from.

Third, it is generally agreed that John 21 is a later appendage to the Gospel proper.[39] After John 20.30–1 the final chapter of the Gospel comes as something of a surprise. However, the debate about whether or not John 21 is entirely compatible with the character and purpose of the

36 R. E. Brown mentions just two of these: Cyril of Alexandria (*In Joh.* 12; PG 74.745) understood 153 as made up of the fullness of the Gentiles (100), the remnant of Israel (50), and the Trinity (3); Rupert of Deutz saw in the number the married (100), the widows (50) and the virgins (3) (*The Gospel According to John*, 2.1075).
37 *The Gospel According to John*, 2.1076.
38 See esp. R. E. Brown, K. P. Donfried, J. Reumann (eds), *Peter in the New Testament* (London: Geoffrey Chapman, 1974), 139–47.
39 A substantial challenge to this consensus view was mounted by P. S. Minear, 'The Original Functions of John 21', *JBL* 102 (1983): 85–98. The challenge has been largely ignored.

Fourth Gospel still continues.[40] For example, in support of linking John 21 closely with earlier chapters in the Fourth Gospel, the story of the miraculous catch of fish portrays the ability of the Beloved Disciple to recognize Jesus on the beach (Jn 21.7); this is entirely in line with his insight and belief at the tomb (Jn 20.5, 8). In both narratives, however, Peter is the slower of the pair to realize what is happening. Or again, when it comes to vocabulary and style the similarities and differences between John 21 and what precedes are difficult to assess.[41] If the number 153 has anything to do with the system of the 364-day calendar, as might be implied by reading its various interpretations in light of 4Q252, then this would possibly be another indication that John 21 is both similar to and different from the rest of the Gospel. Although not widely followed by other scholars, the most promising suggestion for explaining the different chronologies of the Synoptic Gospels and the Fourth Gospel with respect to Passover has been made by A. Jaubert. She argued that while the Fourth Gospel's narrative reflects the luni-solar calendar which was followed in the Jerusalem temple, Jesus and his disciples celebrated Passover three days earlier according to the calendar observed by the Qumran community.[42] Thus, if the 364-day calendar lies behind the number 153 in John 21.11, then the ideology of the pericope may fit with the practice of Jesus and the disciples (according to Jaubert); but this is not made explicit in John 21 itself which may indicate that the writer of the passage needed to gloss over the calendrical significance of the number so that the last chapter remained in agreement with the luni-solar calendar of the overall narrative of the Fourth Gospel.

Fourth, as is widely recognized, the same story, rather than a different incident altogether, features in Luke 5.1–11. The call of Peter, together with James and John (also mentioned in John 21 together with some others), takes place at the outset of Jesus' ministry as in the other Synoptics but Luke uses the story of the miraculous catch, perhaps to explain

---

40 See most recently the literary arguments of B. Gaventa, 'The Archive of Excess: John 21 and the Problem on Narrative Closure', in *Exploring the Gospel of John* (ed. R. A. Culpepper and C. C. Black; Louisville: Westminster John Knox Press, 1996), 240–52.

41 As has been exhaustively pointed out by M.-E. Boismard, 'Le chapitre xxi de saint Jean: essai de critique littéraire', *RB* 54 (1947): 473–501; cf. the summary of the evidence in C. K. Barrett, *The Gospel According to St John*, 479–80.

42 A. Jaubert, *La date de la Cène* (Paris: J. Gabalda, 1957); 'The Calendar of Qumran and the Johannine Passion Narrative', in *John and Qumran* (ed. J. H. Charlesworth; London: Geoffrey Chapman, 1972), 62–75.

the psychology of the moment. The fish are not numbered in the Lukan version. The story is told so as to fit with the generally positive portrayal of Peter in Luke: Luke omits Jesus' rebuke of him (Mk 8.32–3), Jesus' reproach of him asleep (Mk 14.37) and his running to the tomb (24.12). Perhaps the illumination of the background of one aspect of the story of the miraculous fish in John 21.1–14 should encourage a reconsideration of what the Gospel of Luke and the Fourth Gospel have in common. Such commonality may be particularly illuminated by the scrolls from Qumran.[43]

CONCLUSION

This study has shown that in its reworking of the flood narrative according to the 364-day calendar 4Q252 has the ark ground on the mountain tops on the hundred and fifty-third day after the start of the flood, a day which is also the seventeenth of the seventh month. That day is the eve of the Sabbath within the octave of the Feast of Sukkoth. These facts encourage a reconsideration of how the 153 fish in John 21.11 should be best understood. It has been argued that in light of 4Q252 several of the suggestions for interpreting the number can be reconsidered afresh. The links between the flood, Noah and his family and baptism suggest that that is an appropriate backdrop to the generally agreed view that the catch of fish has to do with the mission of the Church. The implicit occurrence together in 4Q252 of 153 and 17 in association with Sukkoth supports reading John 21.1–14 in light of Ezekiel 47. In particular, such a juxtaposition lends yet further support to the suggestion of J. A. Emerton that the place names of Ezekiel 47.10 can explain the number 153 by *gematria*. The numerological interpretation of the 153 fish may also reflect a similar interest among Essenes, if the Qumran community is to be identified with them in some way, since Josephus

---

43 Of the four canonical Gospels, only Lk. 16.8 and Jn 12.36 have the phrase 'sons of light'. The temple orientation of both Gospels may also be a shared feature which depends on an outlook such as can be found in some Qumran scrolls: for Luke see G. J. Brooke, 'Luke–Acts and the Qumran Scrolls: The Case of MMT', in *Luke's Literary Achievement* (ed. C. M. Tuckett; JSNTSup 116; Sheffield: Sheffield Academic Press, 1995), 72–90 (Chapter 9 in this book); for the Fourth Gospel see G. J. Brooke, 'The Temple Scroll and the New Testament', in *Temple Scroll Studies: Papers Presented at the International Symposium on the Temple Scroll (Manchester, December 1987)* (ed. G. J. Brooke; JSPSup 7; Sheffield: JSOT Press, 1989), 186–94 (Chapter 6 in this book).

associates the Essenes with the Pythagoreans, the philosophical school whose metaphysic was grounded in number.

All this fresh juxtaposition of ideas is not an argument that the Fourth Gospel or John 21 alone was written by someone familiar with the writings of the Qumran community. Rather, 4Q252 extends our knowledge of Jewish exegetical traditions which antedate the writing of the Fourth Gospel by about a hundred years. These traditions shed light on the early Christian writings. Together with the obvious use of *gematria* elsewhere in the broader Johannine tradition, the number of fish in John 21.11 seems altogether less esoteric than has sometimes been thought. It is the number that represents the baptized, those brought safely through water, who are the fulfilment of the expectations of Ezekiel 47, especially verse 10 concerning En-gedi and En-eglaim. The calendrical calculations of 4Q252 enable us to tie several interpretative threads together to show what kind of rich net is used in John 21.11 for landing those 153 fish.[44]

---

44 This study has been challenged by M. Bar-Ilan, *Genesis' Numerology* ([Hebrew] Rehovot: Association for Jewish Astrology and Numerology, 2003), 105, n. 208, for putting together calendrical and other numerological data with *gematria*, matters which he considers should remain discrete.

Select Bibliography

There is no overall bibliography in this collection of essays. To have provided one might have suggested some kind of comprehensive coverage of the Dead Sea Scrolls and the New Testament. Such a comprehensive analysis has yet to be done. Readers wishing to pursue any matter of detail or searching for bibliographical assistance should be able to discover what they want in relation to the topics covered in these essays through the judicious use of the modern author index. Nevertheless, since readers of all kinds may pick up this volume, I add here a short classified Bibliography.

The Dead Sea Scrolls

The Dead Sea Scrolls have virtually all now been published in principal editions; the great majority of these are available in the series known as Discoveries in the Judaean Desert (Oxford: Clarendon Press, 1955–), most of whose volumes have appeared since 1990. Those volumes are referred to in this book either by volume number and page (e.g., DJD 22, 157) or with full bibliographical information.

In addition, there are two handy collections of Hebrew/Aramaic texts with parallel English translations:

F. García Martínez and E. J. C. Tigchelaar, *The Dead Sea Scrolls Study Edition* (Leiden: Brill; Grand Rapids: Eerdmans, 2nd edn, 2000), 2 volumes

D. W. Parry and E. Tov, ed., *The Dead Sea Scrolls Reader* (Leiden: Brill, 2003–); this has six volumes: 1. Texts Concerned with Religious Law; 2. Exegetical Texts; 3. Parabiblical Texts; 4. Calendrical and Sapiential Texts; 5. Poetic and Liturgical Texts; 6. Additional Genres and Unclassified Texts

In addition to various electronic resources there is a concordance to the nonbiblical scrolls:

M. G. Abegg with J. E. Bowley and E. M. Cook in consultation with E. Tov, *The Dead Sea Scrolls Concordance*, Volume I, *The Non-Biblical Texts from Qumran* (Leiden: Brill, 2003)

The scrolls in English translation

There are three generally available translations with English texts alone; parts of the first two are incorporated with adjustments in the parallel Hebrew/Aramaic and English editions above.

F. García Martínez, *The Dead Sea Scrolls Translated: The Qumran Texts in English* (Leiden: Brill; Grand Rapids: Eerdmans, 2nd edn, 1996)

G. Vermes, *The Complete Dead Sea Scrolls in English* (London: Penguin Books, 5th edn, 1998)

M. Wise, M. G. Abegg, E. Cook, *The Dead Sea Scrolls: A New Translation* (San Francisco: HarperSanFrancisco, 1996)

General introductions

J. G. Campbell, *Deciphering the Dead Sea Scrolls* (Oxford: Blackwell Publishing, 2nd edn, 2003)

P. R. Davies, G. J. Brooke and P. R. Callaway, *The Complete World of the Dead Sea Scrolls* (London: Thames and Hudson, 2002)

F. García Martínez and J. Trebolle Barrera, *The People of the Dead Sea Scrolls: Their Writings, Beliefs and Practices* (Leiden: Brill, 1995)

L. H. Schiffman, *Reclaiming the Dead Sea Scrolls: The History of Judaism, the Background of Christianity, the Lost Library of Qumran* (Philadelphia: Jewish Publication Society, 1994)

H. Stegemann, *The Library of Qumran: On the Essenes, Qumran, John the Baptist, and Jesus* (Leiden: Brill; Grand Rapids: Eerdmans, 1998)

J. C. VanderKam and P. W. Flint, *The Meaning of the Dead Sea Scrolls: Their Significance for Understanding the Bible, Judaism, Jesus, and Christianity* (San Francisco: HarperSanFrancisco, 2002)

Reference collections

P. W. Flint and J. C. VanderKam, *The Dead Sea Scrolls after Fifty Years* (Leiden: Brill, 1998, 1999), 2 volumes

L. H. Schiffman and J. C. VanderKam, ed., *Encyclopedia of the Dead Sea Scrolls* (New York: Oxford University Press, 2000), 2 volumes

Bibliographies

C. Burchard, *Bibliographie zu den Handschriften vom Toten Meer* (BZAW 76; Berlin: A. Töpelmann, 1959)

C. Burchard, *Bibliographie zu den Handschriften vom Toten Meer II* (BZAW 89; Berlin: A. Töpelmann, 1965)

J. A. Fitzmyer, *The Dead Sea Scrolls: Major Publications and Tools for Study* (SBLRBS 20; Atlanta: Scholars Press, 2nd edn, 1990)

F. García Martínez and D.W. Parry, *A Bibliography of the Finds in the Desert of Judah 1970–95* (STDJ 19; Leiden: Brill, 1996)

B. Jongeling, *A Classified Bibliography of the Finds in the Desert of Judah 1958–1969* (STDJ 7; Leiden: Brill, 1971)

W. S. LaSor, *Bibliography of the Dead Sea Scrolls 1948–1957* (Fuller Theological Seminary Bibliographical Series 2; Pasadena: Fuller Theological Seminary, 1958)

A. Pinnick, *The Orion Center Bibliography of the Dead Sea Scrolls (1995–2000)* (STDJ 41; Leiden: Brill, 2001)

The scrolls and the New Testament

M. Black, *The Scrolls and Christian Origins: Studies in the Jewish Background of the New Testament* (London: T. Nelson & Sons, 1961)

J. H. Charlesworth, ed., *John and Qumran* (London: Geoffrey Chapman, 1972); republished as J. H. Charlesworth, ed., *John and the Dead Sea Scrolls* (New York: Crossroad, 1990)

J. H. Charlesworth, ed., *Jesus and the Dead Sea Scrolls* (New York: Doubleday, 1992)

J. A. Fitzmyer, *The Semitic Background of the New Testament* (Grand Rapids: Eerdmans; Livonia: Dove, 1997)

D. Flusser, *Judaism and the Origins of Christianity* (Jerusalem: Magnes Press, 1988)

N. S. Fujita, *A Crack in the Jar: What Ancient Jewish Documents Tell Us About the New Testament* (Mahwah: Paulist Press, 1986)

J. Murphy-O'Connor, ed., *Paul and Qumran* (London: Geoffrey Chapman, 1968); republished as J. Murphy-O'Connor and J. H. Charlesworth, eds, *Paul and the Dead Sea Scrolls* (New York: Crossroad, 1990)

K. Stendahl, ed., *The Scrolls and the New Testament* (New York: Harper, 1957; London: SCM Press, 1958; republished New York: Crossroad, 1992)

Further reading

There is one series of books which specializes in technical studies of the Dead Sea Scrolls; this series is called Studies on the Texts of the Desert of Judah (Leiden: Brill, 1956–) and includes specialist monographs as well as the proceedings of conferences. There are three recently started series of publications of a more popular sort; in all three series further volumes are planned:

Studies in the Dead Sea Scrolls and related literature

J. J. Collins and R. Kugler, ed., *Religion in the Dead Sea Scrolls* (Grand Rapids: Eerdmans, 2000)

C. A. Evans and P. W. Flint, ed., *Eschatology, Messianism, and the Dead Sea Scrolls* (Grand Rapids: Eerdmans, 1997)

J. A. Fitzmyer, *The Dead Sea Scrolls and Christian Origins* (Grand Rapids: Eerdmans, 2000)

P. W. Flint, ed., *The Bible at Qumran: Text, Shape and Interpretation* (Grand Rapids: Eerdmans, 2001)

J. Magness, *The Archaeology of Qumran and the Dead Sea Scrolls* (Grand Rapids: Eerdmans, 2002)

E. C. Ulrich, *The Dead Sea Scrolls and the Origins of the Bible* (Grand Rapids: Eerdmans, 1999)

The literature of the Dead Sea Scrolls

J. J. Collins, *Apocalypticism in the Dead Sea Scrolls* (London: Routledge, 1997)

D. J. Harrington, *Wisdom Texts from Qumran* (London: Routledge, 1996)

J. C. VanderKam, *Calendars in the Dead Sea Scrolls: Measuring Time* (London: Routledge, 1998)

Companions to the Qumran scrolls

J. G. Campbell, *The Exegetical Texts* (London: T & T Clark International, 2004)

J. Duhaime, *The War Texts: 1QM and Related Manuscripts* (London: T & T Clark International, 2004)

H. K. Harrington, *The Purity Texts* (London: T & T Clark International, 2004)

C. Hempel, *The Damascus Texts* (Sheffield: Sheffield Academic Press, 2000)

T. H. Lim, *Pesharim* (London: Sheffield Academic Press, 2002)

S. A. White Crawford, *The Temple Scroll and Related Texts* (Sheffield: Sheffield Academic Press, 2000)

Journals

Many journals publish occasional articles related to the Dead Sea Scrolls, but two specialize in the scrolls:

Dead Sea Discoveries (Leiden: Brill, 1994–)

Revue de Qumrân (Paris: Gabalda, 1958–)

Index of Bible References

Index of Non-biblical Sources

Index of Modern Authors